Harlan Genealogy

D1202233

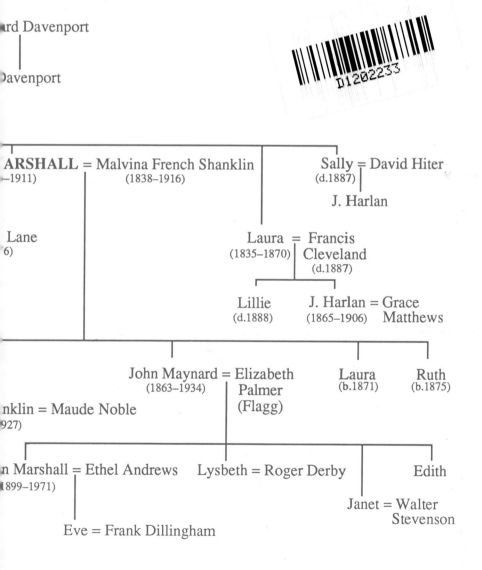

rd Davenport

)avenport

ARSHALL = Malvina French Shanklin
—1911)   (1838–1916)

Sally = David Hiter
(d.1887)

J. Harlan

Lane
'6)

Laura = Francis
(1835–1870)   Cleveland
       (d.1887)

Lillie   J. Harlan = Grace
(d.1888)   (1865–1906)   Matthews

John Maynard = Elizabeth
(1863–1934)   Palmer
         (Flagg)

Laura   Ruth
(b.1871)   (b.1875)

nklin = Maude Noble
927)

n Marshall = Ethel Andrews   Lysbeth = Roger Derby   Edith
1899–1971)

Janet = Walter
     Stevenson

Eve = Frank Dillingham

ROBERT MANNING
STROZIER LIBRARY

Tallahassee

John Marshall Harlan

The Last Whig Justice

Loren P. Beth

THE UNIVERSITY PRESS OF KENTUCKY

KF
8745
H3
B47
1992

Frontispiece: Associate Justice John Marshall Harlan, about 1910. Courtesy of the Library of Congress.

Robert Manning Strozier Library

APR 12 1993

Tallahassee, Florida

Copyright © 1992 by The University Press of Kentucky

Scholarly publisher for the Commonwealth,
serving Bellarmine College, Berea College, Centre
College of Kentucky, Eastern Kentucky University,
The Filson Club, Georgetown College, Kentucky
Historical Society, Kentucky State University,
Morehead State University, Murray State University,
Northern Kentucky University, Transylvania University,
University of Kentucky, University of Louisville,
and Western Kentucky University.

Editorial and Sales Offices: Lexington, Kentucky 40508-4008

Library of Congress Cataloging-in-Publication Data

Beth, Loren P.
    John Marshall Harlan : the last Whig justice / Loren P. Beth.
        p. cm.
    Includes bibliographical references and index.
    ISBN 0-8131-1778-X
    1. Harlan, John M. (John Marshall), 1833-1911. 2. Judges—United
States—Biography.   3. United States—Constitutional history.
I. Title.
KF8745.H33B47 1992
347.73′2634—dc20
[B]
[347.3073534]   91-36140
[B]

This book is printed on recycled acid-free paper meeting
the requirements of the American National Standard
for Permanence of Paper for Printed Library Materials.
∞

Contents

Preface

While I was still in graduate school at the University of Chicago, I first became interested in John Marshall Harlan. My teacher of constitutional law, Robert Horn, regarded Harlan as something of a hero. In those days his was an unusual view, since the Supreme Court had not yet vindicated Harlan by reversing *Plessy* v. *Ferguson.* My first scholarly publication was a summary of Harlan's major dissents, published in 1955. It was at that time that I first conceived of a biography; in my mind it would have been an exercise in hero worship—probably the worst possible approach to biography. The second Justice Harlan, however, held the largest part of his grandfather's papers and had granted exclusive rights to their use to Professor Alan Westin. But Westin's prolific writings went off in other directions, and in the mid-1960s Harlan's great-granddaughter gave the Library of Congress permission to enter the Harlan file in the public domain, thus making it available to me and all other interested persons.

My time has been encumbered with other duties and projects, and it took me many years to collect and collate the materials used for this book and to study and classify all of the thousands of cases in which Harlan participated. The actual writing did not begin until the mid-1980s. Since biography is a new form of writing for me, it took me longer to shape up the manuscript than it should have done. Nevertheless, this long gestation period had its benefits. Primarily, it gave me a chance to face up to the obvious fact that Harlan had faults—both as a man and as a judge. The resulting biography is much more critical than it would otherwise have been, even though I remain on balance an admirer of this much misunderstood man.

Over the years I have accumulated debts of gratitude too numerous to recount or even to remember. Chief in my mind are the various chairmen of the political science departments at the universities of Massachusetts and Georgia: the late John Harris, William C. Havard, and Glen Gordon at Massachusetts; and Frank Thompson and Thomas Lauth at Georgia. These men were uniformly supportive with their personal assistance and their willingness to provide the departmental help—principally secretarial but to some extent monetary—that alone have made the result possible. Also, Thomas L. Owen, then a librarian at the University of Louisville, led me to the extensive Harlan collection at the law school there, and his master's thesis on Harlan's political career was of great help. Of course, no researcher could do without the aid—always willingly given—of the various librarians of institutions that I consulted. The most important of these was, of course, the Library of Congress; the others are mentioned in the appropriate footnotes, and I hope such notice will be a sufficient token of my appreciation. My intellectual debts to the biographers of Harlan's colleagues on the Court and of his political friends and foes, as well as to historians of the period of Harlan's life, are also very great.

Many secretaries and typists have worked on various portions of the manuscript, but I would especially like to thank Marian Thomas, who whipped the whole bundle into shape for submission to the publishers.

Especially for a project that covered so many years, the support and understanding of my wife was both necessary and unstintingly given. A little discreet admonishment may have helped me through some especially slow periods. So I dedicate this work to Carol.

Introduction

When on June 1, 1833, Eliza Davenport Harlan presented her husband, James, with a fifth son, the young parents named him John Marshall Harlan. Just then entering upon his thirty-year career as one of Kentucky's most prominent lawyer-politicians, James was an ardent follower of the great Whig leader Henry Clay. Chief Justice John Marshall had become the elderly patron saint of the Whig party, establishing as constitutional law the central tenets that it espoused. Having already named one son Henry Clay and determined that his sons would be lawyers like himself, James undoubtedly felt that it was most appropriate to name this latest addition to the family after the Great Chief Justice, so known even before his death and ever since.

Father Harlan could not foresee that this red-haired squalling infant would in his turn become one of the most prominent members of the Supreme Court. A focus of conflict and controversy almost from his entry into the legal profession, John Marshall Harlan maintained that role throughout his nearly thirty-four years on the bench. His judicial career was marked by numerous dissenting opinions, often solitary: one of his successor judges even labeled him "an eccentric exception." This probably accounts for the fact that after John Harlan died in 1911, his name passed into that decent obscurity that is the usual historical resting place for all but the great judges. Certainly in 1925 no one thought of Harlan as one of the greats.

Greatness was, in a sense, thrust upon Harlan posthumously by the New Deal and Warren Court liberalizations of constitutional doctrine. Successive decisions broadened the scope of federal power (and thus narrowed state power) under the commerce clause, eliminated the use of substantive due process to block economic regulation by the states, extended to blacks and then other minorities the civil rights that had been denied by Harlan's colleagues, and drew increasingly stricter guidelines for state criminal procedures. All of these had been subjects of Harlan's dissenting opinions, which thus came to seem prophetic. This aura of prescience recalled Harlan to the attention of scholars, and every poll taken since the mid-1950s accords him the status of greatness. Numerous scholarly and not-so-scholarly articles and commentaries in books attest to this renewed respect for the Kentuckian. This increased admiration has been given greater force by two other factors: Harlan so often was the only judge in his era to take the positions he did, and Harlan's family and political background made him a most unlikely man to have dissented in these cases, especially those involving racial discrimination.

It is the dual contrast between Harlan and his colleagues and between Harlan and his own background that makes a study of his life and judicial career of interest far beyond the intrinsic appeal of any prominent person's life. Despite these facts, Harlan's life is the least studied of any well-known Supreme Court justice of the nineteenth century (with the possible exception of Joseph P. Bradley). The rough outlines, of course, have been well known to scholars for half a century now: Born to a Kentucky slave-owning family, John Harlan was himself an owner of household slaves until the Thirteenth Amendment freed them. Like his father, he became a Whig politician who upon that party's demise became a Know-Nothing (apparently accepting the anti-Catholic and antiforeign tenets of that short-lived movement); from this he evolved over several years into a Constitutional Unionist supporting John Bell in 1860. He was staunchly Unionist but anti-Lincoln even to the extent of supporting McClellan for president in 1864. He fiercely opposed the Reconstruction Amendments upon their adoption, but by 1867 he turned up in the Republican party as an equally fierce proponent of these amendments. Finally, as a Supreme Court justice he issued the long string of dissenting opinions for which he is best known.

But until his papers became available to scholars, one had little opportunity to study his early life in an attempt to trace the reasons for this apparently plotless succession of events and attitudes. The documents that are now available do not, unfortunately, permit the mystery to be entirely cleared up, but one can at least make intelligent assumptions. In this book I suggest that Harlan's Southern Clay Whig nationalism accounts for most of his major subsequent actions.

As the Northern and Southern Whigs split over the question of slavery, the party quickly died. Southern Whigs either gravitated to the Democratic party with its secessionist tendencies or had to create a new political home for themselves. Clay Whigs felt above all the need to preserve the Union, and so the Harlans were placed in a dilemma. No politician could be successful in Kentucky if he took an openly antislavery position: thus they could not join the new Northern parties that did so—Republican or Free Soil. In an attempt to remain politically viable, they chose "native Americanism." This was only partially and temporarily successful; it was also to prove morally repugnant. Native Americanism was followed by the organization of the state-based Opposition party, which attempted to downplay nativism while emphasizing Unionism and proslavery tenets. By 1860 the

Opposition party members had become able to combine with other former Whigs in the border states to create the Constitutional Union party. This group, unable to support the Republican Lincoln with his Northern anti-slavery base; the northern Democrat Stephen A. Douglas, who was suspected of being soft on Unionism; or the southern extremist John C. Breckinridge, who was supported by out-and-out secessionists, was doomed to failure. Harlan and his Kentucky Unionist friends thus remained in a nationally frustrated political movement, although they were able to control the state and prevent secession until the Civil War ended. Even while fighting on the Union side, Harlan's group retained its basic anti-Lincoln (i.e., proslavery) stance, to the extent of supporting the Democratic presidential candidate in 1864, General George B. McClellan.

Following the war the former Kentucky secessionists rapidly gained control of the state, and the Harlan group was increasingly frustrated by its inability to gain public support even though it opposed the freeing of the slaves and the other Reconstruction Amendments. The anti-Democratic voters were in a minority and were additionally split as Republicans gained strength. Political success in Kentucky for John Harlan became hopeless under these conditions. He could never bring himself to join the secessionist Democrats, and with the slavery issue settled, the Republican party—the apparent inheritor of Whig principles—was the inevitable choice. Although Republicans could not win state elections either, this situation might change gradually; in addition, there was the powerful incentive of patronage from Republican administrations in Washington.

Whole hog or none, once he became a Republican Harlan soon came to support even the hated Reconstruction Amendments, and he gradually drifted into the anti-Grant reform wing of the party. His partnership with a leading reformer, Benjamin H. Bristow, and the latter's unsuccessful bid for the Republican nomination for president in 1876, propelled him in this direction; they also brought him forcibly to the attention of the successful nominee, Rutherford B. Hayes. He was thus soon to become a justice of the United States Supreme Court.

As a judge, freed from immediate partisan concerns, Harlan espoused, on the whole, the old Whig doctrines supporting the national government as against the states. Thus he argued for interpretations of the Fourteenth Amendment and of the commerce clause that would maximize the powers of Congress. With the support of his "old Yankee" wife and his three sons (who all settled in the North), he was encouraged to maintain the rights of the freed slaves even against eight Northern Court brethren who did no such thing.

An intensely partisan man in an intensely partisan era, Harlan often tended to sound as though the apocalypse were at hand, a characteristic that exaggerates the contrasts that abounded in his life. Nevertheless, except in degree, his evolution does not differ markedly from that of most

Northern and border state Whigs who lived through the death of the party and the Civil War. Choices undoubtedly had to be made: Harlan almost invariably made the choices that were most consistent with his Whig nationalism. These specific choices led Harlan to the Supreme Court and then to his great dissenting opinions. The child was father to the man in John Marshall Harlan's life perhaps to a greater degree—if less obviously—than in the lives of most of his colleagues on the Supreme Court.

Part I

THE ROAD TO THE SUPREME COURT

1

Kentucky Childhood
1833-1854

The Harlans were pioneers. From generation to generation they moved away from their native countryside. They were yeoman farmers typically looking for better land.[1] This tradition was begun by George and Michael Harland, sons of Thomas. George was born about 1650 in the hamlet of Monkwearmouth, then in rural County Durham, now part of the city of Sunderland, in England. George and Michael were, or became, Quakers and migrated to northern Ireland, presumably as part of the Anglo-Scottish "colonization" of that troubled area begun under Oliver Cromwell's rule. After George married an Elizabeth Duck, of whom nothing is known, George and Michael moved on, this time to the New World. Being Quakers, they naturally settled in Pennsylvania—in Chester County, about 1687. George, after serving at least once as a member of the Pennsylvania Assembly, was buried in 1714 at Centre Meeting Hall in Pennsbury (Pennsburg?).

A younger son of George and Elizabeth, James Harlan, born in 1692, again moved on, doubtless impelled by land hunger. He settled near what is now Martinsburg, West Virginia (but then Virginia Colony), in the lower Shenandoah Valley, and the Harlans became a Berkeley County family for several generations. Although they probably participated in local affairs, no record exists, and as far as is known they took no part in the Revolutionary War. Some time during this period they ceased being Quakers. Possibly as a result of the Great Awakening in the 1740s, some wandering revivalist converted them to Presbyterianism.

James Harlan's grandson, another James (b. 1755), was to become another pioneer. He and his brother Silas canoed down the Ohio River with James Harrod in 1774. When Harrod established a fort in Kentucky that became the town of Harrodsburg, the Harlans went on along the Salt River a few miles and settled a farm tract that became known to pioneers around 1779 as Harlan's Station. As they became settled they built a solid house of local stone, still called the Old Stone House.[2]

This was the Kentucky of the "dark and bloody ground," still subject to Indian depredations. Silas Harlan, in fact, was killed fighting Indians at the battle of Blue Lick Springs in 1782, and Harlan County in the Appalachians is named for him. John's family, however, occupied the Old Stone House for only three generations. Doubtless their increasing prosperity enabled James's son, of the same name, to give up farming. Born in 1800, he had only what he described as "a good English education embracing mathematics." He went on, "I was intended for mercantile pursuits, and was a clerk in a Dry Goods Store from 1817 to 1821. I then commenced the study of law under the direction of the late Judge John Green and was admitted to the bar in 1823."[3] His practice became so flourishing and its demands so confining that he had to become a townsman. After practicing in and around Harrodsburg for some years,[4] he became a commonwealth attorney and then a Whig member of Congress for two terms (1835-39).[5] It was during this period, about 1821, that he married and established his family. His bride was Eliza Davenport, daughter of Richard, another Kentucky pioneer who came from Spottsylvania County, Virginia.

Thus, on the banks of Clark's Run in the Old Stone House, John Marshall Harlan was born in 1833, "a disastrous plague year."[6] Rural Kentucky—the Bluegrass—in June showed "on every hand a land of peace and plenty, to whose dreamy beatitude the flocks and herds on the quiet hillslopes lent a tranquil charm."[7] By this time the Indians were gone, and the region was civilized, though still to modern ideas quite primitive. John was the fifth son of the eight children born to James and Eliza to survive infancy.

Kentucky politics in James Harlan's day were colorful, often rowdy, and not infrequently violent, not least so in the Salt River country. "A southern congressman reported an encounter with a denizen of the Salt River bottoms who modestly averred that he could jump higher, squat lower, dive deeper, stay under longer, and come up dryer . . . , whip his weight in wildcats, and let a zebra kick him every fifteen minutes."[8] James Harlan himself was a prominent and faithful follower of the great Whig leader Henry Clay, and he served in Congress from Clay's home district. He was, in fact, the only delegate at the 1848 Whig convention who stuck with Clay to the last, refusing to make Zachary Taylor's nomination unanimous. Whigs from Clay's Ashland district were so impressed by this that they presented Harlan with a silver pitcher.[9]

To be a Clay Whig meant being anti-Jeffersonian and, by the same token, pro-John Marshall. John, named after the great chief justice, imbibed these views at his father's knee: belief in a government "that would be supreme and paramount in all matters entrusted to the General Government, its powers, however, to be so exerted as not to infringe upon the rights which remained with the people of the several States." These Whig principles can be clearly seen in the judicial opinions of Justice Harlan.

John, then, grew up with politics and was his father's inheritor in more ways than one. One aspect of his father's career that is most impressive is the wholehearted—even rabid—way in which he espoused whatever he believed. Duels were not uncommon in the South, and many originated in political quarrels. One of these involved James Harlan, who was in 1833 managing the congressional campaign of the Whig, "the portly, dark-skinned, humorous, leisure-loving" Robert P. Letcher. The Democratic opponent, Thomas P. Moore, for some reason challenged James to a duel.[10] His son John later wrote:

> [Moore] arranged to have his challenge delivered to my father at the Central Hotel [in Danville] about two o'clock in the morning. For that purpose his agent caused my father to be aroused from a sound sleep—he supposing no doubt that a man was lacking in nerve or disposition to fight when half asleep. Upon a knock at the door of my father's sleeping room he got up and the challenge was handed to him. He read it by candle light and immediately sat down at his table, in his night gown, and accepted the challenge, and being the challenged party he exercised the right to select the weapons. He prescribed rifles, the rifle of each to be placed at the breast of the other, and they were to fire at a word of command. My father's acceptance of the challenge was promptly communicated to Moore at Harrodsburg. Moore declined to fight on the terms prescribed, contending that they were barbarous. . . . Thereupon my father printed a small hand bill (one of which I remember to have seen . . .) in which he denounced Moore as a liar, scoundrel and coward. He went personally to Harrodsburg on the next county court day, where there was a large crowd, and . . . distributed the hand bills among the people. He finally came to a small crowd in which Moore was standing, and handed one of the hand bills to Moore himself, who took, read it, and then walked off without saying a word. . . . Moore never afterwards appeared in politics, or became an aspirant for office. It was said, in Kentucky, that [Andrew] Jackson had great admiration for Moore (who served one term in Congress) and had determined to make him his successor as President. But the frauds developed on Moore's side in the . . . election were so flagrant . . . that the result of the contest was to impair his chances for advancement.[11]

Letcher's gratitude resulted in James's later appointment as Kentucky's secretary of state, an office that he held from 1841 to 1845 and that necessitated the family's removal to the state capital, Frankfort. The family drove from Harrodsburg to Frankfort, a distance of about thirty miles, in a wagon, "one of the old fashioned affairs," in which was packed "all of their plunder." They settled at first in a house that stood where the home of the superintendent of the state cemetery was later built.[12] Here the eight-year-old John found the atmosphere even more political. The young boy's first distinct memory of politics involved his father's taking him to a speech delivered by the great Henry Clay in Lexington, in which Clay accused the Democrats of unnecessarily bringing on the Mexican War. Harlan recollected that "I was a mere boy at the time and did not know what the occasion meant. But I remember that . . . I sat at his feet, and was charmed with his magnificent bugle voice."[13]

James Harlan remained active politically while building a busy—though hardly lucrative—law practice. He was a member of the Kentucky House of Representatives from 1845 to 1851, the state's attorney general from 1851 to 1861, and a U.S. district attorney from 1861 until his death two years later. As the Whig party declined and died, James cast about for a viable alternative, as did Whigs all over the country. For some reason neither the Free Soil party nor the fledgling Republican party attracted him, and he became instead one of the Kentucky leaders of the American party, whose members were better known as the Know-Nothings. He was evidently not proslavery enough to desert to the Democrats. Today, the Know-Nothing movement seems radically extreme, attempting, as John Harlan observed, "to restrict and destroy the influence of foreigners and Catholic priests in our political affairs." In this desperate effort to revitalize the shell of the old Whig party, John joined his father, pledging in 1854 to support only "native Americans."[14] They both eventually gave active support to Bell's Constitutional Union party in 1860.

Details of John's boyhood are sparse. Growing up in country and small town, with a sizable and no doubt boisterous set of siblings, he probably enjoyed the kind of life common to other Kentuckians of his generation. His brothers—Richard Davenport (b. 1823), William Lowndes (b. 1825), Henry Clay (b. 1830), and James (b. 1832)—were enough older both to tease and to lead. Champ Clark, who grew up in the same area a generation later, recalled the joys of childhood: making popguns of alder stalk and whistles of pawpaw limbs. Children blew up hog bladders, tied up the necks, and left them to dry—and "when the proper time came we would jump on them, and there would be considerable of an explosion." They slid down hills in the winter on homemade sleds; they "wrestled, ran foot-races, turned handsprings, played leapfrog, jumped, swam, climbed trees, swung in grapevine swings, and alas! sometimes we fought." They fished "by every method known to the rural districts of the time—with hook, with seine, and with our hands. If a big fish got under a rock and we could not get him any other way, we would break the rock and catch him. In the winter we would spear them. . . . We learned to shoot and hunted such game as there was. . . . everybody in Kentucky could shoot, generally with a rifle." They had, for entertainment, candy-pullings, spelling bees, country dances, corn-shuckings, log-rollings, and house-raisings. They ate molasses candy, ginger cakes, doughnuts, maple sugar, black walnuts, hickory nuts, hazelnuts, cider and persimmon beer, not to speak of "the luscious pawpaw." Their sweethearts "were fair to look upon, though clad in simple calico, gingham, and linsey-woolsey."[15]

County court days were festive and often rowdy affairs, with people gathering from all around. They were, as well, political occasions, as the story about James Harlan's "duel" indicates. Whole families packed up and went to town—the county seat—for court day. Held once a month on Mondays, county court day was, for the Kentuckian, "the centre of his public social life, the arena of his passions and amusements, the rallying-point of his political discussions, the market-place of his business transactions, the civil unit of his institutional history." County court day was the "monthly Monday on which the Kentuckian regularly did his fighting." He drank, too: "The drinking led up to the fighting, and the fighting led up to the drinking." Whiskey was sold in half-pint "ticklers," and on county court day "wellnigh a whole town would be tickled." It was a day for politics, perhaps preeminently: "The politician, observing the crowd, availed himself of it to announce his own candidacy or to wage a friendly campaign, sure, whether popular or unpopular, of a courteous hearing; for this is a virtue of the Kentuckian, to be polite to a public speaker, however little liked his causes."[16] One fight, which took place on such an occasion in front of the courthouse in Frankfort between Pete Swigert and Demijohn Johnson, was fondly recalled by young Harlan, who said that "after the first fight started, there were soon a score or more of men pounding each other indiscriminately."[17] Whether he was old enough at the time to be one of the participants is not recorded. John Harlan undoubtedly "hung around" county court days from early childhood: certainly he spoke at many of them after he grew up.[18]

Kentuckians were, by and large, religious folk in the middle years of the nineteenth century, especially in the small town and rural atmosphere that characterized so much of the state. The Harlans were devout Presbyterians—and not merely for business reasons. Churchgoing was, then, both customary and frequent, and Harlan never broke that habit. While his religious feelings were no doubt reinforced by the example of his wife, there is no reason to suppose that his beliefs would have been substantially different in any case.[19]

John also grew up in a slave society and in a slave-owning family. His father, Clay Whig that he was, did not believe in the extension of the slave system or in the harsh treatment of slaves. He doubtless felt that slavery was basically an evil and hoped that it would gradually die out. His daughter-in-law Malvina Shanklin ("Mallie") Harlan recounted an incident that illustrates his "inborn hatred for the dreadful institution."

One Sunday morning, on his way to church, he passed in the main street a company of slaves that were being driven to the "Slave Market" in a neighboring town. The able-bodied men and women were chained together, four abreast, preceded by the old ones and the little "pickaninnies," who walked unbound.

This pitiful procession was in charge of a brutish white man belonging to a class which in those days were called "Slave-drivers," because their duty was to drive gangs of slaves, either to their work or to the place of auction. Their badge of office was a long, snake-like whip made of black leather, every blow from which drew blood.

The sight stirred my Father-in-law to the depths of his gentle nature. He saw before him the awful possibilities of an institution which, in the division of family estates, and the sale of the slaves, involved inevitably the separation of husband and wife, of parent and children; and the dreadful type of man which the institution of slavery developed as slave drivers seemed to my Father-in-law to embody the worst aspects of the system.

My Father-in-law could do nothing to liberate the poor creatures then before him; but he was so filled with indignation that any one calling himself a man should be engaged in such a cruel business that, walking out to the middle of the street and angrily shaking his long fore-finger in the face of the "Slave-driver," he said to him, "You are a damned scoundrel. Good morning, sir." After having thus relieved his feelings, he quietly pursued his way to the House of Prayer.

To those who heard and saw this, that day, there was no suggestion of profanity in his language. Like some Old Testament prophet he seemed to be calling down Heaven's maledictions upon the whole institution of Slavery.

My husband, who was then very young, and was with his father on that peaceful Sabbath morning, never forgot the impression that was made upon him by his sudden indignation at the brutal and typical incident. It was the nearest thing to "swearing" that he had ever heard from his father's lips.[20]

She also remembered that James Harlan made it possible for two of his slaves to purchase their freedom: one of them "struck it rich" in the California gold rush and sent back a gift of a fine piano when John's sister Elizabeth was married.[21]

In the Harlan papers there occur occasional references to Robert, or Colonel Robert, Harlan. These must seem mysterious, since no one of that name appears in the official family records. In fact, Robert James Harlan was closely related to John. There exist two stories about this relationship. Robert was the son of a mulatto slave, Mary Harlan; his father was either John's grandfather or his father. According to one story, Robert was born in Virginia in 1816—which would make it likely that grandfather James sired him while on a visit to his old home.[22] But another source claims that Robert was born in Harrodsburg and that his father was the sixteen year old who later became John's father.[23] So he was either John's older half-brother or his half-uncle.

Accounts agree that Robert, although officially a slave, was brought up in the Harlan home as a member of the family. Although he was not sent to school, he was tutored by John's older brothers. Purchasing his freedom for five hundred dollars earned through being a barber and grocer, Robert journeyed via the Panama route to California, where he accumulated a small fortune in the gold fields. Returning east, he settled in Cincinnati, invested his money sucessfully in real estate, and became wealthy, owning racehorses. He married a white woman, Josephine Floyd, the daughter of John B. Floyd (governor of Virginia and secretary of war under President Buchanan, and a Confederate major general). Encountering prejudice probably not least because of his marriage, he immigrated to England in 1859.

Unfortunately, England proved economically unprofitable, and Robert returned to Cincinnati in 1868, where he resumed his active social and political life. He became a trustee of the city's public schools, a colonel in the state militia, a member of the Republican State Committee and delegate to the national conventions in 1872 and 1884, and a prominent member of the state legislature, in which he sponsored the abolition of Ohio's "black laws." When he died in 1897, the Cincinnati *Enquirer* ran two stories about him: he had a little known, but remarkable, career.[24]

The Harlan family apparently kept in touch with Robert throughout his life. Close family friends must have known of the relationship, for one wrote to John: "I saw Robert Harlan talk of England here this week. He seems to have improved by eating English beef and breathing English air."[25] John's brother James, in his ceaseless search for the means to support his drinking habits, was not too proud to ask Robert for money, which was apparently forthcoming, for James wrote his brother that "Bob Harlan has for two years been unusually kind to me, not however putting me under obligation."[26] As late as 1878, Robert was requesting John to renew a note.[27] Mallie, however, discreetly ignores the relationship in her memoir.

Like all wars, the Mexican War touched off tremendous enthusiasm among lively young males. In addition, the Harlans' political idol, Henry Clay, though opposed to the war before it began—as a proponent of good Whig doctrine—fully supported the war effort once hostilities were definitely under way. So his namesake Henry Clay Harlan, although only sixteen, organized a company, of which he became captain. James and John—only fourteen and thirteen—were accepted as noncoms in the unit, which became part of the Twenty-second Regiment of the Kentucky militia. The oldest brother, Richard, was a lieutenant in the Kentucky cavalry and fought at Buena Vista. Despite a good deal of drilling and equipping, Henry Clay Harlan's regiment was never sent to Mexico, nor indeed did it even leave Frankfort.[28]

John's precocity extended beyond his abortive attempt to be a soldier and visit Mexico; he was also extremely literate for a young person. He had what was for his day in Kentucky a fine education. There being no public schools in Kentucky, he was sent to a local school in Frankfort conducted by B.B. Sayre, which had a fine regional reputation. He received a traditional classical education. Dr. Sayre, like Harlan's mother some years later, thought he should be trained as a merchant. Father James, however, would have no truck with such an idea. His sons were to be lawyers, and even though three elder brothers were already destined for the law, he obviously felt that there would be no purpose in having a name like John Marshall if one were to be only a businessman.[29]

First, in any case, he was to attend college. John was the third Harlan boy to enroll at Centre College in Danville, which under the leadership of President John Clarke Young enjoyed a great reputation in the 1840s and 1850s. Nevertheless, its orthodox Presbyterianism probably had as much to do with the attendance of the Harlans as did its academic reputation. Henry Clay Harlan had preceded John there by two years, and no doubt his experience was influential in the selection of the college for John also. James Harlan deeply felt his own lack of a good education, wishing his sons to be better off in that regard. He wrote to a friend that "my education was very imperfect, as you will perceive from this letter."[30] Along with his brother James, John went off to Danville in 1848, rated as a junior at the ripe old age of fifteen. When he graduated with honors two years later, his mother apparently tried again to steer him away from the legal career his father had determined upon. But even though Mother Harlan had already made arrangements for John to work under a distant kinsman in a Philadelphia mercantile house, his father stuck to his original purpose.[31]

Centre College was one of the first institutions of higher education established west of the Appalachians, and it educated a high proportion of the "Western elite" during most of the nineteenth century. It was small (by standards of today, that is), enrolling perhaps 150 during the years of the Harlan boys' attendance. The college claimed that there was "no place where their [the students'] morals and health would be more secure" and that discipline was rigorous enough so that students were not exposed to "such disorders as are frequent in many institutions." As a matter of fact, the college was proud that its discipline was largely self-enforcing: at times, three or four years went by with no college-enforced discipline beyond simple admonition.[32]

The college was apparently to a large degree the extended image of its president. His attitudes toward religion, discipline, and education were the college's attitudes. John Clarke Young came to Centre as president at the tender age of twenty-seven. A man of outstanding character, with a Scot's sobriety and practicality, he established the college on a sound financial basis, even using his personal life to bolster the college's status: his first wife was a Breckinridge, and his second, a Crittenden. Except for Clay himself, one could go no higher in Kentucky political and social circles.[33]

One of his successors, in noting Young's great influence, remarked: "He was a great teacher and a greater preacher. He was a prince among teachers and preachers, and he was singularly gifted in his power to adapt himself to young men. He secured their respect; he won their confidence; he awed them, if it became necessary to do so; he dominated them by his will; he could, on occasion, overwhelm with his indignation or wither with his scorn. He had the precious gift of imparting knowledge. He had the rarer and higher gift of inspiring love for learning and strengthening the purpose of doing something."[34] While he was a deeply religious man, President Young does not appear to have been pious or antirationalistic; certainly neither trait shows itself in his inaugural address in 1830, in which he said:

> In a college like ours, to which all denominations of Christians may send their sons for instruction, no sectarian dogmas should be inculcated; those truths only should be taught which are common to all—those general and clearly revealed truths which will draw forth the affections towards God, and cause us to walk in His ways. But for making the youth acquainted with these truths, and making them feel their power, every means should be used. The Bible should be placed in the hands of all—it should be studied and recited. Besides, there should be a constant commixture of efficacious scriptural truth with the ordinary instructions in literature and science.[35]

Despite the religious emphasis, education basically concentrated on the classics. Had John Harlan attended ten years later, he would have been faced (as a junior and senior) with the following curriculum, which was probably not very much different from the program in 1848:

JUNIOR YEAR
First Term: Cicero, Greek, Evidences of Christianity, Rhetoric, Chemistry, Differential Calculus.
Second Term: Cicero, Greek, Moral Philosophy, Political Economy, Physiology, Rhetoric, Natural Philosophy, Integral Calculus, Geology.

SENIOR YEAR
First Term: Quintillian, Plato contra Atheos, Natural Philosophy, Mental Philosophy, Logic, Criticism.
Second Term: Juvenal, Aristophanes, Constitution of the U.S., Lectures on International Law, Butler's Analogy, Logic, Astronomy, Civil Architecture, Zoology.[36]

In addition to the formal curriculum, there was a "weekly requirement of reading and declamation for all students with original speeches required of juniors and seniors."[37] This requirement may be the source of John Harlan's essay—done at the age of fifteen—on the impact of the American Revolution. This rather high-flown piece of rhetoric, complete with quotations of poetry, can best be evinced by direct quotation: "The name, the fame, the achievements of our heroes, were sounded abroad, and served as a watchword to the lovers of liberty all over the world. Our country was the birthplace of modern freedom; but no sooner had her opinions acquired strength and maturity, than she flew forth in other climes, to establish her temples on the ruins of baronial castles and feudal prison-houses."[38]

Biblical instruction was a part of the daily regimen. There was chapel every day, church as well as a Bible lesson on Sunday, and "an opportunity of attending a religious lecture from the President, once during each week."[39] Rules were strict, even if punishment was in most instances moderate. Obviously, taverns and many stores, houses, and shops were off-limits; nor could students attend any "theatre, ball, dancing-party, or horse-race." They could not have guns or sword-canes. "Profane swearing, intemperance, obscenity, licentiousness, impiety, playing at cards or at any game of wager" were prohibited—as were boisterous noises.[40]

Costs seem to have been minimal, even taking into account the lower general price levels of the day: room, board, and laundry, including fuel, might run to a maximum of $3.00 a week in private homes, and perhaps $2.25 in college. Tuition was similarly low, as no doubt were faculty salaries.[41]

One might think that Centre students had no time for play, but of course given the exuberance of youth this was not true. John Harlan was as high-spirited as the next youth, as a college acquaintance later recalled in a letter to him: "Do you remember the years spent at Centre College and the fight between Sam ——— and yourself, which seemed so serious at the time, but over the recollection of which you have doubtless often smiled since? I know I have—and although at the time I was ———s friend, and consequently not yours—the whole matter has long since ceased to occur to me in any light other than the ridiculous."[42]

President Young's views on slavery, like his attitude toward religion, were moderate. The slavery question tore churches apart, but up to his death in 1857 Young and his college slid through without great difficulty despite the fact that the president was well known as a "gradual emancipationist." He freed some of his own slaves, and in 1849 he spoke in favor of a gradual emancipation clause for the proposed new state constitution.[43] He was not, however, an abolitionist, and he was unable to protect the position of one of his faculty members, James C. Birney, who espoused that doctrine and was forced out.[44]

Before the Civil War, American lawyers were almost all office-trained through an apprenticeship arrangement. There were few law schools, and it was not generally thought necessary to have formal legal training. In fact, when Harlan joined the Supreme Court in 1877, none of his colleagues had graduated from law schools.[45] The first law school was Harvard's, established in 1817, although quite a few colleges had law lectureships or professorships earlier than that. Even in 1850 law schools were few, especially west of the Appalachians.

Therefore there is occasion for comment that Father James Harlan—who could have trained all his sons in his own office—chose to send two of them (James and John) to attend the law department of Transylvania University in Lexington. The oldest institution of higher education west of the Alleghenies, Transylvania also had the first law school. It had a strong law faculty and a formal two-year program. The program was at its height from the 1830s to the mid-1850s; after that it declined very rapidly and was abolished about 1858. The mainstay of the faculty, undoubtedly, was George Robertson, former congressman, state representative, and chief justice of Kentucky, who taught at the institution from 1834 to 1857. Thomas A. Marshall, another noted Kentucky jurist, was also one of Harlan's teachers.

These men were of the Whig persuasion, and both were Unionists during the Civil War. Judge Robertson gave the valedictory address to Harlan's graduating class in 1852. It was a chapter-and-verse attack on the Virginia and Kentucky Resolutions of 1798 and 1799, aimed primarily at the consequent concepts of nullification and secession.[46] It so impressed young John Harlan that he became one of a committee of three to urge the judge to have the address published, a request to which Robertson duly acceded, in the belief (as their petition stated) that it would "have the tendency to check the monstrous doctrines of nullification and secession."[47] One of the cosigners was George Graham Vest, who, his early antisecessionist views notwithstanding, went on to be an officer in the Confederate army and, much later, a distinguished senator from Missouri.[48]

Robertson, like Young, was basically opposed to slavery but could see no way to get rid of it easily. In an address given to the people of Fayette County about the proposed new constitution of 1849, he said:

> I am not one of those who believe that domestic slavery is a blessing, moral or physical, to the white race. I cannot believe that it makes us richer, more moral, more religious, more peaceful, more secure, or more happy—nor can I admit that, under its various influences, our children become more industrious, more practical, or more useful; and I am sure that free labor is degraded, and laboring freemen greatly injured by slavery. If, in the dispensation of an all-wise Providence, it could be obliterated from the face of the earth, I should consider the achievement as most glorious and beneficent to mankind: . . . But I apprehend that day is not our day.[49]

Many years later Harlan, by then an old man "looking back through memory's haze" and no doubt thus exaggerating days that he fondly recollected, had this to say about his law school:

> I remember when here of sitting at the feet of some of the greatest judges and lawyers that ever appeared in this or, I believe, any other country. George Robertson, Thomas A. Marshall, A.J. Woolley and Madison C. Johnson were the professors or teachers in this law school when I had the honor to be a member of it, and I undertake to say that no law school that has ever existed in this country or, in my judgment, in any other country has had at the same time

as professors and teachers of the science of law four greater lawyers than those four that I have named. If George Robertson and Thomas A. Marshall had been placed upon the bench of the Supreme Court of the United States in their early youth, they would have left a royal heritage as jurists of our Nation. No greater lawyers in the largest sense of the word ever lived in this country, in my judgment, than Madison C. Johnson. He deserves to be ranked by the side of Daniel Webster and lawyers of that kind.[50]

Hyperbole aside, there is no doubt that Harlan's formal training—in both college and law school—was the best that the West could provide at that time.

Harlan also had the opportunity while at Transylvania for his first contact with sophistication and culture. While it would be too much to say that up to 1850 he was a rustic (his college experience and his life in the state capital prevented that), Danville and Centre College provided at best an idyllic small town atmosphere and a rather narrow if sound education. Frankfort offered little beyond an exclusive concern with politics.[51] Lexington was a different matter. A small city even in those days—although it probably seemed large to young John—Lexington had by 1850 lost its commercial predominance in the state to the growing river city of Louisville. The coming of railroads would speed up this process. But at midcentury Lexington retained an urbanity and sophistication that made it the social and cultural center of the Kentucky-Tennessee West and gave it the title Athens of the West. In addition to the university, Lexington boasted a group of academies and schools for girls, a natural history museum and library, and a school of art. One visitor—perhaps overly impressed to find such a place as far west as Kentucky—called it "a Paris in miniature," a town in which "a taste for elegance and luxuries prevails, [and] the fashions and manners of polished Europe are found."[52] Lectures, concerts, and literary gatherings were available, and even though we have no direct evidence that John Harlan took advantage of them, there is little doubt that the aura of the town had its effect in broadening his horizons and giving him some idea of life outside the rural Bluegrass. Also, the aged idol Henry Clay had his famous home, Ashland, in the town.

Harlan's political career, one might say, also began during his Transylvania period. In the spring of 1851, before he even reached the age of eighteen, John was offered the post of adjutant general of the state. When Governor John L. Helm made the offer, rather casually, Harlan assumed he was joking and reminded the governor of his tender age. "No matter," Helm replied, "you can fill the place." The following autumn Harlan was indeed appointed. The post was largely a sinecure: the state had practically no military organization, and the job consisted primarily of keeping a few old military records from the War of 1812 and attending some meetings as presiding officer of the board of the two private military institutions holding state charters. The latter task Harlan performed "with all the dignity I could command." He also was the state's official representative at the commencement ceremonies of the two schools. At one of these he met young James G. Blaine, who was then teaching at the Western Military Institute at Drennon Springs, earning the princely sum of $1,200 a year. Harlan himself was paid $250 a year for performing these onerous duties, and he retained the post under successive governors for eight years.[53]

For a budding young lawyer the post was of some value, nevertheless, in expanding Harlan's acquaintance around the state and providing him with some statewide visibility that would prove helpful a few years later when he became active in elective politics. He also gained the appellation "General," even before the Civil War, a title that stayed with him until his Supreme Court appointment.

The years immediately following John Harlan's Transylvania period were spent largely in getting his feet on the ground as a lawyer. He was admitted to the bar in 1853, but he was already occupying a desk in his father's law office in Frankfort. James Harlan had a thriving though not outstandingly remunerative practice and was able to absorb the energies of the remaining three sons. The other two had died young: Henry Clay Harlan of what was probably tuberculosis in 1849, and Richard Davenport—the veteran of Buena Vista—in 1854. Both young James and William Lowndes Harlan were to remain in their father's office until his death in 1863. Nothing further is known of William except that he died in 1868; but the later life of James will be referred to from time to time in this narrative.

John seems during this period to have practiced law mostly as his father's clerk, while at the same time gradually taking on some clients of his own, sometimes traveling to nearby county seats. Since he had no clerk, he at times pressed his young wife, Malvina, into service in copying legal documents.[54] He no doubt took part in the thriving social life of the little community. Finally, he began to take an active interest in politics, being elected city attorney of Frankfort in 1854, a position to which he was reelected in 1856.[55] Although running for office was a political act, the duties of the position were not. They consisted of prosecuting petty offenders: breach of the peace, drunkenness, selling liquor to slaves. For such offences the punishments would normally be small fines. The fact that the job took little of John's time is indicated by his ledgers, which record only thirty-five cases during his first year.[56]

Even in the 1850s life in rural Kentucky could be adventurous. There were many Harlans scattered around Boyle County, and one of the young lawyer's cousins was inevitably named John also. Young cousin John, Harlan later recalled,

> was a remarkable young man in intellect, but with a tendency to irregular habits.

A few years after 1850, I now forget the date, he was "in the hills" of Boyle County, at an improper place, and there came into contact with a dangerous man named Pitman. They quarreled, and Pitman advanced upon John as if to attack him. The latter drew a pistol, and killed Pitman. That aroused the Pitman "gang," and they, it was believed, formed the purpose to kill John, at the first opportunity, when it could be done safely. I say safely, because they knew that John would kill the man who assaulted him, unless he was first killed. John was indicted for murder in the Boyle Circuit Court, and Hon. Joshua F. Bell, the leading lawyer and orator in that part of Kentucky was employed to defend him. Well, the trial came on, and my father and myself attended the trial. The Pitmans were all "around" in the court room. They could be seen during the trial whispering and conferring with each other as if planning mischief, and it was feared, indeed, believed, that they intended to kill John as he came into or went out of the court house, from time to time, during the trial. So "Big Jim," my cousin Wellington Harlan, and myself, were immediately around John every step, going and coming, between the jail and the court room, and at his side in the court room during the trial. Our purpose was to make it impossible for the Pitmans to get at him, without encountering his brother and two cousins in deadly conflict. Our plan was successful. The trial resulted in John's acquittal, and he went out of the court house, free, with Big Jim, Wellington, and myself at his side. My father and I immediately left for our home at Frankfort, taking John with us and keeping him for several months, until the excitement, in Boyle County, among the Pitmans and their partisans, subsided. I should, in candor, say that during the whole of John's trial, Big Jim, Wellington and myself were heavily armed. The man the other side most feared was Big Jim, who was believed to have on his person (as he did) an enormous bowie knife, which he had the strength, skill and willingness to use, if necessary, for John's or his own or our safety.[57]

2

Kentucky Lawyer-Politician
1855-1860

John Harlan as a young man had the normal interest in the fair sex; nevertheless he does not seem to have had any serious affairs until he met his future wife. Thomas T. Crittenden—a nephew of the famous senator, and a future governor of Missouri—was living in Frankfort during the 1850s, and the two young lawyers were good friends. Tom later wrote that they "often visited together the beautiful young ladies of the city and State." In fact, Crittenden continued, John Harlan "introduced me to the fair, handsome Kentuckian who afterwards became my wife, and he was one of my attendants at the wedding."[1]

Nevertheless, Harlan's chosen bride was not one of the local belles. His older sister, Elizabeth, had married a physician, James G. Hatchitt, from Evansville, Indiana, and had gone there to live. Both James and John Harlan visited her occasionally despite the long trip, taken by stage or horseback and steamboat; and both found their wives in Evansville. But John's wife's memoir tells the tale more interestingly than an outsider could.

One day during the late summer of 1853 in Evansville, Indiana, a small but growing town in the Southwestern part of the State—a young girl of fifteen, suffering from some slight affection of the eyes, had been confined by the physician's orders to a darkened room.

. . . Happening at the moment to peep through a narrow crack of the almost closed window-shutters, she saw a young man passing by. As she had lived all her life in that small town and was familiar with almost every face in it, she knew at once that he was a stranger.

. . . That was sixty-one years ago; but, as clearly as if it were yesterday, she can still see him as he looked that day—his magnificent figure, his head erect, his broad shoulders well thrown back—walking as if the whole world belonged to him.

. . . On the sixth of the following February, she was invited to take supper with the family of Dr. J.G. Hatchitt, a young physician living in the block beyond her father's residence. To her surprise, as she sat talking to her hostess, a young man—with a rope to each arm, as he "played horsey" for the little nephew that was the delighted and uproarious Jehu—suddenly pranced into the room. The young girl at once recognized him as the interesting stranger that had caught her eye six months before, as she peeped through the narrow crack of her window-shutters, and whom, after the romantic style of that period, she had (to herself) called "A Prince of the Blood."

. . . Very much amused and yet covered with manly confusion at thus being caught by a strange young girl in the act of "playing the boy," the young man—who proved to be John Marshall Harlan, of Frankfort, Kentucky, and a brother of the hostess—was duly presented to "Miss Malvina Shanklin."[2]

Malvina French ("Mallie") Shanklin was the daughter of an Evansville businessman, evidently a successful one. Her mother's family was descended from two old New England families, the Bradfords and the Howes. One of the Howes established the Howe Tavern, known to history as Longfellow's Wayside Inn, in South Sudbury, Massachusetts, and Edith Howe, who lived there, married Timothy Bradford in 1764. Family tradition says that the Howes "were all Tories or Royalists till the war broke out, drinking their tea made on a chafing dish in the cellar, but they soon took up arms for their country. Edith Howe Bradford cut out a web of cloth from the loom and made it into clothes and knapsacks for her brothers and neighbors." Later on, the Bradfords "were invited to dine with Washington at a dinner given by him to his officers of staff, who were each allowed to invite two of their friends or relatives; and Edith Bradford junior, who was a very small child, sat on Washington's knee, and he called her 'a pretty curly-haired little Miss.' "[3]

Malvina Harlan's recollections of meeting Harlan continue:

His conversation during that evening greatly interested the young girl, showing unusual thought and intelligence for a youth of only twenty-one. That night he escorted her home. As was her custom, being an only daughter [she had three brothers], she went straight to her mother's room to tell her "all about" the very pleasant acquaintance she had just made. She showed so much enthusiasm in her description of him that her mother, after listening awhile to her girlish outburst, said, in a very dry, decided and matter-of-fact tone:

"You have talked quite enough about a young man whom you have only seen for an hour or two; now, you can go up to your room. Good night."

During the next week, a daily call from this new friend gave me a new interest in life; and at the end of the week, before he left for his Kentucky home, to my great surprise he asked me to be his wife. . . .

I must mention a style of dress for young men that was in vogue in the days of our courtship—whether it was a fashion in the country at large or was confined to the West and South, I do not know.

It consisted of a dark blue dress-coat, decorated with large flat brass buttons on both sides of the front and at the waist line in the back. The buttons were a generous inch in diameter, wholly without design, the polish of the flat surface equalling gold in brilliancy. This coat was worn with a buff waistcoat and buff trousers, made of a material somewhat resembling in texture the khaki of today. This interesting fashion was not long-lived, as I remember it; but while it lasted it gave an air of its own to the young men of that day. It was used for informal occasions.

This style of dress-suit was most becoming to my young man—the dark blue color bringing out his wonderfully clear complexion and his fine blue eyes. His beautiful sandy hair, which he wore quite long (as was the fashion of the day) he always parted on the right side, instead of the left, as did all the young men of his family, giving them a most marked individuality.

In those days early marriages were quite common, and in my case the young man urged an immediate consummation of his wishes. But the wiser counsels of parents prevailed, and for two years—during which I was at school and he at the practice of law in his father's office in Frankfort—we corresponded, an occasional visit from him making the time seem shorter.[4]

Mallie was sent to school in Glendale, Ohio, near Cincinnati, where she apparently boarded with an uncle. Her niece many years later wrote to Mallie's son Richard that "Uncle Maynard . . . borded [sic] her and dressed her beautifully and she had her hair curled by a barber and went to a dance every Monday night and was called a very pretty girl and had a very happy young ladyhood. He [her uncle] bought her a *$800 piano* which was the *first one ever brought to this city.*" Since Mallie was a fine musician, the acquisition of the piano is believable, even if it was not actually the first in Evansville.[5]

Mallie's parents were more interested in young Harlan's character than in his financial status. Perhaps, she remarks, "if they had known what the young wife afterwards learned, namely, that . . . [John] had to borrow $500 from his father for the expenses of the wedding and for our start in life, my parents might have looked upon their decision as a trifle unwise and hasty."[6] It should, however, be remembered that John, like his brothers, was working for a "law firm" and could only get his share of the profits from his father; that he was only starting out in his own practice; and that living at home cut his expenses to a minimum.

Mallie vividly describes the wedding:

In those days, in the community in which I was brought up, the announcement of an engagement would have seemed somewhat indelicate; and in my case it was *not until* the receipt of an invitation from my parents, announcing simply that they would be At Home on December 23, 1856, and enclosing two cards tied together at the top with a tiny tell-tale bow of white ribbon—one bearing the name of John Marshall Harlan and the other the name of Malvina French Shanklin—*that any of the friends on either side had any idea that a marriage was in prospect.* The only exceptions were the six bridesmaids, who were pledged to secrecy. A dress maker from New York had been smuggled into the house and was carefully hidden from view for two whole months, during the preparation of my simple trousseau.

Thus bidden in the quaintly reserved fashion of those early days, a large company of our friends gathered promptly at nine o'clock on the evening of December 23, 1856, in the large front parlor of my father's house, to witness what was called a "Tableau Wedding"—which at that time was quite an innovation.

In the smaller back parlor, which was shut off by folding doors from the front room, until the great moment arrived, the bridal party of fourteen were grouped in a semi-circle facing the wedding guests—six bridemaids alternating with six groomsmen, the Bride and Groom standing in the centre. At weddings in those early days (as I recall it) there was no best man—at all events, at *my* wedding the Groom (to one person, at least) was the only best man; so that in the semi-circle that formed our "Tableau," a bridesmaid, instead of a groomsman stood at the Groom's right hand, while a groomsman stood at my left.

Two of the bridesmaids were dressed in pink, two in blue and two in buff, the Bride, of course, being in white.

The Groom wore the traditional black dress-coat; but his waistcoat was of black velvet, and his neck tie, instead of being white, was an old fashioned black stock, rather broad and fastened in the middle with a gold scarf pin. He wore a high standing collar, with a broad opening, the slightly flaring points coming well above the line of his firm and strongly marked chin—the quaint stock and collar, together, giving him a dignity and maturity beyond his three-and-twenty years.

The immediate members of the two families and the officiating clergyman were the only other persons in the back parlor.

When all things were ready, the folding doors were then thrown open, thus revealing the Tableau, and the ceremony was performed in the presence of the large company of friends who were gathered in the front parlor.

At every entertainment in those days, amateur music, both vocal and instrumental, made part of the pleasure of the occasion. And in marked contrast to the formality and conventionality of social life at the present time [1915], I may recall the fact that the Bride on that December night . . . was escorted to the piano by the young husband, that she might contribute to the pleasure of the evening. I had had advantages in the way of musical education that were rather unusual in those days in my part of the country, and it was not until I had sung three or four of the popular ballads of the day that I was allowed to leave the piano.[7]

After a short honeymoon in the home of the bride's parents—a customary arrangement at that time—Mr. and Mrs. John Harlan took up residence with the elder Harlans in Frankfort. In addition to constituting Mallie's first face-to-face experience with slavery, it was also the first time she had lived in a large extended family household. This consisted of the older couple, Mallie and John, James and his wife (he had married Amelia Lane of Evansville on April 2, 1856), William, and the two remaining unmarried sisters, Laura and Sallie. In addition, Elizabeth ("Bettie") Hatchitt usually brought her two children to Frankfort for the summer. Together with the household slaves, this group required a large house. Actually the

Harlans had two houses—one in the center of town that they occupied in the winter, and a summer house on a bluff overlooking the town. The town house was "an old-fashioned frame mansion, with spacious rooms, standing at the corner of an unusually wide and deep lot." [8]

In this large household the father and mother were still relatively young and active. Father Harlan was fifty-seven, though he appeared older to Mallie's still girlish eyes, but "he was as straight as an arrow, with firm, elastic step, his head well set on a magnificent set of shoulders. His manner was very reserved—the result of great modesty and shyness, and not from a lack of interest in those around him. He was indeed the head of his house, and his wife and children adored and revered him." His wife, nevertheless, "was the moving spirit and comforter of the entire household." [9] (Mallie never describes Eliza Harlan's physical appearance.)

During Kentucky's long, hot summers the entire household moved to the top of "Harlan's Hill" to escape the worst of the heat. Unfortunately the slope was so steep that the place could be reached only on foot or by horseback, which made carrying clothing and supplies up and down rather difficult. Originally a "small summer home," it must have eventually been fairly large, since "as the boys, one by one, brought their brides to the family home, or the girls their husbands, room after room was added to the rambling house, which was only a storey-and-a-half in height, and one room deep. A broad vine-covered latticed porch, which ran the full length of the long-drawn-out cottage, served on very warm days as sitting room and dining room and library—for books were everywhere." [10] Summers were thus made livable if not comfortable.

The Harlan houses, with their lively young people, were inviting places for the younger crowd to gather, and Mother Harlan did nothing to discourage all comers. Mallie relates: "Many a party of young people, after enjoying the steep climb to the house on the hill, found such a welcome as gladdened their hearts. They felt sure that, even if the rain should come up in the evening (and I remember many such an occasion), the girls, at least, could count on comfortable housing for the night and a good breakfast in the morning. . . . A way was always found by my capable and hospitable Mother-in-law to make room for one more, even if the younger members of the household, both married and single, had to be put up with cots laid on the floor." [11]

Living in this style would have been possible, if not as easy, without slavery. After all, the extended family system provided almost automatically for a supply of young wives and husbands who would have been available to help with the work. For families like the Harlans, slavery enabled most of the ladies of the household to constitute a kind of leisure class; they could concern themselves with visits to the state legislature (a favorite form of social activity), with parties, and with their frequent pregnancies and the children resulting therefrom. The men of the house-hold, on the other hand, were hardly leisured. Wives, children, and slaves constituted for them an economic burden. Nor was the task of Mother Harlan—of running this large household enterprise—by any means a sinecure.

James Harlan, Sr., was by no means a wealthy man, if one considers wealth to be cash, either in income or in savings. The family law firm provided what was necessary to run the household and provide clothing for the senior Harlans, the unmarried daughters, and the slaves. The married males had to have their own practices to provide clothing and other necessaries and luxuries for their own wives and children. Being the state capital, Frankfort was a flourishing place for the law. The senior Harlan's practice—with his sons often acting as clerks—included a great deal of appellate work; not only was he admired as a lawyer, but the state's highest court, the court of appeals, was located in Frankfort. For that reason, many of the state's best lawyers congregated in the capital. As Mallie discovered, it was therefore

> necessary for my Young Lawyer, in his efforts to build up his practice, to go upon the Circuit. For the first four or five years of our married life, he was away from Frankfort for practically half the year, though it was only for a week or ten days at a time; so that we had to be contented with what snatches of home life we could get in the intervals between.
>
> It was a period of steady growth for him, and was just what he needed to prepare him for his future career. The contact with comparative strangers and with men of learning and standing in every profession greatly widened his outlook, giving him an experience that he would not otherwise have had. Many of these trips were made by the old-fashion stage-coach lines, and some of them were on horseback, with saddle-bags to carry his clothes and law papers.[12]

· In fact, the need to enlarge his practice to take care of his growing family, together with the increasing pressure being placed on him to con-duct an expensive and quite possibly fruitless second race for Congress, led John to decide to leave the family firm in 1861. John, devoted to his profession, at the same time felt that he needed a larger field for its practice. The little family therefore moved to Louisville, where John went into partnership with an experienced and "very prominent" local lawyer, Judge William F. Bullock. By this time there were two children. Edith Shanklin Harlan was born on November 14, 1857, and Richard Davenport Harlan, on the same date two years later. The third child was born later in the year of the move: he was James Shanklin Harlan, born on November 24, 1861.[13]

The Harlans were not abolitionists. They owned slaves, and they had always lived in a society in which slavery surrounded them. On the other hand, John imbibed from his teachers—his father, President Young of Centre College, and Judge Robertson of Transylvania—a deep dislike of involuntary servitude in any form. Mallie had been taught to oppose slavery strongly, and there is no doubt that she exercised some influence over her husband, in this as in his active religious faith. Prepared to dislike everything about the peculiar institution, she nevertheless was impressed that all the Harlan slaves were "carefully looked after, not only physically but morally." She found that the elderly, who could no longer work, were "cared for like . . . babies"; they were visited daily and took a great interest in what went on in the "Big House." "The close sympathy existing between the slaves and their Master or Mistress was a source of great wonder to me as a descendant of the Puritans, and I was often obliged to admit to myself that my former views of the awful institution of slavery would have to be somewhat modified."[14]

These attitudes were doubtless shaped by society; they were also deeply influenced by the political interests of the family. Father James was an elected official, and John himself soon would get caught up in elective politics. Although there were out-and-out abolitionists in Kentucky, they were not elected to public office. Even those who were publicly known as gradual emancipationists stood mostly on the political sidelines.[15]

There has been a lot of speculation on the origins of John Marshall Harlan's remarkable stands in favor of Negro rights as a Supreme Court justice, which seem to demonstrate a transformation that has never been satisfactorily explained.[16] My own attempt is set down later in this volume; at this point it is sufficient to say that his private attitudes were probably to some degree different from his public statements as early as 1855. He was led by partisan enthusiasm and the desire to win elections, once he became a candidate, with a resulting split between the private and the public man.

One specific event, interesting in itself, may bring some additional evidence to bear upon John's general attitudes on the race question. (It is well to point out that to antebellum politicians the slave question and the race question were not the same thing: doing away with slavery was one question; the belief in the equality of the races was another.) In the fall of 1858 Father Harlan wrote to a friend, "Both myself and my son John have been prevented from attending to any business for several weeks, having had our hands badly burned. This will account for our delay in answering."[17] Thus noncommittally did he pass over what were really quite serious injuries, especially to John. Nor did he reveal the tale of heroism involved. Mallie was not so reticent in her memoirs.

In October 1858 the family as usual planned to move down from Harlan's Hill to the town house for the winter. In the hubbub of packing one of the slave girls was working late on her own mending in a sitting room kept warm by the embers of a log fire. The girl fell asleep on the floor and accidentally knocked over the candle by the light of which she had been working. Her clothes caught fire; she screamed in fear and agony. Everyone was awakened and, running into the sitting room,

> found the poor girl a veritable pillar of fire . . . like a wild animal making the circuit of the large room in her awful agony.
>
> My husband, catching her with one hand as she was about to pass the door by which he entered, held her fast, and, with the other hand, tore her clothes off as best he could. His father and mother both joined him in his efforts and were badly burned, though not so severely as he was.
>
> The excitement and terror of the moment made us lose sight of every one else except the poor suffering girl; but I can never forget my husband's muffled and agonized cry (My God), as he held out his poor hands to me. The left hand, with which he had gripped the girl with full strength, was seared to the bone and the right arm from the finger tips to the elbow was almost unrecognizable, as belonging to a human body. He was a hero in his suffering, and with unsurpassed bravery he lay waiting until the poor girl could be relieved, though the shock to her was fatal. She became unconscious in a short time, and lived only a few hours.[18]

In addition to the horror of the girl's death, John and his parents were badly injured, and in John's case recovery was especially painful and slow. On the third day following the incident he had serious convulsions, which the doctors felt were probably the first symptoms of tetanus (in those days invariably fatal).[19]

> The paroxysms were most severe . . . [and] my poor husband's face was so changed as to be almost unrecognizable. He knew me, however, and in a short time he seemed more quiet. Two physicians from town soon came to his relief, and they gave him quieting potions that produced a change for the better. The burns were dressed afresh, and all excitement quieted, the family physician calling me aside to say that it was a most alarming change; but that, if perfect control could be maintained and no anxiety exhibited on the part of any one of the family, he hoped that, as nature was now beginning to do her healing work, the spasms might become less by degrees, although they would probably return before very long.[20]

This doctor's guarded optimism proved indeed to be justified. Later spasms became progressively lighter and there was no other complication to John's recovery. Nevertheless, the occurrence left its mark. Many years later—perhaps in 1903 or so—John accidentally spilled "scalding-hot tea onto the same hand," and the same spasms briefly recurred.[21]

The incident indicates not only individual courage but also the fact that basically the Harlans regarded slaves as human beings, not merely chattels. It is doubtful that John's campaign rhetoric, which at times sounded extremely racist, convinced even himself.[22]

John Harlan's political career beyond the local level really began in 1855. Though its beginning was accidental, there is no doubt that he was destined for politics. John's entrance onto the statewide political stage coincided with the decline and eventual disappearance of the Whig party, which also was affected drastically in Kentucky by the death of Henry Clay. Basically, the party's troubles stemmed from the sectional and emotion-laden character of the slavery issue, especially as it was influenced by the battle over the extension of the peculiar institution to the territories. Clay's last great political act, the Compromise of 1850, sounded the death knell for the Whigs; by providing for the admission of California as a free state while the rest of the territory gained from Mexico was inferentially open to slavery, it opened the way to the argument that the Missouri Compromise of 1820 was no longer in effect and that the people of each territory—regardless of its location—had the right to adopt slavery if they wished. Stephen A. Douglas, using this argument, pushed the Kansas-Nebraska Act through Congress in 1854, allowing those two territories the right of "squatter sovereignty." The whole controversy had the result of splitting the Southern slave-owning Whigs from the Northern Whigs. While the Southerners might oppose slavery in principle, they felt (as the Harlans did) that states should decide for themselves and that slavery should not be legally abolished but rather allowed to wither away with the aid of state laws prohibiting the slave trade. Northern Whigs, on the other hand, while they might not be out-and-out abolitionists (though they increasingly became so), felt strongly that slavery should not be extended into any of the territories or new states.[23]

The 1850s thus became perhaps the most confused decade in our history as far as the party situation was concerned. Northern Whigs mostly became Free Soilers or "native Americans" (Know-Nothings) on their way to their eventual home in the new, abolitionist Republican party. Southern Whigs had a more difficult choice, for basically they had to choose between favoring slavery and favoring its abolition. It is understandable that, faced with this Hobson's choice, many of them sought some sort of middle way. Regardless of personal attitudes toward slavery, Whigs like the Harlans could not (as they saw it) become Republicans without dooming themselves to permanent minority status. But all of their political heritage made the Democratic party, with its proslavery, states' rights tradition, an inhospitable group. So although many Southern Whigs did make this choice, the "conscience Whigs" like the Harlans found it impossible to do so.

Yet they had to do something. In Kentucky, the Whigs lost the governorship for the first time in a decade in 1851. Although they managed to hold on to the other state offices—James Harlan, Sr., was elected attorney general—the events of the following few years demonstrated the futility of attempting to keep the Whig party afloat.[24] General Winfield Scott, the party's presidential candidate in 1852, suffered a calamitous defeat even though he managed to carry Kentucky. He was, however, the last national candidate the party fielded.

All the leading Kentucky Whigs, of course, had the same problem, and most of them took the same path, even though it proved an eventual failure. Politicians live to run for office and to hold office; the test of success is election. Judged by this test, John Harlan was a comparative failure, for despite twenty years of active political life, he was only once elected to any significant office. His failure, however, must be judged in the light of the political possibilities open to those holding his beliefs. Despite his record of expediency, adjudged the key to his political career by some writers,[25] Harlan never did the one thing that would have practically guaranteed his political success: he never became a Democrat, nor is there any sign that he ever even seriously flirted with the idea. He quite deliberately chose political alternatives that enabled him to continue to espouse the Whig principles of nationalism and antisecession—alternatives that made electoral success almost out of the question. His father did the same, as did Crittenden, Letcher, and most other leading Whigs. This course John continued even after the Civil War.

This underlying core of principle—nationalism and unionism—explains John Harlan's successive shifts in party allegiance and campaign rhetoric: to the Know-Nothing movement; to the Constitutional Union party of John Bell for the presidential election of 1860; to the support of the Democratic candidate in 1864 (General McClellan was, after all, a Unionist); to the Conservative Union state party immediately after the war; and eventually to the Republican party. If this appears to be a record of loyalty to no party, it is because none survived, until the Republican party.

The Kentucky Whig attachment to the American party was born of this desperation. By concentrating on one major aim—"to restrict and destroy the influence of foreigners and Catholic priests in our political affairs"—the new party hoped to turn the country's attention away from slavery with its strictly sectional divisions.[26] But this meant achieving whatever electoral success was possible by playing to the fears and animosities of the old Anglo-Saxon Protestant population as against the large recent immigration of German Catholics stimulated by the Revolution of 1848 (substantial numbers settled in the river towns, especially Louisville) and Irish Catholics escaping the economic distress and starvation occasioned by the Potato Famine.[27]

Aside from their profound Presbyterianism and John's temporary attachment to the Younger Brothers of Temperance Society,[28] there was little about the Know-Nothing movement that would affirmatively attract the Harlans. One is driven to conclude, therefore, that they saw the American party merely as a means to keep the Old Whigs together and perhaps win elections. Harlan's own recollections (somewhat self-serving, no doubt) are true to the probable reactions of a twenty-two-year-old fledgling politician on joining the organization in 1854.

> I was very uncomfortable when the oath was administered to me. My conscience, for a time, rebelled against it. For a moment I had the thought of retiring; for while I was intense, as I still am, in my Protestantism, I did not relish the idea of proscribing anyone on account of his religion. But looking around the room in which the initiation occurred, I observed that the old whig leaders of the city, including my father, were present, and I had not the boldness to repudiate the organization. So I remained in it, upon the idea that, *all things considered*, it was best for any organization to control public affairs rather than to have the Democratic party in power.[29]

It was not in John's nature to be halfhearted in his attachments, and he thus plunged enthusiastically into the activities of his new party. His close friend Tom Crittenden was already involved in campaigning in 1855 for the Know-Nothing gubernatorial candidate, "the impressive, stately, flaxen-haired, honey-tongued" Charles S. Morehead.[30] Harlan's father was also running for reelection as attorney general.

> [Crittenden] had an appointment to speak at Bridgeport, near Frankfort, and asked me to ride out with him. He spoke in a country school-house which would not hold more than a hundred people, and spoke only about three-quarters of an hour. He seemed to have run dry in that time. When he concluded, it was raining very hard, and the people could not go out. Immediately some one cried out, "Let's hear from John Harlan." This surprised me, but I said nothing. The demand for me to speak became general and persistent. I said that I was only twenty-two years of age and had never made a political speech of any kind. They replied, all over the house, "That don't matter; tell us what you think." "Well," I said, "if I must, I must, seeing that the rain keeps you fast in the house." So I commenced, and without notes, or previous preparation, spoke for about three-quarters of an hour. The crowd seemed to be much interested in what I said, and applauded me generously. It seemed to me that a new career was then opened up before me, and I felt that I have *some* gifts for talking to a miscellaneous crowd.
>
> When I went home that afternoon (it was Saturday) and told my father what had taken place at the Bridgeport meeting, he seemed to be pleased, and said I had acted rightly. Turning the matter over in my mind, the next day, I concluded that as my profession would require me to talk, I must go farther, and speak in the city. So, on Monday morning, without consulting anyone, I went to a printing office and had handbills struck off, announcing that I would address the people of Frankfort at the court house that evening on the political subjects of the day.
>
> The handbills were stuck up all around the city, and when I saw one of them, fear came upon me for the consequences; but I could not well retreat. So when I went to the court house in the evening (Monday) and saw a crowd of men and women that filled every seat in the room, I "trembled in my

knees. . . ." But I went ahead, and my success on the occasion was very flattering, and never halted for a word, although the words chosen may not have been the best. When the meeting closed, I was congratulated on all hands, and I went to bed that night feeling that a "big thing" had been accomplished.

The next morning's paper contained an account of the meeting, and some handsome things were said of me by the editors. There was at least one young man, of twenty-two years of age, who at that time thought himself "large" and began (to use a common phrase) to "feel his oats." I so felt, not because I imagined myself as possessing any particular power of oratory, in the true sense of that word, but because I had become conscious of a capacity to say what I desired to say, and to make myself understood by those who heard me.

By the next morning I had become quite confident and said to my father that, as my living depended upon speaking, I would make a speaking tour of the State if he would provide me a horse and give me a silver watch. He said, "All right," and I ordered handbills to be printed announcing appointments for about twenty different counties in the mountainous parts of Kentucky. These handbills were sent to postmasters with requests to have them put up. I took it for granted that if crowds came to hear me, it would be because they thought it was my father who was to speak.

In about ten days I left Frankfort on horseback, carrying no clothes except such as could be put in a pair of saddle bags thrown across my saddle. My first speech was at Danville, and from there I went into various counties—large crowds came to hear me. It so happened that at every appointment some Democrat asked for a division of time—a debate—and I complied with his request. At some of the meetings my adversary would be a man of fifty years of age and a practiced debater. The result was many joint debates, in which I did not always suffer, in the estimation of my side. Those debates were of great value to me as a speaker. They destroyed whatever bashfulness I had, and gave me a readiness of speech and a steadiness of manner that served a good purpose when addressing juries. My father was evidently delighted, although he did not in words express his gratification.[31]

Indeed his father was delighted. As an old campaigner himself, the success of his son was meat and drink to him. Malvina Harlan records an incident from a few years later that plainly depicts the older man's pleasure.

One night, not long after our marriage, when my Father-in-law was seated with the family at supper, he took from his pocket a clipping he had made that day from a Lexington newspaper giving a description of a speech which my husband had made at some political meeting in Lexington. Carefully unfolding the clipping and pushing his heavy gold-rimmed spectacles upon his forehead (as he was apt to do when he wished to speak to any one near him) he passed the clipping on to me with a courtly gesture, without saying a word. I always sat next to him at the table. As might be supposed, the young wife eagerly devoured the complimentary references which the paper made to her husband's speech, in course of which the editor described him as one of the rising young men of the State, predicting a great future for him. Looking up I said:

"Why, I knew that long ago."

"Oh, you *did*, did you?"

"Yes, I always knew it."

"Oh, you *always* knew it? Then you are not *surprised?*"

"Not at all; I am only pleased that others are beginning to discover it." And then, after a pause, I asked, "Do you want this clipping, Mr. Harlan?"

"Would you like to keep it?"

"Yes, very much,"—whereat, bidding me to keep it, he looked as pleased and proud as I felt.[32]

It was a day of oratory, when men made reputations through public speaking, and Kentucky abounded in orators who aspired to fill Henry Clay's shoes. Thus it is all the more remarkable that Harlan's success was immediate and pronounced. A scant year later, for instance, a Louisville paper referred to him as "the young giant of the American Party."[33]

Even earlier, his tour of the eastern part of the state had effect and drew favorable attention from the newspapers. With what became his usual vigor, he lambasted the Democrats; like most political orators of his day he used hyperbole to great effect and freely predicted the apocalypse were his opponents to win. One writer proclaimed that John's speech in Columbia was "one of the best I have listened to for a great while. . . . He traversed the whole range of discussion between the American and anti-American parties, and left the poor anties prostrate at the feet of his Holiness and the foreigner begging for office."[34] Another, unconsciously perhaps summarizing Harlan's effect on the campaign, averred that he "came amongst us unknown to fame, and utterly unheralded, but he left an impression behind him that will not be effaced for a long time."[35]

What effect Harlan's personal efforts had is, of course, unknowable, but he found it sweet that the election was a triumph for his party: not only Morehead, but the whole state ticket, swept to victory—a victory that was probably in large part a legacy from the Whig predominance in the state. But victory had its bitter side as well. Know-Nothing orators, including John and his father, made the campaign one of vilification. They charged that foreigners were antislavery; accused them of pauperism and criminality; and feared the European ideas and practices that might undercut the sturdy values of traditional America.[36] Then too, the election day riots in Louisville between nativists and immigrants have usually been blamed on the Know-Nothing campaign: the day went into history as Bloody Monday.

One should not, perhaps, be too critical of the Harlans for their temporary, politically expedient attachment to nativism. The 1850s exhibited a tremendous groundswell of Protestant hostility to Catholicism, which was for the first time backed by the numbers to make it politically threatening. The Irish, and secondarily the German, Catholic immigration was the heaviest, proportionally, in our history, and Protestants saw a danger that their ascendancy would be completely overwhelmed. Then, too, almost uniquely in the South, which was not the recipient of most of this immigration, Louisville became a German Catholic center as did the other large Ohio and Mississippi river towns such as Cincinnati and St. Louis. It is to the credit of the Harlans that their attachment to this movement lasted such a short time.[37]

The Know-Nothing fortunes were, however, to collapse in Kentucky as quickly as they had arisen, despite John Harlan's efforts. The young Kentuckian stumped the state again on behalf of the Millard Fillmore candidacy for president in 1856. The Democrats, with James Buchanan— but perhaps more important in Kentucky, the state's Democratic leader, John C. Breckinridge, as the vice presidential candidate—swept not only the country but the state as well. Harlan's campaign oratory was as extreme as before, although he "triumphantly vindicated the American party from the charge of religious proscription, proving clearly that it denounced none but those who owed allegiance to a foreign power."[38] A fragment from Harlan's records gives some of the flavor (if none of the substance) of Harlan's oratory, which was probably not atypical of the period:

> All over this great country, from the icy regions of the North to the burning sands of the South; from the stormy capes of the Atlantic to the golden shores of the Pacific, the shout goes up for Fillmore and the Union.
>
> "From break, and beck, and holly glen" it comes—Oh, never let it cease or die away until this beloved land is freed from the curse of partisan administrations and traitorous sectionalism and we once more behold the glorious sight of a free, united, prosperous and happy people.[39]

The party lost, but Harlan did not. His reputation as a stump speaker was enhanced as he criss-crossed the state, and he came out of the campaign a seasoned veteran of the political wars, known throughout the state and marked as an up-and-coming man. His own reelection as city attorney of Frankfort was small consolation, even though it was repeated the following year.

By 1858 the American party was, if not dead, certainly dying, and the Old Whigs of Kentucky could no longer have any hope of electoral success under its banner. With the Republican party—despite the large vote given to its presidential candidate, John C. Frémont, in 1856—looking more and more like a strictly Northern sectional party, close to advocating the abolition of slavery, the only hope was to attempt to revive the Whig party at least temporarily. The results of the 1858 state elections gave point to this endeavor, for the Know-Nothing candidate for judge of the state court of appeals was soundly beaten by a Democrat openly in favor of "Southern slave rights."[40] Harlan's continuing local popularity enabled him once more to buck the tide, and he was elected county judge for Franklin County, the presiding judge of eleven who normally sat separately.

The post of county judge was not a particularly significant office. In fact, the man who sponsored the constitutional provision for the creation of this position was of the opinion that it would best be filled by nonlawyers: "God forbid that they should be lawyers. Good lawyers could not afford to take the office, and a little lawyer is the biggest fool in the world. He has just enough law in his head to drive out common sense. He is like an oyster smack with the canvas of a man-o'war. Every flaw of wind capsizes him. The convention intended that these judges should be farmers."[41] John Harlan was neither a "little lawyer" nor a farmer: he was merely young and ambitious. To the twenty-five year old, being a judge was an honor, a promotion, and a duty to his political friends. Considering the state of the Know-Nothing movement, Harlan had to run hard. He "visited every house and shook hands (as was the fashion) with nearly every man, woman and child in the county, and spoke nearly every day."[42] He won in a relatively close race, 868 to 749. He was to remain on the county court for about two and a half years, resigning when he moved to Louisville in 1861.

In 1859, giving up all the old party designations, the groups that had composed the Old Whigs and the American party formed a statewide organization that was called merely the Opposition. It was with some relief that the Harlans and their friends were able to give up the extreme nativist elements of Know-Nothingism and to concentrate on what really concerned them: the maintenance of the Union, preferably without abolition forced by federal action. At their state convention in February, the Opposition nominated James Harlan for a third term as attorney general. A congressional district meeting in May selected John Marshall Harlan as its candidate for the congressional seat once held by Henry Clay himself.[43] Also the home of the state's Democratic leader, John C. Breckinridge, the district was thus of tremendous moral value to both sides.

The Opposition party convention in the Ashland district, then, wanted a strong candidate to oppose the Democratic choice, William E. Simms, who was especially detested because he was a turncoat Whig: he had served two terms in the state legislature in the 1840s as a Whig.[44] It would seem, then, rather odd that the Opposition forces would nominate a young and relatively untried person like Harlan. Indeed, his nomination came as another political accident.

Breckinridge had, in fact, made the district Democratic when he won the seat in 1851 and 1853, leaving only to accept the vice presidential nomination in 1855. The seat was captured by the Know-Nothing Alexander K. Marshall in 1855, and it was, in an odd historical twist, returned to Democratic control in 1857, being won by Clay's son James in a close race over the Old Whig Roger W. Hanson.

It would have been normal for Hanson to have run again in 1859, but perhaps having lost once—however closely—he had the taint of defeat. In any case, there was stiff competition from George S. Shanklin, a veteran state legislator (apparently no relation to Mallie Harlan). John Harlan was a member of the Franklin County delegation. The convention was approaching a deadlock when, Harlan recalled:

> In the progress of the balloting, Thomas T. Vimont, of Bourbon [County], to my great surprise, rose and said, with great vehemence of voice and manner, that the party needed a young man as its candidate, and he placed me in nomination. I was sitting at the time in the rear of the hall; greatly agitated by the fact that I was to be voted for by some of the delegates, I started to jump up and say that I was not a candidate and could not think of being one. But a member of the Franklin County delegation, who was delighted at the suggestion of my name to the convention, pulled the skirt of my alpaca frock coat so strongly as to tear it nearly off. The balloting proceeded before I could say anything, and to my amazement I was nominated. Immediately a cry arose that I should take the stand. I did so, and when I turned to address the delegates, the condition of the skirt of my coat was so manifest that I referred to it as proof of my efforts to prevent my being nominated. I commenced my talk, intending to decline. But the crowd said, "No, No," and I concluded by accepting.[45]

Harlan's father was, of course, surprised at this turn of events. Also, according to John, perhaps he was a little annoyed: he had wished for a lawyer son, not a full-time politician. Nevertheless, he could not help being proud of his son and agreed to support him unstintingly.

John entered the campaign with little hope of success, but with characteristic energy: if he should lose, it would not be for lack of effort. He immediately challenged Simms to a series of debates, an arrangement typical of campaigning in those days, and the two proceeded to debate all over the district over a period of five or six weeks.

As a speaker Harlan had the advantage. After the first engagement—in Georgetown late in May—Vice President John C. Breckinridge, who was in attendance, was reported to have told Simms, "If you don't do better that young fellow will beat you."[46] One favorable newspaper found in Harlan a speaker whose "personal appearance, and his dignified and manly bearing are exceedingly attractive, inspiring and commanding confidence in all his hearers."[47]

In many ways, however, it was not a happy situation for Harlan. If Simms could be called a turncoat Whig and charged with inconsistency, Harlan in his turn could be accused of rejecting the nativist principles he had espoused only two or three years earlier; he could also be suspected of being soft on slavery. The campaign was enlivened—although not made easier—by the personal attacks made by an Opposition leader, Garrett W. Davis, against Simms, which almost resulted in a duel. The effect, however, was to turn lukewarm Simms supporters into enthusiasts. Democrats,

Harlan later said, "were aroused at what they regarded as the attempt of one of my supporters to bully their candidate. . . . the quarrel of Davis and Simms had done me great harm."[48]

Slavery was inevitably the great issue of the campaign. The two candidates vied with each other in supporting the slave system. Harlan came out for federal protection of slaves in the territories and accused Simms of supporting Stephen A. Douglas's "squatter sovereignty" proposals. Douglas's doctrine was, Harlan charged, a sellout of the rights of slave owners, based on "the mobocratic idea which levels destruction of all written contracts by which the weak are protected against the strong, that majorities can make and set aside constitutions at pleasure."[49] He accused the Democratic administration of extravagance and corruption and used other standard issues. Playing down attacks on foreigners and Catholics—after all, some of them voted in his district—Harlan, in line with his orthodox Presbyterian views, nevertheless attacked the Mormons in Utah.

Even though one newspaper called him "the standard bearer, and defender of Southern rights, and Southern interests," Harlan was really on the defensive where the slave issue was concerned.[50] Democrats charged that he was secretly in league with the abolitionist "Black Republicans." They accused him of defending a slave who sued his master and charged that he had written a letter in an Indiana newspaper in support of the Republican candidate for governor of that state, Oliver P. Morton. (Harlan produced evidence that not he but his brother William had done these things, but voters probably felt that it made no difference).[51] Harlan was, like Simms, vulnerable to charges of inconsistency. His new proslavery views, it was said, contradicted the views on slavery in the territories espoused by the Know-Nothings just a few years earlier. One opposing journal called him plainly a political "trimmer": "Young as he is he has exhibited a facility to drift in the current popular sentiment, and change his opinion as the hour demands. . . . Once a Whig, then a fanatical and violent American, and now a hybrid opportunist, he has accomplished as many sommersaults in his brief career as any man in the country."[52]

In Harlan's defense, he was only doing what most of the Old Whigs were doing: trying desperately to find issues that would provide common ground for the maintenance in a slave state of an opposition party. The difficulties in so doing, given the out-and-out proslavery position of the Southern wing of the Democratic party, are obvious. His private views of slavery had been shaped by his father, his teachers, and his own experience with the household slaves with whom he had grown up.

Harlan failed to win the election. It was an extremely close contest, in which he lost by only 67 votes out of 13,797.[53] John himself always felt that the election had been stolen by the Democrats, since he claimed that there was evidence that voters had been imported from outside the district. Nevertheless he refused to contest the results, pleading the necessities of making a living and the time and expense of a contest. He came out of the campaign, he said, with debts "of about $9,000 and without any money to pay it off." [54]

He later rationalized that he had not wanted to be a full-time politician anyway and that his professional success as a lawyer would have been hampered by service in Washington. He also wondered what his status as an "independent" would have been in the halls of Congress: "I . . . belonged to a local political party known as the Opposition Party. Its members were all old Whigs by training and by association. We had, however, no national political alliance. If I had been given a seat in Congress it would have been [in a contested election] by the votes of the Republican or Free Soil Party, and that fact alone would have sufficed to destroy our party in Kentucky and would have ruined me politically—so bitter was the feeling in Kentucky, at that time." [55] In a nation seemingly headed for dissolution, Harlan had thus found that expediency, even adopted in the name of national unity, was not sufficient for victory. Any doubt left in his mind should have been erased by the results of the 1860 presidential contest.

Actually, the Harlans did not expect the lackluster Tennesseean John Bell to win the presidency. There might have been some hope with a more attractive candidate such as John J. Crittenden, but he was too old. Bell's "personality was cold, his manner formal, his speech calculated and uninspiring." [56] The platform of the Constitutional Union party as summarized in its name was negative yet inspiring; with an attractive candidate the party might have drawn more support from moderates than it did and might even have managed to bridge the growing gap between the North and South to some extent. Even so, events had gone too far for the party members to hope for national success; voters were mostly either Northerners or Southerners and voted as such. The Harlans knew this. There was, nevertheless, some hope at the state level. As the inheritors of Henry Clay, the Old Whigs who composed the Constitutional Union party still had tremendous latent support in the state, and preserving a state base has always been more important to leaders of American parties than national success. This hope that they could win in Kentucky, or make a strong showing, impelled Crittenden and his followers to support Bell.

John Harlan plunged into the 1860 campaign with his accustomed energy and with, perhaps, even more emphasis than usual on the apocalyptic importance of the election. He was a signer of the "Address of the Union State Central Committee," which pledged support of the Union and "unalterable hostility to Northern Republicanism [read *abolitionism*] and Southern Secession." As a delegate to the party's state conclave, he also had a major part in the framing of a resolution acknowledging that the South had been unfairly treated but reasserting a faith that the matters at issue could be better resolved inside than outside the Union.[57] In the campaign itself, beyond acting as an elector for the Bell ticket, Harlan stayed close to home. He engaged in joint debates with electors of the other parties (excluding the Republicans, who had no support in the state).

The result, nationally, of the election is well known. Bell, of course, ran rather poorly in the four-sided race; even the forlorn hope of throwing the election into the House of Representatives did not come to fruition. Bell's support came strictly from the South, mostly from the northern tier of slave states. His Unionist ticket garnered the electoral votes only of Kentucky, Tennessee, and Virginia. This was a triumph for the Kentucky state party, particularly since the Southern Democratic party had the state's own John C. Breckinridge as its candidate.

While the 1860 election signaled the final breakup of the national party system and the victory of secessionism in the Deep South, it had an entirely different significance in Kentucky. It turned out to mean that this crucial slave state would not secede and that it would eventually and officially give its active support to the Union cause. In 1861, again with Harlan's effective support, the Unionists carried the state's congressional elections; they kept control of the state legislature and were able to block Democratic governor Beriah Magoffin's efforts to call a secession convention.[58]

As the war clouds gathered, John Harlan took his little family and moved to Louisville. Part of the motivation for the move was the feeling that he would have to run for Congress again if he stayed in Frankfort, and the economic facts of life were that he could not afford to do so. He hoped to secure a larger law practice in the growing Ohio River metropolis. His political reputation now extended statewide, but he would need to rebuild his legal practice from scratch. In fact, the coming of the war prevented him from doing so, at least for some time.

3

Kentucky Unionist
1861

Louisville on the eve of the Civil War was Kentucky's largest city and only real metropolis, with a population approaching seventy thousand. The eleventh largest city in the country, Louisville had just enhanced its importance by the construction of railroads to Nashville and to Memphis, and it enjoyed a thriving interchange business between a prosperous hinterland and the rest of the nation as well as, more generally, between the Mississippi River and the Northeast. Although a canal had been built around the Falls of the Ohio, it was not large enough to accommodate the new generation of steamboats, so transshipment remained a major part of the city's business.[1]

Nineteenth-century American cities did not enjoy modern amenities. Many of Louisville's streets were unpaved, and even those that were suffered from neglect: one editorialist complained that "in dry weather we are suffocated with constant clouds of dust, and in wet weather the streets are almost impassable on account of the accumulated mud and filth." The filth, it was said, might be composed of "fire-wood, . . . hog and pig fecus, dead animals, stable manure, shavings and litter from buildings." Like other nineteenth-century cities, Louisville used bands of hogs to consume the garbage and refuse deposited by the local citizenry. Charles Dickens, who visited the city in 1842, wrote that the streets were "perfectly alive with pigs of all ages, lying about in every direction fast asleep, or grunting along in quest of hidden dainties." Most of the streets were unlit, and the city's new police force was untrained and largely ineffective. The equally new fire department was somewhat more useful—when it could secure water. The city was proud of its brand new water works; city-supplied water largely eliminated the danger of the plagues that recurred during the nineteenth century.[2]

These conditions were, of course, common in American cities. On the whole, Louisville was a prosperous, growing city with solid public buildings, an extremely congested waterfront, and some cultural pretensions. It certainly provided much potential business for John Harlan and the other lawyers who congregated there.

Aside from the institution of slavery, Louisville in 1861 was perhaps as much a Northern as a Southern city. Certainly it depended on the North for much of its trade. As a developing center of industry it was not typical of Southern cities; unlike most of them, it had received a sizable number of foreign immigrants (almost sixty thousand were in the state by 1860), mostly from Germany, and after the nativist scare of the 1850s had died down, these became solid citizens who contributed greatly to the business life of the community.[3] The parents of future Supreme Court justice Louis D. Brandeis were more successful than most, but they illustrate the point.[4] The Germans almost all supported the Union during the Civil War, and they provided a solid bloc of voters that Harlan could tap after he became a Republican. But the business ties of the community with the North also accounted for its strongly Unionist sympathies, and it was doubtless Louisville sentiment more than any other single factor that prevented the state from joining the Confederacy, although the Clay Whig inheritance of the state meant that Unionist feeling was strong throughout Kentucky.

By the spring of 1861, when the young Harlans made their move to Louisville, disunion was already a fact—South Carolina started the procession by formally seceding on December 20, 1860—and civil war was a strong likelihood. In this situation a political animal like John Harlan was not likely to be able to devote full attention to building up his law practice. His partner, William F. Bullock, was an older lawyer, well established in Louisville. He had been a judge of the Louisville circuit court from 1846 to 1855 and was, naturally, a strong Unionist. The new partnership, then, was probably as much concerned with the political crisis as it was with providing legal services. One has to wonder, in fact, how Harlan supported his family during the period before his resignation from the army in 1863: certainly it was not through his law practice.[5]

On only one question were Kentucky Unionists sure and united: they were opposed to secession. This principle guided them throughout the difficult days and even after the war ended. Beyond this, however, they were both ambivalent and ambiguous. The exigencies of the changing situation led them to change also, leading to frequent charges of inconsistency and bad faith from their opponents. For while the so-called Southern Rights party—the extreme Democrats—could rest on its policies of secession, slavery, and opposition to the attempt by the federal government to coerce the seceded states back into the Union, the Unionists mostly favored slavery (or at least the right of the state to decide on it), opposed secession, and favored conciliation by the federal government that, they hoped, would lure the Southern states back into the Union without violence. When it became obvious that neither the federal government nor the Southern extremists would accept the kind of compromise they had in mind, Unionists were left without a policy. Some of them continued to oppose the use of force, and thus they favored letting the South go, even though that meant dividing Kentucky from the other slave states. This attitude led them to propose and to try to adopt a neutrality policy for the state. Since in the circumstances of civil war they could not in the long run be neutral and still remain part of the Union, they were forced to choose individually whether to break their allegiance to the Union or to stay with it even at the price of accepting federal actions (such as coercion and emancipation) that they disliked.

Most Kentucky Unionists were led step by step—driven, one might almost say—to adopt the latter course. The evolution of John Harlan's position is thus typical of the period. He helped to shape these attitudes and at the same time reflected them, and the changes came in response to both real and perceived political demands, just as did those of the 1850s. It is easy to call Harlan an inconsistent "trimmer" who would do anything to win public office for himself or his party; but this ignores both the real difficulties of the situation and the core of principle that he never abandoned. Harlan's belief in the desirability of the Union and in a fairly strong national government that yet allowed some autonomy to the states never wavered. Indeed, it was as marked during his career on the Supreme Court as it had been earlier. There is little doubt that if he had joined the Confederate army and become a Democrat, he could have had a successful political career: for him, however, trimming could not go that far.

Harlan's first recorded thoughts on the subject after Lincoln's election and the secession crisis came in a letter to the Kentucky lawyer Joseph Holt, who had become President Buchanan's secretary of war but was a strong Unionist.[6] In this letter, dated March 11, 1861, Harlan claimed his political connections and his opportunities "to learn the sentiments of the people" as justifications for writing. In order to strengthen the Union cause in Kentucky, Harlan felt that

> prudence and wise statesmanship demand an immediate withdrawal of the Federal troops from the Seceding states, especially the troops at Forts Sumter and Pickens. If that were done *now*, the secession cause would die in Kentucky and in my opinion throughout all the slave States which have not seceded. The chief cause of the excitement . . . is the constant fear that Lincoln's Administration will attempt coercion, or war between *"him"* and the Seceding states. No matter how it may be produced, no matter who may be in the wrong, whenever war commences between the Federal Government under *Lincoln,* and any of the Seceding States, that moment the Union cause [in the other slave states] will receive a blow from which it may never recover. . . . An immediate withdrawal . . . would be regarded as an act of magnanimity, . . . [and] would be followed by two results of great importance, *first,* in the border slave states the Union cause would be placed upon an immovable foundation; *second,* a formidable party would immediately spring up in the seceding states in favor of a return to the National Union.[7]

Harlan admitted that the federal government had a right to the forts, but he favored political practicality over insistence on those rights. But he went on:

> It must be admitted that if whenever it becomes a settled fact that the people of the seceding states are unalterably opposed to the Federal Government they should be allowed to go in peace. To subdue by arms under an attempt to enforce the laws would be madness in the extreme. What would more likely produce an undying hostility to the Federal Government than a civil war, and what would certainly produce civil war than an attempt now to reinforce Major Anderson or to collect the revenue[?] Now, that the Government has shown its *ability* to maintain Fort Sumter, now when reinforcements are unnecessary, now when it is not compelled to abandon the forts, is the most propitious time to display a magnanimity to a misguided people which can but be followed by the happiest results.[8]

Holt's reaction to these ideas is not recorded; it is not likely that he agreed with them, but in any case events overtook the possibilities. Fort Sumter was not reinforced, nor did the federal government attempt to collect taxes; but the troops were not withdrawn, and South Carolina forced the issue by attacking the forts only a month after Harlan's letter. Lincoln's call for troops followed a few days later, and the war that Kentucky Unionists feared most was on. Hindsight renders Harlan's proposal unrealistic; but he did not have hindsight, and mature statesmen were making proposals even more farfetched.

What would Harlan do once war became inevitable? Together with other Kentucky Unionists, he saw the problem as a twofold one: he wanted to prevent Kentucky from seceding and (as an instrument to that end) to keep the state at least for the moment out of the developing conflict. During the following six months the ultimately futile drama of Kentucky neutrality was played out. It is likely that most Unionists knew that neutrality was illogical, illegal, and doomed to failure. But they needed time in which to organize Kentucky sentiment for the Union, to prepare militarily against the possibility of a secessionist coup, and to gain firm control of the state government. Governor Beriah Magoffin was a Democrat who believed in the right of secession and would have liked to take Kentucky out of the Union, albeit democratically. The state guard, the only military force, was honeycombed with suspected secessionists and led by Simon Bolivar Buckner, who became a general in the Confederate army. The legislature, elected in 1859 before the crisis, was so thinly balanced that no one knew in which direction it might go.[9]

In response to the secession movement, the governor called a special session of the legislature for January 17, 1861, to consider the state's reaction. At this point the Unionists were uncertain what they should or could do, but they wished to be sure that Kentucky itself did not secede. Leaders of all factions scurried around the state attempting to influence public opinion. In addition, the Bell Old Whigs and the Douglas Democrats—both strongly Unionist groups—held conventions in Louisville beginning January 8, timed of course to sway the legislature. John Harlan was the secretary for the Constitutional Union meeting. The two groups drafted a joint resolution that argued that the injustices meted out to the slave states were insufficient to justify withdrawal from the Union and urged politicians of all sections to adopt the Crittenden compromise proposal. Harlan successfully fought to prevent the insertion of language that would support federal coercion of the seceding states.[10] The two groups also agreed to a practical merger, forming the Union State Central Committee, of which Bullock was a member, as were George D. Prentice, editor of the Louisville *Journal*, and James Speed, a close friend of Harlan's who later became Lincoln's attorney general. Since the editor of the Louisville *Democrat* was also a member, two of the most powerful newspapers in the state were aligned behind the Union.[11]

What the governor wanted—supported by the Breckinridge faction of Democrats—was a "sovereign convention," which, as he expressed it, would be able to arrive at a "full and final determination [of] the future of Federal and interstate relations of Kentucky."[12] But it was a convention that the Unionists were at that time determined to prevent. Secessionists hoped that the wave of enthusiasm sweeping the South would carry Kentucky along; Unionists wanted to wait until the excitement had died down a bit so that the more settled aspirations of the people would be reflected. The legislature, however, refused to call a convention and in fact did nothing except pass a joint resolution calling on the Southern states "to stay the work of secession" and protesting against the "use of force or coercion" by the North.[13] The legislators then adjourned on February 11 to meet again March 20. This further session lasted until April 4 but resulted in no significant action.

The adjournment came before the attack on Fort Sumter and Lincoln's consequent call for seventy-five thousand troops, to be supplied by the individual states. Since the state was still in the Union, Kentucky was assigned a quota, which Governor Magoffin refused to supply. Both sides, it is obvious, still felt that there was some possibility of compromise. Kentuckians, with the history of Clay and Crittenden behind them, felt that Kentucky's proper role was that of mediator. For this reason few protested Magoffin's action. There was some fruitless talk of organizing a border slave states confederation or even a Mississippi Valley union, but by May it was obvious that the time for mediation was past, that a third federation was impractical, and that Kentucky must choose some other course.

There was still, at this time, almost no support for Lincoln or his policies; even a strongly Unionist paper wryly called the president a "fourth-rate fool."[14] The Unionists had to tread a narrow line between support of the Union and support of the national administration. Politically, they could not support Lincoln's call for troops; logically, they could not refuse to do so. The uneasy and constitutionally impossible position of neutrality was their solution, but it could be only a temporary one.

A large and enthusiastic public meeting was held by the Unionists in Louisville on April 19, at which the speakers urged a neutralist position, which had already been advocated by Crittenden and the Union State Central Committee. While the throng assembled that night enthusiastically adopted a neutral resolution, all the evidence seems to indicate that to most Unionist leaders this was only a temporary solution. Though they sincerely desired neutrality, they realized that if the state were to stay in the Union, such a course would in the long run be impossible. Since the fundamentally important objective was to stay in the Union, they decided to take what they could get and then await developments.

Governor Magoffin, still seeking a convention, called another special session of the legislature for May 6. This session was thought to be the critical one for Kentucky's decision, and Unionist leaders staged around-the-clock lobbying sessions in Frankfort. Summoned to the capital by his father, John Harlan spent three weeks aiding in this effort. "I labored," he later wrote, "constantly for the purpose of defeating the scheme for calling a Sovereignty Convention—believing that the defeat of that scheme could result in holding the State in the Union and depriving those intending to assist the rebels of the pretext that in their so doing they would obey the command of the *State*." Mallie added, "My husband and a few others of the younger men actually slept in the State House during several all-night sessions when that dangerous resolution was being discussed."[15]

The legislature did not call a convention, nor did it even pass a neutrality resolution. The only significant action taken—which was favorable to the Unionists—was to create a new militia in addition to the state guard, which Unionists regarded with justifiable suspicion. The home guard thus created was rapidly organized with Union sympathizers, thus establishing a balance of military power in the state. Many companies were formed in Louisville, one of which—the Crittenden Union Zouaves—was organized and led by Captain John Marshall Harlan. The Louisville units were called out when, in late September, General Buckner (by now commanding a Confederate army) was thought to be threatening Louisville. The home guard was joined by a new Kentucky regiment of Union troops; but Buckner retreated, and there was no actual fighting. Mallie and the children were left with the Bullocks on this occasion.[16]

The summer of 1861 was an uneasy one, with both sides still jockeying for position. Harlan, Speed, and other Louisville Unionists, Harlan wrote,

concluded that the people needed to be educated as to the value of the Union, as well as to the danger that would come to Kentucky, as a Border State, from armed conflicts between great armies occupying its territory. We raised a little money and with it hired a few bands of music. During the month of May, June and July, 1861, there was hardly an afternoon when I did not, while standing on a store box, on the pavement, address a public audience in the line just suggested. The crowds were brought together by the music of the bands that we employed.[17]

Unionists still felt at a serious disadvantage, knowing that the state guard and the state's store of weapons were controlled by men who were suspected of disloyalty. The home guard, a potential counterbalance, had no arms. During the summer, with President Lincoln's private support, weapons were slowly distributed to Union men throughout the state. The distribution was organized by a committee on which the Harlans, the Speeds, and Crittenden were prominent members. Union men established unofficially a camp near Lexington, Camp Dick Robinson.

William Nelson, who masterminded this secret distribution (which was not really all that secret), was determined to arm the men at Camp Robinson. He arranged for a supply of guns to be shipped from Cincinnati by rail to Lexington. But, as Harlan wrote,

> In some way the rebel sympathizers at Cynthiana obtained information as to these guns being on the railroad train, and when the train got in sight of Cynthiana, . . . the conductor saw a large crowd at the depot, apparently under the control of Captain Joe Desha. Correctly supposing that they intended to seize the guns, . . . he immediately ordered the train to be stopped, and returned with the train and the guns to . . . , Covington. I communicated the facts to Joshua F. Bullitt . . . , [and] requested Nelson to ship the guns by boat from Cincinnati to Louisville on a named night, marked to my address at Louisville, Kentucky. I wrote to Dr. Ethelbert L. Dudley, the leading physician at Lexington and the captain of a company of Union Home Guards, telling him of what we proposed to do with the guns. I informed him that the guns would leave Louisville before daylight on a certain day and would reach Lexington precisely at a named hour. We were enabled to be thus specific as to time, because the Superintendent of the railroad from Louisville to Lexington— Colonel Sam Gill—was a Union man and cheerfully cooperated with us. I should say that there were two companies of volunteers at Lexington, composed of the first young men, socially, in the city—one commanded by Dr. Dudley, the other by John H. Morgan, who subsequently joined the Confederate military forces and became a noted cavalry officer on that side.
>
> The guns were shipped from Cincinnati to Louisville on the regular boat, which arrived at the Louisville wharf about two or three o'clock in the morning. I was at the wharf to receive them. Bullitt was with me. We had them put on drays previously provided, and carried them across the city to the depot of the Louisville and Lexington Railroad on Jefferson Street—Bullitt and myself walking in the street by the side of the drays, each being well armed to resist any attempt to take the guns. The train carrying the guns left Louisville on time and arrived at Lexington exactly at the hour fixed.[18]

In the meantime, of course, politics went on. There were, in fact, three elections in Kentucky that summer, all of which resulted in sweeping victories for the Union side. The first, for delegates to the abortive border states convention, came on May 4. The so-called Southern Rights party, sensing defeat, did not put up a slate. The Union candidates, however, piled up a large vote—more than two-thirds of the total vote in the previous November's presidential contest. The regular elections for Congress came on June 20. Kentucky had ten seats: nine Union candidates were elected. In a light vote, with many Southern sympathizers staying home, the result could be interpreted variously as a vote for the Union, for neutrality, or for both.[19]

Finally, August 5 was the date for the elections to the state legislature. It was a campaign in which Joseph Holt played a great part, speaking throughout the state. Again the Union candidates won a decisive victory: they won control of the House, 76-24, and of the Senate, 27-11. The vote was no doubt influenced by the tremendous victory the Confederate army had scored on July 21 at the first battle of Bull Run.[20]

The Harlans had moved into rooms at the old National Hotel on Jefferson Street. John was away much of the time, and Mallie, who was pregnant, was left with the task of caring for two small children. Nevertheless, she later wrote, "we were never out of my husband's thoughts, and he did everything he could to make us comfortable and happy."[21]

Possibly the most unusual and perhaps the most useful of Harlan's activities was necessarily kept secret at the time. Newspapers were a prime factor in the formation of public opinion throughout the nineteenth century. It was an era of great editors, who wielded tremendous influence, who were often openly partisan, and who sometimes made or broke even presidential candidacies. Murat Halstead, Henry Watterson, Joseph Medill, and others are as important in American political history as are most presidents: indeed, more important than some. Perhaps first among all these editors was George D. Prentice, editor of the Louisville *Journal*. Watterson later evaluated Prentice:

> From 1830 to 1861 the influence of Prentice was perhaps greater than the influence of any political writer who ever lived; it was an influence directly positive and personal. . . . He had to build upon an intellect naturally strong and practical, and this was trained by rigid scholarly culture. He was brave and aggressive, and though by no means quarrelsome, he was as ready to fight as to write, and his lot was cast in a region where he had to do a good deal of both. By turns a statesman, a wit, a poet, a man of the world, and always a journalist . . . there can be no doubt that the vast influence he wielded through the *Journal* prevented the secession of Kentucky.[22]

It is not generally known, however, that for about two critical weeks in 1861 John Marshall Harlan, not George D. Prentice, guided the newspaper's editorial policy and, indeed, wrote its political editorials. The story can be best told in Harlan's own words.

Prentice had been an intimate friend of Henry Clay and his word carried great weight with every Old Whig in the country. In the spring of 1861 he had combatted the movement in the South for a dissolution of the Union, and up to the time of which I am about to speak, all of his editorials were in that direction. But his environment and associations were unfavorable to a further advocacy by him of the Union cause. His wife was an intense rebel. He had two sons who had become open advocates of the Southern cause and I believe had joined or were about to join the rebel recruits. He was the only member of his family who had avowed his adherence to the Union and his opposition to the contemplated rebellion. But it was observed that his paper was beginning to weaken in its support of the Union party, and he was beginning to educate the popular mind in Kentucky in the belief that the true policy of the General Government was to "let the wayward sisters go": that it was unwise to attempt the use of force in preventing a secession of any State if the people of that State in any proper way indicated a desire to withdraw from the Union. His views evidently were making an impression upon the popular mind and greatly discouraged the Union men of the State.

At that time there lived in Kentucky a very distinguished man who had been its governor from 1855 to '59. I allude to the Hon. Charles S. Morehead. He was a very able lawyer, highly respected by the people of Kentucky; but his interests were all in a cotton plantation in Mississippi, and doubtless believing that a war between the General Government and the slave-holding States would result in his financial ruin, he insisted that the Union could not be preserved by force and that a civil war would be the utter destruction of the material interests of Kentucky. He therefore approved the policy of not using force to preserve the Union against armed secession. The rebels in Kentucky believed, and there was reason for their believing, that if the policy then advocated by the Louisville *Journal* was adopted by the States, that their cause would win, and it was deemed a matter of prime importance to secure Prentice's support to this view of the question.

On the *Journal* at that time was Paul R. Shipman, who was by birth and education an eastern man. He was assistant to Prentice and a favorite with the great Whig editor. At that time he was only about twenty-seven years of age, but he had impressed himself upon the Whig men of the State and was regarded as the real editor of the *Journal*, Prentice, by reason of advancing years and perhaps bad habits, having become a writer of editorials only upon great occasions. He had been unfortunate, too, in some financial matters and had lost a large part of his interest in that company. The principal owner, or the owner of a majority of its stock, was Isham Henderson, a man of large business enterprises, and who it was supposed did not care for public affairs and took no interest in them. I do not recall the exact date, but I am quite sure it was in August 1861, Shipman came to me and said that a formidable movement was on foot to secure the support of the *Journal* for the rebel cause; that in the prosecution of that movement Charles S. Morehead had had a conference with Prentice and urged upon him the danger to Kentucky of a war between the United States and the secessionists. He also urged upon Prentice the writing of a series of editorials distinctly in favor of the view that no attempt should be made to employ force against the secessionists and that they should be permitted to depart in peace if they elected to do so. He further said that Morehead had, as an inducement to Prentice, proposed that he should receive the sum of $100,000 if he would agree to take that course, and that he could take that money and go out of the country and remain abroad until the war was over. The whole scheme was to destroy the power of the *Journal* and precipitate such a condition of affairs in Kentucky as would leave the Union men utterly powerless. Shipman said that Prentice had repeated to him a conversation to the above effect which he had had with Morehead, and that he (Shipman) said that he would not only oppose any such course on the part of the *Journal*, but would expose it if it was carried out. He also said that he had mentioned the matter to Henderson, and that Henderson had said to him that before the *Journal* should be used for such a purpose he would see the whole paper "sunk to hell." But Shipman was afraid that Prentice would commit the paper to Morehead's view and take the money and leave the country, and he asked me What should he do? After conference with him we agreed upon a certain plan. In execution of that plan I telegraphed to my father at Frankfort, to Col. Orlando Brown, also of Frankfort, and to Joshua F. Bell of Danville. They were all Whigs and had had a lifelong acquaintance with Prentice. Each of them was fond of Prentice, and Prentice was an admirer of each of them. I telegraphed them to come to Louisville by first train, without indicating why I had so telegraphed. They knew I would not telegraph them to come unless there were reasons for it, and they promptly came, and to each of them Shipman and I communicated the exact situation as to the *Journal*. After conference as to what was to be done, my father "dropped in" on Prentice one evening in his editorial room, and without indicating that he knew what was going on referred to the rumor as to what Morehead was trying to accomplish in that State and as to what Morehead wanted the *Journal* to do. He assumed that Prentice would not do what was asked of him and took occasion in very strong language to denounce such a proposition as Morehead's as treason to the country for which the author deserved to be hanged. Brown and Bell at different times called to see Prentice and had similar conversations with him. The object of the talk of these three gentlemen was to stiffen Prentice's backbone and let him understand that no Kentuckian could accept Morehead's view without danger of disgrace among all the people whose good opinions were of value. To my utter surprise in a day or two afterwards Shipman told me that he was compelled to go East. I protested against his absence from the City, but he said it was impossible for him to avoid going. I said, "What is to become of the *Journal* while you are away? The very thing that we have up to this time attempted to defeat will be accomplished." "No," said he, "you are here." But I said, "I am not an editor of the *Journal* and have no authority there." But he replied, "I have made arrangements that whatever editorials you write on the subject of the Union cause of Kentucky will go into that paper as editorials." Said he, "Henderson at my suggestion had instructed the foreman to put into the paper as an editorial anything you write on the subject without consulting Mr. Prentice." I had no alternative but to try this plan, and for two or three weeks I was at the *Journal* office every night, sometimes until after midnight, watching the editorials that went into that paper and by brief editorials written by myself committing the paper from day to day more distinctly and emphatically to the Union cause and every day making it the more difficult for Prentice to change the policy of the paper without its becoming apparent to everybody that disreputable means were employed to bring about such a result. In a little while the skies cleared. The scheme inaugurated by Morehead failed, and Prentice's natural love of the Union and the Union cause came up again and he commenced to write editorials against the rebellion and the rebels of Kentucky that exhibited extraordinary power and did much to stiffen the backbone and encourage the hopes of the Union men of Kentucky and give them courage for the future.[23]

Law as well as politics could be useful to the Union cause. One aspect of this was to prevent state courts as well as the executive from treating the Confederate States of America as a legal government, recognized by Kentucky. Harlan, working with other Unionist attorneys, argued in July 1861 a case before the Jefferson County Circuit Court in Louisville, which was regarded as a test. In May the U.S. Treasury Department ordered an embargo on the carrying of provisions or arms to the Confederacy, a trade that had flourished ever since the beginning of the secession movement. Louisville was the rail funnel for much of this trade, which went south to Nashville, Memphis, or farther, on the Louisville and Nashville Railroad. James Guthrie, the powerful financier who controlled the railroad, was willing enough to make money on this trade and decided to ignore the embargo until the courts had determined its legality. Harlan and his friends argued that the embargo was justified, because it aided the attempt to suppress an insurrection. The court accepted this argument, in effect denying legal recognition to the Confederacy.[24]

Harlan also played a role in an abortive attempt to dissuade Northern generals from making obvious incursions into Kentucky, especially when there was no military purpose involved. Harlan recalled:

> Mr. Lincoln was extremely anxious to avoid any movement in Kentucky on the part of the Federal Government that would give the rebels an excuse for resorting to measures of force; and therefore he did not allow any camps to be formed in Kentucky at that time, of men who were regarded as, or who volunteered to become, a part of the armed force which was then being raised for the defense of the Union. One of the results of that policy was that Lovell H. Rousseau, a Union leader in the State, established his camp across the river at Jeffersonville. In August '61, or about that time, it was rumored that Rousseau had received an order from the War Department to take such men as were in his camp at Jeffersonville and report for orders to the Union commander in Missouri. It was also rumored that before he left with his force (about 3,000 men) he intended to come over to Louisville from his camp and parade through the streets, that his soldiers, who were mostly Kentuckians, might bid farewell to

their homes. Many Union men in the City believed that that might provoke a difficulty which would be attended with serious results, as the Union men of the State had not become fully organized and did not have arms sufficient for their protection. So, at the instance of many of the Union leaders, Col. George P. Jewett (who was afterwards killed at Perryville) and I went across the river to see Rousseau and to suggest to him that in the judgment of his friends in Louisville it would not be wise for his command to come over to Kentucky at that time. Rousseau heard us with great attention and kindness, but replied in substance that Kentucky was a part of the Union, that the soldiers of the Union had a right to tread its soil, and that as a large part of his command were from Louisville and other parts of Kentucky, he intended to march over to Louisville and through the streets, and if any interference occurred the streets of that city should be made to run with blood. He announced his purpose to cross the river and he did so and paraded through the streets of the city, every house on the line of march being crowded with lookers-on. No trouble occurred, and he went back with his troops to his camp.[25]

By September the time for negotiation, and for neutrality, had passed. Fighting had begun. The Unionist sentiments of the large majority in the state had become clear, and it had become politically possible—indeed, necessary—for Unionists to give up the idea of neutrality. They now had to decide whether they felt that the "departing brethren" should be allowed to go in peace, by either sitting on their hands or joining the Confederate army, or, alternatively, to support federal coercion. Most of them opted for the military solution; certainly, and predictably, James Harlan and his son did. This necessitated closing their eyes to—or trying to dissociate themselves politically from—Lincoln's evolving policy toward the slave question. Despite this problem, James Harlan accepted the president's appointment as U.S. attorney for Kentucky in May 1861. His son, torn between his family and his desire to enlist, was told by Mallie, "You must do as you would if you had neither wife nor children. I could not stand between you and your duty to the country and be happy."[26]

Accordingly, on September 27, immediately after the return of his home guard company from Muldraugh's Hill, Harlan announced in the *Journal* that he was forming an infantry regiment, inviting volunteers. An emotional statement accompanied the announcement, with the following peroration:

Their invaded State appeals to them. Their foully-wronged and deeply imperiled country appeals to them. The cause of human liberty and Republican institutions everywhere appeals to them. All that is most glorious in human government is now at stake, and every true man should come to the rescue. . . . Come, then, let us gird up the whole strength of our bodies and souls for the conflict, and may the God of Battles guide home every blow we strike. For one, I am unwilling to see the people of my native State overrun and conquered by men claiming to be citizens of a foreign government. I cannot be indifferent to the issue which an unnatural enemy has forced upon Kentuckians.[27]

The regiment was to be formed at Camp Crittenden, near Lebanon. Sending Mallie and the children to her family in Evansville, Harlan plunged into the work of recruiting and training the regiment of which he became colonel.[28] On November 12 the regiment, minimally supplied and trained, was mustered into Federal service as the Tenth Kentucky Infantry and assigned to a division commanded by General George H. Thomas, later to gain fame as the "Rock of Chickamauga." Fortunately, the military situation was such that the regiment saw no action for another month.

It must be repeated that Harlan was fighting for the Union, not for the abolition of slavery. He held this position in common with most Kentucky Unionists, and their stance was seemingly endorsed by Congress when it adopted a resolution sponsored by Crittenden that made the restoration of the Union the sole war aim. Events again overtook this position, of course.

4

Union Soldier
1861-1863

Harlan's military experience began with the expedition to Muldraugh's Hill in September 1861. The war had come to Kentucky, ending the dream of neutrality, when Confederate forces occupied Columbus and Hickman in the west, Bowling Green in the south, and Cumberland Gap in the east. Federal forces reacted by throwing troops into Paducah to protect the Ohio River line. Early in September Simon Buckner had declared for the Confederacy, taking most of the state guard with him; he was promptly appointed a brigadier general and given command of the forces around Bowling Green, which was seized on September 17. Buckner sent troops ahead to occupy Munfordville, along the Louisville and Nashville railroad line, and they eventually went as far as Lebanon Junction, only thirty miles from Louisville. William T. Sherman, who was placed in command of Union forces around Louisville, marched south to meet Buckner's army with a force composed entirely of raw recruits: the Fifth Kentucky, which was being trained at Jeffersonville, Indiana, and various units of the Louisville home guard, which were practically untrained and poorly armed into the bargain. The little army advanced by rail, reaching Lebanon Junction without incident, and found that Buckner had withdrawn.[1]

Sherman set up headquarters in the village's hotel, and Harlan's Zouaves, on account of their "military appearance," were assigned to guard the hotel.[2] With space at a premium, Harlan slept on the floor of Sherman's room for the week that the army remained there. Harlan's opinions of Sherman as a result of this contact were almost wholly complimentary. Besides being extremely energetic, the general absorbed information like a sponge: he had Harlan "up at all hours of the night in order that he might obtain information . . . about roads, people, etc." Harlan's political campaigning experience around the state enabled him to inform Sherman readily. Sherman was a chain cigar smoker; Harlan also smoked. When the general needed a light, which was often, he would say, "Harlan, let me have the light of your cigar—mine is out." "Certainly, General." Sherman would then take Harlan's cigar, light his, and throw Harlan's away. Said Harlan, "It never occurred to him that he threw my cigar away, but went on talking."[3]

A week later Sherman moved forward to Muldraugh's Hill, leaving Harlan's company at Lebanon Junction. When Harlan was ordered to bring ammunition forward, he was presented with his first military puzzle, since the railway bridge over Rolling Fork had been destroyed by Buckner's retreating Confederates. He solved the problem by loading a railroad handcar onto a farm wagon, fording the river, and then putting the handcar on the tracks; his men then pushed the car through a long tunnel and delivered the ammunition.[4]

On the way back to Lebanon Junction a small personal drama occurred. Basil W. Duke, a former Kentuckian who had joined the Confederate army, was with a companion on a recruiting trip into central Kentucky. Walking along the railroad hoping to catch a train, they came to the tunnel entrance just as Harlan's handcar arrived at the same place. Stepping aside to let the car pass, Duke carelessly threw back his hat and looked up. Since he and Harlan were acquainted, recognition was inevitable. Harlan thought Duke was on his way South, probably to see his wife. "Some of my men believing that Duke was on his way to join the rebel army, insisted that I should stop the handcar and arrest him," Harlan recalled. "But I declined to do so."[5] Duke's own recollection of the incident is similar:

> When Judge Harlan recognized me it at once occurred to him that I was trying to make my way to Lexington to see my wife; but he also realized that if captured I would be in great peril of being tried and punished as a spy. I was dressed in citizen's clothing and within the Federal lines on no ostensible military business. Under ordinary circumstances, he would have taken me without hesitation, but was unwilling that I should be put to death for an offense of which he believed me innocent. So he quietly placed his foot under the brake, and the efforts of his companions failed to stop the car. Judge Harlan's foot, like everything in his make-up, mental, moral, and physical, is constructed on a liberal, indeed, a grand scale, and might affect the motion of a passenger coach, not to mention a handcar. It was an exceedingly generous and kindly act.[6]

More than most wars, the Civil War was full of such small incidents, and the "capture" of Harlan in October while he was out recruiting for his regiment provides one of the more amusing of these. One evening found Harlan in Hodgenville with a friend. Recalling that Confederate troops were at nearby Munfordville, the two Union recruiters felt that it would not be safe to stay there, so they took to their horses and started toward New Hope, sixteen miles away, where a Union detachment was stationed. As they rode along they encountered a troop of infantrymen who commanded them to halt. Breathing a sigh of relief when they saw that the soldiers were Union, the two men obeyed. A sergeant, in heavy accent, commanded, "Dishmount!" A ready bayonet convinced Harlan that he had better comply. He showed the sergeant his papers, which were examined with great care, and then the sergeant disconcertingly concluded, "Dis may all be true, an' yet you might pee a damn shpy."

Then the two men were forced to walk with the soldiers all the rest of the way to New Hope—perhaps eight miles. Arriving in the small hours of the morning, the prisoners were taken to Colonel Willich, and eventually a captain was located who could vouch for Harlan. After that the atmosphere thawed, wine and beer were served, and Colonel August Willich remarked—as Harlan had already guessed—that the pickets were German immigrants (from Indiana) who had not yet had time to learn English very thoroughly. The next morning Harlan was invited to speak to the regiment. "I did so in English," he wrote, "but not a word of what I said was understood, although I was rapturously applauded, usually in the middle of my sentences."[7]

The first major action of Harlan's Tenth Kentucky Infantry came at the battle of Mill Springs (or Logan's Crossroads) on January 19 and 20, 1862. A small Confederate army under Brigadier General Felix Zollicoffer, a peace-time newspaper editor who had just been succeeded by Major General George B. Crittenden, a son of the famous Unionist senator, had invaded Kentucky through Cumberland Gap and occupied the southeastern portion of the state, resting at the tiny village of Mill Springs on the south bank of the Cumberland River. Zollicoffer, who seems to have possessed more enthusiasm than military skill, had encamped, however, north of the river, and continuous rains had put the river over its banks, making it difficult for him to pull back.[8]

George H. Thomas commanded a Union force of about the same size—four thousand men. His men had been continuously on the road for weeks; the heavy rains had turned the roads to sloughs of mud, and the army had been able to make only a few miles a day. He finally camped about nine miles from the rebel army on January 17, wishing to rest his men before attacking.

Harlan recollected the role of his regiment:

The route to Mill Springs was over a dirt road, and the earth was so thoroughly soaked with rain that Thomas's troops could make only a few miles each day. The regimental wagons sank into the earth up to the hubs of the wheels, and had to be lifted out by the soldiers. There was not a day when I did not myself join in that work in order to encourage my men. All along the route we had to cut down trees and saplings and make what were called "corduroy" roads, over which the wagons, when lifted out of the mud, would be placed by the soldiers.

Finally, the advance regiments of the division reached Logan's Field, three or four miles from the Cumberland River. . . . The Fourteenth Ohio and the Tenth Kentucky were then ten miles in the rear on the march. That night, after our camp had been established, an order came from General Thomas, who was with his advance regiments, directing Colonel Steedman and myself to take our respective regiments early the next morning, Saturday, and go off to the right to a certain point five or ten miles distant and capture a rebel forage train which was supposed to be in that part of the country. . . . But no such train could be found, and it became certain that the information received by General Thomas was incorrect.

The next morning, Steedman and myself prepared to resume our march and join the other regiments of our division, say about eight o'clock. Just as we were starting, a cavalryman belonging to Wolford's Kentucky Cavalry regiment came galloping up, and brought an order that we must hurry to the front, as the rebels, under Zollicoffer, had, early in the morning, advanced on Thomas, and that a fierce battle was raging. It was a magnificent sight to see how the boys struggled through mud and rain to reach the field of battle. The ground was so wet and muddy under them that their feet slipped at every step. I see now with great distinctness old Father Nash pushing along on foot with the boys. Equally earnest with him was a Catholic priest from Washington County, who had come with Catholic soldiers from that county. There were many Catholics in my regiment.

Well, we missed the battle, although we tried hard to be in it. When we reached the battle-field, the battle had ended, and the rebels had fallen back or retreated to their fortifications on the river. We went through the battle-field and saw many dead. It was a most harrowing sight to me. We passed right by the body of General Zollicoffer, which had been placed on a plank on the ground.

We did not halt at the battle-field, but moved on to join General Thomas who, with such of the Union troops as were in the fight, followed the Confederates to their fortifications on the Cumberland River. We caught up with General Thomas about five or six o'clock in the afternoon, and found the Union troops in front of the rebel fortifications, which appeared to be quite formidable. It turned out that if Thomas had, before dark, attacked the rebels in their fortifications, he could have carried the day and perhaps captured all the fleeing rebels with their guns. But the General thought otherwise, and made up his mind to defer an assault until next morning, when all his troops would be on hand.

At dawn our men were aroused and formed in line, and they immediately moved forward to the rebel fortifications, looking every moment for the rebels to open fire upon us. But they did not fire, and we went into the fortifications ahead of all the other troops, without resistance, and found no rebels there. The rebels, it was ascertained, had quietly crossed the river in the night, on a steamboat they owned or had impressed into their service, and had fled south into east Tennessee. Early in the day I crossed the river with one or two others in a skiff, and went a mile or so down the main road on which the rebels had retreated, and took dinner at the house of a man by the name of West. While at dinner word was brought that a flag of truce had appeared near by, and that the officer bringing it wished to confer with us. I went down to the road and met that officer. It was Lieutenant Ewing of Tennessee, who was on Zollicoffer's staff. His object was to obtain the body of General Zollicoffer. I informed him that it could not be done—that arrangements had been made to send the body through Louisville to Nashville for delivery to Zollicoffer's family. In a conversation with Ewing, I learned that the rebels, when they retired from the battle-field, were of opinion that the Union forces amounted to more than 10,000 men. But such was not the fact. The only Union regiments engaged in the fight were the Tenth Indiana, Fourth Kentucky, Ninth Ohio, Second Minnesota, a part of Colonel Hoskin's Kentucky infantry, and a company of Wolford's cavalry regiment, not exceeding 3000 men fit for duty.[9]

Joining Don Carlos Buell's army around Nashville, the Tenth Kentucky was now part of Thomas's division of a much larger army. With the fall of Fort Donelson, Tennessee, in February, the Confederates withdrew from Kentucky completely. They also left Nashville open, and it was occupied without fighting by Buell's forces. When General U.S. Grant's army, which had come up the Tennessee River after Fort Donelson's capture, was embroiled at Shiloh in April, Buell was ordered to Grant's support, and his reinforcements provided the margin of victory. Thomas's division, however, was last in the line of march and did not arrive in time to participate. Harlan recalled another minor incident that reveals something about his character: his concern for his men.

When the battle of Shiloh opened, Thomas' Division was many miles away, but after Nelson, Wood, and Crittenden were on the march to join Grant, Thomas was ordered to go forward with his men. He did so with all possible speed, but it rained more or less all the time and the men were compelled, time and again, to wade creeks. We reached Pittsburg Landing late in the second day of the battle, after the battle had ended, and were transported by boat up the river to Shiloh Landing, where Grant's Headquarters then were. We arrived there about 9 o'clock and were immediately ordered to leave the boat and go into camp, as the boat was to go back to Pittsburg Landing for other troops. We thought at the time that it was a cruel order, as Thomas' troops had no wagons or tents with them and had nothing for their protection against bad weather, except the ordinary army blanket. But the order had to be obeyed, and the men were ordered to go out on the hill-side, and make such provision for their comfort as they could. Upon the dismissal of my men for the night, some of them went to the Government Supply quarters, and cut open for their use many bales of hay. They brought the hay to camp and spread it out over the ground so as to protect their bodies from dampness. In a few moments they were all asleep. But a rain came up about two o'clock in the morning and soon their earth-and-hay beds were so drenched with rain that they were compelled to get up. There they were, on a dark night, in a drizzling rain, and apparently chilled from head to foot. I determined that the situation should be changed, whatever might be the consequences to me. Right before my eyes was a large steamboat, brilliantly lighted, with no one occupying it except a few officers and subordinates. It did not have even a private soldier, except a few to *guard* it. I called my regiment into a line and marched down to the boat, but my men were stopped at the plankway leading to the boat. I said, "Who dares to stop my men or to interfere with my orders." The guard replied that the boat belonged to Headquarters, and they were ordered to prevent its being used by others. I said to him that I only desired that my men should go on the lower deck of the boat and around its boilers so as to dry their clothes. The guard was obdurate and rightly so because he was only obeying his orders. But I had much concern for my soldiers, and called upon one of my best captains, and told him to bring his company with him. I ordered him to move ahead to the boat, and said that if any one attempted to prevent him from going on the boat with the men of the regiment, "to pitch them into the river." The Order was given to Capt. Frank Hill of Washington County, Kentucky. He replied, "All right, Colonel." He started on the boat gang-way with the men, but was stopped by the guard. Hill made his squad fix bayonets, and said to the guard, "Now, young man, I am going on that boat, and if you put yourself across my path, you will go into the river." Turning to the soldiers, he gave the order, "Forward." The guard stood to one side and the men of my regiment went into the boat, and in a little time they were all asleep, with their clothes on, lying on the deck of the vessel around the boilers. When day light came, and all those constituting Headquarters, were asleep, I had the men quietly aroused, and we went to the Shore. After reaching the Shore, I began to turn over in my mind what had taken place, and learned that the boat was the Headquarters of Gen. Grant and that he was then actually in his room. All at once it occurred to me that I was in great peril, and that as I had the night before willfully broken a guard, I was subject, perhaps to be *shot*. But luckily the soldiers on guard did not report us to Gen. Grant. At least, I have always thought that Grant knew nothing of our lawless conduct in forcing our way onto the boat in violation of his orders. But if he was informed of the facts, he had the courage to recognize the extraordinary circumstances of the case and to overlook our lawless acts.

On the next day after our arrival at Shiloh, I walked out to see the battlefield over which the contending armies under Grant and Johnston, respectively, on the day previously, had engaged in a battle which was momentous in its consequences. During this walk I happened to meet Gen. Sherman who had been in command of the Department of Kentucky for a time. He remembered me and invited me to accompany him to see Gen. Grant. I gladly accepted the invitation, and we found the latter in his office on the boat at the River Landing. He was then under a cloud because of the belief that he failed to accomplish some things in the battle of Shiloh which it was supposed he might have done and which would have enabled us to capture the great body of the rebel soldiers engaged in that battle. But great injustice was done Grant in this matter. Subsequent events in his life showed great capacity as a military commander. He overcame the opposition of his enemies and it was not long before he was recognized as the greatest of all the Union officers.[10]

Following Shiloh, the Union army moved to occupy western Tennessee and northern Mississippi, as well as the north side of the Tennessee River in Alabama. Most of this was more or less mere garrison work; the Tenth Kentucky went with Buell to Corinth, Mississippi, and in June to Tuscumbia, Alabama. In July it was stationed at Eastport, Mississippi. In late July two companies of Harlan's regiment, under Captain Henry G. Davidson, were sent to guard Courtland Bridge east of Tuscumbia, where there was an important railroad crossing. Being attacked by a larger force of Confederate cavalry, Davidson was surrounded and forced to surrender, but only after a stubborn fight. The size of the rebel unit can be gauged by the fact that it was commanded by Brigadier General Frank Armstrong.[11]

In August when the Tenth moved to Winchester, Tennessee, the regiment, Harlan said, was forced to march through hostile country where, if attacked "I could not have expected aid from other Union troops."[12] During the march, Harlan had occasion to demonstrate a strain of toughness that one might not suspect from the rest of his career.

> Our route was through Shelbyville, Tennessee. When we got within a few miles of that place we saw, much to our regret and horror, two negroes, wearing Union uniform, hung up at the roadside, dead. This caused me to be very uneasy for the fate of my sick men who were trudging along the road and endeavoring to keep up with their regiment. I feared that they would be killed by rebel guerrillas and determined to use every exertion for their safety. We reached Shelbyville about 11 o'clock, and as I was passing through the town I discovered about 30 to 40 well-dressed men in citizens' clothes, sitting quietly under the shade trees. It occurred to me, all at once, that here was a chance to protect my sick soldiers from rebel guerrillas. I halted my regiment in the main street and sent one of my captains, with a squad of soldiers to where the crowd was, with orders to arrest about a half dozen of them and bring them to me. My orders were to select well-dressed, young men who appeared to be influential and well to do. This was done and the arrested citizens were put into line with my men. Some of them wore pumps and white socks and seemed to be contented with their lot and with the situation. I then rode up, alone, to the crowd of citizens and said to them in substance: "It is proper to inform you as to what all this means. As we came along this morning we saw near here two negroes, hung up at the roadside and dead. They had on the uniforms of the Union Army and were hanged, no doubt, for that reason. They were, of course, murdered by rebel guerrillas, who were prowling around in that country. You know who they are, or could find out all about them. Now, I warn you that for every soldier absent from my camp this evening, two of these arrested citizens will be shot by my orders." Of course, I did not really intend that this order should be executed literally. But I suppose the rebel citizens deemed me to be in dead earnest. I then rode off, and moved ahead with my regiment, taking the arrested citizens with me and having them walk with my men in the dust. I adopted this plan at every town through which I passed on my way to Deckard. I heard no more of rebel guerrillas after leaving Shelbyville and none of my sick soldiers disappeared or were killed.[13]

At Winchester the Tenth Kentucky rejoined Buell's main body. Buell had been under orders to attack Chattanooga, but he was so slow about it that Braxton Bragg, the new Confederate commander, decided to forestall the attack by marching into Kentucky. This turned out to be the major Confederate invasion of the Bluegrass State. Edmund Kirby Smith started it off with an important victory at Richmond, coming into Kentucky from the southeast. He went on to occupy Lexington and Frankfort at the beginning of September 1862. Meanwhile Bragg marched with about thirty thousand men straight for central Kentucky from Chattanooga. Don Carlos Buell felt it necessary to defend Kentucky—especially to protect the Ohio River line—so he set out from Winchester in pursuit, with fifty-six thousand men. The chase, in which Harlan's regiment took part, proceeded along parallel lines, with Buell trying to protect his supply bases at Nashville and Bowling Green. On September 14 Buell found himself at Bowling Green, while Bragg was only thirty miles east at Glasgow—closer to Louisville than was the Union army and well placed for joining Kirby Smith.

Instead of joining in battle, the armies avoided each other: the Confederates went due north and attacked a small Union force at Munfordville. This done, Bragg headed northeast toward Bardstown. On his part, Buell lingered at Bowling Green until Thomas's corps, including the Tenth Kentucky, could catch up; thus he arrived at Munfordville after Bragg had left. The road to Louisville was open, though, and Buell went there to reorganize and receive reinforcements.[14] Buell's Army of the Ohio was apparently a hotbed of discontent during this march, since many officers felt that the general was not aggressive enough and should have attacked the rebel army. Harlan later wrote:

> While our army was en route for Louisville there occurred an incident which was well calculated to disturb any one who desired the success of the Union troops. Somewhere on the line, South of and not very far from Munfordsville, our army was halted for some reason, and thus an opportunity was given for officers to confer with each other as to the possibility of an encounter by the Union army with Bragg's forces. Some of the officers thought it was a great mistake not to hunt for and attack Bragg; for, it was well known that he was not far to the East, and was steadily moving in the direction of Louisville and Central Kentucky. A few others predicted that Buell would not attack Bragg until after he had received the reenforcements then being gathered at Louisville. Others intimated, and, indeed, some said that Buell was untrue to his country and to his [army], and would ultimately so manage his forces that Bragg would escape from the State and go back into Tennessee. I expressed no opinion on the subject, being a young colonel, only a little over 28 years of age. But I did say to Col. Sill of Ohio, another young colonel, that it was distressing to think that we might, at any time, get into battle, under a commander, some of whose officers distrusted his fidelity; that if they really believed Buell to be untrue or unsafe as a commander, they should take active measures to have him put out of command.[15]

The army arrived at Louisville on September 24 and 25, and by that time Lincoln, too, was dissatisfied with Buell's performance and had ordered his removal. Thomas, who was to be Buell's successor, however, did not want to take his superior's place under such conditions and refused the post, asking that Buell be kept. This was done.[16]

Buell remained in Louisville until the end of September, increasing his forces to seventy-five thousand. During the week spent there, Harlan was able to bring Mallie and the ten-month-old baby, James Shanklin Harlan, for a visit. The couple had not been together for almost a year, although they wrote each other daily—a habit that Harlan had established whenever they were separated and to which he remained faithful all of his life.[17]

The Tenth Kentucky was by now attached to Major General Charles C. Gilbert's Third Corps, First Division, under Brigadier General A. Schoepf, Second Brigade, under Brigadier General Speed S. Fry.[18] Marching southeast from Louisville, the Union army encountered Bragg's forces just outside Perryville, and the Federal troops were on "a line running substantially through the farm or plantation of several thousand acres, which was once owned by my grandfather, James Harlan, and near by the house erected by him as a residence."[19] The weather had been extremely dry, and both armies needed access to whatever water was available: this fact gave rise to the battle. The Confederates had only sixteen thousand troops at the spot, and they attacked McCook's Union corps vigorously in the afternoon of October 8. Gilbert committed some of his troops to aid McCook, who was hard-pressed, but he was loathe to detach many, since he knew he might also be attacked. He did eventually do so and even attacked with his right wing. Crittenden's corps, on the other hand, was not engaged at all, nor was a substantial portion of Gilbert's corps, including Harlan's regiment. The number of troops actually engaged on the Union side was not much greater than that on the rebel side. Casualties were, however, extremely heavy. Due to tricks of wind and topography, Buell did not even know there was a battle on for hours; due to poor coordination Crittenden never got into the battle. By the next morning Buell was ready to attack, but the Southern army had wisely retired. Buell got credit for a victory only because his foe left the field: he had greater casualties than his opponent, and he had completely mishandled his forces.[20] Moreover, his subsequent pursuit of the retreating army was lackadaisical.

Harlan's regiment did not get into the battle at all, and Harlan himself was acting as brigade commander. The Second Brigade was stationed at Buell's headquarters, and like his chief, Harlan did not realize there was a battle on.

The battle took place in a small valley, and at the time of the fighting the wind was blowing heavily from the locality of Buell's Headquarters, towards the battle of Perryville. This accounts for Buell's not being able to hear the sound of musketry or cannon. If he had known what was going on, it cannot be supposed that he would have failed to rush to McCook's assistance. I speak of these things without any doubt as to the correctness of what I say, because I was within one hundred yards of Buell's Headquarters during the whole time of the battle. At that time I was in command of a Brigade, and being about to march with my men for the purpose of joining the main body of our corps, Buell sent me an order to stay where I was until further orders, but holding my command ready for action, if any occasion therefore should arise. Later in the afternoon a soldier came from the direction of McCook's corps and gave notice that a great battle had been fought in the early afternoon of that day several miles distant. This was the first intimation that I had had of any battle having been fought. I heard no firing from the direction of the battle field, and if I did not hear it, Buell could not have done so. If I had heard any firing Buell should have also heard it, for we were not more than a hundred yards apart at any time during the battle.[21]

Following the unsuccessful pursuit of Bragg and Kirby Smith, the Union army went into camp near Lebanon. Renewed dissatisfaction with Buell was manifest, by both his superiors and his staff.

The next day after we went into camp, a message came that a meeting of the field officers of our corps, Gilbert's, would be held at the little schoolhouse up the creek and that my presence there was desired. The object of the meeting was not stated, but in view of the ugly feeling that Bragg had been permitted to escape with all his troops, I suspected that the proposed meeting had some mischievous or dangerous purpose in contemplation. But I determined to know what was going on, feeling that whatever was said or done at the meeting, I knew my duty and could take care of myself. So I went at the appointed time, and found about twenty officers there—what for I had not then ascertained. Gen. Speed S. Fry, whom I had known from my earliest boyhood, and in whom I had every confidence, was called to the chair. Soon the talking commenced, all that was said for some time being directed against Gilbert, our corps commander. He was pronounced as incompetent for his position and it was said that his removal was vital to the army. It was suggested that a telegram on the subject should be sent directly and at once to President Lincoln. Finally, a Lieutenant-Colonel or Major of an Illinois Regiment— whose name, I think, was McClellan or McLellan—rose and said with impassioned voice, "Mr. Chairman, I rise to say that, in my opinion, we are a pack of cowards." "What do you mean?" said Col. Fry. He replied: "I mean that we have spent all this evening talking about Gen. Gilbert, when our real objection is to Buell as our commander. In my opinion, Buell is a traitor, is untrue to the army and untrue to the country." When he sat down, I arose, feeling that, although not expecting to say anything, I could not pass in silence what the Illinois officer had said, without expressing my own views. So I said, in substance: "Mr. Chairman, I do not concur in what has been said about Gen. Buell. He no doubt has made mistakes, and may have views that I do not share. But I do not believe that he is untrue to the army or that he purposely or treacherously allowed Bragg's army to escape. Nor will I sign any telegram to the President which would question Buell's integrity or his fidelity to his troops." "What sort of a telegram," broke in the Illinois officer, "will you sign?

Put down on paper what you are willing to say." Thereupon I sat down at the table, and wrote a telegram such as I would consent to be sent to the President. It ran about in this wise: "Gen. Buell having lost the confidence of the Army of the Ohio, we think the public interests would be subserved by a change of commanders." "That," the Illinois officer said, "is satisfactory." We all (including Gen. Steedman and Gen. Fry) signed it and, much to my surprise, the telegram was committed to me to be sent to Washington. The next day I started for Lebanon, where a telegraph office was located, intending to send the proposed telegram. On my way, it occurred to me that the telegram would go through Buell's headquarters, and that all of those who had signed it would get into trouble. But I made up my mind to do what my brother officers desired, and which I had agreed to do. Luckily for us, upon my arrival at Lebanon, the Louisville papers of that day announced that by order of the President, Buell had been superceded by Gen. Rosecrans in command of the army of the Ohio and Buell temporarily deprived of authority. I took the responsibility of withholding the telegram.[22]

For whatever reasons, Buell was relieved of command and replaced, not by Thomas, but by Major General William B. Rosecrans, who, it must be admitted, compiled a record very similar to that of his predecessor in his dilatoriness and lack of aggressiveness. The army was reorganized into the Army of the Cumberland, and Colonel Harlan was promoted to brigade commander of the Second Brigade, Third Division (under Fry and then Steedman), Fourteenth Corps (under Thomas). In this role he was to play a major part in the Union army's attempts to combat the raids of the Confederates' famous cavalry leaders, Joseph Wheeler, Nathan Bedford Forrest, and John Hunt Morgan. It was Harlan's misfortune to draw Morgan. The army returned to Nashville, and Harlan's brigade was stationed in and around Gallatin, covering the northeastern approaches to Tennessee's capital city. By late November the brigade had been enlarged (although it lost Harlan's own Tenth Kentucky Infantry) to include twelve infantry regiments—close to ten thousand men if all regiments were at full strength.[23]

Harlan's first tangle with Morgan's Raiders, a relatively minor action, took place early in December. The brigade's headquarters was at tiny Castalian Springs a few miles east of Gallatin. Still further east, at Hartsville, was another federal garrison. The famous Confederate cavalry commander John Hunt Morgan (another Kentuckian) attacked Hartsville with a cavalry and infantry force on December 7. Basil Duke recalled, "The snow lay upon the ground and the cold was intense."[24]

Although outnumbered, Morgan's troops overwhelmed the Union force: in a very short time, 58 were killed, 204 wounded, and 1,834 captured or missing.[25] Morgan's losses were comparatively light. General Duke added that "the enemy from Castalian Springs began to press upon us so closely" that Morgan's men had to retreat precipitously: "Nothing but the rapid style in which the fight had been conducted and finished saved us.

We had no sooner evacuated the ground than the enemy occupied it," but there was no further pursuit.[26]

The Union rescue force was, of course, Harlan's brigade, which got there too late to save the garrison but soon enough to restore the situation. The attack, though brilliant, thus served no particular purpose. Harlan's own version of the story, written during his tenure as a Supreme Court justice, is of some interest.

> I was put in charge of the Union troops stationed at Castalian Springs, in Tennessee, which was about ten miles from Hartsville, in that State. At the latter place we also had some troops, but they were under the command of an officer who, it was said, had no experience, nor any idea of discipline. He allowed his men "to prowl around the country" and depredate upon the property of private citizens. He did not seem to know the necessity of having pickets out constantly in different directions, so as to inform him of the advance of the enemy. The result was, what might have been expected—a surprise of our troops by the enemy. Early in the morning John H. Morgan "burst out of the woods" and attacked the Union troops when the latter were quietly eating breakfast. After a short contest he captured the whole of our troops, about 2,100 in number, and took them across the Cumberland River. As soon as I could hear from my camp at Castalian Springs, the firing of musketry and cannon in the direction of Hartsville started and I rushed to the aid of our troops at Hartsville. The march made by my troops to Hartsville was extraordinary in its swiftness. But when we reached the battle-field at Hartsville we saw only the dead and wounded lying around, while Morgan's men were a long way off going up the hill on the opposite side of the river, each rebel horseman having on his horse behind him a Union soldier as a prisoner. The rebels were too far ahead to be reached by the light cannon we had for use. When we got to Hartsville, I observed a two-horse wagon crossing the river. As it was evidently under Morgan's control and was being taken to his camp, I ordered the wagon party to be fired upon, and the order was promptly obeyed. Along with the wagon was a rebel soldier recently ascertained to be Horace H. Lurton of Morgan's command, and now a colleague of mine in the Supreme Court of the United States.[27]

Parts of Harlan's brigade, along with other Union troops under his command, were to tangle with Morgan again at the end of the year. It would prove to be his final military action, as well as his most important as an independent commander. Like so many such events, it is surrounded by controversy. The occasion was Morgan's "Third Raid" into Kentucky in December and January 1862-63. Duke later reported that the mission of the raid was to destroy the Louisville and Nashville Railroad, Rosecrans's major supply line, and that Morgan had for this purpose 3,900 men, mostly cavalry but with some artillery as well. The force left its base at Alexandria, Tennessee, on December 22 and reached the Cumberland River that night. They reached Glasgow, Kentucky, the night of December 24, driving a

Union unit from the town. On Christmas Day the march was resumed, with another skirmish, and the horsemen crossed the Green River, camping at Hammondsville (now Hammonville). On December 26, in "steadily pouring rain," moving through mud "which threatened to engulf everything," they struck toward the railroad above Munfordville, destroying the railroad bridge over Bacon Creek, obtaining a surrender of the Union forces garrisoning the bridge, and encamping just south of Elizabethtown. This important rail town was taken on December 27 after a brief battle with outnumbered Federal troops. The raiders captured the entire garrison of some six hundred men. They had now reached their major objective: moving up the railroad toward Louisville, they destroyed all they could, including the two great trestles at Muldraugh's Hill and the Cane Run bridge only twenty-eight miles from the Kentucky metropolis. His mission accomplished, Morgan prepared to return to Tennessee, or at least this is the version of the story given by Duke.[28] Morgan's troops camped on the Rolling Fork the night of December 28, and on December 29 and 30 they were forced into skirmishes—Duke calls them rearguard actions—with Federal troops brought up by Colonel Harlan, at the hamlet of Boston and on Rolling Fork. Duke's version holds that "we knew that a force of infantry and cavalry was cautiously following us, but did not know that it was so near." He admits that they were in a tight spot, since part of Morgan's men were still on the south side of the river. Duke maintains that Harlan's force was not adequately led: "This force, which, if handled vigorously and skillfully, if its march had even been steadily kept up, would have, in spite of every effort we could have made, swept us into the turbid river at our backs, approached cautiously and very slowly." Morgan succeeded in getting across the river and withdrew toward Bardstown without pursuit, eventually returning to Tennessee.

This rather severe indictment of Harlan's conduct of the "battle" was written, it is true, many years afterward and by a man who had every reason to make both himself and Morgan look good. On the other hand, Duke was there and knew the situation, at least from the Confederate side of the battle lines. If true, his version detracts considerably from Harlan's military reputation. It should, of course, be recalled that this was John's first independent command and the first time he had ever handled forces of such a size: Duke estimates the Union forces present as five thousand infantry and two thousand cavalry (Harlan had never handled cavalry at all).

The Union point of view, Harlan's, is vastly different, even though it suffers from the same defect of self-interest. Nevertheless, his official report, written just after the battle, does not reflect the disadvantage of poor memory. Harlan's brigade was, of course, in Tennessee when the whole episode began. When Morgan's expedition was first reported, the raiders had already reached Glasgow. Harlan gathered what forces were available and could be spared. Reports vary about what units were actually involved, and undoubtedly some of them, especially the cavalry, were picked up along the way. But it probably consisted of about five infantry regiments and one cavalry, with one battery of light artillery.[29] This represents a considerably smaller troop strength than Duke's estimate, probably under five thousand total, but still larger than Morgan's force.

Harlan moved rapidly to follow Morgan. He had the advantage of the railroad, but only as far as Munfordville, since the bridges north of there had been destroyed. He was thus in the unenviable position of pursuing cavalry with a force composed mainly of foot soldiers. Harlan's command moved on up the railroad as speedily as possible, aided by the fact that Morgan was proceeding slowly by that time, destroying the railroad as he went. The Union forces finally caught up at Rolling Fork. Harlan reported:

> I went to the front in person, and from a high hill I saw quite distinctly a very large body of cavalry formed in line of battle near the river. Their officers were riding along their line apparently preparing to give us battle. Knowing that Morgan had a larger force than I had, I proceeded cautiously, and yet as expeditiously as the nature of the ground and the circumstances admitted. My men were formed in two lines; skirmishers were thrown out from both infantry and cavalry, covering our whole front, and were ordered to advance and engage the enemy, the whole line following in close supporting distance. The firing commenced, on the part of the rebels, on our left; it was promptly and vigorously responded to by my skirmishers and the artillery. After a while the rebels were driven away, and they then made some demonstrations to occupy an eminence upon my right. To meet this movement the 10th Ind. (Col. Carroll) was ordered to occupy that eminence, from which four companies were ordered to clear the woods on the right on my line. The 4th Ky. (Col. Croxton), 14th Ohio (Col. Este), 74th Ind. (Col. Chapman), were ordered to form on the left of the 10th Ind. A section of the battery was ordered to occupy the eminence, and the 10th Ky. (Lieut. Col. Hays) ordered to support it. This left the 13th Ky. (Maj. Hobson), on my left, supporting the section of the battery stationed there. The firing now became general all along the right of our line of skirmishers; but the rebels, after an obstinate resistance, broke and fled precipitately in every direction. Some struck out into the woods; some went up the river as far as New Haven; some swam the river with their horses. Further pursuit that evening was impracticable, and I may say impossible, in the exhausted state of my men, they having left Munfordville Sunday morning, and come up with the enemy the succeeding day at one o'clock, forty-three miles distant.
>
> I claim for my command that it saved the Rolling Fork bridge, and most probably prevented any attempt to destroy the bridge at Shepherdsville.[30]

Harlan thus claimed that his action probably prevented Morgan from committing further destruction and forced him to return to Tennessee. Neither the colonel nor other Union commanders, of course, knew what

Morgan's plans may have been. Duke says that the dashing cavalry commander's withdrawal was according to plan and according to Bragg's orders. But if there had been less effective action against him, Morgan was hardly the man to forego additional opportunities. The nudge given him by Harlan, in any case, prevented any thought of continuing the raid.

Harlan and his troops returned to Nashville to rejoin the Army of the Cumberland, arriving after the conclusion of the battle of Murfreesboro, in which, like Buell, Rosecrans was left in possession of the field but could hardly claim a victory and in any case did not pursue Bragg's weary army. Late in January parts of Harlan's brigade were again in action against the rebel cavalry around La Vergne and Nolensville, Tennessee; the brigade remained at La Vergne until after Harlan's resignation from the army.[31] He had gained enough credit as a military commander that in late February his name was submitted by President Lincoln to Congress for promotion to brigadier general, a capacity in which he had, after all, been acting for several months. By that time, however, he knew that he was going to have to leave the army, and at his request Senator Crittenden withdrew his nomination.[32]

The proximate cause of Harlan's resignation was the death of his father on February 23, 1863. James Harlan had been ill all winter, and at least once during this busy time John had taken leave to visit Frankfort. Harlan referred to his father's passing as

> an unspeakable calamity to the family, even if looked at only from the standpoint of business. At the time he died my father had the largest practice of any lawyer in Kentucky and the support of my mother and the family depended upon the right hand of the business left by him. My three oldest brothers were dead, and my only remaining brother had become incompetent for business. I was connected with my father in business and alone knew of what was necessary to be done in order to preserve from loss or waste what he had fairly earned by hard work in his profession. So, in every sense, I was compelled to return to civil life.[33]

The officers of Harlan's brigade passed a resolution of regret upon his resignation, asserting that "having been associated with Colonel Harlan for nearly 18 months, during which time he has won the love and esteem of his whole command, by his amiable manners, unflinching integrity, and his indefatigable attention, to all his duties, we hereby extend to him a fond farewell."[34]

5

Into the Political Wilderness
1863-1867

The reasons Harlan adduced for his resignation from the army were, as far as they went, valid enough. Certainly his superior officers accepted them. But one must read the dominant motivation between the lines. What Harlan did not say was that his father's financial support was no longer available, for his mother of course, but just as certainly for himself and his family, who had probably been at least partially dependent. In view of the incapacitation of one brother and the unreliability of the other, John Harlan was now the breadwinner for the whole family.

The family posed problems. Unhappy marriages were as common then, seemingly, as now. John's brother James was already showing signs of the alcoholism that was to ruin his life; his wife Amelia suffered from poor health. William Lowndes Harlan (apparently unmarried) was an insignificant figure who had to be supported. John's sisters were at the Frankfort home almost as much as they were with their husbands. Dr. Hatchitt was a surgeon in Harlan's Tenth Kentucky, and while he was away, Bettie lived with her parents. Laura, too, was unwell, and she died in 1870. Sallie's marriage to David P. Hiter was more successful. The family, indeed, needed John Harlan, not only for financial support but also as the head of the family.

An income, then, was a major reason for Harlan's return to civilian life. But scarcely less important was the settlement of his father's estate. Although James was joined with him as an executor and law partner, it seems certain that the major decisions devolved upon John. There were at least two houses, as well as other property, to be managed or sold; his father's interest in the Old Stone House and the accompanying farm had to be handled to the satisfaction of his cousin Wellington Harlan, whose father had had a share in the property.[1] And John's father had put up large sums as surety for the freedom of some old friends who had been charged with disloyalty by the military "governor," Brigadier General Jeremiah T. Boyle, and these affairs had to be settled.[2] Finally, his mother's portion of the estate had to be figured out and, as it turned out, augmented.

Eliza was entitled, under Kentucky law, to only one-third of her husband's estate.[3] As far as the houses were concerned this posed no major problem, since Harlan was moving back to Frankfort anyway, and he and James would merely continue to live with their mother. The ownership of the slaves was a little more troublesome. The Emancipation Proclamation, although it had been issued two months before Harlan left the army, did not apply to Kentucky, so slavery existed there until the Thirteenth Amendment took effect two years later. Harlan felt that it was best to leave these slaves—perhaps ten of them—in his mother's possession. He had concern for his mother's comfort no doubt, but he also hesitated to put the slaves on the market (as well he might). Not only did he, in Mallie's words, have "a real affection for his father's servants," but he "could not bear to think of them falling into other hands through the barter and sale of human beings that was then still in vogue." So he made himself financially responsible to the estate for all the slaves. When they became free he paid the proper amount into the estate.[4]

Settling the estate meant the necessity of living in Frankfort at least temporarily. Consequently a notice appeared in the local papers: "John M. Harlan, Attorney at Law, Frankfort, Kentucky, will practice Law in all the Courts held in Frankfort and the adjoining Counties. He will give especial attention to the collection of claims in any part of Kentucky. Office on St. Clair Street."[5] Perhaps fortuitously, in view of the need for a steady income, Harlan was nominated by the Union party as its candidate for attorney general of Kentucky only three weeks after leaving the army. This conjunction of events leads to the speculation that Harlan's resignation may have taken place in the foreknowledge that his nomination was likely. Once nominated, his election was almost certain, because the party then completely dominated Kentucky politics. With a steady, though not large, income assured, John could afford to live in Frankfort.

Harlan's nomination was almost a formality, since there was no opposition at the March 19 Union party convention. In accepting, Colonel Harlan (as he would henceforth be known, except when he was called "General") urged upon his party its "earnest prosecution of the war" and rejected peace "on any terms other than submission of the rebels to the laws which they had outraged."[6]

Nevertheless, he attacked, with his usual vigor, the president: for suspending the privilege of the writ of habeas corpus and for issuing the Emancipation Proclamation; he regarded both acts as unconstitutional.[7] This apparently Janus-faced posture was typical of Union party spokesmen during the state campaign that ensued: it undoubtedly represented their personal convictions, but it was also a political strategem that enabled them to retain the votes both of those radicals who might otherwise gravitate to the still unpopular Republican party (men like Harlan's future law partner, Benjamin H. Bristow) and of the "peace Democrats," who had become increasingly bitter about Lincoln's policies.[8] The Union party ended up with Thomas E. Bramlette for its gubernatorial candidate; he was suspected of being a radical, however, and many peace Democrats (including Harlan's old partner, Bullock) jumped the party and put up Charles A. Wickliffe as a rival candidate. They claimed to be the regular Democratic party and stood for peace with union. Lurking in the background of this whole situation was the attempt of the military authorities to dominate the state's politics, which had soured many Kentuckians who had been staunch Unionists on the war itself.

During the summer Harlan campaigned actively; he chaired the district convention of his party, and he gave several non-campaign speeches that were definitely pro-Union.[9] It was, in general, a heated campaign in which neither side gave the other credit even for common honesty. Union party candidates were accused of being Lincoln men in disguise; Democrats were similarly charged with being "stay-at-home secessionists" (both charges were mostly false). The Federal army was an important factor both during the campaign and at the polls. Intimidation was widespread. Even so, the victory margins of Harlan and his associates were so great that one must doubt that any other result would have been achieved even without the military.[10]

A graphic picture of Harlan the campaigner was penned later by Champ Clark, who as a boy in 1863 attended a campaign rally:

> When in the flower of his years and the prime of his splendid powers, he was candidate as Attorney-General of Kentucky, to which office he was elected. He was as magnificent a specimen of a physical man as one would have found in a month's journey—standing six feet three in his stockings, weighing two hundred avoirdupois without an ounce of surplus flesh, red-headed, blond as any lily, graceful as a panther, he was the typical Kentuckian in his best estate.
>
> His mental and educational equipment was superb. On a glorious day in October, at a great picnic in Henry Isham's sugar-grove, in the outskirts of Mackville, Colonel Harlan and Colonel Thomas E. Bramlett, candidate for Governor, spoke to a great concourse of people. I played hooky to hear them speak. Governor Bramlett was a large, handsome man and made a good speech, but Harlan easily overtopped him mentally, physically, and oratorically. Mere chunk of a boy as I was, I could see that Harlan was the greater man.[11]

The attorney generalship was, as it turned out, to be Harlan's only major elective office. An inveterate politician, he must also be considered in many respects a failure. In any case, by 1864 he was once again wandering in the political wilderness, a man without a party. This process began with the presidential campaign that pitted Lincoln against the Democrats' choice, George B. McClellan. General McClellan was chosen, apparently, because he was popular, especially with his troops, and because he seemed to believe that the North could not defeat the Confederacy in offensive campaigns, preferring a defensive strategy. He could thus appeal to the large number of Northern Democrats who were disaffected with the war policy of Lincoln. At the same time he could not be accused of sympathy with the South or even of defeatism.[12]

John Harlan, together with many Kentucky Unionists, still did not feel able to support Lincoln. The president's acts freeing the slaves and his policy of encouraging black enlistment in the army produced major disaffection among Kentucky Union leaders. These men took the lead among Conservative Unionists (as they were called) to find an alternative to Lincoln. Such men as Bramlette and the Harlans' old friend John B. Bruner helped to organize a meeting of the national committee of this group in Cincinnati in December 1863. The committee plumped for McClellan as the only person "around whom conservative people, without regard for former predilections, can rally."[13]

In April 1864 the Kentucky Union party's central committee met. Since it was not attached to either major national party and could hardly expect to constitute a major force as a third party, the balance of the group swung to support of the national Democrats, especially if they would nominate McClellan. A minority felt that the state party should support Lincoln and broke off to become explicitly Republican. The result was that the majority group sent a delegation to the Democratic National Convention in Chicago in August.[14]

To Harlan, this was merely another in the series of events that had started in 1861, when Unionist Conservatives had cooperated with Unionist Democrats to secure Kentucky's loyalism. It did not mean that he became in any sense a Democrat. His support, and that of his political friends, was keyed to the man, McClellan, not to the party, and to his acceptance speech, not the official platform.

A third group also existed in Kentucky, made up of Unionists who were now willing to become Democrats: peace Democrats held their own state convention in Louisville on June 28, led by such prominent men as Wickliffe, John G. Carlisle, and John H. Harney of the Louisville *Democrat*. They asked for, if they did not expect, an immediate armistice and a peaceful settlement.[15] Efforts to combine the Unionists with the peace Democrats failed, and each sent a delegation to Chicago. The credentials committee of the convention settled the conflict by using King Solomon's solution: it admitted both delegations, giving each delegate only a half-vote.[16]

Harlan campaigned for McClellan as vigorously as he had done for others in the past. In his enthusiasm he sounded almost like a Democrat himself. In truth, he said that he had "buried the hatchet" so that he could support a Democratic candidate.[17] But had the candidate been John C. Breckinridge he would hardly have given his support. It was a quixotic move, like others in the past, since McClellan could not win. But Harlan campaigned against Oliver P. Morton's gubernatorial aspirations in Indiana, too, for the sole reason that Morton was regarded as a Republican extremist. In a speech at New Albany Harlan earned Morton's lasting enmity, and the speech was later used to question his integrity when he became a Republican—and again when he was nominated to the Supreme Court bench.[18] His position is best summarized by his own comment, made a few years later: "I did not vote for McClellan because I was a Democrat, or because he was a Democrat, but because I *then* believed that his mode of prosecuting the war was most likely to bring it to a speedy conclusion, with the Union preserved intact. . . . [I supported McClellan because] of his letter of acceptance, in which he repudiated the platform upon which he stood, and declared for the preservation of the Union, in favor of furnishing the men and money to whatever extent might be necessary to maintain the unity of the country."[19]

With the election over, McClellan having carried only three states (one of which was of course Kentucky), Harlan could, for a short time at least, devote his full attention to his duties as attorney general and to his private law practice in Frankfort. The ineffectiveness of these in producing a substantial regular income appears only inferentially; for instance, in 1865 the John Harlan family was able to buy a house, but only because Mallie's father provided the money.[20] It was a large house on the corner of Broadway facing the capitol, on a site now occupied by a state office building. The Harlans' move was doubtless prompted by space considerations, since they then had a fourth child (John Maynard was born on December 21, 1863), and the rest of the family showed a pronounced tendency to converge on Mama: James (who was John's law partner at this time) was living at the Frankfort home with his wife; William was there too, increasingly ineffective; and John's three sisters with their children stayed there frequently. Even so, the change might not have been possible without help. Mallie described the new house:

> The lower story of this house was only one room deep, the rooms being very large and opening onto a latticed porch in the rear, with six or eight steps leading to a garden. The part next to the house was planted with flowers, and back of that was a kitchen garden. The house had a frontage, however, of four rooms facing the Capitol Square. The fourth room led to a passage-way to the kitchen, which was the first room in a long-drawn-out ell at the Eastern end of the house, the ell having been added to, from time to time, according to the needs of the former owner, who was a slave-holder.[21]

Mallie recalled that in this house she and John gave their first entertainment, their tenth anniversary party. She was amused at her mother-in-law's anxiety that the party should be successful: "Although *she* did all the managing and the superintending, *I*, as the hostess, was given all the credit. That was her generous way of coming to the rescue of every member of the family."[22]

John and Mallie still kept a few household slaves, and John had, in fact, just hired a cook, paying the owner a hundred dollars for a year's hire. Mallie's vexation showed even fifty years later as she recounted her inability to control "Aunt" Fannie.

> She was a woman of decided ideas as to her own importance. Being very much older than I was, she bitterly resented the mildest suggestion I could make as to her preparation of certain dishes. On one occasion she said to me:—"You don't know nuthin' 'bout cookin'. I allus done it dis way foh Miss Eddie." To which I replied, "But you are working for *me* now and not for Miss Eddie, and you must do it *my* way." With a look of scorn she said again, "I jus' tole you, you don't know nuthin' 'bout cookin'." Once or twice, taking me by the shoulders, she actually put me out of the kitchen and locked the door.[23]

The upshot of this difficulty was that "Aunt" Fannie was given her freedom. But this did not end the episode. Finding it impossible to locate another cook, Mallie in despair went to one of Mother Harlan's old slaves, "Aunt" Emily, and asked why no one wanted to work for her. "With a look on her face of mingled amusement and sorrow (lest she might hurt my feelings) she said, 'Ole Fannie done gib you such a bad name, Miss Mallie, dat it's gwine to be hard fer you to get a good cook. She say that Marse John is a puffect gen'lman, but dat *you*'se nuffin but a She-Debbil.'"

Luckily a cook was found. A neighbor was breaking up his group of slaves by sending them away, and one older woman who would have been separated from her husband this way was willing to take the chance of working for that "She-Debbil" in return for the opportunity to stay with her George. "Aunt" Charlotte proved to be an enormous improvement over her predecessor and became a very affectionate retainer, as this sequel relates:

> At the time of our "Tin Wedding" we had several visitors in the house. After I had gone to bed, I remembered that I had failed to give explicit orders for the next morning's breakfast. I therefore slipped down to the kitchen door through the passage way, to speak with "Aunt" Charlotte. Reaching the door that led from the kitchen to her bedroom, I heard her voice lifted in prayer—old "Uncle" George (her husband), I had no doubt, was kneeling with her. She prayed for every member of the family by name, especially asking that the little boys and "all the children" might be a comfort and blessing to their Father and Mother. I quietly stole back to our own room, telling my husband as I closed the door, that I did not care whether we had any breakfast or not, so long as there were such prayers going up for us from the kitchen.[24]

As attorney general, Harlan had to give opinions on unusual legal questions. Must a man pay taxes on property taken from a bank by Morgan's

Raiders or on slave boys taken from his farm who enlisted in the Union army?[25] What did Kentucky law provide for justices of the peace who failed to qualify for the position after being properly elected? If qualification includes an oath, can it be taken much later?[26] What is the duty of a county judge in relation to collection of fines for the nonperformance of required militia duties?[27] Can a sheriff elected in 1864 still pay his required bond in 1865?[28]

More interesting were the occasional court cases that had political implications. In Kentucky in 1863 and 1864 these mostly related to slavery, and knowing that Harlan had opposed emancipation and would also oppose the Thirteenth Amendment, one gains a clue about how he as attorney general might approach such cases. Thus, he argued that federal authorities were subject to indictment by the state when they took slaves (private property) without some attempt to show immediate danger or necessity.[29] Similarly, General John M. Palmer was found to be indictable on a Harlan argument for the crime of aiding in the escape of slaves; he had ordered the owners of railroads and ferries to transport blacks who had military passes. The indictments, however, died because Palmer had left the state by the time they were issued.[30] Harlan also felt that the state's right to prescribe the rules of evidence for its own courts was preserved intact despite the war. The federal Civil Rights Act of 1866 allowed blacks to testify against whites; Kentucky law forbade it. The state court of appeals agreed with Harlan that the federal law was inapplicable.[31]

The country was changing as a result of the war. Kentucky would have to change too, but Harlan and many of his conservative friends would fight a last rearguard action against those changes that they regarded as subversive of the American constitutional system. Particularly this meant opposition to the Thirteenth Amendment. Secondarily it involved objections to the operation of the Freedmen's Bureau within the state.[32]

It was commonly felt, both by Democrats and Conservative Unionists, that since Kentucky was a loyal state, the wartime and postwar federal actions abolishing slavery, enlisting former slaves in the army, and providing federal aid (and interference) should not be applied to that state any more than they were to any other loyal state, like New York. Kentuckians usually seemed to feel that they should be allowed to abolish slavery and then to deal with the former slaves in their own way. Harlan, certainly, had always felt that slavery was a question beyond the powers of the federal government.

Nevertheless there was a good deal of sentiment in Kentucky to accept the Thirteenth Amendment by ratifying it. The rather small group of Radicals, including Ben Bristow (then a state senator), accepted the amendment because they agreed with it. Others, like Governor Bramlette, felt that it would be adopted anyway, regardless of how Kentucky felt about it; but he proposed that a compensation clause be added.[33] There is little doubt that John Harlan privately agreed with Bramlette's moderate position, but he apparently felt that no political capital could be built up that way. The Democrats, of course, opposed ratification, and with the support of Harlan's group they had the votes in the legislature to defeat it.

The amendment was adopted, of course, despite Kentucky's resistance. The Radicals in the state turned out to be a small group without effective power, as Harlan had foreseen. The legislature in 1865 selected James Guthrie as U.S. senator over the Radical candidate, General Rousseau. Lincoln removed General Burbridge from military command despite Burbridge's radical record. (His replacement, however, proved to be just as acceptable to Kentucky radicals.) Most important, thousands of returning Confederate soldiers proved uniformly to be reinforcements for the Democrats. Many men who had been Unionists were outraged by army and government actions and joined the Democrats.

But if the Radicals suffered because of their support of Lincoln and the amendment, the Conservatives failed to gain by opposing them. Conservatives always suffered under the suspicion that they were really Radicals. Harlan, who said that he opposed the amendment on principle and that "if there were not a dozen slaves in Kentucky" he would still oppose it as a "flagrant invasion of the right of self-government," could not profit politically from his position.[34] As had almost always been the case since 1856, Harlan was in between at a time when voters were not.

The results of the 1865 Kentucky elections showed victory for the Conservatives, which included all those Democrats who were allowed to vote. It was a narrow victory, however, due primarily to the continued presence of Union troops at the polls and the fact that returning Confederates could not vote. The Conservatives thus won the congressional delegation, 5-4; the state senate, 20-18; and the state House, 60-40.[35]

Harlan had declined the opportunity to run for Congress, as a Conservative, largely on personal grounds. But he publicly denounced the Thirteenth Amendment: he felt that it indicated a resort to complete majority rule, undercutting the right of each state to determine its own policies. In a letter he emphasized that his "opposition is not based on views or wishes which I have in regard to the future of slavery in Kentucky, or in regard to that institution in its moral, social, or political aspect, . . . but on principle." Failure to observe this principle might, Harlan concluded, "destroy our kind of government." In the same letter, Harlan expressed the fear that immediate abolition would stimulate racial unrest. He also predicted future attempts to give blacks the right to vote, and he attacked military rule in the state, specifically that of General Palmer.[36]

John Harlan did not wish to run for Congress, but his brother James was a Conservative candidate for the state legislature. The actions of the brothers brought stinging criticism in the local press, which charged that "the Harlan's [*sic*] want rebel votes, and hence their scurrilous abuse of their government. No persons in this country were more denunciatory of rebels . . . than they were until they believed they could win rebel votes to aid their own advancement for office." [37] The charges are partially true. But it would be more accurate to say that the brothers were trying to be consistent: they had always been for the Union, and they still were; they had always been against abolition by the federal government, and they still were. Nevertheless, this kind of politics gave them strange (and probably somewhat distasteful) bedfellows among the "stay-at-home" Confederates who made up a large part of the Democratic vote. James profited from the association at least temporarily by winning his legislative race. [38]

Unfortunately Harlan was to find that cooperation with the Democrats was a one-way street. The Democrats had their own agenda. Using Conservative votes to permit the restoration of the returning Confederates to "all the privileges of citizenship," the Democrats then took control of the coalition. This control was used, Harlan charged, to choose candidates "who were either in the rebel army, or were most distinguished for the aid and comfort they gave that army." [39] Once back in office, the Democrats could ignore those Conservatives who had helped to put them there.

Part of the reason for the resurgence of the Kentucky Democrats lay in the state's reaction to the adoption of the Thirteenth Amendment, but the policies of the Washington government toward Kentucky after the cessation of hostilities were also important. Lee surrendered at Appomattox on April 9, 1865, and Lincoln was assassinated only five days later. The war was practically over, and the symbol of Northern intransigence was gone. The new president, Andrew Johnson, was pledged to carry out Lincoln's mild Reconstruction policies. Yet even in loyal Kentucky, Union troops remained in occupation, and martial law—imposed in July 1864—was still in force during the August elections of 1865. Although it was finally revoked in October, the operation of the writ of habeas corpus was still suspended and the army remained. Even the hated General Palmer was left in command.

Palmer was finally replaced in March 1866 by Jeff C. Davis, and *habeas corpus* was restored. The legislature zealously repealed the legal disabilities facing former Confederates by early 1866. Its actions doubtless contributed to Harlan's disenchantment with the Conservative-Democratic alliance. Johnson's veto of the Freedmen's Bureau bill in February 1866 seemed to provide Harlan and his friends with another opportunity to stake out a political position that was neither Republican nor Democratic. Conservatives, by supporting the new president in his mild policies toward the South, might be able to regain public support. Harlan, together with other Conservatives, held a giant rally in Frankfort on February 26 "for the purpose of expressing gratitude to President Johnson for the bold and patriotic stand he has taken against the Radicals in Congress." [40] His group called for a state convention that some of its members hoped might form a new party headed by the president.[41] The logic of this was that the Radicals in the state had to go with the congressional radicals. Therefore Conservatives could support the unimpeachably Unionist Johnson without having to associate politically with the former Confederates.

The scheme did not work. As more and more former Confederates filtered back into political life, it became obvious that the Democrats could not be beaten unless Unionists could unite. As the Cincinnati *Gazette* warned, "there are two parties in Kentucky. You must go to one or the other. If you choose to attempt to form a middle party, well and good. In some places the rebels will beat you; in others the Radicals."[42]

Union was, however, preceded by coalition. Without giving up their identity, the Conservatives and the Radicals agreed to support General Edward H. Hobson for the state court of appeals. The Conservatives agreed to drop their candidate, and both groups played down the important issues that still separated them. Thus, one was to drop its criticism of the Radicals in Congress while the other muted its disagreement with Johnson's policies. They agreed on opposition to the extension of the vote to blacks.[43]

The Democrats were happy to fight the campaign of 1866 on a North against South basis, for by that time, now that the war was over and secession an impossibility, Kentucky opinion had veered sharply. The party was strong and well organized; it was united. Even many strong Union men had joined its ranks. The Conservative-Radical coalition never really had a chance to elect Hobson.

But this is hindsight. It is almost certain that when Harlan sponsored a resolution endorsing Hobson's candidacy and when he gave his kick-off speech at Frankfort, he was, like most politicians, optimistic. His was an obvious attempt to rouse the Union veteran vote—there were about seventy thousand Union veterans compared with thirty thousand Confederates—and he lambasted the "Confederate Democrats" hip and thigh. They were, he said, sorry the war was over and regretful of the Union's victory. They hoped to snatch political victory from the jaws of military defeat: "Though beaten on the field of battle, they propose to renew at the ballot box the contest for supremacy of the principles which had much to do with bringing about the war."[44]

Harlan campaigned against the South: warning that the Democratic party represented narrow interests, confined to the South, he argued that its victory in Kentucky would isolate the state from the rest of the country. A truly national party could not afford such an alliance with Southern interests. He pleaded with voters to forget the past disagreements between Radicals and Conservatives in order to focus on the major threat: rule by Southern sympathizers.

It was too late. Only three weeks later Harlan feared that the coalition was breaking apart and, worse than that, that it could not win in any case. In a speech at Glasgow, he spent much time disclaiming the charge that

Hobson was a Radical; obviously the fear was that Conservative voters would desert to the Democrats. He called attention to the fact that Hobson was a prewar Democrat and a Union veteran with a brilliant record: he was the commander who finally forced John Hunt Morgan to surrender during his raid on Ohio. Harlan also feared that a Democratic victory would be taken in Washington to mean that Kentucky had deserted to the South, and thus the federal government's Reconstruction policies in the state would be reinforced and prolonged.[45]

But Harlan himself, true to his political heritage, still tried to locate himself in the middle. He inveighed against congressional Reconstruction and praised President Johnson. He argued strongly against any attempt to give the vote to the freed slaves.[46] He was, in effect, acting against the interests of the very coalition he had helped to form. It is not surprising that he was charged with inconsistency. The Louisville *Courier*, in a scathing editorial, said that "the halting, doubting, dubious course of Harlan during the whole of his political career, has been such that no one is surprised now at any position he may take. . . . His eloquent scathing of the radicals *last summer* failed to bring with it the "recompense of reward". . . *the United States Senate was not reached*. Now he chases the radicals."[47] The same paper called upon the spirits of George Washington, Henry Clay, and James Harlan to persuade John to come back to true conservatism.[48] It was even charged that Harlan had in 1861 promised to turn Confederate before he would accept the abolition of slavery.[49] While it does not seem likely that Harlan made any such explicit promise, various statements and actions taken during the chaotic events of 1861 gave color to the charge.

Hobson lost overwhelmingly, and the coalition immediately fell to charging its constituent elements with being at fault. In particular, the Radicals could with some veracity claim that Harlan had attacked his own supporters.[50]

Harlan's search for a political home thus continued, unavailing. In many ways one might have thought that he would have been ripe for a shift to the Democratic party. Certainly many fellow Conservative Unionists including his former law partner William Bullock, had become Democrats. But the narrow sectionalism of the Kentucky Democratic party and its unwillingness to embrace those who had fought for the Union would have made the party at best an uncomfortable political home. On the other hand, in September 1866 Harlan was still too close to his losing battles against abolition and the continuing radicalism displayed by the congressional radicals for him to join them, either. Thus he remained, for the time being, with the small and diminishing band of Conservatives who knew by now that they had no hope of retaining the offices they held or of being elected to new ones.

The result was, of course, more frustration. When the legislature chose a U.S. senator in January 1867, the conservatives presented their own candidate. Still strong in that body, they were able to force a stalemate for two weeks of balloting. This time the Conservatives went back to their 1865 alliance with the Democrats. Harlan was one of the nominees under this alliance, but his reputation as a strong Unionist prevented him from garnering support from the Democrats: he obtained only eight votes. Finally the two groups got together in support of Garrett Davis, the incumbent, who had been a fiery Unionist but had become disenchanted with congressional radicalism and had deserted to the Democrats. Ben Bristow, the leading Radical candidate, lost in a one-sided vote.[51]

While this might have been viewed as a possibly permanent attachment of Conservatives to the Democratic party, in fact it signaled something quite different. The votes of Democrats in the legislature were uniformly anti-Unionist; no one who still called himself a Conservative Unionist would gain Democratic support. Democrats, in other words, were perfectly willing to swallow the Conservatives, but not to cooperate with them. This was demonstrated clearly when the Democrats, in February 1867, nominated a slate for the coming state elections on which all but one position were filled by former Confederate soldiers or stay-at-home sympathizers. Harlan, for instance, was not renominated by the Democrats.[52]

Faced with this state of affairs the Conservatives resurrected their own party mechanism. At a party meeting in Frankfort early in March, Harlan served as secretary and was elected to the executive committee.[53] Speaking before the group, he castigated the Democrats for being "against the country when the country was in danger."[54] Harlan was assigned the task of reorganizing the party.

With his accustomed energy he set about the task, even though there was little hope that the venture would be successful. He placed announcements in local newspapers across the state asking for the names of five faithful and "efficient" Conservatives in each county.[55] He attempted to collect an assessment from each county to pay for the campaign, particularly for the distribution of the platform statement. He addressed party gatherings in preparation for a state convention to be held in April, and in all of this he maintained the party's position of opposition both to Southern "secessionism" and to radical Reconstructionism.[56]

The Conservative party (usually called by themselves the "Union Democrats" or "Conservative Unionists") met in convention in Louisville on April 11, 1867. Harlan was, of course, nominated for reelection as attorney general. Among other nominees were William B. Kinkead for governor and Benjamin M. Harney for superintendent of public instruction.[57] The party's platform strongly supported the right of the federal government to suppress rebellion and besought the gratitude of the state's voters for those who had fought for the Union. But it also attacked the radicals in Congress. A new note was struck in platform items advocating federal taxes proportionate to wealth and the reduction of tariffs.[58] The party attempted to gain the support of the regular Northern Democratic party, claiming that it was the official inheritor of the prewar Democracy of Kentucky.[59]

The first test of the renewed three-party system came in a special congressional election held May 4. The Democrats won all nine seats by landslides, and to Harlan's dismay the Conservative Unionists ran a very poor third.[60] While the party was committed to the state campaign, its efforts were undoubtedly sapped by creeping frustration after May 4. Harlan doubtless shared this hopelessness, but he went on campaigning anyway. The general atmosphere was not improved by incidents of violence and ostracism aimed at Unionists.[61] One newspaper reported a Harlan speech in which he said that "it was his deliberate judgement, based upon the events of the past twelve months, that no Union man of any kind could, even at this day, live in peace in Kentucky, but for *fear* of the National Government which those persons have who are aiming to place the State under the exclusive control of the men and principles of the rebellion."[62]

The defeat of both Conservatives and Radicals in the August state elections was even more complete than they had feared. On average, the Democrats gained two-thirds of the total vote, leaving both of the other parties far behind. Harlan's old mentor, former governor John L. Helm, was elected again, and John Rodman handily defeated Harlan and John Mason Brown, the Radical candidate, for attorney general. The voters elected twenty-eight Democrats to the state senate, but only three Conservatives and seven Radicals; in the House, the complexion was no different: eighty-five Democrats, five Conservatives, and ten Radicals (James Harlan lost his seat).[63]

Accepting the election results as barring him for the present from any role in politics and not comfortable in Frankfort with its hordes of victorious Democrats, Harlan decided to return to Louisville and reestablish the law practice that he had barely begun in 1861. His years in the political wilderness, however, were numbered: 1868 found him supporting General U.S. Grant for president.

6

Kentucky Republican
1868-1875

John Harlan's decision to return to Louisville was not prompted merely by the political situation in Frankfort. Another reason was doubtless the same as the one that prompted his first move to the metropolis in 1861. It was still true that making a living as a lawyer was likely to be much easier in the large city of Louisville, especially since Harlan no longer had the backing of his father's practice and reputation. His income as attorney general had, of course, been taken away by the voters of Kentucky. He had thenceforth to subsist entirely on what he could earn from his practice. By 1868 John's work as administrator of his father's estate was largely complete. In addition, his brother William died in the spring, and John's moral support was no longer needed by his mother in that regard. There were no longer, in other words, any pressing family responsibilities holding him in Frankfort.[1]

Finally, Harlan undoubtedly felt that if he were to change party loyalties, the comparative anonymity of a large city offered several advantages, principally that in the current state of Kentucky politics it was easier to find a group of like-minded people in Louisville than elsewhere in the state. Indeed, others were making the same move, and Harlan was able to become the partner of one of them. John E. Newman, a much older man who had been a Kentucky circuit court judge during the war, desired to move to Louisville. He, also, was a Unionist turned Republican.[2]

Harlan's marriage continued to be a very happy one, and his family continued to grow: Laura was born on January 7, 1871, and Ruth, on September 7, 1875. Mallie was, however, seriously ill of unknown causes for much of 1873, and she spent most of the year resting and convalescing at Crab Orchard, Kentucky, or with her parents in Evansville.[3] Presumably— no record exists—she had the children with her, and John had to get along by himself in addition to having to make frequent trips to see his family. It was during one of these trips that Harlan almost lost his life. After addressing a Republican gathering in Hopkinsville, Harlan took a train for Henderson, intending to cross over to Evansville to see his wife and children. Shortly before the train reached Henderson, Harlan's sleeping car derailed and fell down a fifteen-to-twenty-foot embankment, the gradual slope of which, however, limited the damage. He related, "As it was, I was much bruised being knocked about in the car as it rolled down. I was compelled to crawl out of one of the windows which I did with very great difficulty. . . . I, however, reached Evansville that night and found my family well. My escape from death was miraculous."[4]

Harlan's mother passed away in 1870. James followed John to Louisville and after about 1873 was associated with the law partnership: this association proved increasingly unsatisfactory as James degenerated into alcoholism, which was compounded later on by drug addiction. James's wife, Amelia, died in 1876. James became more and more unreliable, and he proved to be a financial burden as well as requiring much care and worry, as did his son, Henry.[5]

Laura Harlan Cleveland, John's middle sister, died in 1870 following a long decline. Her husband, Francis Cleveland, was a small town lawyer in Augusta, Kentucky, not overburdened with ambition although seemingly intelligent and capable. He refused an opportunity to go into partnership with John in Louisville, apparently because of his lack of confidence in his own ability.[6] Some years later, still in Augusta, he remarried. John Harlan maintained good relations with him, and his son, Harlan Cleveland, became in his turn a successful attorney: he was U.S. attorney at Cincinnati around 1900 before dying at a rather young age in 1906. His wife was the daughter of Associate Justice Stanley Matthews.[7]

Harlan's other two sisters were apparently happily married. Bettie's husband, Dr. Hatchitt, gave up medicine and was with Harlan's assistance appointed postmaster of Frankfort. He was, obviously, a good Republican, since the job was strictly a partisan reward under the spoils system. Little is known of the other sister, Sallie; she and her husband, David P. Hiter, were living near Frankfort during this period.

Meanwhile, the older children of John and Mallie were attending private schools, first in Frankfort and then in Louisville. It seems probable that Edith, the oldest, did not go beyond grammar school, since that was the most common level of education provided for girls at that time. The two older boys, Richard and James, would have proceeded, around 1870 or 1872, into secondary schools. Richard began his college career at Princeton in the same autumn that his father was appointed to the Supreme Court, the autumn of 1877.

The costs of bringing up and educating six children, in the days before public schools were used by professional families, added to the normal costs of householding, must have been considerable. This factor goes far toward explaining why John Harlan, despite what seems to have been a busy law practice, was usually only a step or two ahead of bankruptcy. The time taken off for campaigning was a major detracting feature as well. While Harlan would often be provided with accommodations by friends, the costs of his travel, meals, and overnight lodgings must have reached very high figures during campaigns. Campaigns, as we have seen, occurred very frequently for John. In addition, he was a generous man who frequently loaned small sums to relatives and close friends, and he invested money in ventures, such as the Louisville *Daily Commercial*, that were not likely to bring any return and, indeed, eventually became worthless.[8]

Whatever the reasons, John's correspondence clearly reveals a strong interest, dictated by necessity, in prompt collection from his clients; frequent complaints from his creditors; and a fair number of cases in which he borrowed money from banks or from his Shanklin relatives.[9]

Although the law practice of Harlan and Newman was not outstandingly remunerative, it seems to have been busy, for they were able to take in another partner, Benjamin H. Bristow, in 1870. Bristow was also a Union veteran, but he had become a Radical and Republican even before Harlan did. He was a former state legislator and lawyer from Hopkinsville who was appointed assistant U.S. district attorney in Louisville in 1865 by his own and Harlan's friend James Speed (then U.S. attorney general). He had gained a reputation as a champion of civil rights for blacks under the Thirteenth Amendment and the various radical Reconstruction laws. Seeing the need for a Republican journal in Louisville (the Unionist *Journal* under Prentice had by now merged with the *Courier* and become thoroughly Democratic), he and a few associates formed a corporation to publish a new paper, the Louisville *Commercial*, in 1869. Colonel Robert M. Kelly was chosen as editor and general manager, although he was succeeded (temporarily) in the latter position in 1870 by another Harlan friend, John W. Finnell.[10] The Harlans and the Bristows became family friends: they vacationed together at Niagara Falls in 1869, and by that time Harlan was apparently pressing Bristow to give up his federal appointment. Eventually, due partly to disenchantment with the Grant administration and partly to the hope of a greater income, Bristow did so. He had by that time become well enough known outside Kentucky so that even a New York paper reported his resignation, calling him a "gallant soldier" and a "civil rights champion."[11]

The firm could also afford to take in a young clerk, Augustus E. Willson, who became a full partner after Judge Newman's death in 1873.[12] James Harlan was also associated with the partnership during those periods when he was able to work. The partners located their office on Jefferson Street opposite the impressive courthouse, designed by Gideon Shryock and built in 1842, and the city hall, which was built in 1873—a location prized by lawyers. The Harlans eventually bought a home on Brook Street at the corner of Jacob, which was within walking distance of the office.[13]

The practice apparently consisted of the normal kinds of cases: claims work, collections, and work for the increasing number of local businesses. Perhaps the number of people associated with the practice was necessary because of the frequent absences of the two major partners, Harlan and Bristow. Harlan was often off campaigning, whereas Bristow was in Washington as solicitor general from 1870 to 1872 (it was a new position) and as secretary of the Treasury from 1874 until after his failure to be nominated for the presidency in 1876.

The professional association of Harlan and Bristow seems to have begun when Harlan became involved in the famous long-running Presbyterian Church case. The political tensions of the time account for the split that took place in 1866 in the congregation of the Walnut Street Presbyterian Church in Louisville (of which Harlan seems to have been a member after 1868), between pro-Northern and pro-Southern factions.[14] The split was partly caused by a dispute over whether to call the Reverend William T. McElroy as pastor, but it shortly became obvious that McElroy was merely the symbol of the opposition of the two factions. The original suit, in Louisville chancery court in 1866, was an attempt to force the court to decide which of the two factions was to have possession of the church and other property. Although Harlan was still attorney general, living in Frankfort, he was one of the lawyers representing the Northern group (Avery). Chancellor Henry Pirtle, a strong Unionist himself, decided in favor of the Northern faction, and the losers appealed to the Kentucky Court of Appeals, the state's highest appellate tribunal. While the case on appeal was ostensibly decided on technical grounds that are of little interest here, it is notable that the court of appeals reversed the chancery court by a vote of 3-1, three Democrats against one Unionist.[15]

Party lines were so strictly drawn that the result was perhaps foregone. With the fertility that one expects of American lawyers, however, the Northern faction contrived to bring the case to the U.S. circuit court. This effort was, indeed, well under way even before the court of appeals rendered its decision and even though a confusing set of maneuvers was being carried on concurrently in the state courts. The device Harlan and his colleagues hit upon was to create a diversity suit: under federal court rules, if the contending parties were from two different states, then the federal courts had jurisdiction. By obtaining new members of the congregation who lived in Indiana, the necessary diversity could be created. William A. Jones thus came to live in Indiana; he moved there. Since he was unemployed, it presumably did not matter greatly where he lived. Jones, thus, brought suit in the federal court in Louisville. The decision came in May 1869. Judge Bland Ballard, with the announced concurrence of U.S. Supreme Court justice Noah H. Swayne, issued the injunction requested by the Northerners, thus giving them control of the church property.[16]

When the Southern faction appealed to the Supreme Court, Harlan had his first (and apparently his only) chance to argue before that tribunal.

He and Bristow (who had already been appointed solicitor general but had not yet taken office) went to Washington in March 1871 to present the oral argument, while the other faction was represented by Thomas W. Bullitt, another prominent Louisville attorney who had fought against Harlan as one of Morgan's Raiders.[17]

Bullitt's argument for the Southern faction was based on two points: that the federal courts had no jurisdiction over a case of this sort, because it amounted to an interference with the legitimate powers of the state courts; and that the state courts had intervened properly, since the ecclesiastical tribunals had departed from "the original principle of society" and therefore had reached an unlawful decision.[18]

Harlan, in an eighty-three-page brief, which was later printed, contended that federal courts had proper equity jurisdiction to right wrongs done by the state, since jurisdiction was given by the residences of the litigants, not by the subject matter of the case. He then went on to claim that the General Assembly of the Presbyterian Church had complete power to make its decision, which was then not properly reviewable by the civil courts. Bristow then extended these arguments.[19]

The Supreme Court held this case for a year after argument, hoping, Justice Samuel F. Miller wrote, that the litigants would settle it themselves. Also, the case was so momentous—in principle it involved many other congregations—that it justified "careful and laborious examination and discussion." In fact, Miller held, the district court had jurisdiction basically because the questions brought to it were different from the questions decided by the state courts. But he agreed with Harlan that civil courts should not substitute their judgments for those of properly constituted ecclesiastical courts and that therefore the circuit court's injunction was properly issued.[20] The decision still stands as a precedent in church property cases, having been used as recently as 1969.[21] Justices Nathan Clifford and David Davis dissented, holding that the case should have been dismissed for lack of jurisdiction.

Harlan was also the lawyer and arbitrator for the Northern side in a similar dispute in the Second Presbyterian Church of Lexington in 1868. This arbitration failed due to a dispute over the proper numbers of communicants belonging to the Northern faction, and Harlan resorted to publishing the entire correspondence in the Lexington newspapers. The case consequently had to be settled in court. Harlan at one point wrote that he wished to postpone the hearing by the Kentucky Court of Appeals until after the elections, because "we know quite well what the present court will decide."[22]

In 1867 the Southern Presbyterian Synod tried to seize control of Centre College and even introduced a bill in the state legislature that would have given them the property. John Harlan was, again, chosen to represent the Northern interest, and his arguments before the Judiciary Committee were largely instrumental in killing the bill.[23] The case then dragged through the Kentucky courts until the Northern Synod won a final award in the court of appeals in 1873.[24]

These cases not only demonstrated but reinforced Harlan's commitment both to Unionism and to his denomination. There is no doubt that his final decision to become a Republican was strongly influenced by the fact that as a lawyer he was constantly embroiled in church cases that exacerbated the North-South cleavage. Not only were the Democrats soiled by their more and more open domination by former secessionists, but they were also to be charged with religious heresy and schism. Then, too, in these church cases Harlan's associates were, of course, all former Unionists and radicals: men like Ballard, Pirtle, and Bristow. The opposing lawyers were often veterans of the Confederate army, like Bullitt. It would have been difficult, indeed, for a thorough partisan like John Harlan to have followed any other course.

Harlan's practice also grew to include cases related to the growing racial tensions in Kentucky, resulting from white reaction to the newly acquired rights of the former slaves. Now, however, he was on the other side of the slavery question. Forgotten was his feeling as the state's attorney general that blacks should not be allowed to testify in court against whites. By 1870, in fact, he was receiving letters from lawyers throughout the state asking him to help in cases in which the result depended on black testimony. Federal law, part of the radical Republican legislative product, gave black claimants the right to pursue their cases in federal courts, where they were allowed to testify, and Harlan had by then (partly as a result of the church cases) become known as an expert on getting cases into federal court.[25] Harlan handled a Negro church case too, defending a Methodist congregation when the Southern (white) Methodist authorities claimed title to its property.[26] One correspondent wanted the firm's help in an election fraud case: the defeated candidate claimed that potential black voters had been kept from the polls. "I can easily prove that a number of Democrats have in Hopkinsville by drawing pistols and by threats and otherwise intimidating and preventing negroes from voting for me," he wrote, rather ungrammatically.[27] The partners gave their advice in such cases, which added measurably to their practice if not to their incomes.[28]

But Harlan also got into political trouble over one case involving race. Even though he had advised President Grant that cases should be brought in federal courts, he ended up defending rather than prosecuting one man who was accused of membership and activity in the Ku Klux Klan. The matter arose when, in 1871, Klan activity around Frankfort resulted in the hanging of several Negroes. Harlan was at the time on his way to Washington to talk with President Grant about Kentucky politics; he wrote to Bristow of his concern at the intimidation of Republicans, both black and white. Since many of these people were afraid to bring cases to court,

Harlan proposed that "the Federal Court . . . have a grand jury in perpetual session," which could then "summon every body until they find out who the Ku Klux are." [29]

When the federal attorney for the Kentucky district, Gabriel C. Wharton, did bring indictments against some of those who were suspected of the hangings, he proposed to Bristow that Harlan be appointed special counsel to assist him in the prosecution of the cases. [30] There is no evidence that Harlan was then actually offered such a position, and he ended up defending at least one of the defendants! He explained to his absent partner:

> There are some matters connected with this KuKlux business which embarrass me—I *must* urge the Gov't to "go for" the KuKlux—and yet I am being applied to [to] defend, as counsel some who are charged with being KuKlux. I once thought that I would have nothing to do with cases of this kind—but, upon reflection, I find that I must play lawyer in these as in other cases, [or] abandon good fees which I am not able to do. While I was urging and endorsing Wharton to get after the KuKlux, here comes Howard Smith after me to defend his son—I could not resist his appeal, and did not feel that I ought to decline—and I am glad that I defended his son for he clearly established an *alibi* and nobody believes him to have been guilty. [31]

While Harlan attributed his action to his need for the money and his friendship with Howard Smith, he no doubt also felt, as most lawyers do, that all defendants deserve legal representation and thus that his own feelings about the Ku Klux Klan were irrelevant. Nevertheless, black Kentuckians could be forgiven for feeling that he had reneged on his campaign promises; he had just run for governor on a strong anti-Klan platform. He wrote further to the solicitor general: "My colored friends, some of them, cannot understand how I [could] defend [the] KuKlux. Some of them think, in their ignorance, that I have deserted them. Altogether my position is embarrassing politically, but I cannot help it." [32] The episode proved to be only temporarily important to Harlan's political position, fortunately for him. In fact, it may have redounded to his credit among the politically powerful lawyers of the state; for it is notable that even many Democratic lawyers supported his appointment to the Supreme Court six years later.

Early in 1873 John Harlan actually was appointed as a special counsel to aid in federal prosecutions for violation of the Enforcement Acts. [33] For some time thereafter he did participate in such cases, thus becoming known rather widely, like his partner, as a champion of civil rights—an appellation that he deserved, but that he earned even more richly as Associate Justice Harlan.

That John Harlan was in the process of becoming a nationally or at least regionally known lawyer by 1877 is attested by a news report that he kept in his clipping file. While the story may be in some respects apocryphal (and neither the paper nor the date are identified in the file), it was not made up out of whole cloth, either. "In the great Pullman palace car case [John Marshall Harlan] was employed on short notice. . . . Locking himself up in his office with Judge Lochrane, of Georgia, and Mr. George M. Pullman, he examined them thoroughly upon it, grasping all the points and arranging his citations. For twenty-four hours, during which time his companions alternated between sleeping and dispensing information, he studied the case, and at the end of that time he had every point at his fingers' ends and was as fresh as a daisy."[34]

There are signs that Harlan became at times a little bored and dissatisfied with legal practice. Commenting on the slight hopes for Republican success in Kentucky in 1872, he wrote somewhat wistfully to Bristow: "I have sometimes thought that, if I could, I would leave this rebel state but if the Democrats succeed in 1872, our place will suit a loyal man as well as another. The probability is that I will plug away here at the law for the balance of my days, and every year that I live increases my comfort in the reflection that I must, of necessity, stick to my profession. It is a hard master, but I love it better than any other except that, if a wealthy man, I would enjoy public life."[35]

In a surprisingly short time Harlan the frustrated Conservative Unionist became Harlan the state Republican leader. This rapid transition was aided by several factors peculiar to postwar Kentucky. One was the fluidity of party lines, especially among antisecessionist politicians. The Republican party was still new in the state in 1868: even those who were regarded as radicals had not dared to call themselves Republicans as late as a year or two after the hostilities ceased. In this sense Harlan was hardly a latecomer to the party ranks. His rapid rise was due also, however, to his own personality and ability. He started out already known favorably throughout the state as a popular campaigner and an attractive and powerful speaker. He threw himself into Republicanism as he had thrown himself into all of his political positions, with every ounce of his energy and with total conviction. Once the choice was made, John Harlan was not one to harbor doubts about its rightness.

Partly due to acquaintances formed during the war and even earlier, Harlan also had something of a ready-made reputation in the North, especially in Ohio and Indiana. He campaigned vigorously in 1868 in Indiana, for Grant and for Governor Oliver P. Morton's reelection, as well as in Kentucky for the Republican candidate for governor, R. Tarvin Baker. His conversion to Republicanism was announced with pride by the Frankfort *Commonwealth*, at that time the leading Republican paper in the state.[36]

The Republican party was, of course, a minority, and it looked as though it might not even survive the immediate postwar period. Harlan himself described it as a "hopeless minority," but he brought to the party qualities it badly needed, leadership and organizing ability.[37] Within a few years he had the party organized in practically every county in the state, visiting most of them personally and conducting a copious correspondence with Unionist friends who provided the core of leadership at the local level. He also worked to consolidate Negro support for the party of emancipation: the problem here was to get Negroes out to vote. They had no great reason to trust the state's Republicans, most of whom had owned slaves or at least had "gone along" with slavery, and they were frequently intimidated by the Klan and other anti-Negro groups.

The exigencies of politics would in any case have forced John Harlan to change his views on the race question. But the need of the Republicans for Negro votes—plus his own conscience, and also possibly his wife's—account for the fact that he shifted so rapidly and completely. Never one to do things by halves, he was also in a position in which, if he were to be able to create trust among the freed slaves and among his fellow white Republicans, he had to become "more Catholic than the Pope." He therefore began immediately to support the Thirteenth and Fourteenth amendments vigorously, just as vigorously as he had previously condemned them.[38]

No doubt Harlan would have preferred at this time to forget his record of the previous few years, as well as his Know-Nothing background. His opponents, of course, would not permit this, and Democratic newspapers had long memories. One thing needed, in the conditions then existing in the state, was a loud journalistic voice that would be solidly Republican, preferably in Louisville. Thus Harlan and his political friends got together in 1869 to establish such a journal, the Louisville *Commercial*. The paper had a checkered career, always in danger of bankruptcy and requiring frequent transfusions of new investments.[39] Editorially, the paper was moderate Republican; like Kentucky Republicans in general, it tried to establish itself as a progressive and liberal voice.

In 1868 Harlan mostly confined himself to speaking in Kentucky on behalf of the national ticket, some campaigning in Indiana, and supporting Republican candidates in Kentucky.[40] He found the fledgling party in disarray, however, and soon became more active in the organizational work that would be his principal contribution to the state party.

Harlan knew that there was little immediate likelihood of winning elections in Kentucky as a Republican. He was, nevertheless, a man of ambition; though he protested, mere legal practice was not to satisfy him for long. Though he unsuccessfully ran twice for governor and once for the U.S. Senate, he began to look more and more at the national political scene. As long as Republicans controlled the national government, preferment through appointment was possible to those who were acceptable to party leaders. In addition, Harlan was ambitious for his partner, who had already been appointed to federal office. Harlan early on began to think about the

Supreme Court, either for himself or for Bristow. In speculating on what would happen if Chief Justice Salmon P. Chase should die, Harlan felt that the likelihood was that Grant would appoint as chief justice either Associate Justice Samuel F. Miller or Associate Justice Noah H. Swayne. In either case, a vacancy would be left on the Court, "and then I trust the President will put on the bench some lawyer in the late slave-holding states," he wrote Ben. "It may be that you will be the man for the vacancy." But Harlan could not help revealing his own feelings about serving on the Supreme Court bench, for he continued, "I know of no more desirable position . . . especially if the salary should be increased to $10,000.—It lifts a man high above the atmosphere on which most public men move, and enables him to become in every sense, an independent man, with an opportunity to make a *record* that will be remembered long after he is gone." Even John J. Crittenden, "great as he was," would be known in fifty years only in his home state, since he was merely a politician.[41]

There is no doubt that Harlan by 1870 saw a position on the Supreme Court as his major ambition. Even so, he knew that if Bristow were appointed, he himself could not be, and he was not the man to stand in the way of his partner and friend. Bristow eventually went high in national politics, but not to the Supreme Court, and neither man would be appointed by Grant to fill any vacancy left by Chase's departure. Meanwhile Harlan did what came to hand politically: he built up the party statewide, campaigned for Republicans in other states as far away as Maine, exerted his growing influence in advising the administration in Washington about appointments in Kentucky or for Kentuckians, and kept Washington fully apprised of the political situation in Kentucky.

His trip to Maine resulted from James G. Blaine's attempts to hold that state for Grant in the 1872 campaign. Blaine as part of this effort invited numerous outsiders in to speak during a two-week period. Harlan was by this time so prominent that Kentucky had tried to secure his nomination for the vice presidency, and Blaine remembered the young man he had first met at a Kentucky military college in the 1850s. During the campaign in Maine, Harlan chanced to be placed next to Frederick Douglass, the noted Negro orator, at dinner; for this he was later criticized by Kentucky Democrats. John wrote many years later that Douglass "had no superior as a public speaker. He would have made a great Senator." When heckled about the dinner during his second campaign for governor, Harlan turned the criticism aside by saying, "I not only do not apologize for what I did, but frankly say that I would rather eat dinner any day by the side of Douglas [*sic*] than to eat with the fellow across the way who sought to entrap me by a question which has nothing to do with the contest." This remark, Harlan reported, was greeted with great applause.[42]

With Republican administrations in Washington and the spoils system in effect, Harlan became the major figure in deciding who would obtain federal jobs in Kentucky. He was not always successful in placing the people he wanted, but he kept busy trying. His correspondence consisted in large part of letters from "deserving" party members who wanted to become revenue agents for Kentucky's flourishing whiskey industry, customs collectors, examining surgeons for Union veterans claiming disability pensions, postmasters, or route agents. Others desired, as one man put it "a good place" in Washington. Sometimes the petitioners wanted these places for friends.[43] At other times, Harlan acted on his own initiative.[44]

Disappointed office seekers could become political enemies. One such was Theodore C. Tracie, who had been associated with the *Commercial* in some capacity and had solicited Harlan's support in his effort to be appointed collector of customs at Louisville. Tracie felt that Harlan had reneged on a promise of support in Washington, in favor of another candidate. His reaction was to accuse Harlan of "the most reprehensible of vices—that of ingratitude."[45] But sometimes Harlan and the rejected petitioner remained friends: John Finnell, for instance, wished to be a court commissioner for Judge Ballard but despite Harlan's intervention was given no such post. Yet he and Harlan were intimate friends until Finnell's death.[46] Harlan was himself frequently disappointed, as when the widow of a local Democratic lawyer, Mrs. Virginia Thompson, was appointed postmaster of Louisville. Harlan wrote to Stanley Matthews, another future Supreme Court justice, that the position ought to have gone to a deserving Republican who had been recommended by him and Bristow. He remarked that "no female can manage so large a Post Office as the one here, and the appointment cannot therefore be justified in any proper view of civil Service reform. It cannot be viewed in any other light than as an act of charity, for a deserving lady, done at the public expense but to the injury of the friends of the Administration."[47]

As a politically aware Kentucky Republican, John Harlan served as a source of information for party members elsewhere as well as for the administration. He wrote to an Indianapolis lawyer, warning him that the Democrats might be hiring Negroes from Kentucky to go to Indiana and vote the Democratic ticket in 1876.[48] After Rutherford B. Hayes's election, Richard Smith of the Cincinnati *Gazette*, a friend and adviser of the new president, visited Louisville to confer with "Bristow, Harlan, Judge Ballard and several other of our friends" in June 1877. Smith's object was to attempt to find the causes of dissatisfaction among Republicans with the administration's "southern policy." He found that in Louisville, as we have seen, there was opposition to local appointments made by the administration, "especially the woman" in the post office. "The Democrats are crowing," Smith reported, "especially over B. [Bristow] and H. [Harlan], bragging they have no influence." Smith's informants, of whom undoubtedly Harlan was chief, told him that while the appointment of a Democrat in

Kentucky might get one new Republican vote, it would lose five hundred old ones.[49]

John Harlan's rising status nationally, however, resulted from his success as a party leader and vote-getter in Kentucky. While he was never again to hold elective office, Harlan has yet been credited as being more responsible than anyone else for creating the Republican party as a viable force in state politics. He did this by good organizing and effective campaigning, which by 1876 had made the party a competitive, though not yet winning, challenger to Democratic supremacy.

Obviously, a complete change had to occur in Harlan's attitudes toward the Reconstruction Amendments and legislation, since without the Negro vote there would be no hope for the Republicans to make inroads on the Democratic majority. Harlan made this shift with remarkable celerity. Indeed, so fast was it that it has given rise to the speculation that one Harlan—either the slave owner who in 1865 inveighed against these same measures or the radical who in 1871 regarded them as an absolute necessity—was merely a self-serving, ambitious politician.[50]

The facts do not permit a definite conclusion on this. Certainly Harlan was ambitious: no political leader who gets anywhere lacks a generous measure of ambition. Ambition, however, cannot alone explain Harlan's transition, since he deliberately chose the losing side, knowing that it would lose. Harlan's true feelings on the race question may, of course, not have been fully developed until after 1866. There is no reason to doubt that his lone dissent in 1883 in the *Civil Rights Cases* was a sincere expression of his matured ideas on the subject; but like most Kentucky Republicans, he probably had to fight his way to these conclusions. The party's background in a Whig slavocracy meant that most of its supporters had at one time either supported or at least acquiesced to the existence of the peculiar institution. Harlan was unusual only in that as a political campaigner his convictions were always a matter of public record.

Harlan's grandson, ignoring the fact that Harlan's change of mind came well before his appointment to the Supreme Court, has a different explanation: "My own belief has always been that this change reflected little more than the strong influence of the responsibilities of judicial office. While he was a man of marked emotion, I remember him as a youngster as being a very just man. I think that in most instances, at least, this quality overcame his personal predilections."[51] This explanation is in any case vastly oversimplified. It does not explain why no other justice was "just" enough to overcome personal predilections, nor does it explore or even question what Harlan's predilections were. Finally, it does not face the fact that as a judge Harlan was noted for finding ways to follow his predilections rather than for reaching conclusions opposing them.

In any case, by the time of his first candidacy for the governorship in

1871, Harlan was a wholehearted supporter of the Reconstruction Amendments and of Negro rights. Admitting that he had earlier opposed them, he now said:

> I have lived long enough to feel and declare . . . that the most perfect despotism that ever existed on this earth was the institution of African slavery.
> . . . With slavery it was death or tribute. It knew no compromise, it tolerated no middle course. I rejoice that it is gone.
> . . . [The Reconstruction Amendments] are irrevocable results of the War; and because the Republicans of . . . Kentucky now acquiesce in these Amendments, or now declare them to be legitimate and proper, it is not just or candid to charge them with inconsistency.
> . . . let it be said that I am right rather than consistent.

Harlan went on to condemn the Democrats for continuing their opposition to what was, after all, a *fait accompli*, to attack the legislature for its failure to act to permit blacks to testify in the state's courts, and to storm bitterly at the Democratic governor for his failure to stand strongly against the breakdown of law and order symbolized by the violence perpetrated by Regulators and Klansmen.

These positions, as Coulter says, commended Harlan "to the reasoning portion of the old Radicals, and commanded the respect of intelligent Democrats."[53] But the Republican campaign would have been insufficent had it limited itself to a defensive position on the race question. Harlan and his supporters went on to develop a broad-ranging progressive platform that they hoped would appeal to business interests and to all who wanted to put the concerns of the war behind them.

Republican speakers therefore concentrated on the state's enormous resources and the failure of the Democrats to exploit them. They called for the development of Kentucky's wealth and tried to turn the attention of voters to the future rather than the past (which included the Reconstruction programs created by the radicals in Washington). Calling attention to the need of immigrants to carry out such a development program, Republicans accused the state administration of driving immigration to other states: Harlan cited the rapid growth of Illinois and Indiana in contrast with that of Kentucky, criticizing the legislature for its failure to supply funds for the assistance of German immigrants.[54] Of course his opponent, Preston H. Leslie, could and did call public attention to Harlan's Know-Nothing background, as did Democratic newspapers. Again on the defensive, all Harlan could do was plead his youth and admit his error.[55] Actually, Leslie's own background included a Know-Nothing episode, but it was he who looked the more consistent.[56]

Harlan also attacked the Democrats for failing to support railroad building south from Cincinnati that would help to develop the central part of the state: he accused the legislature of being under the thumb of the Louisville and Nashville and its interest in maintaining its monopoly on railroad traffic to the interior from Louisville.[57] He broadened this into a general attack on monopoly, which may forecast his later dissent in the sugar trust case.

Harlan saw in the national Democratic policy of opposition to the income tax a willingness to tax the poor through direct taxes on property.[58] On the state level, the equivalent was Leslie's proposal to use a poll tax instead of a property tax for public education. Kentucky had just enacted a rate-bill system by which any deficit in a school system was to be made up from assessment of local families according to the number of children they had in the schools, and this also drew Harlan's strong criticism: "A poor man blessed in the number of his children but unprovided with the world's goods, is taxed while the rich who are able to educate their children in private schools, are exempt from taxation."[59]

Harlan campaigned indefatigably even though his was obviously a losing cause. He spoke every day except Sunday, leading one correspondent to ask, "How in the world did you manage to hold out physically in such a tremendous canvass?"[60] He aroused tremendous interest, and the result was the largest vote in the state's history. Another, less happy, result was an increase in anti-Negro activity. "The KK," one friend wrote, "500 strong warned the colored voters of Cumberland co. if they went to the polls their heads would pay the forfeit. . . . A prominent Democrat came to the polls with his gun & said he would shoot the first Negro voter."[61] Whites responded to Negro attempts to eliminate segregation on Louisville's horse-cars with violence in which Negroes were thrown off the cars, and general race riots were a possibility. Harlan came out strongly against the transit company's segregationist policies and attributed the violence to the Democrats' encouragement of white extremists.[62] He probably lost more votes than he gained, but the events may have made blacks happier to support him and the Republican party in general.

The election was lost: Leslie obtained about 126,000 votes to Harlan's 89,000.[63] While the Democratic majority was thus large, the Republicans gained over 60,000 votes compared with the previous election and proved that they were a factor that the dominant party could not ignore. Harlan claimed that Democrats voted "early and often" and that the total vote would indicate that Kentucky's population was 400,000 greater than it actually was.[64] Largely due to Harlan, "the long, dark, dreary night of Republicans in Kentucky" had ended. Although the party would not capture the gubernatorial prize for more than twenty years, it had become a force that Democrats had to recognize.

For the next three years after 1871 John Harlan was forced by the political situation and his need of income to spend most of his time on his legal practice. He continued his political activities as the occasion presented itself, taking an active part in the campaign for Grant's reelection in 1872. His controversial trip to Maine was his principal contribution, but he was invited to speak around the state and in other places such as Detroit.[65] Some sources also say that Harlan was nominated for the U.S. Senate seat in 1872. Since Senate elections were still in the hands of the state legislature, there was little chance of success and no real campaigning to do: Harlan was defeated by an overwhelming party line vote of 112 to 20.[66]

Harlan was still taking an active interest in the success of the Republicans' newspaper venture, and he wrote frequent letters asking for financial support from wealthy Republicans in and out of Kentucky and even, with W.A. Merriweather, took temporary control of the venture.[67] He also wrote editorials for the paper on occasion, and urged prominent Kentucky party members to stimulate the circulation of the paper throughout the state, even if only for the weekly edition.[68]

At the urgent request of Walter Evans, who was locked in a tight battle for a legislative seat representing Hopkinsville, Harlan did some campaigning in that area in 1873.[69] Regarding his hopes of obtaining preferment from the supposedly grateful Grant, he disclaimed any interest: "As to my receiving office at the hands of the present administration let me assure you that I have no desire for official station at this time. I am in love with the practice of my profession and do not care to go to Washington for any purpose."[70]

By 1874 Ben Bristow had become a Republican leader at the national level. His appointment as secretary of the Treasury, and his conduct of the Whiskey Ring scandals, gave him great publicity, brought him to the attention of reform-minded Republicans—and made him suspect to Grant. The president apparently suspected Bristow of personal disloyalty: as a politician, Grant was never able to separate himself from the actions of his appointees. Like Harlan, Ben Bristow was an ambitious man, and he had his eye on further federal advancement. The presidency or the Supreme Court, he doubtless felt, would be only suitable rewards for his services in cleaning up the party's image. But neither of these was possible without Grant's support, and this situation probably provides the background to an enigmatic note to Harlan from Associate Justice David Davis, Lincoln's friend from Illinois, in which Harlan was informed: "Have just learnt that Waite of Ohio is nominated for CJ—Bristow is now all right, and protected—I began to feel bad at his telegram, for fear he did not approve our course."[71]

While some aspects of this note must remain mysterious, since we do not have records of Bristow's telegram or of the correspondence indicated by the words "our course," the major fact is clear: Harlan was pushing Bristow by this time, proud of his national reputation and probably hoping that if Ben were not appointed in Chase's Supreme Court seat, he would be the most prominent "available" person to put up against Blaine for the presidency two years hence. Harlan spent two years working hard for Bristow's nomination, only to fail at the point of seeming success.

In May 1875 Harlan was nominated by the Republicans to make a second run for the governorship. There is no reason to doubt his frequent protestations that he undertook the race only with great reluctance. His law practice kept him busy; he did not have the money to take time away from it; he wanted to concentrate politically on Bristow's presidential boom; and not least, there was little profit to be gained from another losing race. The convention—depicted satirically but with some truth as consisting almost entirely of federal job holders, such as internal revenue agents, postmasters, judges, attorneys, marshals, and whiskey gaugers—nominated him despite his reluctance and his statement that he could not afford the kind of campaign he had made in 1871.[72] There was no Republican in the state who could come near him as a vote-getter; Bristow, who might have done so, was occupied in Washington. There was even some feeling that Harlan might not have the Negro vote solidly in hand, although John himself made light of this possibility.[73]

The Democrats, confident of victory, nominated a man even younger than the forty-two-year-old Harlan, James B. McCreary.[74] This young Democrat had followed Harlan to Centre College, had served in the Confederate army, and was in the state legislature (with two terms as Speaker). He and Harlan were on good personal terms, a fact that enabled them to travel the state together and debate spiritedly without loss of respect for one another. Despite Harlan's attempts to keep his campaigning to a minimum, he found himself spending most of his time at it. McCreary many years later jovially recalled, "Harlan and I visited every section of the State, mostly on horseback. He was an older and larger man than I, and he had some difficulty in his journeys, particularly when it came to fording streams. He used to ride around streams he couldn't ford."[75]

Early in the debate trip Harlan accused his opponent, who was only thirty-eight, of being too young to be eligible to serve as governor under the Kentucky constitution. Harlan went on to say that "he knew the good people of Kentucky well enough to know that they would not elect a man to the high office of Governor who would have to violate the law to take his seat."[76] McCreary followed on the rostrum, leading off by denying the charge and saying, "I will leave this question of my age to Curtis Burnam, of Richmond, a Republican and a stanch supporter of Mr. Harlan, and any other two Republicans . . . whom Mr. Burnam may select. Now, if they decide that I am not eligible . . . I shall withdraw . . . but, Mr. Harlan, mark you, if they decide that I am old enough you must withdraw." Harlan jumped to his feet and said, "The gentleman's word as to his age is accepted. If he says he is eligible I shall not dispute it."[77] The debate tour proceeded with the two becoming friends. A newspaper report later said that they lived a life almost conjugal for some weeks, riding over the mountains, in the valleys, and sleeping at night in the same bed.

One night they arrived at a little hotel in the hills, worn out with horsebacking and ready to retire. The General, who is a tremendous man, and at the time was in full possession of his health and strength, was the last one undressed and when he crawled in beside Major McCreary, that statesman was ready to topple off to sleep.

"Well, this bed certainly holds the next Governor of Kentucky," said the General settling himself.

Crash! and the slats snapped, pitching the Republican chieftain on the floor.

"You're right, General," called McCreary from under the snug sheets, "the next Governor is still in bed."[78]

Whatever the truth of this story—Harlan's marginal note on his copy says, "It did not happen"—McCreary certainly became governor. The Republican candidate lost again, by almost the same margin as in 1871.[79] Though no one could have predicted it, Harlan had run his last campaign as a candidate. His reputation in the state had reached its height: one admiring supporter remarked that Republicans "can march willingly to defeat when led by such men."[80] More important, he was by 1875 in demand as a campaign speaker far outside his home state and was especially favorably known to the candidate for governor of Ohio, Rutherford B. Hayes.

7

Kingmaker
1876

By 1875 the political and judicial careers of John M. Harlan were inextricably entwined with the destiny of his law partner, Ben Bristow. It is one of the ironies of politics that having achieved so much with each other's help, the two eventually split completely. After Harlan's appointment to the Supreme Court Bristow not only left the firm, but he never even spoke as a friend to John again.[1]

One problem was that the two were not only partners, friends, and political allies: they were also competitors. Both were ambitious, honest, and public-spirited men, and both, at times, allowed their ambitions to get the better of their good judgment. Bristow "arrived" on the national scene earlier than Harlan, with his appointment and successful service as solicitor general. But Harlan's success in creating and leading a strong Republican party in Kentucky and his activities outside the state in the 1872 campaign made him, as well, a national figure.

It was obvious that long-term success as a Kentucky Republican could only be achieved through appointment to some high national office or election to the presidency. The nature of politics is such that there was no room for two Kentuckians in these capacities. If and when Bristow served in Washington, there was no place for Harlan, and vice versa. John supported his partner as long as it appeared that Bristow could succeed. In turn, Bristow often suggested Harlan for office: he proposed that Harlan be appointed attorney general in 1871, for instance.[2]

President Grant had nominated Bristow for the attorney general's post in 1873; but since it apeared that there might be a contest in the Senate over confirmation and it might seem that he was seeking the office, Ben withdrew his name.[3] Bristow, a man of strong moral rectitude, hated playing the game of politics. This fact not only led to his withdrawal on this occasion but also probably cost him the presidency and, later, a seat on the Supreme Court or a cabinet post under Hayes.

After leaving the solicitor's office in November 1872, Bristow spent some time in Philadelphia as a railroad promoter for the Texas and Pacific project: he was heavily involved in the politics of securing grants from the federal and Texas governments. He did not return to Louisville until the middle of 1873, bringing a good deal of railroad business with him. He and Harlan were, however, in the advantageous position of being completely dissociated from the increasing corruption surrounding the Grant administration. There is no doubt that Bristow hoped for— perhaps expected—a Supreme Court appointment at this time. Chief Justice Salmon P. Chase had died, and associate justices Noah H. Swayne and Samuel F. Miller were prominently mentioned as successors. Either appointment would leave a seat vacant. Swayne actively worked for the promotion and asked Bristow to request appointment to the resulting vacancy. There was nothing Bristow wanted more, but he was not the man to ask for preferment, feeling that if President Grant wanted him he should say so. This did not happen. Morrison R. Waite, a relatively nonpolitical lawyer from Ohio, was appointed chief justice, and Bristow stayed in Louisville waiting for the next bolt of lightning to strike.[4]

The gathering corruption in Washington eventually gave Ben his chance. The "negligence, if not actual connivance," of Secretary of the Treasury William A. Richardson in a tax scandal forced his resignation. Although Bristow had refused the attorney general position and no appropriate vacancy had occurred on the Court, President Grant still felt obligated to the Kentuckian. Bristow had served well as solicitor general, had enthusiastically campaigned for Grant's second term, and above all, was a Southerner. He was also a "hard money man," even though no financier, and the businessmen around Grant wanted complete orthodoxy in that respect. So Bristow was appointed in June 1874.

The Treasury, prestigious in itself, offered in addition even greater opportunities to an aspiring politician. He could help the Republican party and the country by restoring the department to his own strict moral standards. In the process he would enhance his own reputation for integrity and probity—qualities conspicuously in short supply among the men surrounding the president and also among the party leaders in Congress. As Associate Justice David Davis reminded him, "*Opportunity* is everything and that you have."[5]

Bristow seized the opportunity. His aggressive attack on corruption in the department—principally the Whiskey Ring—brought him to the favorable attention of reformist elements in the Republican party, men who were disgusted by the moral atmosphere pervading the administration and who favored civil service reform. His name was constantly in the newspapers, and by 1876 he was possibly the best-known Republican in the nation aside from Grant himself.[6]

Such success brought its inevitable penalty, however. The ringleaders of the Whiskey Ring attacked Bristow in any way they could. The machine leaders from the various states—Oliver P. Morton of Indiana, Roscoe Conkling of New York, James G. Blaine of Maine—men who were more interested in political power and position than in honesty, saw in him a competitor for the White House in 1876 and unanimously turned against him. Most important, his success and the rumors of his ambitions made the president, already restive because of Bristow's attacks on his friends, even more suspicious. Grant could not brook "disloyalty" around him, nor did he like the idea that his own appointees might be using their positions to replace him, even though he probably did not really want a third term anyway.

By the middle of 1875, then, lines were already being drawn within the party's ranks. Resurgent Democrats hoped that the bad odor of the administration would give them their first chance since the war. Many Republicans felt that only a clean, reformist candidate could win. John Harlan, Bristow's political adviser, saw Ben as the man. Quietly in correspondence with like-minded Republicans all over the country, Harlan tried to prevent his partner from making any kind of statement that would be interpreted by either side as removing him from contention. He also had to try to persuade Bristow not to resign from the Treasury, for if he did so not only would he lose his daily forum (provided by his legal battles against the Whiskey Ring), but he would also crystallize Grant's growing resentment. Nothing open could be done as long as there was a possibility that Grant might decide to run again. But all hinged on remaining in office: Marshall Jewell, the postmaster general, wrote to Harlan that Bristow should "fight it out. . . . Sumner's advice to Stanton is the thing he wants—'stick.'"[7]

Harlan's letters to Bristow took much the same line. Answering Bristow's question about whether he should retire because of his poor relations with Grant, Harlan advised his partner that "the chief reason in my mind for your retention of your present office is . . . that by so doing you may make yourself President in 1876." He added, "If you have any ambition to go on the Supreme Bench, the chance for it is most probably lost if you give up your present position."[8]

A tricky problem came up when the Kentucky Republicans met in May 1875, for there was much enthusiasm for the endorsement of Bristow for president—a move that Ben and John agreed would be disastrous—and for opposing a third term for Grant, which would probably be equally harmful. Harlan managed to secure a resolution praising both Grant and Bristow and accusing the Democrats of spreading the impression that the president wanted a third term.[9] Thus the convention said, in effect, We know Grant won't run, without having to commit itself on the issue. "I find," wrote Harlan, "that it is entirely acceptable to all except those who would have been glad if we had given the President a slap in the face on the subject of the third term."[10]

Bristow's prospects and strategy, as developed by Harlan, were summarized at the end of 1875 in a letter to a Kentucky supporter: "My candid conviction is that he is the strongest man today that the Republicans can run, and his chances for the nomination are better than those of any one who has been named in connection with the office. He is surrounded by many difficulties, . . . but I believe that he will come out of his present war upon thieves and plunderers with more reputation than has been won by any public man in this country for years past." Harlan went on to say that the state convention should not be held until just before the national conclave in 1876, so as not to "embarrass Bristow's prospects" by a pre-mature declaration. He ended with a disclaimer: "I would not have you to understand that he is scheming for it. Indeed, I know he is not. He has forborne to enter upon any consideration of the subject. . . . But that does not prevent his friends from thinking of him. . . . [In fact,] his great strength with the people . . . consists chiefly in the belief that he is not scheming for the Presidency, but is aiming to protect the Treasury against fraud and villainy. I hope that impression will grow deeper and wider, so that by the time spring comes, there will be a universal demand from every part of the country for his nomination."[11]

One suspects that Ben Bristow, ever the reluctant political virgin, was willing (even eager) to be president but not willing for anyone to think he wanted the office. Despite Harlan's feelings on the subject, a true draft was unlikely, if for no other reason than that there was very strong opposition to Bristow. His great exertions for his partner seem to indicate that Harlan, at least, knew that nominations had to be worked for.

During the winter and spring of 1876 John Harlan was fully occupied in attempting to maintain his legal practice (even Gus Willson was off in Washington working for Bristow in the Treasury Department) and at the same time orchestratng preparations for bringing Bristow's name before the national convention in June. By January the major competitors had become obvious; most of them were, unlike Ben, actively working for the nomination. Indiana's Oliver P. Morton even started to raid Kentucky for delegates on the assumption that Bristow was not interested; he withdrew when Bristow's displeasure became evident.[12] By January Bristow had caught "Potomac fever," even to the extent that he felt he had a mission to save the Republican party from its corrupt leaders. Certainly Harlan pushed him in this direction. Nevertheless, Bristow still refused to do anything that would make him look like an eager candidate, writing to a friend that "it seems to me at best that the Presidential office is not one to be sought, and that no man could better illustrate his unfitness for it than by entering into a scramble to obtain it."[13]

Harlan was heavily engaged in attempting to line up delegates by pushing Bristow at the various state conventions held during the spring, including, of course, Kentucky's. While the Southern states lined up fairly well for Bristow, much competition occurred elsewhere. Morton's abortive foray into Kentucky demonstrated that even Ben's home state could not be taken for granted: the influential O.P. Johnson, who had helped to start the

Louisville *Commercial*, apparently felt that Bristow had used influence to have him sacked from his federal job, and Harlan had to spend some time in cementing Bristow's support in the Kentucky convention, held in May. Harlan promised to use threats if necessary: "I shall let him [Johnson] understand that if there is any effort among Morton's friends to prevent the selection of delegates who are your friends, it may have an effect upon the futures of his friends which he does not anticipate."[14] As usual, he also wrote to Republican leaders all over the state soliciting their support and information.[15]

He was in close touch with reform leaders elsewhere, as well. He met several times, in Louisville or in Indiana, with that state's anti-Morton leader, Walter Q. Gresham.[16] He was in frequent contact with Henry Van Ness Boynton, the prominent newspaper correspondent from Cincinnati, who had taken up Bristow's cause and was writing in his favor, as well as trying to line up other editors and writers.[17] Boynton reported a meeting in Cincinnati in March that included Joseph Medill, Sam Reed, Richard Smith, and Murat Halstead—all leading reform-minded newspapermen.[18] These Western writers felt that no organization politician, not even James G. Blaine, could get the nomination, and that throughout the West Bristow had the greatest strength.

Others felt that Bristow's best chance was to run as an Independent, as Horace Greeley had done in 1872. The fact that Greeley did not win perhaps explains Harlan's opposition to such an idea. In February, when Henry Cabot Lodge suggested this at a meeting in Washington that Harlan attended, the Kentuckian argued that reformism was a very strong force within the party and that it would be better if Bristow could be nominated without causing all the bitterness that a division would engender.[19]

Bluford Wilson of Illinois, another Bristow supporter, also corresponded with Harlan. Wilson was important in Illinois Republican circles and had been a U.S. attorney there; he was appointed solicitor of the Treasury by Bristow and took a major part in the Whiskey Ring investigations and prosecutions. He was an astute political observer who gave reports—perhaps overly optimistic ones—on Bristow sentiment in various states, especially Illinois.[20]

During the spring, political events in Washington—primarily Grant's increasingly obvious suspicion of the motives of his Treasury secretary but also the campaign of vilification carried on by Whiskey Ring people and party regulars—impelled Bristow in the direction of a more active candidacy. "I will make the best fight I can," he wrote, "and, if I must go down will at least fall with my face to the foe."[21] Like Hayes, however, he did not become too personally involved; his change in attitude merely gave permission for his supporters to do what they were already doing: line up delegates for the Cincinnati convention.[22]

This process continued, and by the eve of the convention Harlan was fairly optimistic, more so, perhaps, than the facts warranted. This, however, is endemic among politicians. Amid the hoopla of the few days in the Queen City before the actual opening of the proceedings, Harlan and his lieutenants worked mightily to tie down uncommitted delegates and to obtain promises that delegates pledged to other candidates would switch to Bristow whenever their own candidate released them. This included the crucial Indiana delegation, which was pledged to Oliver P. Morton, its senator and former governor.

Bristow's chances were damaged somewhat by hyperactivity: at least this is what one close observer of the convention thought. Some, such as Carl Schurz, went so far as to say they would bolt to the Democrats if Blaine were nominated. The heavy emphasis on Bristow as a reform candidate actually put off some party regulars.[23] Henry Van Ness Boynton was perhaps overzealous in digging up and publicizing unsavory episodes from Blaine's past, such as the Mulligan letters, which were published toward the end of May. While Blaine succeeded speciously in explaining these away, they undoubtedly hurt his chances. At the same time, they did not help Bristow. Although several newspapermen had participated in uncovering the letters and planning for their publication, the prominent participation of Boynton brought the credit (or the blame) home to Bristow, with the result that the Blaine men were determined to prevent Bristow from being nominated. Hayes actually benefited from this episode, for although his own newspaper supporter, William Henry Smith, was as involved as anyone, Smith managed to keep this a secret even from Hayes. Consequently, Hayes went into the convention with little opposition, even though he had little enthusiastic support, either.[24]

After surveying the situation in Cincinnati, the Bristow backers, in common with many others, were not so sanguine about their ability to stop Blaine. In order to gain time they stalled the nominating and balloting as long as they could. "General" Harlan was chosen to deliver the nominating speech for Bristow: he "arose amid a perfect storm of cheers" and made a "telling speech which was loudly applauded—more however by the people in the galleries than by the delegates."[25] The greatest speech was made for Blaine by the famous orator Robert G. Ingersoll, who actually favored Morton but wanted to make certain of Bristow's defeat. In his "plumed knight" speech Ingersoll sent the crowd wild with enthusiasm and even seemed to make vice a virtue.[26]

The anti-Blaine forces succeeded in postponing the balloting until the following day, but Bristow's men saw their fears realized when, on the first ballot, Blaine secured a commanding lead of 285 votes, compared with 125 for Morton and 113 for Bristow. Since Morton probably knew he did not have a chance, and the other votes for Conkling, Hayes, and Governor Hartranft of Pennsylvania were regarded by many as tokens (except probably by the Hayes people), the question became whether Bristow could get enough votes on later ballots to overtake Blaine.

It was not to be. Despite the herculean efforts at persuasion, Morton could not be brought to support Bristow, and Grant's man at the convention, Zachariah Chandler of Michigan, threw that state's twenty-two votes to Hayes. This seemed a signal that the party men felt that Blaine could not win and would be satisfied with Hayes. On the sixth ballot Morton conceded defeat and threw the Indiana vote also to Hayes, and the rout was on. At this point,

> Gen. Harlan rose from his place and walked toward the stand, and the people divining his purpose at once set up a great cheer, and it was some time before he could be heard. He stood there, his lips trembling with emotion waiting for the storm of applause to be hushed, and then he spoke grandly. He thanked the convention for the support they had given his fellow citizen, and the thanks of Kentucky were especially due to those men of Massachusetts and Vermont, who when it was whispered throughout the length and breadth of this land that Benj. H. Bristow was not to be President because he was born and reared in the South, had come forward and said they were satisfied that a Kentuckian could be loyal; that Benjamin H. Bristow was a man to be trusted (great and prolonged applause).[27]

Harlan then withdrew Bristow's name and cast Kentucky's votes for Hayes, setting off a "scene of wild and tumultuous applause . . . that defies description."[28]

The political eminence of Benjamin Bristow declined as fast as it had risen. He was never again to hold any political office. Yet he came so near to the nomination that historians and biographers are always tempted to second-guess. Did Harlan misjudge the time to switch to Hayes? If he had stuck it out for another ballot, would Bristow have been successful? One charge against Harlan is that of simple political mismanagement. At first, at least, Bristow himself did not share such sentiments: he praised the Hayes nomination and wired Harlan his congratulations "that my friends have helped to do it."[29] When talking to reporters he did not appear excessively disconsolate, and certainly there was no tinge of bitterness.[30] He wrote later to Harlan, "I cannot attempt to express to you the gratitude I owe you for your unselfish support and splendid fight made in my behalf." Harlan, he said, had acted "with consummate ability," and his move to Hayes "was exactly in the right time, and done in the right way."[31]

For his part, Harlan was extremely disappointed but thought he had done the right thing. His explanation to Bristow blamed the Hayes tide on Michigan's switch on the fifth ballot: "As soon as it was done I felt that our case was hopeless." He blamed this event primarily on Morton's refusal to withdraw and the consequent failure of Indiana to change to Bristow. He expressed surprise at the strength of the Blaine movement and even said that it was doubtful whether Bristow could ever have won a "square fight" with Blaine. "As soon as I discovered that we were gone, my determination

. . . was to seize the first opportunity to retire in a becoming manner, and so throw our votes as to . . . secure a good nominee. . . . Altogether you have reason to be proud, not only of the character of the support which you received in the Convention, but of your position before the country."[32]

Hayes's biographer agrees with this estimate, which seems to be the most accurate one available to historians of a very complex situation.[33] Finally, the defeat was due to Bristow's stiff-necked refusal to deal with the party regulars and the consequent enmity of such leaders as Morton and Conkling and, behind it all, Grant. All of these men doubtless wanted Blaine, but they would take anyone in order to avoid having to take Bristow.[34]

A second charge against Harlan is more serious but less likely. Such Bristow supporters as Boynton and Walter Q. Gresham believed—or said they did—that Harlan deliberately threw the nomination. Indeed, Gresham's widow wrote many years later that in a midnight conference "Harlan was promised a place on the Supreme Bench, and he, as the head of the Kentucky delegation, started the Bristow following to Hayes."[35] Nothing in Hayes's papers or subsequent actions gives color to this charge. Doubtless Harlan hoped—indeed he said so to Bristow—that a timely switch would secure a good nominee; beyond that he probably hoped that Hayes would be properly grateful and that the eventual result would be some sort of political plum for Bristow, himself, or both. There is, however, nothing particularly nefarious in such a calculation.

The intimate relations between the Harlans and the Bristows were not resumed, even though officially the partnership remained in existence. Bristow immediately resigned from the Treasury, leaving on July 1, 1876, to the plaudits of the newspapers, some of which called him the greatest Treasury secretary ever.[36] After a vacation in Saratoga with his family, Bristow campaigned actively and enthusiastically for Hayes, as did Harlan. Then the former secretary returned to Louisville and his practice.[37]

Bristow's friends, especially Henry Van Ness Boynton, occupied their time for the next year trying to secure for Bristow what he would not ask or work for for himself: a proper reward for his great services. Once Hayes was installed, these men assumed that Ben's record and his popularity within party and country entitled him to such a reward. As it became more and more obvious that no such appointment, to the cabinet or the Supreme Court, was going to go to Bristow and that instead Harlan was likely to gain office, Boynton undertook a campaign of vituperation against John. Bristow became convinced that Harlan was climbing over his back, and the relations between the two men were permanently ruptured.

8

The Fruits of Success
1877

John Harlan returned to Louisville after the convention disappointed, naturally, that his partner had failed to receive the nomination. On the other hand, he felt that the choice of Hayes was, under the circumstances, perhaps better than Republican reformers might have expected. For there was no doubt that Hayes would represent the reform wing of the party and lure back the Liberal Republicans who had run Horace Greeley on a separate ticket in 1872.[1] The widespread disgust with the corruption surrounding Grant had thus prevented the nomination of anyone tarred with the same brush, such as Blaine. The Democratic candidate, Samuel J. Tilden, was certain to try to take the reform issue away from his opponent; but a Grant Republican would have had no chance to win in November.[2] Hayes had also the advantage that he had, with whatever misgivings, stayed with Grant in 1872 and could therefore not be accused of party disloyalty. On balance, then, Hayes was probably a better candidate than Bristow because he had not incurred the enmity of Grant and the Republican stalwarts. Naturally, whatever his disappointments, Harlan soon became an enthusiastic Hayes supporter.

Hayes's main contribution to the campaign, as was customary in those days, was his letter of acceptance.[3] He called strongly for a return to an appointment system based on merit, a clear, if implicit, criticism of Grantism; pledged himself (unwisely) not to run for a second term; came out for sound money through the resumption of specie payments; called for a constitutional amendment to remove religion from the public schools; and proposed in vague terms to work for a return of normal conditions in the South. Harlan's reaction to the Hayes letter was enthusiastic. He said it was "capital in every respect," and in an excess of hyperbole he continued, "I do not think it contains anything which it ought not to contain—not a sentiment." But he went on, "He might have said more without [injury] to the cause."[4]

Earlier, John had written to Hayes personally, suggesting items for the acceptance letter. His emphasis on economic matters in his own campaigns in Kentucky led him to criticize the Republican platform: "I venture to call your attention to the singular fact that our . . . platform . . . does not contain the word 'retrenchment' or the word 'economy' as applied to the financial affairs of the nation. . . . [This] omission could be supplied in your letter of acceptance."[5] Although the nominee replied that Harlan's "views are mine, thru & thru," he did not accept the suggestion that he emphasize economic matters in his acceptance.[6]

Regarding the Republican chances for victory, Harlan was not without qualms, even in July. "I am constantly apprehensive that some new act of folly will be committed" by "our leaders in Washington." The removal of various reform supporters from their federal positions and the forced retirement or resignation of others—he obviously had Bristow in mind—were major causes of disaffection within the party and led to a consequent loss of enthusiasm.[7] To Marshall Jewell's comment that Hayes could probably not carry Connecticut, he replied, "Then New Jersey and New York are in danger. What next? It is terrible to think of the consequences." He accused the Republican stalwarts of being willing to destroy the party "when it has ceased to minister to their morbid ambitions or their insane follies."[8] If President Grant desired "to defeat our ticket in November he need only continue in the course that he has pursued in the last few weeks."[9]

No matter what his fears and enthusiasms may have been in regard to the Hayes campaign, Harlan still had a living to earn. He had, indeed, spent too much time in the previous few years on his own and others' campaigns. Even though he was by now in exceedingly great demand as a speaker—requests for his aid flowed in from all over the Northeast and Middle West—he felt it necessary to limit his activities. His reply to such requests was almost unvarying: "Our Courts are just commencing here, and it so happens that my most important cases are crowded into the month of October in such a way that absence is almost impossible." Nevertheless, both he and Ben Bristow spent much time in Indiana (a critical state) in September, and Harlan also visited Ohio before its crucial state election in late October.[10]

His Indiana speech is one of the rare ones that has been preserved, although it is incomplete. It is written in the third person—"Gen. Harlan commenced by alluding," and so on—but in his own handwriting. His last extant political statement, it is of some interest as a revelation of his sentiments only a year before his appointment to the Supreme Court, although of course these sentiments were inevitably colored by the specific issues of the 1876 campaign and by Harlan's usual habit of enthusiastic exaggeration, shared, of course, by most politicians of his era.[11]

Harlan began by referring at excessive length to the fact that the Republican party saved the Union while the Democrats would have allowed its dissolution. Resorting to the time-honored technique of whipping up enthusiasm by getting his audience to chant in unison, he claimed that Tilden's men were seeking "diligently to prevent discussion of the question to which" their charges relate. If, for instance, "we refer to the trying times of 1861," then "they say that we are waving the bloody shirt." A string of "ifs" followed, each concluded by the cry, "They say that we are waving the bloody shirt."

Thus having accomplished the difficult feat of waving the bloody shirt while denying that he was doing so and the easier task of warming up his auditors, Harlan proceeded to prove, at least to the satisfaction of the crowd, that the Republicans, having saved the nation, should be trusted to govern it. He referred to the merciful peace terms imposed by Grant at the time of Lee's surrender: remembering the wrongs committed in the name of secession and the tremendous casualties, Grant yet also knew "that Lee and his comrades were to remain our countrymen and that this great nation could afford to accord to them generous and magnanimous terms." Northerners, he recalled, accepted this. He dodged the long conflict between President Andrew Johnson and the Radicals in Congress, preferring to leave the impression that "loyal people" entertained no "feelings of hatred toward those in rebellion." Harlan intended to indicate that the Republicans' basic goal was the protection of blacks in their newfound citizenship and that the carpetbag governments and military occupation in the South resulted from Southern (i.e., Democratic) intransigence on this issue. He laid great stress on the outrages of the Ku Klux Klan and the White Circle League, which, he claimed, Northern Democrats never denounced. From that day to this, he intoned, "the Democratic leaders of the North have continued to tell the people of the Cotton States that they are being oppressed by the government of the United States." To elect Tilden would mean "the destruction of the right of free speech" in the South and "a notice to every white Republican in those sections to quit that country." The truth was, he averred, that the Republicans were "the truest friends of the South, and their triumph . . . would open up a new career for the South." Praising Governor Hayes fulsomely, Harlan promised that a Hayes administration would work for the interests of both whites and blacks and for the eradication of any distinction between the North and the South.

After much more along these lines, including animadversions against Tilden's record and plans, Harlan turned to other issues that, however, he touched only lightly. He spoke favorably of Hayes's plans for civil service reform. "There have been," he said, "corrupt men in all political organizations, and there always will be some," but the Republicans' "record in the prosecution of offenders against the laws of the country [an obvious allusion to Bristow] is a grand record as compared with the Democratic party when it was in power." He jestingly referred to the Democratic candidate for governor of Indiana, Congressman James D. "Blue Jeans" Williams, who "had been so vigilant in watching the interests of the people, as to cut off the supply of lemonade for the members of the House of

Representatives in Washington. . . . notwithstanding that great reform,
. . . the Democratic members of the House could be seen every day during
the hot summer, wending their way to the side room of the Senate Chamber, and drinking the lemonade furnished for the use of Senators."[12]
Harlan also praised Republican measures of financial economy, and lambasted the record of the Democratic House.

Life did not consist entirely of campaign speeches, and in fact Harlan
campaigned less actively in 1876 than he had in the past. For one thing,
presidential campaigns were then relatively brief: they did not gain full
steam until September and ended by early November. The summer of 1876
was the centennial of American independence, and like thousands of other
Americans, the Harlans visited the Centennial Exposition in Philadelphia.

But Harlan's financial situation demanded that he pay greater attention
to his law practice, which absorbed most of his time for the year following
Hayes's nomination. Harlan never made much money from his practice; he
was forced to take out frequent loans, mostly in these years from his
Shanklin relatives in Evansville, and he often found it difficult to repay
them on schedule.

His position as the leading Republican in Kentucky continued to require a good deal of time. He was expected to find federal jobs for deserving
party members, many of whom were personal friends, and he found
protecting these officeholders a losing battle in the waning months of
Grant's presidency. Grant, heavily influenced by the party spoilsmen
around him, adopted a vindictive policy toward his "enemies," that is,
anyone who supported Bristow or other reformers. So Bristow found it
expedient to leave office. There was also a wave of firings of men in lower
positions, and Harlan stayed busy writing to friends in Congress or in the
administration complaining of these firings and endeavoring, usually without success, to secure the workers' reinstatement. Indiana's Morton, hand
in glove again with Harlan's Kentucky Republican opponent O.P. Johnson,
apparently took a hand in this against Harlan's friends.[13]

Other Harlan men were to lose their jobs: Robert M. Kelly, the
Louisville *Commercial* editor, lost his post as pension agent.[14] The U.S.
attorney for Louisville, Gabriel C. Wharton, was similarly treated.[15] Harlan
wrote to another petitioner, "Besides, I am quite sure that my recommenda-
tion would not avail you anything with the P.O. Department. Recently
some of my friends have been roughly handled by that Department, and
my protest has not been sufficient to protect them."[16] Feeling that General
Sherman's friendship with Grant might be of some help (and no doubt
keeping in mind the influence of Sherman's brother, John, the senior
senator from Ohio), Harlan wrote, "A movement is being made to affect
prejudicially some of your old comrades—and to the extent that you can

properly do so, I would be glad if you would interfere for their protection."[17]

Under these circumstances, Harlan and Bristow could do little but stick to their law practice while awaiting the results of the election, which was not settled until March 2, 1877, two days before the inauguration. This is not the place to describe the details of this exciting period when the most hotly contested election in American history led to rumors of renewed rebellion or at least massive riots.[18] Harlan, a deeply interested bystander, played no role in the drama. Ben Bristow, influenced by a constant stream of letters from Boynton in Washington, no doubt had high hopes of a cabinet post. As early as October, Boynton wrote that if Hayes were elected he would immediately become embroiled in a battle with the Republican regulars in Congress and that he could not win such a battle "with an ordinary cabinet. He must have such men as yourself, Cox, Schurz—men who before the country represent" reform.[19] Bristow was told that "the rings" were organizing to keep him out of the Treasury Department but that this would put Hayes "in a place where he would be obliged either to recognize you, or admit at the outset of his official life that he had surrendered to the rings."[20]

During the winter of 1876-77, while the election results hung fire, Harlan concentrated on his law practice and on his family. With six children, including three boys whose college educations had to be financed (it was in those days assumed that the girls would not receive any higher education), an assured income and a prosperous practice were essential. Nevertheless, busy as Harlan was, his income was barely enough, and he resorted again to loans from Mallie's relatives in Evansville. While Bristow apparently resumed an active role in the partnership only briefly, business was handled the more efficiently due to the return of Gus Willson, who had gone off to Washington to help Bristow during the Treasury scandals.

After Hayes was finally declared the winner, the active sparring began for the spoils of office. Hayes had, first of all, to construct his cabinet. It is significant that although Harlan's name appears in various lists of proposed cabinet officials, Bristow was virtually ignored: not only did Senator Morton and all the Grant men oppose him, but Hayes himself probably was reluctant to put in his cabinet anyone with such obvious presidential ambitions.[21] Consequently, even though the new president had at one time thought of Bristow for secretary of war (a post that Ben probably would have refused) and Schurz suggested that he be returned to the Treasury, Bristow was eventually dropped completely from consideration. The new idea was to placate the Bristow reformers by appointing Harlan as attorney general. This was not to be, although one story has it that discussions of the appointment had proceeded so far that Harlan made a trip to Washington to take the oath of office.[22] Arriving in the capital city, he was told that "political complications of a peculiar character" prevented the president from appointing him. Although Harlan apparently never knew what these "complications" were, it seems that they were primarily due to Morton's opposition: Hayes felt that he was in Morton's debt for his nomination and went to great lengths to please him.[23] The basis of Morton's opposition to either Bristow or Harlan is not recorded. Reading between the lines, it appears that Harlan's friendship with Walter Q. Gresham, a prominent Indiana supporter of Bristow, had alienated Morton, who had presidential ambitions himself and regarded Gresham as disloyal.[24] Then too, Morton's attempted incursion into Kentucky had no doubt brewed ill feeling between him and Harlan. In any case, Morton wrote a note to the new president early in March:

> It is among the rumors that you contemplate selecting Gen. Harlan of Ky. for a seat in your Cabinet. I write in frankness to say that his appointment would be disagreeable to my friends for reasons too numerous and lengthy to be referred to here. Kentucky never cast a Republican vote and perhaps will not in our life time, and Kentucky Republicanism never meant much. An appointment from that state would not answer the demand for a Southern appointment and would I think not be generally acceptable to Southern Republicans.
>
> But in view of what you said to me this morning I venture to say it would be personally distasteful to me and my friends.
>
> If it were in your power to select one from Indiana it would be personally gratifying to me and would be territorially proper, but to have Indiana passed and one taken from Ky. would make an impression which I am sure you do not intend and which I should regret.[25]

Faced with this sentiment, which amounted almost to an ultimatum, Hayes capitulated by appointing Richard W. Thompson of Indiana as secretary of the navy, notwithstanding Thompson's somewhat unsavory reputation. Then he turned to Charles A. Devens of Massachusetts, "distinguished mainly as an after-dinner speaker," for attorney general.[26]

Bristow was undoubtedly disappointed not to receive an appointment, but like a good soldier he wrote Schurz, the new Interior secretary, congratulating him and expressing satisfaction with the cabinet's makeup.[27] Harlan's feelings are not known, but displeasure must have been a major reaction. There was still hope for both men. Associate Justice David Davis had resigned from the Supreme Court even before the inauguration in order to accept a Senate seat from Illinois. There was much speculation about his successor, and Bristow's friends, including Boynton, pushed him for the vacancy. One correspondent wrote to Harlan, "I believe Col. Bristow will be appointed to the supreme bench and that you and he will receive at the hands of this administration what is due to you as the men that made the administration."[28]

One of Rutherford Hayes's first tasks was, as promised, to end military government in the South. By this time, federal troops were maintained only in three states: Florida, South Carolina, and Louisiana. In each, the Democrats—former secessionists—claimed to have won the state elections. In Florida, with the support of the state supreme court, the Democratic governor was inducted without violence, although under protest. In South Carolina, rival governments were set up, but Democratic governor Wade Hampton made good his claim by collecting taxes and, again, gaining the support of the courts.

This left Louisiana, where there were also rival governments. The Republicans, led by "Governor" Stephen B. Packard, with his part of the legislature, occupied the state capitol, but they were maintained there as against the Democratic claimant, Francis R.T. Nicholls, only by the presence of federal troops. Since there were also two supreme courts, the Democrats could not use judicial support effectively. Nevertheless, Packard's days as the leader of the last of the carpetbag governments were numbered, unless the troops were kept in place. For Hayes, this was a very touchy political issue; while he and many other moderates felt that carpetbag government had failed and he had virtually promised to remove the troops, he yet had to face the opposition of the radicals, many of whom not only wished a harsher policy toward the South but were opposed to Hayes's reform policies as well.[29]

Various Republican leaders had sought privately to persuade Packard to relinquish his claims, but without effect. Finally, the president decided after consultation with his cabinet to send a commission to Louisiana. The purpose of this is not immediately clear: it was certainly not expected that any federal body could dictate which was the legal government of the state. Perhaps the commission is best seen as a face-saving device by which Hayes could justify the withdrawal of the army without taking too much blame for failure to support Packard's pretensions. In many ways this was a thankless task, and it was some days before Hayes was able to find five men of probity who would agree to serve. The five finally chosen were Charles B. Lawrence of Illinois, Joseph R. Hawley of Connecticut, John C. Brown of Tennessee, Wayne MacVeagh of Pennsylvania, and John M. Harlan of Kentucky.[30]

The five proceeded to New Orleans, and by late April the affair was settled, largely, it must be said, without the commission's assistance. The main contribution of the group was the final information that Hayes was going to withdraw the federal troops. Once this was known, support for Packard rapidly disappeared. Those members of his legislature who had without doubt been regularly elected went over to the Nicholls legislature; together the two groups made a legal quorum in each house and became the official state legislature. Packard issued a statement of withdrawal, and Francis R.T. Nicholls took over as governor. The troops were withdrawn. Nicholls and his supporters had promised to treat the blacks fairly and equally: even if made in good faith, this promise was soon ignored. But "peace" prevailed, and the last formal remnant of Civil War occupation in the South was gone.

While John Harlan took a leading role in the activities of the Louisiana Commission, credit for the settlement, as well as blame, went to President Hayes. What Harlan acquired was largely intangible: the gratitude of the president for his willingness to undertake a task that many others had refused and the political support gained from his new friends who made up the commission. Wayne MacVeagh, particularly, became a lifelong friend and was of use to Harlan during the coming struggle in the Senate over his appointment to the Supreme Court. Secretary of State William M. Evarts, who acted as Hayes's agent in contacts with the commission, also became a strong Harlan supporter.

Meanwhile, Bristow was somehow becoming more and more disenchanted with his law partner, a process aided and abetted by Henry Van Ness Boynton. The details of what transpired will probably never be known. Bristow never wrote his own version; Boynton wrote too much and too partially (he became an open foe of Harlan); and Harlan gave an explanation that is probably true to the facts but may be self-serving in their interpretation. Not the least mysterious event in this series was Bristow's explicit refusal to be considered for Justice Davis's position. When William Dennison, at the request of Hayes, telegraphed Bristow asking whether he was interested in the position, Bristow replied in the negative, adding that the South "should be represented." Being familiar with "the ability and worth of General Harlan," he urged that Harlan be considered "earnestly" for the seat. In a letter the same day, Bristow explained that his financial status deterred him from further public service: "It is hard enough at best," he said, "for one who has been been for a brief period in public life and in politics to recover what he has lost in professional business." [31]

There is, nevertheless, little doubt that Ben wanted the appointment. Why did he respond negatively? Possibly, ever reluctant to seem to be seeking a place, he wanted and expected the president to approach him personally and persuade him. Like the maiden who refuses a proposal of marriage hoping it will be repeated even more forcefully, he had put himself in a dilemma, for what could he do if the invitation was not repeated? Boynton pointed this out to Bristow, warning him that Hayes was likely to conclude not only that Ben did not want that position but also that there "was nothing else near good enough" for him either.[32] In this Boynton proved to be correct. No more feelers went out to Bristow. It is quite possible that the former Treasury secretary would never have been appointed anyway, but Hayes probably concluded that, in any case, there was no use considering someone who would only refuse the position if it were offered.

Apparently Harlan knew about this exchange of letters, for the journalist Richard Smith told Boynton that Harlan told him that Bristow "would not take Davis' place if it were offered."[33] Boynton was working on an opposite assumption: apparently Ben had telegraphed him that he had not actually refused to consider the post, and Boynton took this to mean that Harlan was either exaggerating or lying. Boynton's letters from this point on show a drastic change in attitude toward Harlan, who is depicted as a schemer in his own behalf trying to undercut Bristow. In fact, each of the partners was apparently trying, at this point, to avoid interfering with the other's chances without at the same time destroying his own.

Boynton also showed a measure of cynicism about Bristow's possible appointment. Still desiring his friend to run for the presidency, he suggested that Bristow accept the Supreme Court vacancy; he "could stay on the Bench two years, & then find reasons . . . for resignation" in order to be in position to make another run at the nomination. Bristow's reaction to this idea is not known.[34]

The real trouble between the two Kentuckians came about, apparently, at the time Harlan was traveling from Washington through Louisville on his way to New Orleans. He was picking up his oldest son, Richard, then eighteen, who was going along as an observer of the commission's work. Bristow met Harlan at the station, and the two had a hurried conversation. The only authority for this story is Richard Smith as filtered through Boynton. Smith told Boynton that President Hayes had sent Bristow a message "by Harlan to the effect that you [Bristow] were to be consulted about Kentucky Matters."[35] Although this message seems to have meant merely that Hayes would take Bristow's advice about giving federal jobs to those Kentucky Republicans who had been discharged by Grant, Boynton took it to mean something more; or at least he assumed that Hayes must have said something more, perhaps about the Supreme Court, and that Harlan was "double playing, or double dealing."[36] In the rush of the moment Harlan apparently forgot to deliver the message. At Bristow's inquiry, Harlan wrote from New Orleans that, indeed, Hayes had sent such a message.[37] Boynton asked rhetorically, "Do you think it would have been possible for Murray, or Wharton, or Bluford Wilson, or his brother, or Campbell, or myself to have passed through Louisville with any kind of message from the President, & have forgotten to deliver it?"[38] Assuming that Bristow really did want the Supreme Court appointment, it becomes clear that Boynton could successfully rouse his suspicions of Harlan's motives.

Harlan's own reactions—penned in diary form for only one day, August 21, 1877—were naturally quite different from those of Bristow and Boynton. John did not know of Morton's opposition to the original idea of making him attorney general; he consequently believed that his failure to receive the position, which was really his principal immediate ambition, was due to Bristow's failure to support him. Although Bristow "had frequently said to me . . . that he did not desire to go upon the Bench," Harlan wrote, he had also seen a news item written by Boynton that pointed out that if Harlan were not made attorney general, Bristow would probably be offered the Supreme Court seat. John's deduction, naturally, was that his partner was sacrificing him to his own unacknowledged desire for a Supreme Court appointment. An alternative explanation would be, Harlan felt, that Ben "expected Hayes to do the foolish thing of calling him back to the Treasury."[39]

Harlan's suspicions lessened temporarily when, in response to urgings from mutual friends—Eli Murray, Gabriel Wharton, and Gus Willson—Bristow sent his message to Dennison disclaiming any Supreme Court ambitions and suggesting Harlan for the Davis vacancy. Harlan says he attempted to stop this message from being sent, but it was too late. By this time both men knew that they would not receive cabinet posts, and each was evidently interested in the Supreme Court. But each was also attempting not to stand in the other's way. Naturally their attempts to push each other were halfhearted.

Harlan, for his part, telegraphed Dennison, urging him not to relax his efforts to secure the appointment for Bristow. By this time, however, Hayes was having second thoughts about Bristow's candidacy, although Harlan did not know this. One objection was that Kentucky was in the same judicial circuit as Ohio, and there were already two justices on the Court from that circuit, Chief Justice Morrison R. Waite and Justice Noah H. Swayne (of course, the same argument was later urged against Harlan). Probably more important, however, were Hayes's suspicions that Ben would only use the Court as a springboard for his presidential ambitions. The fact that Boynton was openly pushing for another Bristow candidacy for the White House certainly did not help, nor did the opposition of the machine Republicans, such as Blaine.

Harlan concluded his diary entry with a stinging assessment of Bristow's conduct in the whole affair:

From that day to this he has never alluded to the matter of the Supreme Bench. So far from suggesting any method to aid me, his immediate friends have been, with his knowledge & approval, been pressing his name upon the President— And no one now doubts that he has, from the outset, been anxious to be Davis' successor—& I do not now doubt that his telegram to Dennison was wanting in candor & frankness. Nor do I now doubt that his failure to press my name for Attorney General was because my appointment to that office would endanger his chances for the Bench. He was unwilling to make any sacrifices for one whom he had professed to regard as his most intimate confidential valued friend. He had shared nearly all the honors which had been awarded to Kentucky under Republican Administration. I had shared none—I had remained at home, building up the party in the State, and making sacrifices for that purpose whenever any had been made. He had made none. I had canvassed the State a second time for Governor solely that I might, thereby, strengthen him before the country. When the time came to me to secure what my ambition coveted, he by his actions said, stand back until I am satisfied with additional official station, and then you may come forward—not before. Thus has an exhibition of selfishness snapped the cords of a friendship which, on my part, was as pure and unselfish as any man ever felt for another. I mean only that our confidential relations have ceased, probably never to be renewed.[40]

The truth about this tangled episode will never be fully known. There was, undoubtedly, partial justice on both sides. Boynton was thoroughly convinced that Harlan was angry about his failure to secure the attorney generalship and that he knifed Bristow in the back because of this and then actively worked for the Supreme Court appointment himself.[41] Bristow's biographer, Ross A. Webb, takes the same view.[42] Despite denials by Boynton, there is little doubt that the newspaperman worked undercover to prevent Harlan's appointment, by spreading stories about bribery connected with the Louisiana affair, doubts about Harlan's true Republicanism (based mostly upon his earlier opposition to the Reconstruction Amendments), and tales of his "treachery" to Bristow. Webb does not go so far but nevertheless feels that Harlan's ambitions hampered any chances Bristow may have had.

In fact, opposition to giving Bristow any high positon was widespread. Opponents ranged from his natural political rivals such as Morton and Blaine to others who were friendly to him but nevertheless feared his political ambitions. Justice Samuel F. Miller was one of these, as was, apparently, Chief Justice Waite.[43] Wayne MacVeagh wrote Harlan that he felt Bristow's "career should be political rather than judicial."[44] This opposition was strong enough to influence Hayes regardless of what Harlan might have done.

What Harlan actually did is largely unknown. There is no evidence that he actively opposed Bristow. Up until May, indeed, he supported him. Gus Willson, who as clerk and partner was very close to both men, maintained that the break was basically the result of the Court appointment, "which was Bristow's life long ambition."[45] But Bristow never seemed to want anyone else to think he had any political ambitions, and even his friends could not be much blamed for eventually believing his frequent denials. Harlan, at least, did so; he wrote that Bristow had "frequently said to me . . . that he did not desire to go upon the Bench. Upon one occasion . . . I had suggested that he ought to accept the place upon the Bench if tendered him. But he responded with some warmth, with the suggestion that that would shelve him & that he could not afford it."[46] Regarding his failure to apprise Bristow of the Hayes "message" in April, there is no reason to doubt Harlan's own version. First, he did in fact tell Bristow of it by letter as soon as he reached New Orleans.[47] Second, he regarded the president's remarks as more or less casual conversation, not as a specific "message" to Bristow: "I did not so understand him at the time yet I do not doubt that he expected you to know what he had said to me. Hence I determined to tell you of it as soon as I saw you. My memory is greatly at fault if I did not on the platform at the R.R. repeat substantially what my letter [of April 9] contains. Our conversation was however a very hurried one, and I am not surprised that you failed to gather what I supposed I was communicating."[48] In fact, Boynton made a mountain out of a very minor incident and evidently persuaded Bristow of its importance.

Nevertheless, there is no doubt that Harlan wanted political advancement, first to the attorney general post and later in the Court appointment. Nor is there any reason why he should have permanently stood aside while Bristow waited to be wooed by the president, especially since all the signals seemed to indicate that Bristow would refuse any position that would place him disadvantageously for another run for the presidency in 1880. Few men of normal political aspirations would have done so, and whatever his virtues, Harlan was very much a man of ambition and pride. Seeing himself as fully the equal of Bristow, he felt that there was no reason not to reach for the prize when it was obviously within his grasp.

Finally, we know by hindsight that Hayes decided against Bristow before he decided for Harlan. The president took eight months mulling over the situation caused by the resignation of David Davis. It was early May, though, when Hayes, in conversation with Justice Miller, remarked that he feared the political ambitions of the former Treasury secretary. Miller recorded his own agreement, for he had been on the Court with two men—Chief Justice Salmon P. Chase and Justice Davis—who had similar aspirations, and he knew that political goals only caused trouble for the Court.[49] Also, Hayes early recorded in his diary his determination not to appoint anyone who had been in Grant's cabinet or who had presidential hopes, and of course Bristow was disqualified on both counts.[50] It is thus obvious that even John Harlan's refusal to be considered, would not have helped Bristow. It would have been that rarest of political events, a completely futile bit of excessive loyalty.

The president's indecision is, finally, indicated by the fact that when Harlan visited the White House in July—he was one of a committee sent to invite the president and his cabinet to attend the Louisville Industrial Exposition to be held in September—a confidant of Hayes, Edward F. Noyes, asked Harlan, in the president's name, whether he would accept the ambassadorship to England. This inquiry was repeated the next day by Hayes himself. Harlan replied, as he reported later, "I do not see how a man of my limited fortune & large family could afford to live abroad in official position, and abandon his profession for four years. To be entirely frank, Mr. President, I have never cared for any public position which was not in the line of my profession."[51] While it is clear, thus, that as late as July Hayes had not decided on Harlan to fill the Davis seat, Harlan's reply also implies that he might accept nothing less.

While in the East, John took the occasion to go up to Philadelphia, where, as he put it, he "saw" Wayne MacVeagh and Simon Cameron (the Pennsylvania Republican leader). Boynton, who was by this time seeing conspiracies against Bristow everywhere, inferred that Harlan talked to these men "about his candidacy."[52] But there is no independent evidence that this is true. MacVeagh, indeed, did write Hayes a month or so later recommending Harlan; however, he had already pledged his support (not for any specific position) much earlier.[53]

9

Political Reward
1877

Associate Justice David Davis, "Lincoln's Manager," was elected to the Senate by the Illinois legislature on January 25, 1877, and resigned his seat on the Court effective March 4. Thus Rutherford B. Hayes knew, even before his own election was certain, that a Supreme Court vacancy would need filling. Speculation about the appointment naturally began immediately, but the possibilities, in January and February, were wide open, since there was still a good chance that the new president would be a Democrat. It remains mysterious, however, why Hayes took so long to make his appointment, when one might have expected that the seat would have been filled almost as soon as the cabinet appointments were made.

Two considerations rendered his decision less urgent than it might otherwise have been. First, Congress adjourned shortly after getting itself organized and approving the cabinet appointments in March. Thus any appointment to the Court made before Congress reconvened would have to be a recess appointment, and under the circumstances of Hayes's relations with the Republican stalwarts, such an appointment would likely have caused him nothing but embarrassment: there was a real possibility that a justice who had already taken his seat might eventually be disapproved by a fractious Senate. While Hayes intended to call a special session to deal with the army appropriation, which Congress had failed to enact, it was found possible (and politically desirable) to delay this until October 15.[1] As a consequence, the Supreme Court nomination could not go before the Senate until that date. Scond, the Court was itself nearing the end of its October 1876 session; Justice Davis's resignation did not take effect until March 4, 1877. Any new justice would thus barely have assumed his seat, even assuming prompt Senate action, before the Court adjourned for the summer.

Between these two circumstances, the president found himself with the leisure necessary to take his time about what was likely to be a contentious nomination. There were good reasons, in fact, not to announce the name of Davis's successor until Congress could act on it, rather than letting debate drag on through the summer and fall. There is, however, no reason to suppose that the president actually made up his mind about the appointment until shortly before the special session convened on October 15.

Harlan, along with several other possibilities, was in the mind of the president by early March. In fact, Hayes probably thought of Harlan as soon as he determined that he would not make the Kentuckian attorney general. Justice Samuel F. Miller, who kept up with this affair, partly because of his interest in pushing his own brother-in-law, William Pitt Ballinger of Texas, wrote Ballinger in mid-March assessing the qualifications the president had in mind for the post:

> Caldwell and Wood [sic] have been pressed on his consideration by more men of influence than any other nominees. Judge Bruce of Alabama who is a graduate of my law office had an interview three days ago with the President as I suppose to favor Wood; but of that I am not sure. He told me however, that the President was hesitating between Harlan of Kentucky or possibly Bristow their interest being one, and a *real* Southern man, and in this latter sense he did not consider Wood or Caldwell to meet the requirements. Now the difficulty of selecting a real Southern man is that all the men who before the Rebellion had made high reputation as lawyers are either dead or too old for the place.[2]

Miller could have added that most prominent Southern lawyers were still tainted by their association with the Confederacy, and they were also not Republicans.

Even at this early date, Miller had identified the most prominent contenders. Henry Clay Caldwell of Arkansas and William B. Woods of Alabama were both federal judges. They were not "real" Southerners, being carpetbaggers: Woods was from Ohio and had been a Union army officer; Caldwell hailed from Iowa and was also a Union veteran.[3] Woods was apparently very well liked in his circuit (or else he orchestrated a campaign), for Hayes's good friend James A. Garfield wrote that he "felt that he had never seen as many sincere recommendations as those which supported Woods."[4] Hayes was sufficiently impressed to appoint him to the next Supreme Court vacancy, in 1880.

Woods and Caldwell had, nevertheless, at least two advantages over Harlan or Bristow: they came from judicial circuits that were then unrepresented on the Court. On the other hand, Kentucky was in the same circuit as Ohio, which already had two justices, Chief Justice Waite and Justice Swayne. The chief justice told Miller that it would be a mistake to appoint anyone from Kentucky. In Miller's words, "It would be very unpolitic to fill the place from a circuit which now has two members of the court, and . . . this would give Davis' circuit just ground of complaint."[5] Miller had by May talked personally to the president (Waite apparently never did) and presumably had passed this word on; but the president was by then fully aware of the politics of the situation. He was being importuned by Illinois lawyers and political leaders to nominate Judge Thomas Drummond of that state to fill what they seemed to regard as the "Illinois seat."[6] Illinoisans, David Davis himself included, were not so much against Harlan as they were opposed to another appointment from the sixth circuit.

On the same occasion, Hayes asked Justice Miller for his own opinions. Miller, while pressing the candidacy of Ballinger, nevertheless told the president that both Harlan and Bristow "were fully up to the standard required both by native ability and professional attainments" and that of the two "Harlan was probably a man of the most vigorous intellect, while Bristow was believed to be if any different of the soundest judgment."[7] The two agreed, however, that Bristow's presidential hopes stood in the way of his appointment.

Harlan had other liabilities, which may have given Hayes pause. He had come late to Republicanism and had originally opposed the Recon-struction Amendments: Republican stalwarts thus distrusted him. They were not encouraged by his service on the Louisiana Commission even though that body's work merely gave the president a pretext for doing what he wished to do anyway. There were, moreover, rumors of corruption and even possible bribery related to the Louisiana episode that were to haunt John during the struggle in the Senate over his confirmation. Finally, the stalwarts would never forgive Ben Bristow or the other Republican re-formers who had prevented their man Blaine from being nominated in 1876. Harlan was rightly seen as a member of the reform wing of the party, and any job given him by the administration would be regarded as a reward to Bristow.[8]

If he had weaknesses, though, Harlan also had major strengths. He was the man known to be closest to Bristow, so that if the former Treasury secretary's appointment was seen to be impolitic, Bristowites like Boynton might be expected to regard Harlan as the best available alternative. In general, Hayes needed to maintain his own reputation as a reformer who was willing and able to battle the stalwarts and beat them. The choice of Harlan would do this. The Kentuckian was, in addition, enough of a Southerner to propitiate Southern Republicans and appease Southern Democrats, thus carrying out an earlier version of Nixon's "Southern Strategy."

Most of all, Hayes owed a good deal to John Harlan, much more than he owed to Bristow himself. Bristow had, after all, been a competitor for the presidential nomination and was always seen by Hayes people as a poten-tial thorn in the president's side whenever Hayes might do, or not do, something about which the reformers might have strong opinions. Harlan, on the other hand, had swung the Kentucky delegation to Hayes at a critical moment in the convention. In addition, he had incurred substantial politi-cal risk by agreeing to serve on the Louisiana Commission. Finally, there is no doubt that Hayes knew of Harlan's hopes to be attorney general, and felt

that there was a danger that Kentuckians might turn against him if something else were not offered to either Harlan or Bristow.

Even so, there is some evidence that Hayes would have preferred to
appoint Woods, who had none of Harlan's political liabilities. His offer of
the post of ambassador to the Court of St. James's is probably best viewed
as an attempt to satisfy Harlan without putting him on the Supreme Court.
John's refusal of that offer quite possibly made the Court appointment
almost inevitable.

By August, although Justice Miller continued to press for Ballinger,
Hayes had a fairly clear choice between Woods and Harlan. At this juncture
John's friend from his Louisiana Commission days, Wayne MacVeagh,
wrote to the president,

> I cannot resist the conclusion that you are wrong in the tendency you first
> expressed to fill [the vacancy] from one of the extreme Southern states.
>
> I certainly need not protest that I am absolutely free from any prejudices
> against that section of our common country, . . . but . . . I cannot divest myself
> of the conviction that if a lawyer of unquestioned ability, a statesman of com-
> prehensive views and a thoroughly sound Republican can be found living in
> the more Northern States of the South, it is safer to offer him the position.
>
> I believe General Harlan of Kentucky meets all these requirements and that
> you could not possibly do a wiser and better thing for the country as well as for
> your Administration than offer him the existing vacancy.
>
> . . . I therefore earnestly hope that you will see your way clear to offer the
> present vacancy to General Harlan and to await another opportunity before
> going further South.[9]

Whether or not MacVeagh's words influenced the president, he did exactly
what they suggested.

While all this was going on, John Harlan was concentrating on his law
practice, with time out as usual to try to obtain or retain federal jobs for his
friends or political supporters. His oldest son, Richard, was to start at
Princeton in the fall, and money was as usual a problem. In addition, there
is some evidence that John was actively involved in his own candidacy for
the Court vacancy. By July it was practically certain that President Hayes
was not going to offer the position to Bristow; this left Harlan free to pursue
the position as actively as he wished. He did not want to do anything overt,
but he perhaps worked behind the scenes to stimulate support. This was
nothing more than many others had done and were doing. Caldwell, in
particular, had "campaigned" for the Supreme Court once before and was
doing so again, although this time without the support of Justice Miller,
who was committed to his brother-in-law.

How active Harlan really was cannot be judged with any certainty.
Boynton, as we have seen, accused him of politicking for the position in
Philadelphia with MacVeagh and Cameron as early as July. In September

and October dozens of letters arrived at the White House urging his nomination. Most, but not all, of these came from Kentucky lawyers or other prominent Kentuckians. These could very well have been written without any urging from Harlan himself: some may have been spontaneous, although it is more likely that a few of his close associates, such as Gus Willson, orchestrated a letter-writing campaign. Another evidence of his personal interest appears in a letter from Charles W. Fairbanks to someone close to the White House.

> I have just had an interview with Judges Gresham and [John D.] Howland—the former you know and the latter is Master in Chancery of the U.S. Court [in Indianapolis].
>
> During the interview the subject of Judge Drummond's case came up. I learned that John M. Harlan was, and is, moving earnestly for appointment to the Supreme Bench. He has been here a number of times of late, and I am advised a petition has been started in his favor—though it is not signed to any considerable extent. The petition is not openly circulated as Judge D[rummond]'s was—and such as sign it (if any have) do it with the understanding that H. should be appointed if Judge D. is not. This is as Judge G. thinks.
>
> I understand Judge David Davis is very pronounced against the President's going South for an appointee, and from what Judge G. intimated Judge D[avis] will be very much disappointed if Judge Drummond is not appointed. And he expressed himself to Gresham recently as being most decidedly opposed to Harlan. I was surprised to learn of his strong disinclination towards the selection of a Southern man.
>
> I write this upon request of the Judges whom I have mentioned. They in common with a great many regard it as advisable to appoint a Judge to the Supreme Bench from the Circuit and think no one is entitled to the place above Judge D[rummond].[10]

David Davis was not, in fact, as much opposed to Harlan as he was in favor of Drummond. He seems to have had friendly though not intimate relations with Harlan and was close to Bristow as well. Certainly he supported the nomination when it came before the Senate.

Whatever Harlan himself was doing, other candidates were doing also. Then too, many who were not in the race themselves had candidates to promote. Thus, quite a few non-Kentuckians were called upon to comment on Harlan's ability and political availability. The president asked his political intimate William Henry Smith (then director of the western Associated Press in Chicago) for his frank opinions: "Confidentially and on the whole is not Harlan the man? Of the right age—able—of whole character—industrious—fine manner, temper and appearance."[11]

Early in October, Smith's reply was not wholly favorable.

> Is Harlan the man? I think so. His age, vigor—mental and physical—his agreeable manners and personal magnetism are strongly for him. I think him a

very much better man in every way than Bristow, and if a Southern man is to be taken, he is the man. The appointment will offend a good many people of both parties of this section, who believe the selection should be made from this state [Illinois]. They will complain at first but in time, if the Administration continues in well doing, they will forget about it or overlook it. This remark applies *to the people,* not to a *few* politicians who sympathize with Conkling and swear you have destroyed the party in breaking the machine. I hope, however, the appointment of a judge will not be made at a date earlier than November. The more time you get, the surer of victory.[12]

Although still favorable to Harlan, Smith was less hopeful a few days later about the political reaction that might be expected in the Middle West.

I am troubled about that Supreme Court business. The offense to the people of this District, if an appointment is made out of it, is going to strike deeper than I at first thought. This District is second to none in importance. It will be more important in the future. To appoint Harlan will be to give the Ohio Dist. three members, & deprive this strongly Republican one of any. Then the appointment of Harlan would be less acceptable here than a man from the Gulf States. That is now clear. In view of these facts & the *near approach of the Wisconsin Election* I hope you will postpone the appointment until the regular Session. Hence I telegraphed through Webb today. Give the lawyers of this dist. a fair & full hearing.[13]

MacVeagh, too, was at work. He wrote to another Louisiana Commission colleague, Charles B. Lawrence of Chicago (and presumably to others), soliciting support for Harlan. Lawrence thereupon wrote the president that if a Southern man were to be appointed, "no lawyer could be named from the South who would be more acceptable to the bar of this Circuit than Gen. Harlan and there can be no question of his eminent fitness for the place."[14]

Miller, in a letter to Ballinger just a week before Hayes's decision was made public, seemed resigned to Harlan's appointment, although since he was writing to another aspirant he could not openly give up hope. "I do not see how the President can appoint Harlan, though I think he wishes to do so. If not Harlan then there is much hope for you. His action thus far in making appointments shows the strong perhaps too strong influence of his personal wishes. Next to Harlan I think his wishes are in your favor."[15]

Whether one calls his reasons independence or stubbornness, Hayes disregarded the advice of both Smith and Miller, and on October 16, 1877, he had finally made up his mind, submitting the name of John Marshall Harlan.

In the American system, nomination by the president is far from tantamount to final appointment. The Senate has the power to "advise and consent," and that body is extremely jealous of the power and fairly often uses it to delay if not to block appointment. This is especially true when the president is weak, when his party has a minority in the Senate, or when there is strong feeling against the president within his own party. Although Hayes appears stronger to present-day historians than he often did in his own time, he will never be ranked among our strong presidents. Even a strong man, though, would have had difficulty with the Republican stalwarts. To them the only good president was one who was under their thumb. It is true that Harlan's association with Bristow would have led, in any case, to some opposition in the Senate, but it is certain that much of the opposition and its strength were due to stalwart anger at the president's temerity in daring to nominate anyone not approved by them.

This situation delayed Harlan's confirmation for six weeks. In hindsight, it appears that the stalwarts did not have real hopes of defeating him, but of course Harlan did not know this, and these were anxious weeks for the Kentuckian and his growing family.

The reasons for opposition were varied, and much depended upon who the objector was. Some of the opposition, but not the most serious or intractable, came from the seventh circuit, which would lose a seat. This was certainly true of Senator Davis, who felt that "his" seat belonged to his circuit. He was, however, as Justice Miller reported, "personally friendly to Harlan," and he ended up voting for his confirmation. Senator Timothy O. Howe, a Democrat of Wisconsin, had dual reasons for opposing the confirmation: not only was Harlan from a different circuit, but Howe also had personal ambitions for the seat.[16] Melville W. Fuller, a prominent Chicago attorney and Democratic leader, opposed the appointment almost solely on circuit grounds. Writing to Hannibal Hamlin, Fuller said that he found it "a disagreeable surprise" and went on to say that it "accomplished nothing except to reward a Louisiana Commissioner, a personal and secondary consideration. I hope the nomination will fail of confirmation."[17] It is fortunate that Harlan did not know of this letter, for in the 1880s he was to send his son James to study in Fuller's office; they had become friends while Harlan was "on circuit." Fuller went on to become chief justice in 1888, and the men and their families developed an intimate association that lasted many years.

The most serious attacks, however, came from the eastern Republican stalwarts, joined by such midwesterners as Senator Zach Chandler of Michigan. To a large extent these men were merely trying to deal Hayes a defeat: Harlan was incidental, and anyone else appointed would have had to run the same gauntlet. Even here there were variations in motive, however. The chairman of the Senate Judiciary Committee, George F. Edmunds of Vermont, was a man of rocklike integrity and stubbornness.[18] He distrusted Harlan's Republicanism and, apparently, opposed him for no other reason. He set about to collect whatever information he could that was critical, writing to acquaintances in Kentucky such as Lincoln's attorney general, James Speed. Speed was forced to acknowledge Harlan's sins—his opposition to the Civil War amendments and the Civil Rights Bill, his support of McClellan for president in 1864, and his relatively recent conversion to Republicanism. But he concluded with a strong endorsement of his old friend:

> It is due to Gen'l Harlan to say that eight or ten years ago, he sloughed his old pro-slavery skin and has since been an earnest open and able advocate of what he had thought wrong or inexpedient. This I know from intimate inter-course with him since his removal to Louisville.
>
> From the beginning of our civil troubles till General Harlan became anti-slavery the idea that had led his course was the integrity of the country. For that he was ready to sacrifice everything.[19]

If Edmunds assumed prominence due to his titular position as chairman of the Judiciary Committee, however, his opposition was more or less rational and not self-interested. This was not as true of the real focus of Harlan's opposition, Senator Roscoe Conkling.[20] The New York machine leader and old-time spoilsman, together with Blaine, as Justice Miller hyperbolically said, "would prefer to take the chances of what would come from a democratic administration after the next election, to yielding any of their ancient rights of controlling public patronage and submit to Evarts, Shurz & Co. They profess to dislike the policy. They really want the offices."[21]

Regardless of the reasons for the trouble, it was serious enough to worry Harlan and his supporters. Various advocates went or were sent to Washington to help: his young partner, Gus Willson, spent the entire six weeks there. Willson later claimed that he had been of use "during the several months Senator Edmunds held up the nomination," apparently partly in countering the hostile moves of Henry Van Ness Boynton.[22] Eli Murray also went to Washington at John's request. As Harlan explained to President Hayes,

> I have information from Washington which leads me to believe that there is a purpose with some to postpone all consideration of my nomination until the regular session in December. Underlying this purpose is the desire to defeat my nomination not because my Republicanism is doubted but because I was a member of the Louisiana Commission. In order to cover this plan the air is being filled with charges against me, some of which cast doubt upon my fidelity to the Republican party, and some imputing to the Commission improper practices at New Orleans.
>
> I have requested my trusted friend Gen. Murray to proceed to Washington that he may, if it shall seem necessary, take such steps as he may deem proper for the protection of my good name against those who would assail it.[23]

The Kentucky Democrats supported Harlan almost to a man. This was especially true of Senator James B. Beck, who, as Harlan reminded him, had participated in Preston H. Leslie's campaign for the governorship against Harlan in 1871.[24] House Democrats like John G. Carlisle also helped in lending influence, although of course they had no vote. John's old friend Tom Crittenden, now a Democratic congressman from Missouri, also lent support, providing both advice and help. Remarking that he had just talked with Senator Daniel W. Voorhees, Crittenden admitted that "there is a fight against you," but he went on, "You can't be beat. Keep quiet and be easy. I have reason to believe you will get out of the Committee all right." A few days later the Missourian reported having talked to the new senator from Ohio, Stanley Matthews. Since Matthews was a strong Hayes man, there was no doubt how his vote would go. Voorhees thought that Senator Samuel B. Maxey would support Harlan as well. Tom Crittenden also told his brother in Kentucky to "tell Harlan to keep quiet," judging that he would be appointed unless he did "some more unworthy thing in a few days than he has ever done before."[25] John defended himself as best he could, not in person, since he was not called to testify, but by letter. Beck presumably made the best use possible of the letter Harlan supplied him late in October, in which the nominee summarized his political record, claiming convincingly that he was really a Republican and had fundamentally changed his opinions from the time when he supported McClellan and opposed the Civil War amendments. As he pointed out, there was really no organized Republican party in Kentucky until after 1867, and he had been the most prominent leader of the party since that time.[26]

Harlan also defended his record as a member of the Louisiana Commission. Stalwarts had, of course, opposed the commission itself and Hayes's use of its report to justify the withdrawal of troops from the beleaguered state; but there were also charges, apparently stimulated in part by Boynton, that the commissioners had offered bribes or were at least aware of the use of bribery in persuading Republican legislators to desert to the other side. While Harlan utterly denied that he or any other commissioners had offered bribes, he remained silent about the rest of the charge. The charge was itself minor even if true—Boynton wrote no more to Bristow than that "Harlan knew that forty thousand dollars was raised by the Nicholls men to set the Nicholls government on its feet"—and Harlan undoubtedly did not wish to dignify it by replying.[27]

Harlan defended his resignation from the army in 1863 against the implication that it occurred because of his opposition to Lincoln's Emancipation Proclamation. The only possible defense was his own words written at the time; while they were probably true, he had no further way to prove it. Of course there was no way that John could counter the opposition based on geographical location of circuits, but that was not in itself very serious anyway.

Finally, critics launched the usual attacks made against judicial appointees: he is not a good lawyer, has no judicial experience, and lacks a "judicial temperament." Thus one writer who had lived in Kentucky from 1865 to 1867 wrote to Iowa senator S.J. Kirkwood: "Harlan . . . is not a jurist and never was accredited with being. Is not in full sympathy with the Republican party and never was. Never had any influence in his own state that amounted to anything. . . . He is in fact a milk and water politician[,] a political demogogue who all his life has been after office, but his fitness as a judge never entered the minds of his Kentucky friends."[28] Another critic said much the same: "Harlan is deficient in legal and professional education, such as ought to be had by any one of the Supreme Bench. As for general scholarship or literary attainments, he has *none*. I defy any one to prove from any oral, or written or printed utterance, he ever made that a literature, ancient or modern, ever existed."[29]

Harlan had much active support, as well. His old prewar partner William F. Bullock, although now a Democrat, contradicted the above assessments of John's legal abilities, calling him "justly distinguished for his high legal attainments, his active and discriminating mind, his studious habits, and his high sense of Justice and honor."[30] The judges of the Kentucky Court of Appeals, mostly Democrats, wrote that Harlan's personal character was "above reproach" and that "he is an able, enlightened and learned lawyer, and one of the most laborious and painstaking members of his profession."[31] Lewis N. Dembitz, Louis D. Brandeis's father-in-law, agreed. Harlan, he said, was one of the two leaders of the Kentucky bar. "He has a fine judicial temper—he shows it by the fairness and moderation of his course as an advocate."[32] An Indiana lawyer, doubtless swallowing his disappointment that his circuit would lose its representation on the Court, told the president that Harlan's selection "would give more general and uniform satisfaction to the Republicans of our State than that of any other man in the South."[33]

The remarks in such letters are doubtless overblown, yet just as certainly they contain an element of sincerity. John Harlan had a gift for friendship, a gift for advocacy, and he lived in a small, tightly knit legal community in which no one's defects could be easily hidden. Over a long period in politics he had inevitably made enemies, as well. What seems remarkable, though, is that so many of his political opponents seem to have respected him as a man, as a lawyer, and as a politician.

Over a six-week period the opposition gradually dwindled. By November 19 Senator Beck was able to assure the impatient Harlan "that you are to be reported favorably & I [do not] doubt soon will be confirmed."[34] On November 26 Indiana Democratic senator Joseph E. McDonald announced that Harlan had been favorably reported, apparently without a recorded committee vote. A motion was placed before the Senate, in executive session, on November 29 that Harlan's nomination be confirmed, along with sixteen other Hayes nominations.[35] Conkling, still fighting the stalwart battle against Hayes, moved that the resolution of confirmation be reconsidered, but this motion happily failed. The final confirmation was apparently by voice vote and included all seventeen appointees; it probably occurred on Monday, December 3.[36] The previous Friday Beck triumphantly wrote Harlan that his appointment was finally assured: "Voorhees and I were greatly delighted and went off half cocked. Maxey says [to] say 'unanimously' because I want him to know I was for him, & I was in a humor to oblige everybody. . . . The motion to reconsider, if it does not prevail falls & the confirmation stands & on Monday after 12 P.M. the President will be advised & send the Comm[ission]. . . . It is all right you can't be beaten. I have seen both sides. . . . I think I can get *all* our side [the Democrats] to stand by you."[37]

Many years later Mallie Harlan recollected the day; she apparently got her dates mixed, but there is no reason to doubt the essential accuracy of her tale.

After lunch—as he was, naturally, somewhat restless because of the way in which his nomination was hanging fire in the Senate—his three boys urged him to join them in an impromptu game of foot-ball which took place upon a common in the outskirts of the city. With great glee they afterwards described the way in which their father had played "full-back" on their side, and how everyone had "stood from under" when he advanced, with great deliberation and dignity, to kick away the ball whenever it threatened their goal.

When my *four* "boys" (for my husband was always a boy along with his three sons) returned, late that afternoon, to our Broadway home—tired and happy and hungry for their Thanksgiving Dinner—a telegram was waiting for him, informing him that on that very morning "the Senate had unanimously confirmed his nomination as an Associate Justice of the Supreme Court of the United States."[38]

Part II

JUDICIAL CAREER

10

Associate Justice
1877-1887

On December 10, 1877, at the age of forty-four, John Marshall Harlan was installed as Associate Justice of the Supreme Court. The ceremonies were social as well as legal events in those days. Harlan's induction was attended not only by his own proud wife but also by many Washington dignitaries and friends, including Lucy Hayes.[1] Taking the oath of office, John must have thought of those great Americans who had preceded him on the Court, especially his namesake, the Great Chief Justice; equally, he must have looked back with both affection and nostalgia on the crowded years that had brought him so far. Taking the solemn oath of office was a sobering experience, reminding him that no justice had yet dishonored the Court. "I, John Marshall Harlan, do solemnly swear that I will administer justice without respect to persons, and do equal right to the poor and to the rich, and that I will faithfully and impartially discharge and perform all the duties incumbent on me as Associate Justice of the Supreme Court of the United States, according to the best of my abilities and understanding, agreeably to the Constitution and laws of the United States, so help me God."

John Harlan was not a modest man, but most people confronted by the oath and the known responsibilities of the office would probably undergo moments of self-doubt. In his letter to Hayes accepting the nomination, Harlan had referred to his "distrust" of his "ability to meet the requirements of a position so exalted."[2] Of course, few men have refused appointment because of such doubts, even if they are sincere.

The Harlans proceeded to Washington by train, stopping in Cincinnati to change trains and staying overnight with John's old friend John Finnell, who seems to have been as excited and proud as Harlan himself.[3] Once in the capital, wishing to relieve Mallie of the burdens of housekeeping and caring for the children for a while, the Harlans, she records, "took a suite of rooms at Mrs. Rines' boarding house on Twelfth Street—a well-ordered establishment that for years had been patronized by many well-known Senators and Congressmen with their families."[4]

Lucy Hayes, known as "Lemonade Lucy" because she would not allow liquor to be served in the White House, set the example for many other hostesses, and Washington was a soberer place than it had been in Grant's days. One visitor to the White House remarked waggishly that the "water flowed like champagne." As for the Harlans, John had long forgotten the days when he led a temperance organization in Frankfort, but no one could have called him a heavy drinker. He liked a glass of good Kentucky bourbon, however, and enjoyed giving gifts of it to those of his friends who were so unlucky as not to have their own sources.

In those days it was the custom for the Supreme Court wives to be "at home" on Monday afternoons to entertain callers. Mallie was aided on these occasions by her oldest daughter, Edith, who was twenty when the Harlans arrived in Washington. Mallie records that her own "at homes" began as early as two o'clock and that she "often had as many as two or three hundred visitors."[5] These events must have created a serious drain on the Harlan finances, which were shaky at best.

Washington was, in the 1870s, a city of perhaps 150,000 people whose almost exclusive concerns were government and politics. The year 1877 saw a depressed economy, but this did not affect the number and gaity of the political receptions or the social life indulged in by the women. Nor did it affect the Harlans' financial status: never affluent, John was now restricted to his salary as a judge, $10,000 annually until 1903, when it was raised to $12,500.[6] Social responsibilities must have eaten heavily into this restricted income, even though the cost of living was very low compared with today. John's lack of resources made housing a difficult problem, one which was not to be solved for a decade. Richard was at Princeton, to be followed there in short order by the other two boys; this did not help finances a bit.

Harlan's physical presence was in itself an addition to the Court. Finnell reported the opinion of one correspondent that "John Harlan with his studhoss clothes on is the best looking man on the bench."[7] Another said that Harlan looked like a "born judge."[8] Congressman James A. Garfield, the heir to Hayes's presidency, visited the Court just a few days after Harlan's induction; his opinion was that John had "a fine presence, a good head, and ought to make an excellent judge."[9]

Harlan's new colleagues greeted him in friendly fashion and he soon enjoyed good working relations with all of them. There had been nothing personal about the opposition to his appointment shown by Chief Justice Waite and Justice Miller, and Waite quickly became John's most intimate friend on the Court, one with whom he enjoyed an easy, informal social as well as business relationship. Asking for advice, for instance, in a difficult municipal bond case (the Court handled many of these), Harlan jokingly remarked, "You may come to the conclusion that my mind has become confused by reading the decisions of our court, or that I have seen Ben Butler on his Yacht & tasted some of his New England rum." He went on to comment about the summer activities of some of their colleagues: "The last

I heard from Bro Woods he was at Newark. Bros Matthews and Blatchford will, I fear, get such lofty ideas in the Mountains that there will be no holding them down to mother Earth when they return to Washington. Bro Bradley, I take it, is somewhere studying the philosophy of the Northern Lights, while Gray is, at this time, examining into the Precedents in British Columbia. Field, I suppose has his face towards the setting sun, wondering perhaps, whether the Munn case or the essential principles of right and justice will ultimately prevail."[10]

Morrison R. Waite had been appointed chief justice by Grant, in a surprise move, in 1874.[11] An Ohioan, he was close to the Hayes people. He and Harlan were to disagree frequently about case decisions, but they were kindred spirits. As chief justice he administered the Court's affairs capably but left little personal impress on its decisions. His more arrogant colleagues, Miller especially, had condescending attitudes toward him, although they liked him personally. Miller apparently felt that he, as the Court's intellectual leader, should be its actual leader; he wrote that he was trying to "get all the good out of our Chief and my brethren" that was possible, "but I can't make a silk purse out of a sow's ear. I can't make a great Chief Justice out of a small man."[12] Waite was, however, a prodigious worker who wrote more opinions, including most of the "dull" ones, than anyone else on his Court; a moderate on a moderate Court; and a man who in many ways typified his period. His biographer sums it up: "Engaging modesty, genuine kindness, unquestioned integrity, and willingness to work long and hard—in a word, Character of the highest sort."[13]

The senior associate justice, Nathan Clifford, was a Maine Democrat who had been appointed by James Buchanan in 1858. The son of a poor farmer, he made up for his lack of education by ambition and hard work. He was a large-stomached man with an appetite to match. An ardent fisherman, he sometimes sent samples of his catch to his colleagues; but in the conditions of the day, they usually were a little "off" by the time they were received. He had been attorney general under James K. Polk, and peace commissioner and later minister to Mexico. As a judge, he thought of judicial interpretation as a mechanical process and was generally found on the conservative side, supporting the narrow construction of the Fourteenth and Fifteenth amendments adopted by the Court's majority in the *Slaughterhouse* and succeeding cases. He wrote long and dreary opinions. He dissented frequently from the stands taken by the new Republican majority in the 1870s. By 1877 he was in poor health and was failing mentally as well, and he ended an undistinguished career on the Court in 1881.[14]

Noah H. Swayne, the second Ohioan on the Court, had been appointed by President Lincoln in 1862. When Harlan came on the bench, Swayne was seventy-three years old. He had been prominent in Ohio political and state government affairs for years before his ascension, and he actively worked for the appointment, as he worked later, unsuccessfully, to become chief justice. He has generally been relegated by historians to the ranks of mediocre justices, but perhaps his performance was a little better than that. His dissent in the *Slaughterhouse Cases*, especially, exhibited a broad and forward-looking approach to the Fourteenth Amendment. Yet by 1877 his mental powers were failing, and in fact he seems never to have grown into his exalted position. While he could be charming, the acidulous Miller wrote that Swayne concealed "an absence of any real sincerity and the presence of an ever watchful selfishness." When he finally retired early in 1881, the event was generally felt to be long overdue.[15]

One of the strong figures on the Waite Court was Samuel F Miller. Miller had been born in Kentucky and entered into the practice of medicine in Appalachia. He eventually turned to the law, and when he found that his abolitionism would never lead to legal or political success in Kentucky, he moved to Iowa, setting up his practice in the Mississippi River community of Keokuk. He entered Republican state politics and became very prominent, before his appointment to the Supreme Court by Lincoln in 1862. Not a scholar, Miller was yet the most powerful intellect on the Court. He used a moderate, strict constructionism tempered by a clear sense of purpose. A dominant personality who had scant respect for the opinions of others, Miller nevertheless became fairly close to Harlan, who had some of the same traits. Miller was, however, more influential, making his mark in majority opinions while Harlan did so in dissent.[16]

Stephen J. Field was a colorful Californian, appointed by Lincoln in 1863 to fill a tenth seat created especially as part of an attempt to cement California's Union ties. Combative and stubborn, Field found life on the frontier exciting and full of incident, since he made many enemies there. He was elected to the state supreme court and was by 1863 the logical choice for the new seat even though he was a Democrat. He became, during his long tenure, the one judge who was most willing to use the Fourteenth Amendment's due process clause creatively to protect America's burgeoning business enterprise rather than the freed slaves for whom it had been intended. Unlike Miller, he was never very close to Harlan: they were too much alike and disagreed too often. He left the Court in 1897 after some years of mental decline, having served longer than any justice up to his time.[17]

A Pennsylvanian, William Strong was appointed by President Grant in 1870 as part of a package (with Bradley) that, it was charged, was intended to reverse the Court's initial decision declaring the Civil War legal tender acts unconstitutional. There is no direct evidence to support the charge, even though Strong did later vote to uphold the acts. Strong became the Court's expert on patent law. He was a good judge but not outstanding and not particularly interested in constitutional issues. Since he resigned in 1880, still in good health (he would live until 1895), his term did not overlap

Harlan's enough for their lives to touch intimately either on or off the bench.[18]

The other "strong" judge on the Court, although not well known to posterity, was Joseph P. Bradley of New Jersey. A farm boy, he attended Rutgers and graduated convinced that "hard work, piety, and virtue could lead to unlimited success." In his case they did. He became an outstandingly successful railroad lawyer. He also became a prominent Republican and was appointed to the Supreme Court by Grant, with William Strong, in 1870. Like Strong, he voted to overrule the first legal tender decision. Bradley was not a very likable person; he was self-righteous and had a bad temper, and he apparently believed that moral rectitude was a sufficient guide to judicial decision-making. Predominantly conservative in view, he was nevertheless a fine lawyer. Leon Friedman sums him up well: "In terms of craftsmanship and the marshalling of legal principles in reasoned opinions to guide lawyers and through them society itself, few justices have surpassed Joseph P. Bradley."[19] He sat until 1892, and if he and Harlan were not close, they were at least friendly.

Ward Hunt was the junior justice until Harlan's arrival. A New Yorker, he had been appointed by Grant in 1872 after a career including the chief justiceship of the New York Court of Appeals. His tenure on the Supreme Court was "brief and unspectacular." He wrote few opinions, the most noteworthy being his dissent in *United States* v. *Reese* (1876), in which the Court majority invalidated sections of the Enforcement Act of 1870. Struck by a paralytic stroke in 1879, he was unable to sit after that and finally resigned in 1882. He and Harlan were on good terms and perhaps would have become intimate had Hunt's career lasted longer.[20]

John Harlan thus joined what was, on the whole, a strong court. Miller, Field, and Bradley rank among the greatest of our Supreme Court judges. The chief justice was more than adequate. Swayne and Hunt were weak, but Strong was at least an average judge. How Harlan would fit into this group, with its three prima donnas, would remain for the future to decide.

The Supreme Court that Harlan joined in 1877 was not the great public law court, concentrating on constitutional issues, that we know today. In the 1886 session, for instance, which was not atypical, the *United States Reports* shows that of over three hundred cases disposed of, only twenty-nine had to do with constitutional issues, and most of these were minor. The Court also handled nineteen admiralty cases, eight bankruptcies, eighteen appeals from the court of claims, sixteen cases involving land grants and titles, and twenty-three patent controversies.[21] But most numerous were cases stemming from the states under the Court's diversity and removal jurisdictions. Congress had provided, particularly during and after the Civil War, for the removal of various kinds of cases from state courts or (what amounts to the same thing) for federal district court jurisdiction *ab initio* in various kinds of cases in which Congress apparently felt that claimants from one state might not get a fair deal in the courts of another state. This was known as diversity jurisdiction. While some of these were suits against a state itself or one of its local subdivisions, most were purely private cases.[22] The diversity and removal cases constituted in 1886 over half of the Court's total cases—about 155. These cases involved various issues: the division of a person's assets in insolvency situations; wills; personal injury suits by employees against the railroads for which they worked; contract suits between corporations; and private claims of unfair taxation by states or local governments. Railroad cases bulked large in this category.

Such cases came to the Supreme Court not merely because of the liberal diversity and removal laws, which, after all, were a direct burden on the district courts, not the high court itself. Added to this was the general idea that almost any case could be gotten to the Supreme Court through writ of error procedures.[23] In fact, most of the Court's caseload was accounted for by applications for writs of error that, under the jurisdictional rules then applicable, could not easily be refused.

If the caseload was heavy, it was also largely composed of routine cases, many of which could be disposed of by opinions that in fact amounted merely to jurisdictional statements. This is why the chief justice wrote so many more opinions than the rest of the judges together: he almost always wrote these jurisdictional decisions. One calls them opinions only for formal reasons: that is the way they appear in the reports. Of course, even jurisdictional matters had to be decided by the full Court, and so they encumbered a lot of time.

Supreme Court justices also had circuit duties. Until 1891, at least, each justice spent a part of every year doing duty in the circuit to which he was assigned. This meant actually sitting on the circuit court bench as chief judge on a panel, the other members of which were district or circuit court judges, usually of the district in which the city was located. Usually Supreme Court justices were assigned to their home circuits, but in Harlan's case this was unlikely, since he was the third and junior justice from his circuit. The chief justice, following tradition, had the fourth circuit, comprising the Southeastern states near Washington; Swayne held Harlan's home circuit. John was therefore assigned to the seventh circuit, comprising Indiana, Illinois, and Wisconsin. This meant reading much material, frequent correspondence, and regular summer trips to Indianapolis, Chicago, and Milwaukee. John was disappointed. He had wanted Waite's circuit, and Waite himself would have preferred something nearer his home, but the other judges felt that tradition should rule. Harlan, knowing that much of the opposition to his own appointment had stemmed from the seventh circuit, felt that he might not be well received there. But the chief justice pointed out:

If I had not known that a single term all around would overcome all seeming opposition to you, I would have given you my place. But the feelings of some of the Judges was so decided against my giving up my circuit to *anyone*, that I thought it best on the whole to stay there. Personally I preferred your circuit to my own.

You are sure to *capture* the place. So put on a bold face & "go in."[24]

Harlan did "go in" and proved to be a popular figure on the circuit.

Another pronounced factor in the judges' burden of cases was, of course, opinion-writing; but this was made harder on some judges because of the inability or unwillingness of others to carry their proper share. Illness was the most common, but not the only, factor in this. In his first week on the Court, Harlan wrote to the chief justice, "I incline to think that, in view of the importance of the questions involved in the Oregon case the opinion should come from one of the older members of the Court." Evidently Waite acceded to this request. Harlan also asked not to be assigned cases in which Roscoe Conkling had been counsel, since "I heard last winter that Senator Conkling does not feel altogether *kindly* to me."[25]

Justice Ward Hunt suffered a stroke that rendered him incapable of sitting at all, and not being eligible for a pension, he refused to resign until Congress passed a special pension act for him. He was thus absent for a great part of the 1878 session, all of 1879 and 1880, and part of 1881. The other justices, of course, had to cover for him. During the same period justices Swayne and Clifford were in failing health and wrote comparatively few opinions. Waite wrote plaintively to his wife: "Judge Miller is very blue about himself. He shows it in his face, and talks about his chances very despondingly—Judge Strong was 70 years old Saturday, but must remain until Feb. 1880 before he can resign. He says he shall do it then for sure. With Judge Clifford 75, Swayne 74, Strong 70, Hunt in bad health and Miller likely to go through a dangerous operation it looks as though the next few years would be likely to make some radical changes in the Court."[26]

The Court lost all of Clifford's services and most of Swayne's as well in 1880, so three justices were practically unavailable for that term. By the latter part of the 1881 session the Court was back to full strength with the addition of justices William B. Woods, Stanley Matthews, Horace Gray, and Samuel Blatchford. Since Bradley did not write opinions easily, the chief burden during the intervening years fell on Waite, Field, Harlan, and Miller.

The return of the Court to full strength did not necessarily mean an even spread of opinion assignments. Bradley never carried a full load, although he wrote some of the Court's more important opinions. Matthews and Blatchford became, with Waite, the workhorses. Waite himself was ill for a good part of the 1884 session, during which time Miller served as acting chief justice: he complained that he could not get any work out of Bradley.[27]

Woods was ill for almost all of the 1886 session, dying at its end; his replacement, Lucius Q.C. Lamar, wrote almost no opinions during the whole of the following session. Harlan's own burdens were increased due to the death of Chief Justice Waite in March 1888, because John temporarily took over Waite's fourth circuit in addition to his own. The following year Matthews was ill, and he died late in the session. David J. Brewer, Matthews's replacement, did not take his seat until January 1890.

Thus, except for the few years 1881 to 1886, Harlan's work load was increased because of the physical and other deficiencies of his colleagues. But he was comparatively young and was able to shoulder this extra work without serious effects.

Newcomers to the Court during the 1880s did not, unfortunately, improve its abilities. Justice Strong's resignation late in 1880 brought William B. Woods to the bench. Woods had been Harlan's chief competitor for the position in 1877. Although he was a carpetbagger from Ohio, he has sometimes been considered as a Southern appointment, since he had lived in Alabama for many years. Although Hayes appointed him for largely political reasons, he was not without ability and probably deserves more credit than he has been given by historians. He was apparently well accepted in Alabama, where he gained a high reputation as a circuit court judge. His service on the Supreme Court was too brief for him to establish much of a reputation except as a hard worker who generally was assigned more opinions than almost anyone else, specializing in equity issues.[28]

Although his place in history is no larger than that of Woods, Stanley Matthews was a fine lawyer. He was an Ohioan who, after a controversial struggle in the Senate, replaced Justice Swayne. Matthews was a close friend of President Hayes's and was prominent in Ohio Republican circles. He was a successful soldier and a moderate in politics, and had it not been for his controversial views on the federal occupation of the South and on protectionism, he might have been appointed chief justice instead of Waite. He was influential in the settlement of the dispute over Hayes's election and was rewarded by election to the Senate to replace John Sherman in 1877. His support of silver as legal tender made him even more controversial. When he was nominated by Hayes to succeed Swayne early in 1881, the Senate pigeonholed the appointment. He was renominated by Garfield and was finally confirmed in May.

Matthews was a good judge. He was hard-working, impartial, and sensible. He had already become a good friend of Harlan's, and indeed the families were tied together by marriage, since Matthews's daughter married Harlan Cleveland, Harlan's nephew. Matthews might have become a very good and prominent judge had he lived longer. Unfortunately he became ill before the 1888 session began and died early in 1889. Harlan delivered the eulogy at his funeral, summing up his friend's capabilities thus: "A great judge, a heavy loss to the Court; a rapid worker; accurate and skillful; wide and able; growing all the time." If perhaps a trifle too effusive, Harlan nevertheless put his finger on his colleague's major qualities.[29]

The most nearly distinguished of Harlan's new colleagues in the 1880s was Horace Gray of Massachusetts. A well-known legal scholar and chief justice of the Supreme Judicial Court of Massachusetts, he was the era's most nonpolitical appointee to the high court. Gray was appointed by President Chester A. Arthur at the suggestion of Massachusetts senator George F. Hoar, even though he was so punctilious that he had refused to provide Garfield with copies of his best opinions. Harlan welcomed him as an old and admired acquaintance. Taking his place on the bench as the last of the "class of 1881," Gray brought with him a high reputation as a legalist, one who knew the precedents. Nevertheless, he proved to be something of a disappointment during his relatively long, twenty-year career on the Court. He stimulated unwelcome controversy when he might have shifted sides to provide the majority against the income tax in 1895 (it has always been a matter of doubt whether it was Gray or Shiras). Louis Filler observes that "his forte was largely technical and historical"; he had neither a broad view of the Court's functions nor a forward-looking view of the purposes of the law.[30]

Ward Hunt finally retired in 1882 and was replaced by Samuel Blatchford, a federal circuit judge from New York. Blatchford, too, although a Republican, was relatively nonpolitical. His career as a judge and the fact that he edited the circuit court reports from 1852 to 1887 had given him a solid reputation among lawyers, and his appointment was well received. He proved a workmanlike, unexciting judge who wrote more than his share of the Court's opinions during his eleven-year tenure, being especially relied upon in patent and admiralty cases that, as we have seen, occupied a good deal of the Court's time before 1891. He was apparently not interested in constitutional law, although he took part in the conservative construction of the substantive due process concept. If Blatchford is undervalued by history, it is because historians seldom attribute much value to the routine: at his death, Attorney General Richard Olney paid a just observance to Blatchford's "tireless industry, persistent application, [and] . . . determination to work the powers he possessed to their utmost capacity."[31]

With the accession of Blatchford the personnel of the Court was settled for the mid-1880s. It was by any measure a strong Court. Its weakest members, at least from a public law point of view, Woods and Blatchford, were nevertheless valuable for their contributions to the more routine work that still composed the bulk of the Court's load. Yet the Court of the 1880s has, for historians, an ambivalent reputation. This seems due to the fact that most historians, even legal ones, think of the Court in present-day terms as primarily the arbiter of the U.S. Constitution. But the important constitutional issues of the period were relatively few, and they were often decided wrongly. Justice Harlan's reputation survives the liberal critique of the Court only because he happened to dissent in some of the most criticized decisions, such as the *Civil Rights Cases* of 1883, and because he served for twenty years beyond the decade. Had he died or resigned in 1890 his present reputation would be as low as those of Woods, Matthews, Gray, and Blatchford.

In the 1880s the Court sat in the old Senate chamber on the east side of the main corridor of the Capitol, linking the rotunda with the new Senate chamber. The courtroom had columns of native Potomac marble, gray painted walls, and mahogany furnishings with red draperies and carpeting. The Justices were provided with neither clerical assistance nor office space. By the 1880s some of them were hiring clerks out of their own resources, but for many years their only offices were their home studies. They thus worked largely isolated from each other, which alternately helped and hindered the development of close friendships and the collegial relationships that observers have always wished (usually in vain) that the Court would exhibit.

Thanks partly to the fact that many cases were routine, the judges could then turn out, compared with today, enormous numbers of opinions. Chief Justice Waite, who dealt with most of what were essentially jurisdictional statements, wrote eighty-four opinions in the 1885 session, probably a high mark in the Court's history. But even a normally active associate justice might account for twenty to thirty: in the same session every justice except Bradley contributed that number. Harlan was generally near the average for the Court, never writing fewer than twenty in the 1880s and twice reaching more than thirty. Blatchford, the Court's workhorse, often wrote more than forty and once more than fifty. Many cases did not present difficult political or social issues; nevertheless this is an astonishing level of productivity.[32] Harlan, being an unusually self-confident person, did not often suffer *"Judicial Worms*—that kind of worms which produce doubt and hesitation, and which do not permit the mind to rest in certainty, until a decision of some Master of the Rolls is found."[33]

The Court also worked very fast. While a case might take two to three years to be heard after being docketed, once it reached the oral argument stage things proceeded rapidly. Normally the Court sat to hear argument four days a week from eleven to four. Mondays were usually mostly taken up with the announcement of decisions and reading of opinions, while Saturdays were devoted to the judicial conference, during which the judges discussed and voted on cases heard during the week. Most cases were routine and did not call for extended discussion, and most votes were unanimous. The chief justice assigned cases to individual justices for opinion-writing, and most of the time the opinion was written without consultation with the other judges. It was normally finished for announcement in two to three weeks. Before it was announced it was apparently read to the justices in conference; this method left the writer quite free to say what he wished. During and after Waite's tenure, the Court's sessions began (statutorily) the second Monday in October and lasted until the middle of May, with brief Christmas and February recesses.

Once the session concluded, most of the justices went on circuit, which required varying lengths of time. Harlan usually found himself occupied on circuit at least until the end of June, and often well into July. The "vacation" was mostly regarded as being in August and September. The justices scattered according to preference during these months with, in the 1880s, a pronounced tendency toward New England resorts. Harlan, for several years, took his family to Block Island, where Justice Miller also went. Later, the Harlans vacationed in East Gloucester or Mt. Wachusetts, Massachusetts, and once in Winchester, Virginia.

The Court families had active social lives. Teas for the wives were frequent, while the justices themselves had a weekly whist game in which apparently all of them participated at least occasionally; Harlan, Waite, and Miller appear to have been the most regular. Whist was also featured as a vacation activity; John wrote his chief lightheartedly at the end of one summer, "I wish to give notice that the experience of this Summer has improved my knowledge of whist. So next winter, when opportunity arises, I will not be so modest when Bro. Miller is discoursing upon the fundamental rules of that game." [34] The justices did not devote all of their vacation time to play, however. Each of them almost always had cases from his circuit to work on, or cases held over from the Supreme Court's most recent session.

All in all it was a busy life, although a good deal more quiet and reclusive than John was accustomed to. Nevertheless, he settled into it easily and seldom regretted his choice of a judicial life. The major problem, at least during the early years, was money. The Harlans were not high-livers, but they enjoyed society; they had a fairly large family to take care of, with three boys to put through college; and living expenses in the capital city must have seemed high to them. Harlan was constantly in debt and fending off his creditors. Things became so bad, indeed, that in the early 1880s he seriously thought about resigning from the Court. In 1884 his brother James wrote that he had "seen notices of a rumor that you thought of resigning to resume the practice at Chicago," and he went on to advise that he thought it was a good idea. [35] John even changed his legal domicile to Chicago with the vague feeling that the contacts made there as circuit judge would help establish him as a lawyer. In 1880 he wrote to his old friend and former partner Thomas W. Bullitt (then a bank director seeking to collect a loan from Harlan):

My purpose was to write to you Monday night. Twice I sat down for the purpose but I delayed in the hope that some plan might be devised for my relief and which would at the same time be satisfactory to creditors. But all my plans have miscarried. I see no way to provide for my indebtedness, and my duty is to acknowledge frankly the situation in which I am placed. . . .

When I accepted my present office I hoped that some turn in the sale of real estate would occur that would let me [satisfy my debts]. . . .

At one time I seriously considered whether it was not my duty to quit the Bench, and return to my profession. But I concluded that I could not by practice at Louisville support my family and meet these debts. If I removed to a larger city it was uncertain what I could accomplish.

Since I have been here I have lived with the utmost economy possible. My necessities have compelled me to board, and I do not suppose I will ever be able to own a home. The only thing in my life about which I entertain serious doubt is whether I should, under the circumstances, keep my boys in college. They are all at Princeton, are doing well, living with strict economy, and, indeed, two of them, in ways that are entirely honorable and which I need not refer to, are paying their own board there. They are aware of my condition, and intend as soon as they leave college to bend all their energies to the liquidation of my indebtedness. If I should withdraw them from college, I do not believe that the sums thus saved when distributed among my creditors would be of any consequence to them.

Now, I have written to you, an old friend, what I should have written some while ago. But my pride has held me back and I have lived in the hope that I could devise some scheme for my relief. But in that I have failed. I should say that I owe more than $30,000.

What do you say I shall do? . . . Advise me.[36]

Bullitt's reply has been lost, but ten days later Harlan signed over the deeds to two pieces of Louisville property to Bullitt for sale, with the hope that "the net result of the sales may be such as to largely reduce my debts to the two banks you represent."[37]

Apparently John was successful in meeting at least his most pressing obligations, for a few months later the Harlans rented a house at 1623 Massachusetts Avenue. This prosperity proved to be temporary, however, for 1884 and 1885 found them living in Rockville, Maryland.[38] Rockville was then a quiet country town sixteen miles from Washington. The Harlans rented quarters in a private home. John commuted to Washington for the six days of each week when the Court's duties required his presence, and he began at this time his long career teaching constitutional law at the Columbian Law School, now the law school of George Washington University. This required him to stay in Washington three evenings a week. Although his emolument was not great, he felt, as his wife put it, that "his judicial salary was not large enough to provide for the education and maintenance of our surviving five children and our grand-daughter."[39]

Harlan was finally able, in 1886 or 1887, to secure a house in Washington, but only because of the gratitude and enterprise of his three sons. They acted together to buy three lots on the corner of Fourteenth and Euclid, giving their joint notes for $12,500. A Mr. Hill, from whom they bought the land, was so impressed with the initiative shown by the three that he was persuaded to lend them an additional $20,000 with which to build the house. Justice Harlan was then to pay the taxes and the interest on the mortgage as his rent for the house that the boys actually owned. This episode is the more remarkable since Richard, the oldest son, was just entering his first job, as minister at the Old First Presbyterian Church in New York City. He used most of his first quarter's salary to make the down payment. The second son, James, had just been admitted to the bar in Chicago, where he had studied law under Melville W. Fuller; but at that point his future was uncertain. John, the third son, was still in law school with even more uncertain prospects.[40]

To say that the acquisition of the house ended the family's financial problems would be a major exaggeration. At least one attachment proceeding took place a few years later, in which Harlan's law books remaining in Louisville were sold to pay a judgment against him.[41] His son James, who as a lawyer apparently took care of the loan payments on the house, wrote his father a scolding letter about his failure to pay the "rent" promptly:

It has always seemed to me that it would be much better if you would send me each month a cheque of an amount sufficient in the twelve months to cover the yearly charges on the house.

These charges it seems to me must be paid in any event and ought to come before everything else. I have also thought it perfectly clear that unless some orderly method of meeting these charges is adopted, your account will always be in confusion. For instance, you have not repaid at all the $525 that I paid last July for interest. And the January interest you were compelled to pay all out of one month. Of necessity your accounts for this month are thrown into confusion by such a heavy draft upon your funds. I wish very much that you would accept my suggestion of a monthly cheque. I am sure that it would be very much easier for you if you did that regularly and *let nothing interfere with it.* Try it for this year at any rate. So long as I was unmarried I could usually manage these matters and wait for your cheque, but now that I have other burdens it is not always so easy.[42]

Home life for the Harlans was unusually serene. The relationship between John and Mallie, indeed, began idyllically and seems to have continued that way for their entire married life. There are no stories or rumors of infidelity or any of the more minor difficulties that usually beset marriages. Mallie's own protestations might not be believed, since she would naturally not wish to publicize difficulties, but in the complete absence of evidence to the contrary, we must take them at face value. John apparently never made a major decision—at least one that would affect the family—without consulting Mallie. He was a model of attentiveness and concern when Mallie was ill. In the spring of 1882, for instance, he took her to Atlantic City to recover from "malarial fever" and had to miss many of the Court's sessions. His frequent bulletins to the chief justice about Mallie's condition attest to his deep concern.[43] Mallie apparently made some remark to him about this, for he wrote from Chicago in June (before her complete recovery): "I don't know that you should feel that I have been particularly attentive during your sickness. Certainly all that I have done and all the solicitude I have felt has been due to the best of wives. No man ever had such a wife as I have—that I would submit to the candid judgment of 'the world and the rest of mankind.' I shall be very happy when you are again restored to health."[44]

The children grew into adulthood without apparent problems of any unusual nature. Undoubtedly they went through the normal childhood illnesses; these are not recorded. There is a record of an apparently serious operation undergone by Edith, the oldest daughter, at the National Surgical Institute in Philadelphia; this necessitated several stays in the hospital there and some large payments.[45] The nature of this illness is unrecorded. In 1880 there was an outbreak of typhoid fever at Princeton, and the college apparently adjourned early; despite the natural worries of parents and friends, Richard and James emerged safely.[46] All three boys were academically successful and were apparently popular as well, but little record of their activities remains. One surviving letter from James refers to "football": "I went to New York yesterday and played with my class team in a game of foot-ball with Columbia College. All our expenses, save about a dollar, were paid by the class. We had a very pleasant game and were victorious. They are a very gentlemanly set of fellows and treated us very nicely. We left on the 9:35 train yesterday morning and got back the same night in time to see the bon-fire which our class had made to celebrate our victory. The college bells were rung and the whole affair was very pleasant."[47] Uncle James wrote from Louisville, "I heard that John had got into some trouble about 'hazing.' What is it. I would not mention it, but for the fact that if there was anything in it, you would certainly know it anyway."[48]

John was, naturally, concerned about the future careers of his sons, but little evidence of this is recorded. One letter, written to his son James soon after Richard's graduation from Princeton, expresses a model father's interest:

> If possible I wish to keep Richard at home next year but I will not, of course stand in the way of his interests. I am quite sure of one thing and that is teaching at the same salary, is to be preferred to work in the Departments.
> As to his profession he must decide that for himself—that is, he must not select one in order to please any body else, but that one for which he feels himself best suited. It is not a question of conscience or duty in any other sense.

I am glad you are contented in your present position. The work will do you good. That which you earn can be turned to good account. Next year [at Princeton] I wish you to "spread yourself." I have a fancy that you can speak & write much better than you yourself are disposed to believe.[49]

Richard eventually chose to be a Presbyterian clergyman. James decided to become a lawyer and was placed as an office trainee with Melville W. Fuller in Chicago; after admission to the bar he was taken to Washington by Fuller as the new chief justice's law clerk. John Maynard Harlan, the justice's youngest son, was his father's first government-paid clerk after his graduation from law school.[50]

The three Harlan girls posed, in a way, even fewer problems, since they did not need to be trained for careers. Edith, the oldest, was apparently an attractive and gregarious young lady, who had become a favorite with President Hayes and his family.[51] She took Justice Strong's daughter Mary along on the Harlan vacation in 1880. Justice Strong wrote to his Court colleague:

I am more obliged to you Mrs. Harlan and Edith than I can well express for the care you have taken of Mary during the past summer, and for the kindness you have shown her. . . . Mary writes in glowing terms of her enjoyment, and of the watchful care you have extended over her.

Of course, I have no objection to her going to Princeton [Massachusetts] with you, though I wish her to return to Philadelphia not later than the 15th of the month. She may not have money enough to defray her expenses. I therefore send you my check for $25.00 asking you to apply it as she may need.[52]

But Edith was also to provide the major sorrow of Harlan's family life. She married Linus Childs of Massachusetts in 1881, and her daughter, also named Edith, was born early in 1882. By the end of the year the young mother was dead. The couple had settled in Chicago, and Edith came down with what the doctors called "typho-malarial fever." John and Mallie rushed to Chicago on November 9, which necessitated another absence from the Court. Young Edith, not yet twenty-six, died three days later.[53]

Edith had obviously been Mallie's favorite. She wrote later that Edith

was the life of our household, helping me in all my social duties. She was a girl of rare qualities, kind of heart, and with gracious and winsome manners. In her own very quiet and sensible way, she had keenly enjoyed our life in Washington.

She was a kind of mother to the other children, always speaking of her brothers as "my boys" and exerting upon them (without any conscious effort) a sweet and tender influence for good.[54]

Edith's death struck a great blow to her parents, but of course life went on. Their large hearts embraced the baby Edith, and they took her into their household and brought her up. In 1906 she was married in the same church where her mother and father had wed.[55]

Laura and Ruth, the other two girls, were much younger and were not of marriageable age in the 1880s. Practically nothing is known about them beyond the fact that they lived with their parents during the period.

If John Harlan's immediate family presented a model of the ideal family, the same cannot be said of the families of his siblings. This was especially true of James. His wife's death accentuated James's rapid decline into alcoholism and opium (and later morphine) addiction. This situation caused his brother endless concern. James's letters in the 1880s are full of apologies for his conduct, futile promises of improvement, and pleas for money or clothing. He was left in Louisville as Gus Willson's partner, but after some years of futile struggles to help James, or cover for him, Willson finally had enough and abandoned the partnership.[56] While James apparently took his son, Henry, to Block Island to vacation with John's family in 1880, this seems to have been the last time the brothers were together.[57] Since John's own letters to James are lost, we do not know precisely what his attitude was; but there are frequent letters of thanks from James for help throughout the 1880s. It seems likely that John became more and more disillusioned about James's future and possibly felt personally embarrassed that the brother of a Supreme Court justice should be publicly known as an alcoholic.

James's one son, Henry, continued his father's distressing saga. Like James, Henry had an ailing wife and one child. Also like James, Henry had his problems with liquor, and he was apparently rather shiftless in general. The justice had little sympathy for his nephew and refused in no uncertain terms to help him. His attitude was probably typical of the times, even though it seems callous and perhaps priggish. By 1889, however, John had had enough dealings with alcoholics.

> I was absent recently, and upon my return I found your letter. You are correct in supposing that I had heard your habits were not good, and you do not say in your letter that you abstain entirely from drinking. You only say that the reports about you are exaggerated, and that you are not a *drunkard*. Frankness compels me to say that your case is a hopeless one, if you touch strong drink *at all*. One drop is evidence to me that you are destined to a drunkard's grave at an early day, and, supposing that you now and then drank, I had concluded that it was a waste of time for me to follow after you as I have after others, and try to save you from ruin. Why, sir, you should no more think of drinking one drop than of jumping off the railroad bridge. It is idle to say that you can control yourself. Others as strong as you have said that, and miserably failed. You recall the fact that you borrowed thirty dollars from me, and gave me a draft upon some auction house in Louisville in payment. The draft went forward, came back protested, and with the statement that there was no such house as you described. I wrote to you on the subject, and got no answer. . . .

. . . I have made up my mind that if one of my sons ever contracts the habit of drinking, to break off all connection or responsibility for him, and never allow him to come into my presence.[58]

When Harlan's sister Laura Harlan Cleveland died, Francis lost no time in remarrying. Although his son, Harlan, accepted this and came to love his stepmother, his daughter, Lillie, did not. She had gone to stay with her aunt "Lizzie" Hatchitt in Frankfort, and although she visited her father at least once, she retained her dislike of his remarriage. As she grew older she developed signs of epilepsy and eventually died of it in the absence of effective treatment. The only letter of hers that survives is a pathetic plea to John Harlan for her mother's memory: "I have been thinking of you all day and wondering if you did what I heard. Papa wrote to me the other day and said that you and Aunt Millie wrote them a letter of congratulation. I could not believe that MaMa's brother could do such a thing, so I thought I would write to you and see if you did. If you did, I am very sorry for I always thought you loved my MaMa. He will never get any congratulation from his daughter. I would show more respect for MaMa than that. Papa says that I must come home next month but I do not want to go."[59]

James and Elizabeth Hatchitt moved to Kansas after Dr. Hatchitt lost his postmastership at Frankfort, apparently in the shakeup resulting from Cleveland's election in 1884. He eventually became the Indian agent at the Crow Agency in Montana. During the 1800s John spent some time and effort helping to secure federal and private railroad jobs for the Hatchitts' son, Clay.[60]

Harlan's youngest sister, Sallie, died in 1887. Her husband, David P. Hiter, moved to Kansas City with the younger children and lived for a time with his oldest daughter there.[61] Harlan would eventually have difficulties resulting from his attempts to aid one of the Hiter offspring.

Harlan continued, as he would for the rest of his life, a staunch, rather conservative Presbyterian. His religious ideas were not profound, but they were deeply held. He objected strenuously to official as well as social activities conducted on Sunday. To one invitation from the attorney general to a formal dinner on Sunday, he replied that "a standing engagement which he had to meet his Pastor every Sunday Evening at the Church service" made acceptance impossible.[62] Similarly he objected to government support of the Chicago World's Fair in 1893, when it became obvious that this support included Sunday activities.[63] His conclusions about religion were fully those of a man of faith, as indicated by a letter to his son James:

I observe, from your letter to Mama, that your mind is being occupied, at odd times, with the question of eternal punishment. It seems to me that this is not a question which need concern us very much in this life. At any rate there is no ground to think ill of any one who happens to think that punishment, in another life, for the short-comings in this life, will be eternal.

The important question is whether there will be any punishment whatever. If you and Dave are agreed on that proposition, I don't think it material for you to inquire as to the degree or extent of the punishment which will be inflicted. Whatever may be the punishment it is certain to be more than you or Dave will like, and more than you will, even in that supreme moment, admit that you ought to have. You will remember—of course you do for Mama fancies that you continually read the bible—the occasion when the rich man woke up in hell, and saw Lazarus, the beggar, in Abraham's bosom. The first named individual, who had been "clothed in purple and fine linen, and fared sumptuously every day," was anxious to change his base of operations. But Abraham said: "Son, remember that thou in thy lifetime receivedest thy good things, and likewise Lazarus evil things; but now he is comforted, and thou art tormented."

"And besides all this," continued Abraham, "between us and you there is a great gulf fixed: so that they which would pass from hence to you cannot; neither can they pass to us, that would come from thence." (Luke Ch. 16: 19-31.)

Now, it is certain that there are two distinct places or localities in the next life, between which there is an unpassable gulf. The inhabitants of neither can pass to the other—One is peopled by those who are "comforted," the other by those who are "tormented." There is nothing in the Bible of which I am cognizant, which justifies the belief that the line is ever passed, so that the man who commenced the other life in the torment may join those who are "comforted" from the outset. The thing is not to get into the torment at all. . . .

In other words, we shall have, in some form or way, we know not of, after this life, the capacity to discern the difference between comfort and torment. It is certain that if we are comforted, as the beggar was, we will not know what torment is, will have no occasion to bother our brains with determining the question as to how long the "tormented" will be punished.

I do not bother my brain with these subtle inquiries—If we could solve them all we should know as much as God does, and would claim ourselves to have had some hand in creating the Universe.

Do not fall into the habit too common among young collegians of calling into question the fundamental ideas upon which all religion rests. You are not bound to accept blindly what the fathers have taught but you ought to be slow in striking down the old landmarks, or ploughing up the old ways.[64]

Aside from financial difficulties, John Harlan's position was secure. It offered the dignity of high position, the satisfaction—always great among politicians—of mixing with the important figures in national life, and increasingly the opportunity to participate in decisions that affected American policy directions in significant ways. He became intimate with most of the presidents under whom he served, frequently acting as an adviser on Kentucky politics; for although most of his family had left the state, his continuing relations with Gus Willson ensured that he would always be kept informed. In the 1880s especially, he was still very active as a job-broker, although increasingly this was confined to promoting family members and close friends.[65] John's always active interest in public recognition was satisfied by his developing role as the Court's conscience, for his dissents to decisions such as the *Civil Rights Cases* and *Hurtado* v. *California* brought him widespread praise or notoriety. Harlan even found pleasure in the workaday routine of ordinary cases, although he soon came to feel that the judges were seriously overworked. Nevertheless, he was young and vigorous as judges go, and the work did not stretch his energies beyond his capacity.

It is not my purpose to delve deeply into Harlan's work in the seventh circuit court, to which he was assigned for twenty-odd years. The court sat in the major cities of Indianapolis, Chicago, and Milwaukee and also at times in Evansville, Springfield, and Madison. Harlan's duties, until the practice was changed by the Circuit Court of Appeals Act of 1891, were to sit with a circuit judge to hear such cases as came on appeal from the district courts and that were apparently felt to be significant enough to demand his presence. Supreme Court judges were expected to visit their circuits at least every other year; but Harlan often did so more often. Ordinarily such visits would take place in the late spring and early summer and would last as long as the business at hand required, sometimes into July. Occasionally Harlan went to his circuit during the February Supreme Court recess, but obviously his Supreme Court duties were too onerous to permit this unless there were vital cases to be heard that could not be delayed until spring. Once or twice bringing the circuit court to Washington was even discussed, since Harlan could not leave, but it seems that this last resort did not turn out to be necessary.[66]

The circuit court was much occupied with railroad bankruptcy cases—a constant feature of the era—and these cases bulk large in Harlan's correspondence with his circuit judges. There were also frequent cases involving patent claims, from which, exercising his privilege as a Supreme Court justice, Harlan excused himself, writing that patent cases "involve scientific investigation [and] . . . I have no fancy and but little aptitude for that branch of the law."[67] He extended this attitude toward the Supreme Court as well: the *United States Reports* do not show that he wrote a single opinion in a patent case.

The most interesting and controversial of Harlan's circuit court cases involved Indiana's corrupt electoral politics. One of these cases came about as a result of Simeon Coy's conviction for conspiracy to induce election inspectors to give the tally sheets to someone else for counting the votes in a contest for criminal judge of Marion County. There was no charge that he had interfered with the election of federal officials. When the case was first brought to the circuit court, Judge Walter Q. Gresham ruled that since only a state election was concerned, federal courts had no jurisdiction even though federal officials were being elected at the same time. Later, how-

ever, Judge William A. Woods issued an indictment, and Coy was convicted. The implication is that Coy was being persecuted because he was a
Democrat. The conviction was nevertheless sustained by Harlan and later
by the Supreme Court.[68] The basic question of federal jurisdiction, however, remained bothersome for some years.

An interesting aspect of such cases was that the Supreme Court justice
involved, in this instance Harlan, got to revote when the case reached the
Supreme Court. There was apparently no custom of recusal because the
same judge had ruled below, and there was apparently some pressure on
the other justices to go along on the decision in the interests of good
feelings within the Court.

In a case involving similar issues a few years later, Harlan and Woods
apparently refused to extend this jurisdictional doctrine to Republicans.
Known as the Blocks of Five cases, they began when a letter, purported to
have been written by W.W. Dudley, treasurer of the National Republican
Committee, was publicized. The 1888 election promised to be as close in
Indiana as it had been in previous years, and the Republican presidential
candidate, Benjamin Harrison, a former governor of the Hoosier state, had
pleaded with the national party organization to send aid: Indiana was not
only too close for comfort, but it was a key state if Harrison hoped to win.
Dudley's letter promised financial help, which was innocuous enough; but
it went on to propose that Indiana Republicans "divide the floaters into
blocks of five, and put a trusted man with necessary funds in charge of
these five and make him responsible that none get away and that all vote
our ticket." This open suggestion that voters should be bought caused a
furor, even though both parties had probably been doing that for some
years.[69] Despite the unfavorable publicity about the letter, Harrison won
Indiana and the election. Immediately afterward, however, some Republican leaders proposed indicting Dudley and others. Dudley reacted furi-
ously, saying that he would not be a scapegoat and that if tried he "would
explode a lot of dynamite" about the inner workings of the Republican
campaign.

None of this involved Harlan, of course. But when the U.S. attorney in
Indianapolis brought the indictment, Judge William A. Woods first stalled
by adjourning the grand jury. He finally instructed the grand jury that "a
letter . . . containing advice to bribe a voter . . . is not indictable." Many
naturally speculated that Woods had bowed to pressure from high Republican sources. Woods brought Harlan into this matter by saying that his jury
instruction had the Kentuckian's agreement, and he went on to quash
other indictments associated with the case. No one was ever tried. Of
course Woods felt that his reputation had been sullied and tried to hide
behind Harlan.

Harlan's role in all this was ambiguous and equivocal. On one side,
when a vacancy occurred in the district attorney's office, which would have

to prosecute the cases, he refused to appoint a Republican, writing that the "party in power [in Indiana] has the usual right . . . to be represented in that office." He went on: Besides, if I were to appoint a Republican, it would be said at once that my purpose . . . was to suppress investigation as to the alleged offences. I must avoid doing anything that will impair or lessen the respect which is due the Judiciary. . . . I must appoint a Democrat of acknowledged integrity, who will do justice though the heavens fall."[70] He did appoint a Democrat, Judge Solomon Claypool.

Whether indictments could issue in the Dudley case depended, Judge Woods averred, on the interpretation of the existing federal corrupt practices act. The law forbade bribery in elections, but also attempts at bribery. Dudley had attempted, or more properly suggested, bribery, or at least that was the charge; but there was no charge of actual bribes being offered or taken. So, Woods asked, if A (Dudley) advised B, but B did not actually bribe or attempt to bribe anyone, could A nevertheless be punished? He thought not: it was "only the initiative of an imperfect conspiracy."[71] But he did not wish to rule on the matter without Harlan's advice.

Harlan's original answer disagreed with Woods: "A man that advises another to bribe a voter," he wrote, "commits an offense, although the person so advised does not finally act on the advice."[72] The circuit court judge, however, either because of politics or conviction, insisted that he was right.[73] He felt obligated to act on Harlan's view of the matter, though, which would have meant Dudley's indictment.[74] A week later Harlan changed his mind. He had "reluctantly," he says, concluded that Woods's first interpretation was correct.[75] Woods was, of course, only too eager to accept this change, and it became the basis of his advice to the grand jury that no indictment could issue against Dudley.

There is no evidence regarding the reasons for the justice's reversal. He merely said to Woods that he had "carefully re-examined the questions." Had he figured out, or been informed, how damaging an indictment would be to Republican leaders up to and including President Harrison? Or had his reversal been based on strictly legal considerations? That he felt defensive about the episode is made clear in his lengthy correspondence with Claypool about it. Harlan was refusing to let his letters to Woods be used in a libel action that Woods had entered into against Claypool. Again, the closest he came to a real explanation was in saying that "it has often occurred in my Judicial life that subsequent investigation has shown me that my first impression as to a legal question was wrong."[76] That is as far as we can go in the matter.

If the justice changed his opinion to suit the political needs of his party friends—how wrong, yet how human—then one is led to speculate on the quality of Harlan's ethical standards as a judge. In this episode he does not emerge looking ethical, but one should in fairness recall that he lived in an era of partisan excess, so it is not too much of a surprise to find that partisanship overcame scruple. As we shall see, however, he could also in his votes on the Bering Sea Fur Seal Commission act on his views of what was right as against what were generally perceived as the interests of his country.[77]

In other incidents bearing on the question of judicial integrity, Harlan appears to have been careless of the judiciary's reputation for fairness. He regularly sat and voted in cases argued before the Court by close associates, specifically his intimate friend and former partner Gus Willson, and by close relatives, such as his nephew Harlan Cleveland and even his sons.[78] The cases themselves seem not to have been of particular significance; yet if the appearance of virtue is as important as virtue itself, then Harlan was at least somewhat at fault. True, other judges were not always any more careful than he was: even the great Oliver Wendell Holmes, Jr., voted in a case involving the copyright law as it applied to articles written for magazines by his father, the "Autocrat of the Breakfast Table."[79] On the other hand, Rufus Peckham seems to have absented himself from cases argued by his brother.[80]

Harlan also indefatigably promoted the careers of his sons and regularly, if mostly unsuccessfully, used his political influence in their favor. Such efforts usually involved James. John was settled, satisfied, and successful in his Chicago legal practice, and Harlan's influence was not necessary in Richard's case either; he made his own mark as a Presbyterian minister and college president. But James had ambitions beyond his legal career. His name was regularly proposed, with the justice's support, for federal judicial vacancies in the Illinois district and for the court of appeals as well. James was eventually appointed attorney general for Puerto Rico and, later, to the Interstate Commerce Commission. The fact that cases from Puerto Rico and the ICC might be reviewed by the Supreme Court was obviously not regarded by Harlan *père* as a disqualifying factor.

Although not precisely a parallel to Justice Tom Clark's decision to resign when his son Ramsey became attorney general in the 1960s, one incident nevertheless highlights both the increased strictness of the rules of judicial ethics and the comparative insensitivity of Justice Harlan to such questions. President Theodore Roosevelt had expressed some reservations about the appointment of a sitting justice's son to the ICC. Justice Harlan replied:

> It surprises me me that, in the judgment of anyone, my presence on the Bench . . . stands in the way of the appointment of my son to a place on the Interstate Commerce Commission. If that view be sound, it will follow that the acceptance of a position on the Supreme Court will prevent a son of the Justice from holding a Federal or State Judgeship during the lifetime of the father or while he remains on the Bench. . . . A proposition attended with such consequences ought to be carefully examined. . . .

It should not be overlooked that an Interstate Commerce Commissioner is only one of seven Commissioners . . . , and that a Justice of the Supreme Court is only one of nine. . . . The possibility that a Justice . . . would be controlled by the fact that his son was a member of the Commission is . . . entitled to no consideration whatever. It should be assumed that each Justice . . . recognizes the responsibilities attached to his high position, and, in deference to his conscience will do his duty fearlessly, without fear or favor, and regardless of the personnel of the tribunal whose official action comes under his examination.

There is another consideration. . . . On several occasions you have . . . expressed a fixed purpose to appoint my son to a Federal Judgeship, at Chicago, whenever you had an opportunity to do so. But how could you . . . if the view now urged by some . . . is to be accepted . . . ?

. . . The obstacle which apparently stands in his way might, perhaps, be removed . . . by my announcing a purpose . . . to retire. . . . My self-respect, to speak of no other aspect of the matter, forbids such an announcement. I am sure that you would not desire or have me make such an announcement. And I am equally sure that my son would not care to have an appointment under such circumstances.[81]

Finally, another episode bearing on Harlan's sense of judicial propriety involved his friend Eli Murray. Murray, who had with Harlan's aid secured a federal job as governor of Utah Territory, gave some rather valuable, or at least potentially valuable, mining stocks to Richard. Harlan's lengthy refusal to allow his son to accept such a gift reveals a thorough conversance with at least the financial aspects of the ethics that ought to govern a Supreme Court justice.

Further reflections satisfied me that there were reasons why neither I nor any of my family should become interested in mining stocks. . . . There are now upon the docket of our Ct, several mining cases from the West, and we are likely for many years to come to have such cases before us. These cases may involve questions of great moment to all who are interested . . . , and their disposition might seriously affect the value of such property and stocks. If Richard should become the owner of any mining stocks it might be that his interests could be affected by our decision and that, too, without my knowing, at the time, that such would be the result. I prefer that no such complications should exist, and hence, with Richard's consent, return the certificate. . . . I am sure that you will appreciate my feelings in this matter and that you will concur with me in saying that a Judge should avoid even the appearance of evil.[82]

11

Associate Justice
1887-1897

In May 1887 Justice Woods died, ending the brief period of stability on the Court that characterized the mid-1880s. In fact, so rapid was the turnover that by 1897 Harlan and Gray were the only holdovers from the Waite Court. The transition was the more remarkable in that the strong judges— Miller, Bradley, and Field—were succeeded by appointments of pronounced mediocrity. The Court in 1897 contained only one "great" justice, and that was Harlan. Gray and White, and perhaps Fuller, were above average. The rest, often having short tenures, were average at best.

Harlan's most memorable opinions, of course, came in dissent, often solitary. Mediocrity ruled the Court in the 1890s, Miller having died in 1890, Bradley writing few opinions in the years until his death early in 1892, and Field writing even fewer as he descended into senility preceding his 1897 resignation. Anyone assessing the decisions—especially the great 1895 triad often criticized by scholars (the sugar trust, income tax, and *Debs* cases) but also the final acceptance of substantive due process and the Court's unmatched error in *Plessy*—should bear in mind that they were produced by a Court dominated by judges who had little if any claim to fame even outside these much maligned decisions. The Court's sole strong judge dissented in almost all of them. Not the least remarkable aspect of Harlan's career on the Court is the fact that when history has judged him to be right he was usually dissenting, while when he led, or followed, a majority he has more often been regarded as wrong.

The replacement for Justice Woods, Lucius Quintus Cincinnatus Lamar, was a long-time political leader from Mississippi, that state's first former Confederate senator, and Grover Cleveland's secretary of the Interior. A noted public speaker, he played a role as something of a compromiser in the Senate. His appointment to the Court was opposed by radicals, who claimed that he was not a good enough lawyer and that, at sixty-two, he was too old. Lamar was, indeed, modest about his own ability to fill such a high judicial position, but there is no reason to believe that he would not have grown into the post as so many others have, if he had lived longer. He worked very hard to make up for his supposed deficiencies, and his body—never very strong—failed under the strain. He served only five full terms. Considering the nature of the Court's work at that time, Harlan had reservations about Lamar: "How much interest he will take in dry records involving dry questions of law with no element of romance, I do not pretend to know." But Lamar disappointed him in the expectation that the Confederate veteran would now "vindicate the authority of the Union against State Sovereignty," for Lamar's record is primarily that of a states' rights strict constructionist, although the issues by the 1890s had become complex enough so that such a characterization is only partially correct. Lamar enjoyed good relations with his colleagues and joined with them—if he had been a strong judge he might have led them—in construing the Fourteenth Amendment narrowly. He and Harlan disagreed on this but were nevertheless on friendly terms.[1]

Chief Justice Waite, Harlan's closest friend on the Court, died in March 1888. His replacement was a man whom Harlan could support wholeheartedly, even though Fuller was a Democrat and a private lawyer with a primarily local reputation in Chicago and despite the fact that Miller, Bradley, and Field all had serious reservations. Melville W. Fuller, it was sometimes said, "was the most obscure man ever appointed Chief Justice."[2] He was not a legal giant in his performance, preferring instead the role of moderator, but he was well liked and was regarded by Oliver Wendell Holmes, Jr., as the best chief justice under whom Holmes served. Fuller aided the Court by using his influence to help secure the passage of the Circuit Court of Appeals Act of 1891. A thorough conservative, he represented the attitudes of the majority of the justices. As was usual with him, Harlan sunk his legal and constitutional disagreements in his liking for the man: he had deliberately chosen Fuller, a leader of the Chicago bar, as his son James's mentor, and the two had been close friends for some years. When Fuller visited Washington he often stayed at the Harlan home, and Harlan advised him on tactics during the fight in the Senate over his nomination.

The situation as regards the nomination was rendered more delicate because Fuller was counsel for an important case that was to be argued before the circuit court, known as the *Lake Front* case. Harlan, as circuit judge, was to sit on the case and wished Fuller and his opposing counsel to come to Washington to go over it. While Fuller's nomination hung fire, however, it did not seem desirable for him to visit Washington: "I suggest that it is best for you not to come here about the Lake Front decree. Your presence here would be misinterpreted. It might be published on the house-tops that you came on law business, but the general public would say that you came about the Chief Justice-ship—& this latter view would be embarrassing."[3] Harlan wrote that he would like to come to Chicago to discuss the Lake Front case if it "were at all practicable," but

My nephew [Harlan Cleveland] is to be married next Tuesday and before this week closes he & others will be in our house, remaining until about the 6th.

There is another obstacle in the way—*confidentially*—Some people, who ought to know better, have been talking and writing to me about my being a possibility in connection with the Chicago [Republican] Convention. I *know* very well that this [is] all mere talk, originating from the partiality of a few friends. But I do not intend to give any one an excuse to say that I have a [case?] . . . —hence, I must not be in Chicago before or during the Convention. My purpose is to keep far away from political movements.[4]

The obvious solution was to defer consideration of the *Lake Front* case. So Harlan suggested that the lawyers delay their Washington visit until after Fuller's confirmation: "You and Ayers can talk about the Lake Front case before you are sworn in."[5]

A potential conflict between the two men arose because of Fuller's desire to take the midwestern circuit as his own. While Harlan had not wanted it to begin with, he had in the course of a decade built up close working relations with the judges and did not now wish to change. The two discussed this situation even before Fuller's appointment was assured. Harlan did not conceal his reluctance to move to the so-called Virginia circuit.

In reference to my taking another Circuit, the usage has been for the Chief Justice to take the Va. Circuit. After a little while the Chief Justice must be *settled* here & he is convenient to the Va. Circuit. There is very little there to do, & that fact you will appreciate after being on the Bench for a time. We will talk over the Circuit matter when you come. As my boys are to be at Chicago, my present assignment is agreeable. But that is not central. If the brethren think that the Ch. Justice may properly take some other than the Va. Circuit we can then talk over the whole matter with a result, I doubt not, that will be satisfactory to you. If your comfort, as Chief Justice, is to depend *in any degree,* upon your having the Chicago Circuit, you shall have no difficulty about it, so far as I am concerned. Don't let that give you any concern.[6]

Fuller decided to go with tradition, and Harlan kept his old assignment.

The question of circuit court assignments recurred when President Harrison appointed Harlan to the Bering Sea arbitration commission in 1892. Since this duty would require a lengthy absence from the Court—the arbitration was to take place in Paris—Harlan's circuit duties had to be at least temporarily assigned to someone else. This gave rise to the question whether Fuller still wanted to have that circuit, and by now Harlan had changed his tune on the matter, advising the chief justice that he ought to take Chicago permanently.

I have written to Gresham and Woods informing them of the purpose of our court to assign you regularly to the 7th Circuit in addition to your own. If any assignment to Circuits (besides the one of next Monday) should be made in my absence, and if you should conclude to take the 7th Circuit permanently (which you know that you are [welcome?] to do and which . . . I would be glad for you to do). . . .

I ought, perhaps, to say that given all the circumstances I prefer *any* circuit in the West or South to the Chicago Circuit—the reasons for which you understand. They are not [prejudicial?] to the Chicago Circuit. The truth is, I ought at the start to have acceded to your wishes for the Chicago Circuit.[7]

Although the reasons for Harlan's change of mind are not clear, it seems likely that his relations with the senior circuit judge in Chicago, William A. Woods, had suffered as a result of Woods's connection with the election fraud case from Indiana involving W.W. Dudley and Harrison's election. In any case Fuller refused the offer, and Harlan returned to the Chicago circuit when he came back from Paris. He was, however, eventually assigned his home circuit in 1896 when Howell Jackson died (by that time the sixth circuit comprised Ohio, Kentucky, and Tennessee).

The friendship of the new chief justice with Harlan deepened after he reached Washington and indeed became more intimate than the Kentuckian's relationship with any other justice during his entire thirty-four years' service. Harlan joshed the Democratic Fuller after the Republican victory of Benjamin Harrison in 1888:

I have received today a small supply of Kentucky (whisky) ten years old. The supplier, I know will be glad to be informed that a bottle of it has gone to the Chief Justice of the United States to cheer him up in the midst of the dire calamities that have come upon the grand old party that has stood by the Constitution "as it wuz," with all the "difficulties" that have attended its enforcement. I will drink to your health, on this Thanksgiving Day, in the hope that Bro. Gray will "bring down" not only a large lot of "Drinks"[?] but the Montana case.[8]

Such intimacy enabled Harlan to be very frank with the chief justice at times. Thus he felt able to complain of overwork: "Here I am with 4 cases more to finish and I a *very tired* man. The fact is that I have had no 'let up' for 18 months."[9] He also revealed considerable touchiness about the number of cases he was assigned, overworked or not:

Let me celebrate the 21st anniversary of my judicial life by a slight growl.

Two Saturdays in succession you have not assigned to me any case but have assigned cases and important ones to Justice Gray. I was in the majority in each case assigned to him.

I fear that you have the impression that my health is failing while that of Justice Gray is vigorous. I hope his is on the mend. I know I am in good health and wish to do my full share of the work. The cases on my hands to be written are not as many in number as in the case of some others.

Now tear this up & think no more of the growl.[10]

This note reveals a Harlan who was sensitive about his status on the Court, but he did not really wish to antagonize Fuller by accusing him outright of preferring to have Gray write opinions in some significant cases, so he diplomatically placed his argument on the basis of health and called it merely a "slight growl."

The controversial but brilliant Stanley Matthews died rather suddenly in 1889. His successor was David J. Brewer, a Kansan and a nephew of Justice Field, who had served for twelve years on the Kansas Supreme Court and as a federal circuit judge for six. Despite his thoroughgoing conservatism, Brewer had a wit and joviality that endeared him to Harlan, and the two became close friends. Both men were deeply religious, which gave them a bond that ideological differences did not break. The Kansan remarked publicly that

> All men are said to have their hobbies. . . . Mr. Justice Harlan has a hobby . . . and that is the Constitution of the United States. He has read and studied it so assiduously that I think he can repeat it from one end to the other, forward and backward, and perhaps with equal comprehension either way. . . .
>
> Mr. Justice Harlan . . . believes implicitly in the Constitution. He goes to bed every night with one hand on the Constitution and the other on the Bible [and, as Justice Day is supposed to have added, "his golf sticks under his pillow"], and so sleeps the sweet sleep of justice and righteousness. He believes in the Constitution as it was written; that the Constitution as it was must be the Constitution as it is, and the Constitution as it shall be.[11]

Jocularly intended and received, these remarks nevertheless tell us a good deal about the character of the Kentuckian. They could only have been made by a man who knew Harlan well, who admired him, and who appreciated his always lively sense of fun.

Harlan, for his part, also kidded Brewer. Writing from Paris, he asked:

> What ought to be done with the "blasted Englishman" who made this picture? He has obtained a picture of George Washington's face, as the latter is sometimes caricatured & used it for me.
>
> And then, the putting of the hands up into the arm holes of my vest was pure invention.
>
> I will write to you soon at length, saying, now, that the insinuation as to my eating & drinking in your last, has as little upon which to rest, as some of your judicial views have. But I shall get even with you in some way, but without malice. I bear you no malice.[12]

The crusty Iowan, Samuel F. Miller, one of the great judges in American history, died in the autumn of 1890. Harlan wrote that no judge since Marshall had made a "deeper impression" on American jurisprudence.[13] Miller was promptly replaced by a very highly regarded U.S. district court judge from Detroit who had actively worked for the appointment, Henry Billings Brown. Although Brown served for fifteen years, he largely failed to live up to his promise. A moderate conservative, he nevertheless wrote a bitter dissent when the Court majority invalidated the income tax law. But his most famous—indeed notorious—opinion came when, writing for an eight-man majority, he justified the Louisiana jim crow laws as not being discriminatory. In later years, after he had retired, Brown is said to have developed serious doubts about that opinion. His relations with Harlan seem to have been warm and friendly.[14]

Like Waite earlier, Fuller at times had to worry about the health and performance of his associates. He wrote in 1892: "I am better in health than for many weeks, but not in strength and more anxious than I can tell you. . . . We are in a miserable condition. Joseph Bradley is really wretched and so is Lamar. We are reduced in effect to *seven* & of the seven, Field is far from strong. If I leave there is danger of the Court's being left without a quorum. It is a serious question."[15] Fuller's illness, whatever it was, was mild enough to permit him to continue functioning that spring, but the Court's general condition did not improve much.

George Shiras, Jr., came to the Court in 1892 as an unsatisfactory replacement for another of the strong justices, Joseph P. Bradley. Like Brown, Shiras would retire voluntarily, still in excellent health, after serving only ten years. Shiras was a successful corporation lawyer from Pittsburgh, an independent-minded Republican who had been careful to keep himself free of the taint of association with the Cameron-Quay machine. He proved to be a middle-of-the-road justice who seldom dissented and thus could be regarded as the magnetic pole of the Court during his tenure.[16] For his part, Justice Harlan lost a good friend in Bradley; a whist-playing companion in Block Island days, Bradley had also become an occasional source of aid to his younger colleague. One surviving note illustrates the relationship.

> You know that I greatly rely upon you, while you are on the Bench (and I hope your departure from it is far in the future), to keep me *straight*. But it is important that you be kept straight—and to that end I send you an article from Kentucky—"straight"—It is 21 years old. A small quantity of it will produce delightful sensations, and make you wonder why every sensible man is not an adherent of the Presbyterian or the Dutch Reformed Church. Too much of it, *at one sitting*, may do harm.
>
> This is preliminary to my apologizing for sending you, also, my opinion in the Utah murder case. Knowing your opposition to this way of sending around opinions to be read, I should not send this one, except that others are being handed about. But I really want your guidance in this Utah case.[17]

Lucius Q.C. Lamar's undistinguished career on the Supreme Court ended in 1893, as did the somewhat more important tenure of Samuel

Blatchford. The successor to Lamar was one of the more unfortunate choices ever made, although poor health contributed significantly to Howell E. Jackson's weakness. Jackson was a prominent circuit court judge from Tennessee. He became ill little more than a year after his appointment, suffering from tuberculosis complicated by dropsy. Jackson was perfectly willing to retire but was entirely dependent on his salary for an income. His most important act as a justice was his journey to Washington to participate in the decision in the second income tax case, in which he, with Harlan and two others, made up the minority favoring the law's constitutionality. Three months later, in August 1895, he died. A plaintive letter to Harlan refers to his illness as well as to Court business.

> Your note with opinion in the Plumley case is just to hand. I concur fully in your opinion, which is a most excellent one—clearly distinguishing the case from all others decided by our court. . . . Nothing occurs to me by which the opinion could be improved. I voted to affirm and am fully satisfied with the [manner in which you handle?] the decision. Please send me copies of all your opinions whether I have heard the cases or not, as I am interested in what is being discussed and wish to keep up. I have ample leisure to read them, and enjoy the change from [novels?] and such light literature to something more substantial. I am getting on comfortably and feel hopeful of substantial improvement from my winter in this balmy climate. My cough is gradually growing less violent and troublesome—and I am resting much better at night. But the time hangs heavily on my hands and my thoughts turn with longing to the Court and Brethren whose work I would like so much to be sharing. I am, however, making a business of trying to get well so that I may be of some assistance in the future.[18]

Unusually for the 1890s, Justice Blatchford was succeeded by someone as good as he, if not better. Edward Douglass White is well known to scholars, but mostly because he eventually became chief justice (1911-21). In the realm of public law, White is noted primarily for his sponsorship of the "rule of reason" to guide courts in their application of the Sherman Antitrust Act. He was generally conservative and business-oriented; nevertheless, he joined Harlan in dissenting from the income tax decision. White was a Southerner and a Catholic, the son of a prosperous plantation owner, and a Confederate soldier who served briefly on the Louisiana supreme court and later as a U.S. senator. In fact, he remained in the Senate for weeks after his nomination to the Supreme Court (by Cleveland) had been confirmed, because he wanted to battle against the Wilson-Gorman tariff bill, which would seriously harm the sugar interests of his native Louisiana. Although he and Harlan often disagreed about Court actions, they were on friendly terms, often walking home together from the Capitol.[19]

Howell Jackson's short-lived term on the Court ended in the summer of 1895. His successor was Rufus Peckham, who largely because of his majority opinion in *Lochner* v. *New York*—a bakers' hours case—became known as possibly the most extreme advocate of laissez-faire in the Court's history. The New Yorker came from a prominent legal family: his father was a judge of the New York Court of Appeals (as was Rufus), and his brother Wheeler Peckham was a prominent corporation lawyer. Peckham was not a leader and is not responsible for any innovative doctrines; except in the antitrust cases, he lined up invariably with the faction wishing to protect business against government regulation.[20]

The last of the changes of the 1890s came as the result of the long-delayed retirement of Justice Stephen J. Field. The Californian was of less and less practical use to his brethren during the 1890s, but he had a deep-seated ambition to break Chief Justice Marshall's longevity record. As a result, he refused to retire until that event was long overdue. One of the most famous but now it appears inaccurate stories about the Supreme Court involves Harlan and Field and the latter's retirement. Despite their frequent disagreements the two were good friends, so much so that Field stood as guarantor for one of Harlan's frequent bank loans. When it became obvious that the cantankerous Westerner ought to retire, it was natural for Chief Justice Fuller to ask Harlan to visit the old man and suggest that he do so. The younger man, trying to be diplomatic, roused the somnolent Field and asked him whether he remembered being deputized twenty-five years earlier to suggest to Justice Grier that he ought to resign. Suddenly wide awake, Field answered wrathfully, "Yes, and a dirtier day's work I never did in my life!" At this Harlan could do nothing but withdraw, having failed in his purpose. Once he had achieved his aim of serving on the Court longer than Marshall, Field was ready to retire. He asked Harlan to look at his retirement letter, and Harlan wrote to Fuller:

> This morning he sent for me and read what he had prepared, most of it in print. He finally wished for suggestions when I said to him that in my judgment it was too long & had too many references to his own opinions. As it is, it will not do at all. Having said that he had consulted yourself & Brewer about his letter to the President, I advised him to consult you again and take your judgment. If he brings to you the letter he read to me, it will be seen at once that it will not do. I spoke frankly to him, in order to make your work the easier.[21]

Unfortunately, Field's replacement was markedly inferior to his predecessor. Joseph McKenna was certainly the most inappropriate choice of the era. A thoroughly political man, McKenna had built his California power base into a position in the House of Representatives in which he became a chief ally of William McKinley. He was appointed to the ninth circuit court of appeals by President Harrison in 1892, where he spent four obscure years before being chosen as attorney general by McKinley in 1897. He held the position for less than a year before being elevated to the Supreme Court in 1898, despite criticism even from California that he was not up to the job. McKenna himself felt inadequate, and nothing in his performance makes him look any better. He served until 1925 and wrote hundreds of opinions. He was a hard worker, but his voting seemed almost random, following no consistent pattern. He tended strongly to follow Justice White. For some years, Chief Justice Fuller "took care to assign to him the simpler cases," but McKenna eventually wrote some important constitutional decisions. His relationship with Harlan seems to have been friendly but not close.[22]

The judges of the Supreme Court finally received some relief from their excessive work load when Congress passed the Circuit Court of Appeals Act of 1891.[23] Among other things, this law created a new set of courts of appeal that were to have general appellate jurisdiction over cases from the lower federal courts, especially the diversity and removal cases which had taken so much of the Court's time, and the customs and patent cases. In exchange, it is true, Congress vested the Supreme Court with increased jurisdiction over criminal cases. Nevertheless the act was effective, at least in the short run: whereas the *United States Reports* record 281 decisions for the Court in the 1890 session, they show a low of 172 by the 1898 session, and the load did not begin to increase again until after Harlan's death. The number of opinions assigned to Harlan to write fell from thirty-seven in 1890 (the highest on the Court except for the chief justice) to only eighteen in 1898. On the other hand, he wrote only two dissents in 1890, and eleven in 1900.

At the same time, by reducing the number of essentially private law cases coming to the Court, the 1891 act accentuated the tendency for the Court to become more and more a public law body, with a greater emphasis on the decision of constitutional issues than ever before. This profound change was congenial to Harlan, never at his best with technical legal issues anyway. It was, of course, in this new kind of case that he made his reputation as the Great Dissenter, since these were the issues that most disturbed the public.[24]

Senility was a problem that afflicted the Court not only because of Stephen J. Field. The Supreme Court reporter also had an indefinite appointment. The reporter during the 1890s was J.C. Bancroft Davis, a former assistant secretary of state and judge of the U.S. court of claims, who had served as reporter since 1883. Fuller's biographer reports that Davis, no doubt because of his previous eminence, felt that his work for the Court was a little beneath him. In any case, justices frequently complained to Fuller about corrections to the reports that Davis sometimes failed to make, assuming that he knew better than the justices did what they should have said. The chief justice hesitated to discipline or discharge Davis, however, partly because he was a remote relative, but mostly because Fuller was a kindly man who hated to cause pain to anyone. The problem grew more serious as Davis aged.[25]

One incident related to Davis provides a good illustration of Harlan's warm relationship with the chief justice. Harlan was dissenting in a case, while Fuller had written the majority opinion; moreover, Harlan's opinion had originally been intended as a majority one, but apparently Fuller's had been persuasive enough to cause one justice to reverse his vote. Nevertheless, Harlan was disturbed at the quality of the headnote written by Davis for the case. He wrote to Fuller: "I have read the head-notes in the Bank case. They are awful and are enough to make you and not me sick. There is time to correct them. Make the corrections and send to Banks Brothers [the printer] and tell them they must be made. It will require some of the opinions of the next term to complete Vol. 141 and hence you have time to have the corrections made."[26] Instead of adopting Harlan's suggestion, Fuller wrote a gentle letter of reproof, enclosing the corrections, to Davis; but for some reason the changes were never made.

Whether Supreme Court justices should serve the country in non-judicial capacities has been a subject of controversy for many years. It is nevertheless true that they have done so at various times in our history, notably when five justices served on the electoral commission that arbitrated the Hayes-Tilden election in 1877. It is also true that ideas of judicial propriety have evolved over the years, and judges might not serve in ways today that they would have done without much thought a hundred years ago.[27] Certainly Harlan, his colleagues, and the public had no particular objections to the Kentuckian's selection in 1892 as one of the American representatives for the Bering Sea arbitration in Paris. Fuller and Brewer, indeed, both served as arbitrators in the Anglo-Venezuelan boundary dispute in 1899.

Harlan's acceptance of President Harrison's request that he go to Paris came only partly out of a sense of civic duty. The Harlans had never been abroad, and the state of their finances was such that they might never have been able to travel to Europe on their own. The fur seal controversy provided them this opportunity. In fact, Harlan accepted only after the president had assured him that his wife and youngest daughter (Ruth, age eighteen) could certainly accompany him.[28] The Harlans rented their home to the Brewers and sailed in August 1892 on the French liner *La Touraine*. John thus missed almost all of the 1892 session of the Court, voting in only six cases. After a few days in Paris the family journeyed to Switzerland, where they spent the rest of the summer with Richard's wife and Laura. On the train to Switzerland the family was awestruck by the Alpine scenery (they had not traveled in the American West, either). Mallie described this vividly.

From his window on one side of the carriage, he drank in the wonderful scenery, while I looked out, awe-stricken, . . . the other side. To my son and his wife, we must have seemed like two children; for my husband kept calling to me "come and look" at the scenery on *his* side, while I kept calling to him to "come and look" at the marvels on my side.

He was always very shy and undemonstrative in expressing his feelings. But on this occasion the sight of the sublime in nature, such as he had never seen before, overwhelmed him. His eyes filled with tears and he was too much moved to speak. All he could say was to stammer, "This looks like the Gate of Heaven."[29]

John left his family in Switzerland late in September 1892 while he returned to Washington, having found that the process of translating the records into French would last into the winter. He sailed back to France in time to spend Christmas with his family in Paris. The arbitration sessions began in January 1893, but during a recess in February, John and Richard spent ten days in London, where John met such dignitaries as Lord Chief Justice Coleridge, the lord chancellor, and the Master of the Rolls and was tendered a dinner at the houses of Parliament by James Bryce. He returned to England after the conclusion of the arbitration in order to prepare his opinion, taking a side trip to Scotland when he had finished. The Harlans sailed back home from Liverpool in October 1893, in time to spend a few days at the Chicago World's Fair (and for John to sit on another round of the *Lake Front* case before the circuit court) before returning to Washington for the remainder of the 1893 session.

The United States had been concerned about the decline in the number of fur seals in Alaskan waters ever since the purchase of Alaska in 1867. The popularity of the fur as an item of fashion led to tremendous slaughter of the animals, which breed in the Pribilof Islands and feed in the Bering Sea or the North Pacific. It was, however, difficult to do much about the situation as long as other nations did not cooperate. Although the American government threatened to seize sealers in international waters (and sometimes did), this was obviously unsatisfactory and even led to threats of the use of the British navy to protect Canadian sealers. Although other countries, particularly Russia and Japan, were involved, the chief conflict was thus between the United States and Great Britain, representing Canadian interests.[30] International arbitration doubtless appealed to both sides as a means of quieting animosities if not settling the problem. Consequently an arbitration commission was formed, consisting of two Americans, two Anglo-Canadians (both sides adding numerous lawyers and advisers), and one each from France, Italy, and Norway/Sweden. It was as a member of this seven-man tribunal that Harlan went to Paris; the other American representative was the Democratic senator from Alabama, John T. Morgan.

The Harlans became close friends of the Morgans'; the judge's family spent several months traveling in Italy with the Morgans while John was back in Washington, and the two Johns—attempting to distance themselves somewhat from the Americans who were to present the U.S. side of the argument—were thrown into each other's company a good deal. Harlan made other friends, especially the senior British judge, Lord Hannen. Hannen, although unwell much of the time, sponsored Harlan's introduction to London legal and political circles, and the favor was reciprocated a year later when Lord Hannen visited Washington (unfortunately he took sick and died there).[31]

The Americans' interest in protecting the fur seals was praiseworthy, but unfortunately they did not have a strong case in international law. They basically argued that the destruction of these valuable animals was *contra bonos mores*. The British replied that, even granting the morality of the American claim, there was nothing in international law that had received "the assent and consent of the civilized nations" of the world that gave one country the right to enforce its own version of morality against the nationals of other countries who were merely following perfectly legal pursuits. Under such circumstances it is not surprising that the arbitration commission ruled against the United States on each of the five questions submitted to it. Senator Morgan dissented from the findings in four of the five, while Justice Harlan voted against his own country in four. The votes did nothing directly to protect the seals, although the two sides did conclude a separate agreement, of which it has been said "that it was a victory for arbitration and the pacific settlement of disputes—not for the seals."[32]

Harlan, naturally, did not return to his country with the plaudits of the multitudes. It was, indeed, charged that he had been brainwashed by the suave Britishers into accepting their arguments on everything. But he took the position of arbitrator as an important job, regarding the work as "the most serious that has ever been committed to me." He further defined his position:

> The average American will assume that the Arbitrators designated by our Country will decide every question submitted to them in favor of our Government, overlooking the fact that we sit as Judges obliged by the highest principles of honor to determine the case in all its aspects according to the principles of law and justice. At any rate I take this view of my position, and do not permit myself to doubt that the other Arbitrators will look at the matter in the same way. The questions to be determined by us are of very great consequence and some of them not at all free from difficulty. I shall aim to know all about the case that may be necessary, and all that can be known by hard work. And I hope the result will not be discreditable either to me or the principles of right and truth.[33]

Certainly there was nothing to Harlan's discredit about the arbitration commission's work or about his own activities and votes. Indeed, he showed rather rare impartiality, especially considering that his pre-Court life had been that of a partisan and that historians often classify him as a judge who tailored the Constitution to suit his preferences.

The Harlans conducted an extensive correspondence from abroad, most of which has unfortunately disappeared. One good example of the fact that the judge was not always as stern and serious as his portraits make him appear is a letter that he wrote (in French) to Justice Brewer.

> You will understand that I am known [here] as a Judge of the Supreme Court of the United States. . . . Beware not to approach me with any familiarity!
>
> Sir Judge [Henry B.] Brown writes me that he is watching you closely but that it is almost impossible to keep you in line. I believe I understand that he is jealous of your fame which is increasing day by day; your reputation being unique as an eloquent orator, as having more ideas and common sense up to the roots of your hair (as they say), and having no colleague up until now able to surpass you on either side of the ocean.
>
> . . . I want to call your attention to the calming qualities of Coal Tar Soap Le Boeuf (the Ox). What attracted my attention to this is the announcement of the inventor in his advertisement here: he promises to regrow hair and to save from anxiety persons who are worried because of their personal appearance; and to relieve from perpetual torment the man who needs to brush his lock of hair from one ear to the other in order to hide the bald places. Sir Judge Brown will no doubt be happy to hear about this remedy.
>
> The time that both of you have wasted in trying to cover the bald places on your heads, if you had spent it studying my judicial opinions, especially my dissenting ones, would have added a great deal to your reputations already so famous and so well deserved as judges.[34]

Harlan knew that the American claim was not legally sound, it seems, for despite his words there is an undercurrent of fatalism in what he wrote to former president Benjamin Harrison:

> I had a sort of "feeling in my bones" that however good our claim to an exclusive jurisdiction . . . there was a strong probability that the tribunal would deny them. . . .
>
> Our country did not get all that it was entitled to have, but if the present [Cleveland] Administration will do its full duty, the seals will be saved from extermination.[35]

Consequently Harlan returned to his judicial duties with moderate satisfaction. Although he was always thin-skinned about public criticism, in this case he did not allow the adverse sentiment to bother him much.

The Circuit Court of Appeals Act of 1891 had another effect on the justices: it relieved them of the necessity of participating in decisions at the intermediate level. Senator William M. Evarts, who guided the act through the Senate, "hardly expected any more circuit attendance by the Justices in the future than in the past, [but] he did not disturb the deep sentiment behind the old tradition by explicitly eliminating them . . . from the composition of the circuit courts of appeals."[36] Active participation in cases did decline rather rapidly, although it did not disappear completely. Gregarious as he was, John Harlan had mixed feelings about this development. On the one hand, he knew what a burden it was to attend circuit courts, almost invariably in the hottest part of the year and at a time when the justices were already played out from a full session's work in Washington. But he obviously relished the chance to mix with the important lawyers and judges and for years had found among them close friends.

In the late 1890s, after his transfer to the sixth circuit, Harlan demonstrated this capacity for friendship by becoming intimate with three of the court's judges. The sixth circuit was based in Cincinnati, a city with which Harlan had long been familiar. Indeed, he was already a very good personal friend of the chief judge, William Howard Taft. He quickly established good relationships with the other Ohioan, William R. Day, and with Horace H. Lurton of Tennessee, with whom he had the chance to share Civil War memories.

The Harlan-Taft friendship had developed over a period of years. Taft was himself almost a quarter of a century younger than Harlan, and the Kentuckian's first contacts undoubtedly came when Taft was still a child. Taft's father, Alphonso, was a successful Ohio lawyer-politician who served for a time in Grant's cabinet; John Harlan apparently knew Alphonso fairly well in his Louisville days. The younger Taft went to Washington as Benjamin Harrison's solicitor general, and this had the effect of ripening a friendship that would last until Harlan's death. Harrison appointed Taft as circuit judge in 1892, and Taft and Harlan continued to see each other frequently and exchanged letters that combined filial affection, humor, and business. Whether Harlan exerted any influence with Harrison in Taft's favor is not known, even though he was fairly close to the president; but he did write to Gus Willson that "Taft will make a good Circuit Judge. He is very agreeable in manners and has personal qualities that will make him popular with the Bar. He has had marvelous success for a young man."[37]

Even more significant in the relationship of the two, when the Harlans finally found a permanent summer home—at Murray Bay on the St. Lawrence in Quebec—they found that the Tafts were already regular summer residents there. The two men had many things in common: both were large men who were also overweight (Taft, indeed, came to weigh over three hundred pounds). Both were lawyers who were mainly interested in being judges, and they had their circuit court business to discuss. Perhaps most of all, they both developed an interest in "the game of Golf," as Mallie Harlan customarily called it.[38]

In the early 1890s Harlan's brother James finally died after years of recurrent bouts of alcoholism and drug addiction. During the last year or two John kept his brother in a Louisville hotel.[39] James was apparently hit by a switch engine in the Louisville railroad yards.[40] Fraternal feelings aside, the justice must have felt, and suppressed, some relief. James had made his own life a misery and had been a constant trial both for John and for their close mutual friend in Louisville, Gus Willson, who later wrote to Richard that James "was a lovable man and learned lawyer but could not let liquor alone."[41]

Harlan's troubles with alcoholic relatives did not end with James's death. He, together with his nephew Harlan Cleveland, supported another of John's nephews for his college education; but J. Harlan Hiter fell into bad habits and was eventually expelled from Washington and Lee in 1900.[42] From this point Hiter apparently went from bad to worse, for one of his other relatives wrote to Harlan in 1911 that "for ten or twelve years I have put up for him, paying his debts, buying new clothes and giving him a fresh start."[43]

Harlan had a fellow sufferer on the Supreme Court, for one of Chief Justice Fuller's daughters was an addict and became a homeless tramp on the streets of her native Chicago, while his father-in-law committed suicide.[44] Possibly this bond of suffering was one of the things that drew the two men to each other.

John Harlan had no such troubles within his immediate family. His marriage remained a happy one, and both he and his wife were on the whole healthy. His two remaining daughters, Laura and Ruth, grew into adulthood with no obvious problems; his granddaughter Edith was sent to the Misses Shipley's School, "Preparatory to Bryn Mawr College," near Philadelphia. The three boys were by the 1890s settled into their professions and making their own marks in the world: all would be successful. Richard, the oldest, was a prominent Presbyterian minister in Rochester, New York. He married but had no children. James was a successful lawyer, in partnership with his brother John, in Chicago. James was, however, ambitious for a judgeship and was prominently mentioned for a U.S. district court position several times during the 1890s; his father used his influence in these instances, but unsuccessfully.[45] John Maynard Harlan became involved in reform politics in Chicago. He was elected to the city council in 1897 and served one term, refusing to run for reelection.[46] A year or so later he was the unsuccessful reform candidate for mayor. But between these bouts with politics he was an extremely successful lawyer. He was also the only one of Harlan's children to have children of his own except, of course, the ill-fated Edith, and one of them, his only son, John Marshall Harlan, was eventually to become a Supreme Court justice in his own right.[47]

Justice Harlan continued his many activities outside the Court. He regularly taught a class of adult men in Sunday School at the New York Avenue Presbyterian Church; he taught constitutional law at the Columbian Law School; and he served on the national committee that was at the time planning to build a cathedral in Washington for the national Presbyterian Church. He gave occasional speeches, taught at the summer session of the University of Virginia Law School, and gave a series of lectures on the Constitution at Northwestern University.[48]

Another sidelight on Harlan's character is his love of a good time in convivial or family surroundings. From football with his sons in 1877 to golf as he approached old age, he always maintained this characteristic, which again gives the lie to the picture of stern dignity shown in his portraits. One admirer reported:

> For years Justice Harlan was the regular and favorite guest of the Bar Association of the District of Columbia in its annual Shad Bake River Excursion to Marshall Hall opposite Mt. Vernon on the Potomac River. Other Justices of the Supreme Court including Chief Justice Fuller who went once and Justices Brewer and Horace Gray who went often, were guests of the Bar Association but Justice Harlan was their standby. His popularity with the judges and lawyers was never greater or more evident anywhere. From the time when he got on the steamer at the Seventh Street Wharf until he said good-by on his return he was always the center of interest and admiration. He entered with youthful zest into the enjoyment of the day, told stories and exchanged repartee, took part in the athletic sports especially baseball, shot at the mark in the shooting gallery, bowled in the bowling alley, ate the planked shad dinner with obvious pleasure, led in the singing of the college songs, and generally was the jolliest and apparently the youngest member of the party. Everybody agreed that he contributed to it more than any one else. The last time he went on the excursion he distinguished himself by knocking a home run in the baseball game (Though, of course, one of the young limbs of the law ran round the bases for him) the first time he went to the bat. Then, as on other occasions, he hit the bull's eye in the shooting gallery practically every time he tried and this with the greatest ease.[49]

The 1890s were a period of stability for the Harlans, a time of relative prosperity and health, and the justice had the satisfaction of being perhaps the best-known member of the Court, primarily for his dissenting opinions in the race and income tax cases.

12

Associate Justice
1897-1911

Justice Stephen J. Field's long-awaited retirement in 1897 left Harlan the senior justice. It also brought up, not for the first time, the question of the sixty-four-year-old Kentuckian's own retirement. This was a question upon which Harlan had frequently speculated, without reaching a firm conclusion. In Paris in 1893 he had written that a professorship at a law school, with a pension, was a position for which he would be "greatly tempted to surrender my present position. . . . I could imagine nothing more agreeable to me than to spend the balance of my life in that sort of work."[1] Similarly, in 1906, at a time when he was indeed under some indirect pressure from President Roosevelt to give way to a younger man, Harlan wrote, "My inclination is to retire." But he went on to speak of his desire

> to participate in the decision of some great questions which will confront the court within the next five years.
>
> Of course, the question would be easy of solution if I was physically or mentally incompetent to meet the requirements of my position. This is a matter which could not be referred to myself alone. Ordinarily, an old man will not recognize the fact that he is steadily going down the hill. If my judgment on the subject is to be trusted, I am physically equal to my judicial work, although I know that I am not as *Keen* for it as I was a few years ago. Many friends—in perfect good faith I do not doubt—have assured me that my opinions of last term are as clear and rigorous as any I have written, and that is the judgment of the profession. They urge me to stand, and not to think of retiring.
>
> So you see, the question is up to me, and I must take the responsibility of deciding it. When I think of the matter at all, five dates come up for retiring: 1. On the 10th of December next, when I shall have been on the Bench twenty-nine years: 2. December 23d, when I shall have been married fifty years: 3. March 4th 1907, so as to enable Congress to confirm the nomination of my successor: 4. *At the end of the next term, June 1st 1907,* when I will be, if alive, 74 years of age: 5. *December 10th 1907,* when I shall have been on duty *thirty* years. To put all those dates aside would mean that I would remain on duty until death removed me. My sons say, stick! They assure me that when the time comes that I should retire, *for the benefit of the public,* they will tell me frankly.

The general question has occurred to me, and doubtless will to you, whether, all things considered, it is not best for a Judge, to have it asked *why he retired,* than why the old man did not retire, and give way for one younger or more vigorous in health. Let me say that I am myself conscious of failing in several respects. I cannot endure physical labors as well as I did a few years ago—my capacity to *concentrate* my reasoning faculties and hold them steadily and continuously on the work in hand and my memory of dates, names and people is . . . not quite what they were. Yet, *generally,* I feel that I am almost as competent for mental work as I ever was.[2]

The Justice was also on record as feeling that he would never resign. In writing to Taft about the possibility of Field's retirement in 1892, Harlan said, "I think you can rely upon it that he will not retire until he makes a permanent removal to the Field cemetery at Stockbridge, MA. In this I think he will be right. I cannot understand how anybody would wish to retire from his regular work after he has become too old to pursue any other course of life with comfort. My own conclusion, long ago formed, is to stay at my post on the Bench until I die."[3] Yet Harlan was thinking seriously, indeed, about leaving the Court in 1906. Aside from his extended comments to Willson, he apparently spoke to Secretary of War Taft about the subject, leaving his old friend with contradictory impressions. Taft wrote to Attorney General William Moody: "I think the President has heard from Harlan, but in a very indefinite way, and with an indication that Harlan wishes to decide himself when the public interest will permit his retirement. I am inclined to think that the old man wants to hang on."[4] Later the same month, however, Taft reported a different feeling to Moody: "I think Harlan is going to retire. He has not been well this summer, and the appointment of James [as a member of the Interstate Commerce Commission] I think has reconciled him to leaving."[5]

Only the next year, however, Harlan was definitely not thinking of retiring. He wrote to Gus Willson: "I have *now* no purpose to 'lay down the shovel and the hoe' of judicial life. I must move ahead in the course of life, and calmly await the end, which cannot, in the nature of things, be *very far off.*"[6] Whatever his tergiversations on the subject and despite political pressures, Harlan never made up his mind to retire, and death claimed him so suddenly that the question was finally beside the point.

By all odds the most significant and the most famous of Harlan's new judicial colleagues during the first decade of the twentieth century was the redoubtable New Englander Oliver Wendell Holmes, Jr., who came to the Court in 1902 as Theodore Roosevelt's choice of a replacement for Horace Gray, also from Massachusetts. A lengthy absence preceded Gray's final decision to resign: he had been absent since mid-February 1902, and his successor was not confirmed until December. Holmes was an aristocrat from an old Boston family and the son of the "Autocrat of the Breakfast Table," a famous writer and poet. Severely wounded in the Civil War, Holmes became a prominent lawyer and legal scholar, writing the seminal work *The Common Law* in 1881. He was appointed to the supreme judicial court of Massachusetts, again succeeding Gray, in 1882, and served for many years as its chief justice. Roosevelt had his doubts about Holmes—at least about whether he was a good enough Republican—but appointed him anyway.

Like Harlan, Justice Holmes was famous partly because of his dissenting opinions. They often dissented in different cases, or if in the same cases for different reasons: the best example perhaps is the New York bakers' case.[7] For many years a large and enthusiastic Holmes cult existed, and there is no doubt of his secure place in Supreme Court history as one of its great judges. A great prose stylist, Holmes was somewhat prone to let a pithy epigram take the place of a clear or profound thought. One commentator appropriately says that "Gray, Harlan and White could make good ideas uninteresting: Holmes made the dullest case a literary adventure." Yet, "the constitutional opinions of Holmes' first years are substantively not very satisfying."[8]

John Harlan was never close to Holmes. Perhaps he disliked having his own intellectual leadership of the Court usurped. Holmes, for his part, was distinctly patronizing toward the senior justice, which must have made Harlan furious at times. The Bostonian privately referred to Harlan as "the last of the tobacco-spittin' judges," which was patronizing even though true! In the Court's conferences he often prefaced a counterargument by calling Harlan "my lion-hearted friend."[9] Holmes was not one to suffer fools gladly; sure of his own intellectual superiority, he could be unfeeling and cutting toward those he regarded as his inferiors. On one occasion he said that Harlan's mental processes were "like a great vise, the two jaws of which cannot be closed closer than two inches of each other."[10]

A comparison of these men, the two dominant figures on the Supreme Court until Harlan's death, is a fascinating study in contrasts. Holmes the aristocrat was intellectual, possibly nihilistic, and brilliant, but withal facile and superficial, a man who loved to play with ideas but was not in the end a profound thinker. Holmes was a literary stylist and phrasemaker but not too proud to appreciate a bawdy story. Harlan, on the other hand, was very much a man of the people, who even in his seventies was marked by the frontier character of early Kentucky. Proud but not intellectual, he held firm if oversimplified convictions and believed in Truth as he saw it. He was not a phrasemaker, and his heart governed his conclusions. It is no wonder that the two did not become close friends, despite a shared Civil War background, the common love of a funny story, and, sometimes, shared conclusions in cases before the Court.[11]

Parenthetically, Harlan did chew tobacco, and of course in the nineteenth century the Court's facilities were liberally supplied with spittoons, as were public buildings generally. Harlan, who liked to reminisce, recalled that

> his father, an old fashioned silver gray whig, abhorred the chewing of tobacco, and often stated that no gentleman would use it in any way. He himself never thought of doing it until one day at school when the school master asked an anaemic youth named Foster what he had in his mouth, and when he was told that it was tobacco rated him soundly telling him that with his poor physical constitution he was hastening his end. Then, turning to young Harlan he said, "Now if you were as strong and tough as John Harlan you might chew with impunity, but as it is you are preparing for an early grave." This, Judge Harlan said, started him that very day to chewing tobacco secretly so far as his father was concerned for a long time, and that he thought his father never became reconciled to it.[12]

George Shiras's resignation early in 1903, after a tenure that left scarcely a trace in Supreme Court jurisprudence, created another vacancy to be filled by the new president, Theodore Roosevelt. His choice fell first on Taft, who declined with great reluctance, and then on Taft's Ohio colleague on the sixth circuit court of appeals, William R. Day. William Rufus Day had been a long-time political ally of President McKinley, who also was from Canton, Ohio. He nevertheless avoided political office until his mentor appointed him an assistant secretary of state in 1897. John Sherman, the secretary, was elderly, crotchety, and despite his illustrious career, entirely undiplomatic, and Day was left with many of the real responsibilities of the department. He headed the American delegation to Paris to settle the Spanish-American treaty and upon his return was rewarded with a seat on the sixth circuit court in Cincinnati, where he made friends with John Harlan. He was to remain there only four years. Roosevelt wished Taft to assume Shiras's seat, but Helen Taft had her eye on the White House, and Taft himself thought he ought to remain as governor general of the Philippines, so Teddy fell back on Day. Harlan was happy to have another close friend on the Court, but in truth Day did not prove to be a great judge. His ideological position on the Court was ambiguous, but on the whole he was conservative regarding federal regulatory programs, while he generally opposed the development of substantive due process limitations on the states.[13]

William H. Moody, another Roosevelt appointee, replaced Henry Billings Brown in 1906. He was the last new justice who would serve with Harlan for any significant length of time. Moody was from Massachusetts, where he had been a successful corporate attorney and a public figure of some importance in Haverhill. Among other tasks, he served as a prosecutor in Lizzie Borden's famous murder trial. A friendship with Roosevelt, begun at a political meeting when Moody was running for Congress in

1895, led to a close association throughout Moody's four terms in that body and to his appointment as secretary of the navy in 1902 and as attorney general two years later.[14] Active and successful in both positions, as attorney general he successfully argued the *Swift* case, one of the administration's most publicized antitrust actions.[15] He was then elevated to the Supreme Court. Whether or not Moody would have been a strong judge is unknown, for unfortunately he fell seriously ill after two years, although he remained on the Court for two more sessions, during which he was unable to function. He would likely have been a moderately liberal justice and, as such, probably would have voted with Harlan frequently.[16]

The other two justices, appointed by President Taft, came to the Court so near to Harlan's death that questions of interaction become relatively insignificant. Horace H. Lurton, the third of the sixth circuit judges to rise to the Supreme Court, was elderly by the time of his appointment in 1909 (replacing Peckham) and served only until 1914. Charles Evans Hughes, the most significant appointment since Holmes, served only six years before resigning in order to run for president in 1916. The Lurtons and the Harlans were already close family friends, and the two old men enjoyed swapping Civil War stories.

> My husband's circuit, during the last years of his services on the Supreme Court, comprised the States of Ohio, Kentucky and Tennessee. Among the Federal Judges in that Circuit was Judge Horace H. Lurton of Nashville. My husband and he often held court together on the Circuit and they had become greatly attached to each other, although they had served on opposite sides during the Civil War.
>
> Hearing my husband's glowing account of Murray Bay as a summer resort, Judge and Mrs. Lurton went there in the summer of 1902 or 1903. We saw much of them, for we were anxious to make the summer pass pleasantly for them. One evening, we invited some friends to meet them at supper—the "simple life" being the rule at Murray Bay, "dinners" were rarely given.
>
> There were perhaps a dozen people at the table, and my husband, being in the best of spirits, began to tell the company some of his experiences in the Civil War. He was describing a hurried and exciting march which he and his regiment made through Tennessee and Kentucky in pursuit of the daring Confederate raider, John Morgan. He came to a point in his story where he and the advance guard of the pursuing Union troops had nearly overtaken the rearguard of Morgan's men, who had just crossed a little stream near Hartsville, Tennessee, and were being fired upon by the Union men from the opposite shore.
>
> Suddenly, Judge Lurton . . . laid down his knife and fork, leaned back in his chair, his face aglow with surprise and wonder, and called out to my husband in a voice of great excitement, "Harlan, is it possible I am just finding out who it was that tried to shoot me on that never-to-be-forgotten day?"
>
> In a tone of equal surprise and wonder my husband said, "Lurton, do you mean to tell me that *you* were with Morgan on that raid. Now I know *why* I did not catch up with him; and I thank God I didn't hit *you* that day."[17]

Harlan also welcomed Hughes to the Court and indeed was apparently somewhat of a father-figure, if indeed the sturdy, independent Hughes needed such a thing.[18]

The chief controversy surrounding Harlan's later years was his role in the selection of a new chief justice upon Fuller's death in 1910. As early as 1904 Republican politicians were looking forward to the vacancy on the Supreme Court that would occur when the chief justice resigned. For their own differing reasons, both President Theodore Roosevelt and William Howard Taft, then secretary of war, were, in the words of Taft's biographer, "a little ghoulish as [they] pondered the unreasonable longevity" of the chief justice. After all, Fuller was seventy-one, old for the times, and his wife had died in August. Taft wrote that her death "leaves the poor Chief Justice a stricken man." He also commented hopefully that Fuller "was getting very tired of cases."[19]

President Roosevelt, for his part, embarked on an undercover campaign to persuade Fuller that it was time to leave. Two years earlier, in fact, when Taft had declined the nomination to replace Associate Justice George Shiras, Jr., this campaign had begun. While Taft refused on the very reasonable grounds that he wanted to finish his work as governor of the Philippines, he had never made any secret of his ambition to be chief justice. It is not unlikely that Roosevelt, who felt himself to be under a deep political obligation to Taft, set out to create conditions that would be impossible to refuse. The chief justiceship would probably have been such a position. Then too, in 1902 TR possibly wanted to eliminate the popular Taft as a possible rival for the presidential nomination in 1904. In any case, a "White House story" leaking the nomination of William Rufus Day for the Shiras vacancy went on to speculate: "The suggestion is made that Chief Justice Fuller may soon wish to retire and that Governor Taft would be a suitable man for the vacancy." Shortly after this sentence appeared, the president's close political friend Wayne MacVeagh visited the chief justice, at Roosevelt's request. MacVeagh diplomatically referred to the newspaper story and asked whether there was any basis for it. Fuller, who had been rather insulted by the whole idea, denied it.[20]

Whether or not Chief Justice Fuller had ever thought of resigning, he certainly did not do so in the face of this somewhat clumsy attempt at persuasion. He told Justice Holmes that he was not about to be "paragraphed" out of his position.[21] In 1902 and also 1904, Fuller was in good health and performing his duties as capably as ever; Holmes, who served with him during this period, later remarked that Fuller was the best chief justice under whom he served—a remark that compared Taft himself, White, and Hughes with Fuller. The Chief Justice did not resign, then or ever. Taft's interest in the position continued, as did the newspaper speculation. When Associate Justice Henry Billings Brown resigned in 1906, it recurred. The then secretary of war's concern for Fuller's health was rather touching: "If the Chief Justice would retire, how simple everything would become," he wrote to his wife.[22] Again Roosevelt offered Taft an associate justice position, and again Taft declined. He was holding out for the chief's position, but eventually he became the Republican nominee for president in 1908. He ran, won, and entered the White House on March 4, 1909, with Fuller still holding on to his place.

As president, Taft's priorities naturally changed. No longer dangling for the chief justiceship himself, he nevertheless continued to feel that Fuller had outstayed his proper time on the Court, as had several other of the justices. One cannot, at this distance, tell with any certainty how serious the president was about this. His much quoted comment to Horace Lurton stands on one side: "The condition of the Supreme Court is pitiable, and yet those old fools hold on with a tenacity that is most discouraging. Really the Chief Justice [then seventy-six] is almost senile; Harlan [also seventy-six] does no work; Brewer [only seventy-two] is so deaf that he cannot hear and has got beyond the point of commonest accuracy in writing his opinions; Brewer and Harlan sleep almost through all the arguments. I don't know what can done. It is most discouraging to the active men on the bench."[23] One should add in fairness that "the active men on the bench" in 1909 were not necessarily much better off. William H. Moody was ill and was forced to resign in 1910, despite being, at fifty-six, the youngest member of the Court. Rufus Peckham was seventy-one and also ill. Holmes was a comparative stripling of sixty-eight, Edward D. White was sixty-five, William R. Day only fifty-nine, and Joseph McKenna sixty-six. The latter had difficulty writing clear opinions, and seemingly the bulk of the Court's work fell on Holmes, White, and Day.

One might also recall that Harlan was a close friend of Taft's: they had vacationed together, with their families, in Quebec since the 1890s. Taft also knew that Harlan was a great friend of Lurton's and would possibly have been reluctant to criticize Harlan seriously in a letter to a close mutual friend. Then too, Taft was an extremely verbal man, and often seemed to write letters in order to get immediate concerns off his chest regardless of whether they represented settled convictions.

There was, however, an obvious element of truth in what Taft wrote: the Court was unusually old, and illness did not help. Even so, there is little or no independent evidence that Fuller was senile or that Harlan was lazy. The younger justices, except for Holmes and perhaps White, did not help the Court much. They were mediocre at best even if healthy. The names of Day, McKenna, Moody, and Peckham do not ring down through American history. Taft should have complained about the weakness of the Court rather than merely its age.[24]

If President Taft felt that old age was a serious problem, he went about correcting the situation rather strangely. His first appointment was the selfsame Horace Lurton, sixty-six years old when he replaced Peckham late in 1909. While his other appointees were younger than his friend Lurton—Charles Evans Hughes, indeed, was only forty-nine—they were not of a caliber to raise the prestige of the Court. Willis Van Devanter, Joseph R. Lamar, and Mahlon Pitney were, like their predecessors, at most mediocre. The Court continued to be, on the whole, weak. This was the situation when Chief Justice Fuller died at his summer home in Maine in July 1910. Ironically, Taft now had to appoint someone else to the place he had so long coveted for himself and might not now ever attain.

The standard version of the story of the appointment is told with only minor variations by such writers as Merlo J. Pusey, Henry F. Pringle, and, more recently, John E. Semonche.[25] The front-runner was undoubtedly Hughes, but there was speculation about Holmes, White, Harlan, Senator Elihu Root of New York, and Secretary of State Philander C. Knox of Pittsburgh. Root was sixty-five, Knox only fifty-seven. Knox had already turned down two chances to ascend to the bench: he had been Roosevelt's second choice each time Taft had refused. Taft apparently did not consider him very seriously, despite his initial preference for a man who was still fairly young, under sixty-five, at least. Root, on the other hand, was considered by the president to be too old. In another of his chatty letters, Taft wrote that "if Mr. Root were five years younger I should not hesitate a moment about whom to make chief justice . . . but I doubt if he has in him that length of hard, routine work and constant attention to the business of the court and to the reform of its methods which a chief justice ought to have."[26] This is an ironic statement, certainly, considering the eventual outcome of Taft's search.

Charles Evans Hughes, with a great reputation as a progressive Republican governor of New York, was the junior associate justice and the man who was most entitled to think he had a right to the position. Without making a promise, Taft had in his typical expansive fashion hinted broadly that Hughes would get the job; in fact, there is some doubt that Hughes would even have accepted the post as successor to Justice Brewer had he not expected to be elevated when Fuller left the Court. Taft wrote, "The chief justiceship is soon likely to be vacant and I should never regard the practice of never promoting associate justices as one to be followed. Though, of course, this suggestion is only that by accepting the present position you do not bar yourself from the other, should it fall vacant in my term." Taft was about as explicit as one could well be without making an actual promise. He went on to qualify his statement: "Don't misunderstand me as to the chief justiceship. I mean that if the office were now open, I should offer it to you and it is probable that if it were to become vacant during my term, I should promote you to it; but, of course, conditions change so that it would not be right for me to say by way of promise what I would do in the future."[27]

It is not known whether Hughes really counted on this semipromise.

Nor is it known why the president failed to deliver on it. Hughes was not even seated yet when Chief Justice Fuller died, and there was no bar at all, not even that of custom, in the way of his translation to the chief justiceship. Some speculated that the former New York governor was too young to suit Taft. Semonche is the most explicit in this regard: Taft's "appointment of a young man like Hughes to the top spot would probably place the chief justiceship permanently beyond his reach."[28] If the president still had the ambition to become chief justice, however, there is no direct evidence of it. Two other factors also militated against the appointment of Hughes. One was that Teddy Roosevelt, still the most powerful man in the Republican party and still (in 1910) Taft's close friend and adviser, did not like Hughes. Taft himself had once remarked that Hughes was "a man without magnetism," although what magnetism has to do with the functions of chief justice is a little uncertain.[29] But Roosevelt had the idea that Hughes was "a very, very self-centered man" and opposed his nomination.[30] Finally, the president perhaps mistakenly asked for the opinion of the Court itself: feeling on the Court was that a sitting justice ought to receive the appointment, and when Attorney General George W. Wickersham polled the justices personally, he found that White rather than Hughes was their choice.[31]

Although White was sixty-five, the same age as Root, Taft had by now apparently given up age as a principal factor. Semonche, indeed, believes that age had become a positive asset: perhaps White would last just long enough as chief justice so that when the seat became vacant again Taft would no longer be president but would still be young enough to be appointed.[32] There may be a good deal of hindsight involved in Semonche's view, since that is exactly what happened. Partly due to the intervention of the Democrat Woodrow Wilson's two terms, however, it may have happened some years later than Taft hoped. In fact, Taft accepted the position from President Warren G. Harding in violation of his own earlier feeling about the unfitness of elderly judges. He, too, was sixty-five.

Justice Holmes was never, it would appear, very seriously considered. He wrote to Sir Frederick Pollock that he thought White was the most logical choice aside from Hughes. Harlan was too old, he said, and "I have always assumed absolutely that I should not be regarded as possible—they don't appoint side Judges as a rule, it would be embarrassing to skip my Seniors, and I am too old. I think I would be a better administrator than White, but he would be more politic."[33] Holmes had been a very successful chief judge of the supreme judicial court of Massachusetts for a decade.

Regarding Harlan, the standard version has it that, he "was obviously hungry for the honor."[34] The next episode is well known: "Word had reached the White House [from whom, the historians never divulge] that Associate Justice Harlan . . . thought he should receive the elevation as a final ornament to his judicial career. His retirement would soon come." On hearing this, the story goes, Taft "exploded."[35] (Another writer says he "stormed," while a third uses the more neutral term "responded."[36] Considering Taft's fat-man reputation for geniality, his close friendship with Harlan, and his general penchant for overstatement, perhaps *responded* is the most accurate term.) "I'll do no such damned thing; I won't make the position of chief justice a blue ribbon for the final years of any member of the court. I want someone who will co-ordinate the activities of the court and who has a reasonable expectation of serving ten or twenty years on the bench."[37]

Verbiage aside, the president was undoubtedly right. Harlan was too old, as were Holmes, Root, and, arguably, White, not to speak of Taft himself twelve years later. Only one of White's predecessors as chief justice (Roger Brooke Taney) had been even sixty. The chief justice has a wearing task, perhaps especially during his first few years, and while experience may be essential, so is energy.

The standard version of White's appointment goes wrong in its assumption that Harlan was, or thought himself to be, a potential nominee. Except for the White House episode quoted above, there is no evidence that he was even interested in the position. The only authority for such an interest is the comment of Hughes to his "official" biographer. Hughes was not an unbiased observer, although he was at the time fairly close to Harlan, nor did he say that Harlan told him of his interest, an event that in any case would seem unlikely considering Hughes's own interest in the position, of which Harlan undoubtedly knew. Hughes, in fact, makes more of Justice White's "hunger" to be chief justice than of Harlan's: he told Merlo Pusey that during the period when Taft was pondering the matter, with Harlan presiding as senior Associate Justice, White "had little to say in conference and his usually amiable disposition seemed to have passed under a cloud. Throughout the fall he was offish and disgruntled."[38]

It is true that the two senior justices, Harlan and White, were not close friends. White was a Catholic, a Democrat, and a former Confederate; Harlan was a devout Presbyterian, a rabid Republican, and had been a Unionist in Kentucky when that stance was politically risky. They had frequently disagreed about the cases before the Court, especially on the interpretation of the Sherman Antitrust Act and in the insular cases. Yet this line of reasoning can be carried too far. There is little doubt that Harlan was unhappy to see White become chief justice, but this was probably more due to disagreement on the Court than to any personal feelings between the two. Harlan was entirely capable of accepting former Confederates: Lurton, in fact, was a friend of many years' standing despite his record as a Tennessee Confederate officer. The relations between the Louisianan and the Kentucky colonel were, if not close, at least correct, as a rather charming, though possibly apocryphal, newspaper story indicates:

> Chief Justice White and Justice Harlan are widely known for pedestrianship. They enjoy the exercise, but Justice Harlan finds automobiles disquieting and

has grown to dislike them with a fervor not inferior to that manifested by Senator Bailey and Champ Clark.

The two jurists recently started up Pennsylvania Avenue on their way home. When crossing a side street an automobile came whizzing around a corner and Justice Harlan was saved from possible injury by Justice White, who dragged him out of harm's way.[39]

They were intimate enough to walk home together, at least, even if White did not actually save the elder man's life.

From whom did Taft get the idea that his old friend from Kentucky was "hungry" to be chief justice? Possibly he had no such idea. It almost certainly did not come from Harlan himself, nor with Harlan's knowledge or consent. A George Dorsey, of Fremont, Nebraska, sent a letter to Taft, and an editorial appeared in the Salt Lake City *Tribune;* copies of these were sent to Harlan, but he had nothing to do with their writing.[40] Possibly most influential would have been the fact that Lurton, who was a friend of the president and of Harlan dating back to circuit court days, apparently interceded in the Kentuckian's behalf; at least he did not oppose Harlan. He wrote the Kentuckian that "it looks like Hughes for Chief though I only know from press reports. Occasionally I am gratified to see your name. This would be a most graceful compliment well bestowed and gratifying to me as your friend." It is not known what Harlan thought of this. His reply is noncommittal: "The mention of my name in connection with the place has been without my knowledge or procurement. I do not suppose that I will be thought of."[41]

This would seem to indicate that Justice Harlan was realistic enough to know that he did not have much chance for the place; it stops short, however, of proving that he did not want it. His other known remarks on the subject bear out these points but go a little farther toward personal renunciation of ambition. In one letter he merely repeated the substance of his comment to Lurton: "In view of my advanced years—if there were no other reason—the President will not think of me as Chief Justice. I do not know to what extent my name has been mentioned. Certain it is, I have not moved in the matter nor will do so."[42] Earlier, in a letter to Justice Day, Harlan commented that some friends in Louisville had proposed him. He continued: "I wrote to them to forebear any action in my behalf and I think they are conforming to my request. Of course, the President will never think of me in connection with this matter. My years forbid his consideration of my name, even if he had no other objections. Who will be appointed no one can guess. I do not think Hughes's chances are as good as they would have been had he not been appointed an Associate Justice. I now doubt whether the President has made up his mind finally on the subject."[43]

The most convincing evidence that Harlan did not expect the appointment to fall his way is the fact that he was pushing for another candidate. In a letter to the president, he urged Taft to appoint Justice Day.

Although the question as to the vacancy caused by the death of the late Chief Justice is one of great importance to every citizen of the United States, especially to the present members of the Supreme Court, I would not volunteer my expression of opinion as to a successor, if a former vacancy had not been heretofore the subject of some conversation between us. I beg to make a few suggestions touching this matter.

Up to this time, there has been, I believe, only one instance of the Chief Justiceship being offered to an Associate Justice of the Court. That occurred in the case of Mr. Justice Cushing who, it was supposed, declined on the ground of infirm health. The usage referred to has, I think, no sound reason in its support. Indeed, I have always thought that an Associate Justice ought, as a general rule, to succeed a Chief Justice, who had died or resigned, unless, in the judgment of the President, he was disqualified for the position by advanced years, or by ill health; *provided, always,* he was, in character, sound judgment, sagacity and legal attainments *equal* to the place.

I beg to say that there is on the Supreme Bench an Associate Justice who is equal to the Chief Justiceship, and whose appointment would, I am confident, meet with general approval by the Bench and the Bar, as well as by the people at large. He was born in 1849 and is by no means too old for the place, especially when that fact is considered in connection with his experience in active, judicial life. His appearance at first might impress one with the idea that he was not very strong, physically. But President McKinley once told me that Justice Day was as "hard as a knot," and would likely reach an advanced age. You will know whether he was often absent from his post as a Circuit Judge on account of sickness. Since coming to the Supreme Bench he has not, that I can recall, missed but a few days, if any, on account of sickness. I have found him to be as represented by President McKinley. He has exhibited, on our Bench, an unusual capacity and fondness for judicial work. He has been indefatigable in his judicial labors. Indeed, since he has been with us no member of the Court has held to his work more persistently or steadily nor done a greater amount of work, than Day. His opinions, in my judgment, will always be highly regarded. They show unusual care in preparation. They are not overrun with *dicta* nor with immaterial suggestions. I regard him as a first-class lawyer—sagacious, cautious, as firm as a rock, eminently wise in consultation. And what has become a necessary qualification in a Chief Justice (however great his legal attainments or mental power may be), he has fine executive power and is a "man of affairs." His experience as a Judge would enable him to take up the work of the Court where the late Chief Justice left it, and go right ahead without delay or any friction whatever. He would not be under the necessity of becoming trained in details, upon the "handling" of which with ease and promptness so much depends. He is already fully informed as to the manner in which the business of the Court is transacted. My conviction is strong that, all things considered, the best interests of the country, and the efficient administration of the law will be promoted by his selection as Chief Justice.[44]

Day, too, disclaimed any expectations. On receipt of a copy of the above letter, he wrote to Harlan: "I am not vain enough to think that the President will seriously think of me in connection with the office of Chief Justice, but I will not deny that your opinion of me in this connection has been pleasant reading."[45]

Coming as it did only a week after Fuller's death, Harlan's letter perhaps accomplished several things other than its ostensible purpose. Taft apparently never considered Day as a serious possibility, but the letter did suggest to him the utility of appointing an associate justice with experience of the Court's operations. Harlan may, in fact, have been the first person to suggest this to the president. It was a congenial suggestion: as Robert B. Highsaw suggests, the Court was at the time composed of four relative newcomers and had only four experienced judges. This made strong leadership from the chief's position more important than it might otherwise have been. Taft also felt that White's judicial record was similar to what his own would have been.[46] Taft, then, did agree that elevation of an associate justice would be a good idea. His reply to Harlan did not, of course, say so: it was for Taft unusually noncommittal. "I have your letter of July 11th, with respect to the Chief Justiceship, and I shall give it the full consideration that advice coming from such a source is entitled to. Moody is going to retire, so that I shall have the appointment of a Chief Justice and an Associate Justice, in addition to those already made. I shall keep your letter in order to give it full weight when the time for final decision comes."[47]

In summation, Harlan would probably have liked to be chief justice, and he would also probably have preferred someone other than White. He certainly did not expect to be appointed, however, nor did his feeling about White affect his performance on the Court in the year of life remaining to him. Justice Hughes wrote that "Harlan concealed whatever disappointment he felt in not being made Chief Justice [or, perhaps, in White's elevation] and continued his work through the 1910 term with but little apparent abatement in his vigor."[48] On the other side of the scale, Senator Joseph B. Foraker of Ohio remarked, on attending a judicial dinner late in 1910,

I met the new Chief Justice and had with him a very agreeable conversation. I also met Mr. Justice Harlan. In the course of my conversation with him I remarked that I had tried to imagine how he felt when swearing into office the new Chief Justice. "On this hint he spake," and told me that he felt disappointed when the President, after he concluded to appoint an Associate Justice, passed him by and selected one so much his junior in service and, as he thought, less entitled by their past records to such a recognition at the hands of a Republican President; but he said, straightening himself up and evidently feeling every word he spoke, "I was careful to wear on that occasion my Loyal

Legion button, and I took pains to so stand before him that he could not help but see it; and when I read him the oath I placed emphasis on the requirement that he should uphold the Constitution."[49]

It is difficult to know what to make of this. It is doubtful that Harlan was intimate enough with Foraker to express his innermost feelings in that bald a fashion. He may have been joking, at least about the Loyal Legion button. There is no evidence at all that Harlan was ever mean or petty about other people. He had known White for many years, and if they were not the closest of friends, they were certainly not enemies. Nor did the Kentuckian ever show that much prejudice against former Confederates: Lucius Q.C. Lamar had been a good friend, and Horace Lurton and his family were intimate with the Harlans. Nevertheless, an undercurrent in what Foraker said that Harlan told him is probably true: Harlan would have liked the position himself, and failing that he would have preferred others—Day or Hughes—to White. There is, however, no solid evidence that Harlan either wanted or expected the position for himself. Of course he knew that others were suggesting him as a possibility, and he was human enough to harbor, probably, some inner hopes. "Obvious hunger" is, however, a figment of some historian's imagination.

Chief Justice Fuller died on July 4, 1910, and White was sworn in as his successor on December 19 of the same year. In the interim John Harlan, as senior associate, acted as chief justice. During the rest of the summer the work would not have amounted to a great deal, but Harlan undoubtedly had to be in Washington ahead of his colleagues in September in order to make sure the cases were properly scheduled and everything was ready for the coming session.

Harlan presided over the Court in its hearing of arguments, which began on October 13 with a federal criminal case, *Holt* v. *United States*, involving the admissibility of evidence under the Fifth Amendment.[50] The task of assigning opinions also devolved upon him: for this first case he selected Holmes. He also, of course, presided over the judicial conference. Harlan had, it is true, presided occasionally since 1897 when Fuller had been unable to attend Court proceedings. During this more formal period he was at the helm of the Court for the hearing of the argument of about seventy-five cases, the reports of which include over 914 pages in the *United States Reports*.[51] Of these cases, thirty-three involved constitutional issues, but only two—*Muskrat* v. *United States* and *Bailey* v. *Alabama*—survive to be studied by constitutional law students today.[52] Dissents were reported in only eight of the seventy-five cases. Harlan has left no record of his feelings regarding this episode, nor (apparently) did anyone else comment on the adequacy of his performance. The Court as an institution can carry on through such periods without any outward sign of stress or inefficiency.

Besides his occasional lecture series at Northwestern and Virginia law schools, Justice Harlan was a long-time professor of constitutional law at Columbian Law School. He was for years a favored lecturer, drawing large enrollments of young men, one of whom wrote fondly to Richard in 1930:

> Your father was one of those few men who influence young men to an extent that, a quarter of a century afterwards, they quote and actually bear him in mind during their daily work.
>
> Judge Harlan lectured to our class of two hundred members (1903). . . . The spontaneity of the applause that frequently marked the beginning and close of his sessions, was sufficient evidence of the appreciation the members had of him.
>
> He greatly impressed me the first day that I heard him in class . . . when a green student asked him some question, to which Judge Harlan said he was not sure of the answer but he would look into the subject and reply definitely at the next session. For one of the greatest judges . . . to avoid any degree of evasion . . . naturally gave the students confidence that anything he told them in the future would be a thing to be relied upon.
>
> His sense of humor was always entertaining. He always got a good laugh when he would explain a majority opinion of the Supreme Court and then outline his own sole dissenting opinion . . . , and after a sufficient pause, add: "But of course I was wrong." The simplicity of his character was indicated by a remark he made in class one day, to the effect that he liked to stand on the outside platform of the street car on his way home from court, as he never found a street car conductor from whom he could not gain some information.[53]

Despite this success as a teacher, John's career at the law school ended sourly in 1910. Due either to financial exigencies, personal spite against Harlan, or a real feeling that he was too old, a new university administration cut the length of his course in half, with a corresponding reduction in salary.[54] Harlan, who greatly enjoyed the contact with "his young men" and who was proud of his teaching, attributed the event to the dislike held for the Harlans by the wife of the new president, Harry Snow; she was a cousin of Mallie's and apparently felt that she had been mistreated by the Harlans when the Snows first moved to Washington. She wrote to Harlan, "You all thought we were to be patronized when we came here. *Why*, only you know."[55] Harlan wrote to a member of the university's board of trustees: "My surroundings have become very disagreeable. The Chairman of the Executive Committee [Snow] has without cause become hostile to every member of my family and to myself. His wife was writing unfriendly letters about us in many directions. The husband, of course, knew of these letters and originally or subsequently approved, or failed to control her action. Besides, the unjust action taken in reference to my son's [James's] salary was largely due to him as Trustee. . . . To this I may add, that I did not like the proposition made in reference to my own salary."[56]

John Marshall Harlan, about 1880. One friend remarked that the junior justice looked "like a born judge." Harlan Papers, Library of Congress.

Malvina ("Mallie") Shanklin Harlan (1838-1916), possibly about 1900. She seems to have been an ideal wife for a Supreme Court justice. Harlan Papers, Library of Congress.

Harlan's parents, in portraits by an unknown artist: left, Eliza Shannon Davenport Harlan (d. 1870); right, James Harlan (1800-1863). James was a Whig congressman and Kentucky Attorney General, but his wife was reportedly the moving force in the household. Courtesy of the Kentucky Historical Society. Below, *The County Election*, by George Caleb Bingham, 1851/52. Harlan probably attended dozens of such occasions, which were typical of Kentucky in the 1840s and 1850s. Courtesy of the St. Louis Art Museum, Museum Purchase.

Above, the home of John Marshall Harlan and his family at the corner of Broadway and Madison, Frankfort, Kentucky, purchased about 1865. The howitzer was broken down for scrap during World War II; the house was razed in 1970. Photo by Cusick, courtesy of the Kentucky Historical Society.

A rare informal snapshot of Justice Harlan playing golf, probably about 1905. Harlan Papers, Library of Congress.

Two of Harlan's law partners and longtime friends: left, Augustus Willson (1846-1931), later a Republican governor of Kentucky. Right, Benjamin Helm Bristow (1832-1896), who split with Harlan because of rivalry for the Supreme Court post. Both courtesy of the Kentucky Historical Society. Below, the Old Senate Chamber, "home" of the Supreme Court throughout Harlan's tenure on the bench. Collection of the Supreme Court of the United States.

The four "great" associate justices of the Supreme Court during the second half of the nineteenth century. Above left, Joseph P. Bradley (on Court 1870-1892); above right, Stephen J. Field (1863-1897); below left, Samuel F. Miller (1862-1890); below right, Harlan (1877-1911). Collection of the Supreme Court of the United States.

The three chief justices under whom Harlan served. Above left, Morrison R. Waite (on Court 1874-1888); above right, Melville Weston Fuller (1888-1910); below, Edward Douglass White (1894-1921, chief justice 1911-1921). Waite and Fuller were Harlan's closest friends on the Court; White was perhaps his greatest antagonist. Collection of the Supreme Court of the United States.

The Supreme Court in session, probably in 1887. An unusual depiction of the Court in action. Harlan is the third justice from the right. Library of Congress. Below, "Our Overworked Supreme Court," a cartoon by Keppler in *Puck,* April 1885. During the 1880s the Court had probably the heaviest caseload in its history. Library of Congress.

PUCK.

OUR OVERWORKED SUPREME COURT.
It is Unequal to the Ever-Increasing Labor Thrust Upon It. Will Congress Take Prompt Measures for the Relief of the People?

John Marshall Harlan dur-
ing his later years on the
Court. By 1910 he was the
senior justice and the oldest.
Library of Congress.

Associate Justice Oliver
Wendell Holmes, Jr. (on
Court 1902-1932). Holmes
was the sole great justice ap-
pointed during the first dec-
ade of the twentieth century.
Collection of the Supreme
Court of the United States.

The Justice resigned his faculty position in July 1910. Looking back on his years as a law teacher, he wrote to a friend, "One of the pleasantest features of my labors was the receipt of letters from students, in every section, who attended my lectures and who said that the time passed with me was both delightful and instructive. I was buoyed up with the thought that my lectures had much to do with spreading safe and sound thoughts about our National Government and the Constitution under which it was organized."[57] There can be no doubt that the old man's pride was hurt; but at seventy-seven he had probably reached the point at which he should have stepped down anyway.

John Harlan's activities spread widely during the latter part of his life. He served as president of the board of trustees of the Garfield Memorial Hospital in 1907 and 1908, which proved a most responsible and time-consuming activity.[58] He was active in the campaign to build a national cathedral for the Presbyterian Church in Washington.[59] He shared with an Anglican colleague the trusteeship of the union church at Murray Bay during the pleasant summers that the Harlans and Tafts spent there.[60] He was also a national officer in the Presbyterian Church in addition to maintaining his Sunday school class in the church in Washington.[61] As if this were not enough, Harlan drew up a detailed plan for the government of the District of Columbia, which he sent to Teddy Roosevelt in 1908.[62] It was not adopted.

Although deeply religious, Harlan was not a pious man, and he retained his sense of fun even in religious matters. An old friend of his later recalled:

When Justice Harlan was Vice Moderator [of the national Presbyterian Church] at Winona, Indiana, a Bull of Bashaw voiced commissioner moved
    That all deacons, elders and ministers be enjoined not to use tobacco in any form.
    It was adopted with a whoop.
    I went up to the platform and said to the Judge
    "I have here two six inch cigars—will you join me in vindicating the sacred 'right of private judgment' out front as the commissioners file out?"
    He said "I will."
    He did—
    Handing over the gavel . . . he and I went out the rear stage door and as the anti-tobacconists filed out they saw the Vice Moderator . . . in the solemn process of "vindicating."[63]

Harlan was an enthusiastic, but not a very good, golfer, and he early began to extend this interest beyond the summers at Pointe-au-Pic, Quebec. He became a member of the Chevy Chase Country Club in 1897 and was soon a familiar figure on the links, playing perhaps in a foursome that might include that even more weighty personage William Howard Taft, or Philander C. Knox. In one of his frequent joshing letters to Taft, John wrote:

> You will be remembered in history as the Father of the Fillipinos, the Builder of the Panama Canal, and the Slayer of Boss Cox. Now add to your titles by becoming the Slayer of Judges and Senators who think they can play Golf, but can do no more than play *at* the game.
>
> I saw Senator Knox yesterday at Chevy Chase, and proposed a game with you. He liked the idea. What say you as to a three-some on Monday or Wednesday at 2 o'clock sharp?[64]

Harlan's financial situation improved little over the years. If he was out of serious debt, it was yet true that, as Richard wrote to Taft (then president-elect) in 1909, his father had "not been able to save a single dollar," despite the fact—well known in Washington social circles—that he lived "with democratic simplicity,"—having few entertainments and not even maintaining a carriage (Harlan greatly disliked those newfangled automobiles). Even had he wished to retire, Harlan could hardly have afforded it.[65]

Harlan was fortunate in his sons. Not only did he and Mallie enjoy close relationships with all their children, but the boys were successful in their own careers and in their family lives as well. The two remaining daughters, Laura and Ruth, never married and lived with their parents in Washington. Years later, Laura apparently was a personal secretary to the wife of President Warren G. Harding.[66]

Richard, the oldest son, became a very successful Presbyterian clergyman. He served the congregations of the Old First Church in New York City and the Third Presbyterian Church in Rochester. In 1906 he moved to Washington as a faculty member of George Washington University, where he became known as a social reformer and was influential in the establishment of the graduate school. From 1901 to 1906 he was president of Lake Forest College in the suburbs of Chicago.[67] He had no children.

James, the second son, had become a lawyer with a tendency to depend on his father's influence but apparently the ability to succeed in his own right. He practiced in Chicago for some years in the 1880s and 1890s, and his name became familiar as an unsuccessful candidate for every federal judgeship that became vacant in that city, despite the justice's aid. He went to Puerto Rico as attorney general from 1901 to 1903 and was praised by local leaders for his work there. After a short law partnership with his brother John in Chicago, he was finally appointed as a member of the Interstate Commerce Commission by Teddy Roosevelt in 1906, a position in which he served ably until his retirement in 1918.[68] He and his wife, too, were childless.

The only one of the sons who engaged actively in politics was the youngest, John Maynard. In addition to serving as alderman in Chicago for one term (1896-98), he ran unsuccessfully for mayor as a reform Republican in 1897 and again in 1905, and for governor of Illinois as an Independent in 1920. In between these campaigns he was a highly successful lawyer and civic leader. He was chiefly responsible for the Chicago Traction Ordinance of 1905, regarded as an important piece of progressive legislation.[69] As faithful friends of William Howard Taft, the Harlans supported his campaign for reelection in 1912, and John Maynard followed TR around as one of the Taft Truth Tellers. He moved to New York in 1925, apparently to join his son, John Marshall Harlan, Jr., in legal practice there. Justice Harlan's grandson, of course, became the second of that name to serve as a highly respected Supreme Court justice, from 1955 to 1971. John Maynard had three other children and there were also grandchildren. But as of 1985, there seemed to be no remaining direct descendant of John and Mallie.

John Maynard Harlan wrote to Gus Willson on October 13, 1911: "Father is seriously ill and has been so since the adjournment of the Court on Tuesday last. For some days he has had a slight cold. The matter was aggravated on Tuesday by an intestinal disturbance which brought on a high fever that has rapidly impaired his strength. His wonderful vitality has enabled him to hold his own surprisingly well, but I cannot say that he is as strong this morning as he was yesterday."[70] Death came to John Marshall Harlan a day later; the cause given by his wife was pneumonia.[71]

Harlan had returned to Washington from Pointe au Pic only a few days before the opening of the Court's 1911 session, which began on Monday, October 9. According to Mallie, he had been in good health during the summer but had taken cold during a weeklong stopover in New York with his son John. Nevertheless he attended the Court's opening in "apparently good health."[72]

J.E. Hoover, James's secretary at the ICC, was at this time close to the family, and he wrote a long letter to Richard describing the events of that Monday and Tuesday. Richard was in Paris, but all the other children were in Washington.

> According to a long-established custom, nothing was done in Court on Monday besides the admission of new members to the Bar and the formal submission of motions. At the hour of twelve the members of the Court, as heretofore, filed into the courtroom, in single file, with the Marshal in the lead. I was present. It was gratifyingly remarked by several of the older members of the Bar, as the different Justices resumed their respective chairs, how fresh and well your dear Father looked, which was true. He exhibited as much vim and alertness in all that went on as any of the younger members of the Bench. Yet, the excellent state of health which your Father displayed on Monday underwent a change yesterday. It appears that he was in the very best condition when the Court interrupted its daily session for luncheon, at which time the Judge

partook of more than he had usually been in the habit of taking at such times. This apparent overloading of the stomach seemed to have a depressing effect upon him during the remainder of the day, although, with the exception of a brief absence of five minutes for the purpose of visiting the toilet, he continued upon the Bench until the Court adjourned, at 4:30—the customary time. When the Court's session ended he arose from his seat and proceeded to leave the Bench. As he approached the few steps which lead up to the Bench he was taken charge of by Mr. Harry Butler and one of the Pages and led into the Marshal's Office, where he was detained until a taxicab came when he was accompanied home by Mr. Justice McKenna, who was with him in the Marshal's Office while the cab was being summoned. It was observed by your Mother, however, as soon as the Judge settled down on his lounge in the big study, that he was very weak, and fearing that he was pretty sick, she immediately telephoned to Dr. Hardin, who . . . discovered that your Father had considerable fever—103°.[73]

Despite rallying the following morning, Justice Harlan grew weaker and more ill. Death came at 8:13 Saturday morning, October 14. The story, doubtless apocryphal, is that he awakened from a troubled sleep early in the morning just long enough to say to the watchers, "I am sorry to have kept you waiting." Even if he never said it, it was a fitting last remark by a man who had always practiced the courtly manners of an earlier era.

Part III

JUDICIAL OPINIONS

13

Interstate Commerce

True to his Clay Whig inheritance, John Harlan maintained a strong nationalism throughout his judicial career. This is nowhere better exemplified than by his record on antitrust cases, an area that typifies his constitutional jurisprudence in other ways as well. The Supreme Court's treatment of antitrust law in the period up to Harlan's death is a more than twice-told tale.[1] At the same time, Harlan's differences with his colleagues strikingly demonstrate the pervasive American love-hate relationship with "big business," a feature that still exists today.

Harlan himself, characteristically, was in no doubt about the dangers of monopolies or trusts in general. The Sherman Antitrust Act of 1890 struck a responsive chord in the Kentuckian. Some years later, for instance, he wrote to Gus Willson:

> The greatest injury to the integrity of our social organization comes from the enormous power of corporations. [We live by corporate money.] We must have corporations. We could not get along without them, but we must see that they do not corrupt our government and its institutions. Men in charge of corporations will use their money in ways and for purposes that would not be practiced by them in respect to their own money. We had reached that point in the management of politics when educated men, being at the head of national and State committees would be willing to receive from officers of corporations money for political purposes which they knew was practically stolen from stockholders and policyholders. We are now passing through a crisis upon this subject of private and public honesty.[2]

Harlan in the same letter referred to the "great railroad systems which threaten to dominate the country."[3] Indeed, he had earlier put much the same sentiments into his dissenting opinion in the sugar trust case, warning that as a result of the majority's decision the country might "pass under the absolute control of overshadowing combinations having financial resources without limits and an audacity that recognizes none of the restraints of moral obligations controlling the actions of individuals; combinations governed entirely by the law of greed and selfishness—so powerful that no single State is able to overthrow them."[4] He would repeat, in the twilight of his life, the warning against "the slavery that would result from aggregations of capital in the hands of a few individuals and corporations controlling for their own profit and advantage exclusively, the entire business of the country, including the production and sale of the necessaries of life."[5]

These attitudes, reinforced by Harlan's inherited tendency to accept a broad reach for the power of Congress under the commerce clause and his strong tendency to read both statute and Constitution literally, led him to take the strictest possible interpretation of the Sherman Act.

Of the two major legal problems stemming from the antitrust law, one was constitutional while the second involved semantics. The Supreme Court majority was concerned, apparently, to narrow the applicability of the law, for both political and ideological reasons. The Court's lack of belief in either the efficacy or the propriety of federal interference with the freedom of corporations to operate as they saw fit has often been remarked; but even Justice Holmes would probably have agreed with Harlan that the law could constitutionally extend to manufacturing. (Holmes thought that the government did have the constitutional power to regulate even though he had no belief in the law's effectiveness and felt that the law was constitutionally defective as applied to smaller companies or to situations in which voluntary cooperation seemed economically desirable.)[6]

Justice Harlan's approach to the constitutional issue presented by the sugar trust case was broad and forward-looking. The case as it came to the Court involved the constitutionality of applying the Sherman Act to a practical monopoly of the sugar refining business in the United States. While in no doubt that the act was itself constitutional, the seven-man majority held that refining was a purely local activity and that in any case it was not commerce: "Commerce succeeds to manufacture, and is not a part of it."[7] As a business, it could be regulated by states, but it was not interstate commerce and therefore congressional power did not extend to it. Nor was its effect on interstate commerce through buying and selling direct enough to provide a pretext for the exercise of national power. Chief Justice Fuller, writing for the Court, seemed to envisage an economic system in which most productive activity was confined by state boundaries.[8] Such a belief might have been realistic fifty years earlier, but it failed to recognize that the economy was becoming a "seamless web" in which local business was inevitably intimately related to interstate commerce and could only be effectively regulated at the national level. "It followed," wrote Professor Wallace Mendelson, "that for a generation and more Congress was powerless to deal with many vexing problems of the American economic revolution."[9] The Court's doctrine, although seriously undercut by the beef trust case, was applied by the Court at least through the 1930s.

Although he had silently acquiesced in the Court's 1888 opinion in *Kidd v. Pearson* that manufacturing is not commerce, Harlan probably felt that he was not bound by his own convictions in the *Kidd* case, since the questions concerning state power involved there were not determinative in questions of congressional power.[10] His dissent in the sugar trust case was based on the theory that Congress not only could constitutionally regulate manufacturers but had actually intended to do so. The shift in Harlan's attitude possibly stemmed from two factors: his nationalism, which led him to give Congress the benefit of any doubts, or a basic change of mind about the reach of the word *commerce*, at least when Congress has acted. Whatever the reason, he alone on the Court now adopted a broad reading.

Justice Harlan first pointed out that contracts "in restraint of trade" had long been illegal under the common law, both in England and in the American states. He asserted that Congress could use this same power to "remove unlawful obstructions, of whatever kind, to the free course of trade among the States." Then, conceding that Congress probably could not prohibit sugar refining entirely, the Kentuckian declared that nevertheless the national legislature could strike at manufacturers when combinations acted to restrain trade. Buying and selling constitute commerce even when they precede and follow manufacturing, and Harlan emphasized that a monopoly in sugar refining had no other purposes than to control the buying of raw sugar as cheaply as possible and the selling of the refined product at the highest possible price. This seems obvious enough in the twentieth century, although it was seemingly not so apparent to Harlan's colleagues. Charging that the Court's decision defeated the main object for which the law was adopted, Harlan ended by calling attention to the dangers of monopolies in manufacturing and to the increasingly obvious fact that only national legislation could control or regulate them effectively.[11]

Harlan's dissent is powerful and persuasive: one authority calls it "more perspicacious than the majority" opinion and claims that it voices "the constitutionalism of a distant future."[12] But the future did not arrive until 1948, when in another case involving sugar refining, the Court finally interred the sugar trust doctrine, at least to the extent of holding that manufacturing is so intimately related to interstate commerce that Congress can regulate it.[13] In the *Swift* case in 1906 the Court used the famous "stream of commerce" theory, which Harlan had rather cloudily suggested in the sugar trust case, in order to draw within congressional power many productive enterprises.[14]

The problem of what the Sherman Act meant produced a serious split on the Court, which became in part an almost personal battle between Harlan and Justice White. In a number of cases the Kentuckian first provided the dominant interpretation, only to lose his majority as new justices came to the Court, principally Oliver Wendell Holmes, Jr. Congress, many have remarked, either did not really want an effective antitrust policy or did not know how to create one, since both the purposes and the wording of the law lend themselves to varying interpretations.[15] Perhaps one should not overstress this factor, since it is true to some extent of all great laws dealing with complex problems. Harlan being Harlan, he saw no serious ambiguities in the act; he always tended strongly to be a literalist in matters of interpretation, especially when this produced a result he found satisfactory.

The question was whether the law prohibited all "combinations in restraint of [interstate] trade" or only some of them. Since the law says *"any* combination," Harlan simply concluded that it barred *all* combinations. This is surely a tenable, if simplistic, argument. But to realists like Holmes and White it seemed more logical to assume that Congress really meant to bar only undesirable trusts. To judges, who are accustomed to having the last word, the White approach had the advantage of leaving the courts to judge in individual cases which combinations were undesirable, and thus in restraint of trade.

Basically, one had to try to define the intentions of Congress. Harlan thought that the legislators intended what they said, but this answer is always partially unsatisfactory when semantic ambiguity exists. His opponents held that Congress could not reasonably be assumed to intend an undesirable result, so they wished to apply the so-called rule of reason (which actually meant rule by *judicial* reason). Strangely, although all the justices referred frequently to congressional intent, they did little to ascertain what that intent was. Finding intent is fraught with the possibility of error, however, so they may merely have felt that what was said was more significant to judges than what was meant.

The first cases to come before the Court after the sugar trust case raised this issue, although the fact that they involved railroads may have made it somewhat easier for Harlan's argument to prevail: Justice Rufus Peckham wrote, "Railroad companies are the instruments of commerce, and their business is commerce itself."[16] While not disagreeing with Peckham about this, Justice Edward D. White, writing for four dissenters, argued that under common law only unreasonable restraints on trade were illegal and that the majority view was "tantamount to an assertion that the act of Congress is itself unreasonable."[17] This was in response to Peckham's assertion that the terms of the law were absolute, thus going beyond the common law rule. White did not explain why going beyond the common law was unreasonable, nor did he consider that the defects of the common law may have led Congress to legislate in the first place. Peckham also incidentally set a fashion in antitrust cases by announcing that "debates in Congress are not appropriate sources of information from which to discover the meaning of the language of a statute."[18]

White tended to view the Peckham/Harlan position as creating a deprivation of freedom that was not only unreasonable but also an unconstitutional violation of due process of law under the Fifth Amendment. Peckham gave this argument short shrift, pointing to the fact that even contracts that were not immoral or bad in themselves could be prohibited by Congress, and Congress therefore could, if it wished, control all restraints of trade, both reasonable and unreasonable.[19]

Thus to Harlan and Peckham the job of the Supreme Court was simple; if the case involved interstate commerce, any restraint of trade accomplished through a "combination" was illegal. Following from the sugar trust case, nevertheless, other cases were argued in which Harlan disagreed with Peckham because the Kentuckian felt that interstate restraint was involved, whereas Peckham found (in two stockyards cases) that "where the stock came from or where it may ultimately go . . . is not the substantial factor in the case," that is, these factors may affect, without being, interstate commerce.[20] But the Court could vote unanimously if the justices all found, as they did in the *Addyston Pipe & Steel* case, that an attempt by manufacturers to divide their sales territories had the direct purpose of controlling prices, thus operating on sales, transportation, and delivery of a product, not merely on manufacturing.[21]

The addition of Holmes to the Court provided another spokesman who sometimes agreed with Harlan, usually in defining interstate commerce, but the Boston Brahmin strongly disagreed with his senior colleague about the rule of reason. In *Swift & Co.* v. *United States*, another stockyards case that he unconvincingly distinguished from the earlier Peckham analysis, Holmes wrote for a unanimous Court that the stockyards are a "throat" through which commerce passes and that therefore an attempt to combine to control stockyard charges constitutes a single connected scheme that cannot be broken down into its component parts. This analysis inferentially called into question the whole rationale of the sugar trust case: Why could not a factory be regarded as a throat? The Court as a whole, however, was not ready for such a radical step.

Holmes and Harlan's split on the rule of reason highlights their profoundly dissimilar intellectual qualities. The Kentuckian's insistence on a literal application of the Sherman Act's words was doubtless simplistic; more than that, it was probably unrealistic. While the Yankee "from Olympus" could at times evade serious issues with a striking epigram, he was nevertheless aware of the probable effects of such a literal application. Holmes's approach was, however, more sophisticated than that of his ally, White. These differences showed up clearly in the famous *Northern Securities* case decided in 1904.

The *Northern Securities* case was the fruit of a compromise between the two warring railroad barons, E.H. Harriman, who controlled the Northern Pacific, one of the two major northwestern trunk lines, and James J. Hill, who controlled the Great Northern and (backed by J.P. Morgan) also the Chicago, Burlington and Quincy. The combination would have created a stranglehold on the traffic between Chicago/St. Louis and the Pacific Northwest. The compromise took the form of a holding company, which controlled the railroads through stock ownership while the operating companies remained technically separate.[22]

The Court, faced with a challenge from the new president, Teddy Roosevelt, and his capable attorney general, Philander C. Knox, had to deal with the question of the legality of such a sophisticated evasion of the Sherman law. It is not surprising that, in view of the political power of big business and the ambivalent feelings of the public toward antitrust measures, the Supreme Court was itself split. The case produced four opinions and no majority, although five judges agreed that the holding company was illegal. Harlan's opinion announcing the Court's decision was supported by only three others, and the fifth member of the majority, David J. Brewer, disagreed specifically with Harlan about the Kentuckian's literal reading of the law. He felt only that the Northern Securities Company was acting in unreasonable restraint of trade.

The five could thus agree that the holding company device was indeed illegal. As Harlan wrote, "No state can, by merely creating a corporation . . . , project its authority into other states, and across the continent, so as to prevent Congress from exerting the power it possesses." Emphasizing, but with the agreement only of Brown, McKenna, and Day, that the law forbade *every* kind of combination in restraint of interstate commerce, Harlan delineated a severely limited role for the Court, asserting that judges could have no proper interest in the effects of a statute: "If the Court shared the gloomy forebodings in which the defendants indulge, it could not refuse to respect the action of the legislative branch . . . if what it has done is within the limits of its constitutional power. . . . [This] court has no function to supervise such legislation from the standpoint of wisdom or policy."[23]

In dissent, White wrote for the four-man minority an opinion holding mainly that stock ownership "is not commerce at all."[24] He also joined the separate dissent of Holmes, which focused on reason and a prudential application of the law. To suppress competition by the use of contracts, the method found illegal in earlier cases, was one thing, but to suppress it by "fusion is another," since the law is aimed not at the suppression of competition as such, but at the suppression of contracts and combinations. The Bostonian also emphasized the unwisdom of a decision the implications of which extended to small local mergers or partnerships as well as to large national ones. He ended, referring to Brewer's concurring opinion, by saying, "I am happy to know that only a minority of my brethren adopt an interpretation of the law which in my opinion would make eternal the *bellum omnium contra omnes* and disintegrate society so far as it could into individual atoms."[25]

While Holmes has almost universally been praised by his admirers for his judicial restraint, he appears here as an activist allowing the Court an explicit policy role, in, of course, a good cause. The ebullient Teddy's response to Holmes's opinion, which he regarded as almost treason to the man who had appointed him, supposedly was "I could carve out of a banana a judge with more backbone than that."

Evaluating the four opinions, it has been well said that

> what the opinions . . . reveal so well are the personal predilections of the writers. Harlan was in tune with the government's campaign against mammoth business enterprise; Brewer thought railroads with their monopolistic tendencies should be regulated even where that regulation was once removed; White was worried about the tendency to restrict economic growth and development and the intrusion of the power of the federal government into the realm of the states; and Holmes indicated that, despite his disclaimer, the government campaign against bigness was unwise and that the general theory behind it threatened the liberty of the people.[26]

In one other little-known case in 1909 Chief Justice Fuller jumped into Harlan's camp at least temporarily to provide the fifth vote in a 5-4 holding that a group of wallpaper manufacturers who organized a selling company through which their entire output was sold had violated the Sherman Act. Brewer joined the other three dissenters.[27] This was, however, the last case in which Harlan could amass a majority in a rule of reason case. By 1911 wholesale changes had occurred on the Court, and only the embattled Kentuckian was left to uphold a literal reading of the law; even McKenna and Day deserted him.

The shift was made official in the Court's opinions in the *Standard Oil* and *American Tobacco* cases. With Chief Justice White taking the lead, the Court in both cases held that the companies had violated the Sherman Act. Of course Harlan agreed. After extensive reargument of the cases in January 1911, however, an eight-man majority "reversed" Harlan and enshrined the rule of reason in antitrust law. In other words, White held that the two companies had violated the law not because they had restrained trade, but because they had done so "unreasonably."[28] White took pains to "distinguish," disingenuously, the decisions from those in the *Trans-Missouri* and *Joint Traffic* cases, in order to isolate Harlan as completely as possible. The tactic succeeded, since Harlan could not garner a single supporter for his continued view that all restraints were illegal. Since no one was left on the Court who had participated in the 1890s cases but Harlan and White, no one except Harlan felt it necessary to defend the Court's previous record.

Since in those days judges often delivered oral opinions even before they had finished writing their dissents or concurrences, it is natural, though seldom recorded, that their remarks in Court sometimes went beyond their more considered written opinions. That this occurred in the *Standard Oil* case is known now only because Justice Hughes recalled it in his autobiographical notes.

> Justice Harlan's opinions were verbose and tended to be demagogical. In the Spring of 1911, Justice Harlan was disturbed by the serenity of the Court and complained to me that there were too few dissents. With a passionate outburst seldom if ever equalled in the annals of the Court, he brought his service to a dramatic conclusion. This was his oral dissent [actually a concurrence] in the *Standard Oil* case. He went far beyond his written opinion, launching into a bitter invective, which I thought most unseemly. It was not a swan song but the roar of an angry lion. Almost at the opening of the next Term, he was gone.[29]

Unfortunately Hughes does not tell us just what Harlan said. Hughes was, of course, new to the Court and unfamiliar with the bitter Harlan-White dispute that had raged behind the conference doors earlier. Then too, the proper Hughes had strict ideas about courtroom etiquette, which he was able to enforce to some extent when he became chief justice years later.

Harlan's written concurring opinion was indeed the doughty Kentuckian's last trumpet blast. He excoriated the majority in no uncertain terms, averring that it had "not only upset the long-settled interpretation of the act, but . . . usurped the constitutional functions of the legislative branch." He went on to point out that if Congress had disliked what the Court had done earlier, it had had fifteen years in which to amend the law, and it had not done so.[30] He called the majority's action "scarcely just" to the earlier majorities now no longer on the Court to defend themselves: it was, he said, wrong for the Court "at this late day to say or intimate" that their predecessors had interpreted the law unreasonably.[31]

Harlan feared that the Sherman Act's enforcement would be rendered difficult or impossible (he was right in this). The opinion would "throw the business of the country into confusion and invite widely-extended and harassing litigation, the injurious effects" of which would be felt for "many years to come." He also pointed to what he regarded as the opinion's dangerous results for the American system of separated powers: "To overreach the action of Congress merely by judicial construction, that is, by indirection, is a blow at the integrity of our governmental system, and in the end will prove most dangerous to all."[32]

The Court, then, hesitated to enforce the Sherman Act in such a way as to make it effective against small or large manufacturing and producing combinations. It can be argued that the rule of reason was a more realistic approach to the problems of the American economy than was that taken by Harlan. All of his life the Kentucky judge had tended to be an "all or nothing" person: this tendency made realism difficult, since it led to a belief that interpretation was not necessary because the law said clearly what Harlan wanted it to say. One could almost say that when he was right, it was accidental.

In any event, neither Harlan nor his colleagues had any doubt that the Sherman Act applied to labor organizations, even those that included only manufacturing workers. No nonsense about a rule of reason was spoken of here. John could think of strikes or boycotts as restraints of trade whether reasonable or unreasonable, and his associates, with their general antilabor bias, could agree. Thus the Court was unanimous in the Danbury Hatters case, holding that a boycott against manufacturers of fur hats, in an attempt to force them to unionize, was an illegal restraint of trade.[33] The Court, again without dissent, reached the same conclusion in a case involving a stove and range factory.[34] It was not clear, of course, that Congress had ever intended the act to be applied to unions, as was made obvious by the passage of the Clayton Act a few years after Harlan's death. His penchant for literal interpretations played him false in these cases.

Justice Harlan's Whig inheritance, favoring the exercise of national power, was exhibited again in a string of cases involving the interpretation of the Interstate Commerce Act of 1887, which created a commission to regulate railroads and steamship lines. A clue to his attitudes can be found in a 1905 letter to Taft. Commenting on his reception during a visit to Louisville, Harlan wrote: "One thing was particularly observable and that was the affection and admiration of all without distinction of party, for the President [Roosevelt]. I did not meet anybody who was not with him in his fight for the regulation of railroad rates by the ICC or some like executive body, subject, of course, to such judicial control as would secure the rights of parties concerned, with out unnecessary delay."[35]

The Supreme Court had no doubt that the act involving the creation and powers of the Interstate Commerce Commission was constitutional. But the majority was concerned to construe its granted powers as narrowly as possible, and this attitude was shown in many cases between 1892 and 1911. Most of the time Harlan dissented, but often without bothering to write an opinion. The burden of his dissents, as in the antitrust cases, was that the majority was rendering the commission ineffective and negating the will of Congress. He charged, for instance, that "taken in connection with other decisions, . . . the present decision . . . goes far to make that commission a useless body for all practical purposes, and to defeat many of the important objects designed to be accomplished [by Congress]. . . . It has been left . . . with power to make reports, and to issue protests. But it has been shorn, by judicial interpretation, of authority to do anything of an effective character." Harlan's personal predilections sometimes showed through, as when he claimed that "the acts of Congress are now so construed as to place communities at the mercy of competing railroads." He ended by averring, "I cannot believe that Congress intended any such result, nor do I think its enactments, properly interpreted, would lead to such a result."[36] Various judges, such as Day, McKenna, and Brown, sometimes agreed with Harlan, as did Congress, which in successive acts of 1903 and 1905 explicitly gave the commission the powers that the Court majority had withheld. By the time of his death, the Kentuckian had effectively won this battle.

An exception was provided by the section of the Hepburn Act of 1906 (which substantially enlarged the powers of the ICC) prohibiting the ownership by railroads of products that they themselves transported. The Court, it said, in order to uphold the clause's constitutionality, construed it narrowly so as to apply only to products owned by the railroad at the time of hauling. Harlan would have none of such sophistry, regarding it as, in reality, a disallowance by narrow construction. In order to "save" the law, he said, the court had defeated altogether the purpose of Congress.[37]

Harlan was, nevertheless, a child of his times in many ways: for example, he shared to some degree the rest of the Court's marked antipathy to the rise of organized labor, even to the extent of limiting the power of Congress under the commerce clause. When state action was concerned, however, he was hospitable to labor claims in many instances, as we shall later see.

In the famous *Debs* case Harlan agreed with the Court majority that the federal government could use troops, and that the federal courts could issue injunctions, to end a railroad strike in Chicago. The protection of the U.S. mail and the general power of government to preserve order were the major principles relied on by the Court, but the fact that interstate commerce was disrupted had been regarded by the lower courts as a combination in restraint of trade, and the high court justices specifically refused to disagree with that approach.[38]

The majority went farther than Harlan in the *Employers' Liability Cases* of 1908. Justice White held for the Court that an act of Congress making railroads liable for injuries to all their employees was unconstitutional because it included workers who were not directly involved in interstate commerce. White clearly implied that had the law applied only to interstate workers it would have been valid. Three judges concurred but felt that the entire law—abrogating the traditional master-servant relationship—was invalid. Three others dissented (Harlan, Holmes, and McKenna), feeling that the act should be construed to save the interstate applications. Justice Moody, alone, argued for the constitutionality of the entire act.[39] Congress accepted with alacrity Harlan's invitation and reenacted the law to apply to interstate workers only.[40]

But when Congress attempted to outlaw "yellow dog" employment contracts on railroads—contracts that allowed the companies to fire employees who joined unions—it was too much even for Harlan. Writing for the Court with only Holmes and McKenna dissenting, the Kentuckian averred that even though the act applied only to railroads in interstate commerce, it had no reasonable relationship to commerce and in addition violated due process rights. In the absence of contractual terms, an employer (even an interstate railroad) could hire and fire anyone he chose.[41]

Although Harlan participated in many other decisions regarding the powers of Congress under the commerce clause and wrote for the Court or dissented in quite a few, perhaps the most important of these was the lottery case. The issue arose after Congress had prohibited the carriage in interstate commerce of lottery tickets and raised the question of whether the word *regulate* in the commerce clause included the power to prohibit. Conservatives argued that prohibition is not regulation, or alternatively that the transport of lottery tickets is not commerce at all. The Court was so evenly split that the case had to be argued three times, and even then only a narrow 5-4 decision resulted.[42] Nevertheless, it has never been reversed, and Harlan apparently led the majority: at least he wrote the opinion of the Court, holding that the law was constitutional because regulation can encompass prohibition. "The prevention of harm to the public morals," one commentator has remarked, is "an appropriate goal of the commerce power, without any showing of effect on the safety or efficiency of commerce."[43] Harlan, ever the moralist, regarded lotteries as a form of moral pollution: this leaves open the question of whether he would have accepted a congressional prohibition of an innocuous or beneficial item. In any case the doctrine was soon used to uphold the Pure Food and Drug Act and later many other laws.[44] The only major exception was the child labor case that came up after Harlan's death.[45]

While John Harlan's nationalistic ideology may have dictated his opinions in the cases involving the power of Congress to regulate interstate commerce, he had no such compelling motivation to guide his ideas about the residual powers to regulate commerce left to the states. The Supreme Court had to decide numerous cases that questioned whether state regulations of commerce were valid in the absence of congressional action.

As indicated earlier, much of the development of the commerce clause during Harlan's tenure resulted from the tremendous expansion of interstate trade stimulated by the spreading network of railroads. Not only did they come to blanket the populous and long-settled East, South, and Midwest, but they followed closely behind (in some cases, indeed, they forged ahead of) the advancing western frontier. Every town wanted one, and states competed with each other and with the national government in granting the railroad companies large tracts of land that they then sold off at huge profits.[46] At the same time, the railroads became so powerful that at times they threatened to take over whole states politically: such novelists as Winston Churchill and Frank Norris exaggerated this phenomenon, but only slightly.[47] In reaction to the overweening arrogance of the railroad barons, states enacted a spate of laws regulating not only the railroads themselves but also river transportation. Nor was their political power the only problem:

> Besides, the railroads were corrupt, excessively capitalized, overloaded with debt, controlled by out-of-state interests, monopolistic. Among themselves they were vicious and quarrelsome. They were weak in the infant skills of public relations, but big in manipulation of state governments, in the black arts of lobbying, and the seduction of men in public office. They cheated each other, their contractors and their stockholders. They floated great balloons of debt that burst during panics and crashes, ruining the greedy hopeful people who put their money into stocks and bonds. They were deeply immersed in local politics; and they were at the mercy of the business cycle, and the prices of cotton, coal, wheat, tobacco and corn. In the space of one short generation, they changed from engines of salvation to smoking black devils.[48]

Transportation companies naturally objected to being regulated by states, and numerous Supreme Court decisions turned on the judges' opinions of the constitutionality of such regulations. In handling such cases, David P. Currie writes, "the Waite Court," and, later, the Fuller Court as well, "wielded the commerce clause with unprecedented vigor to clear away state measures that it thought interfered with the free flow of commerce. In the process, however, it left the law an intellectual shambles."[49] Of course, not all state regulation involved transportation: much was aimed at protecting the public health, safety, or welfare—the rubric dubbed the "police power." Often the narrow definition of interstate commerce caused the Court to deal with state actions as though only the police power was in question, especially after 1890. But even when interstate commerce was admittedly concerned, the Court might allow state regulation or taxation.

Although Currie calls this area a "shambles," the Court's—and Harlan's—approach did have some underlying logic. The judges had (or developed) a largely discretionary conception of what legislation was "reasonable" under the police and tax powers of the states. If the law was considered reasonable, even if it regulated interstate commerce, it would be upheld in the absence of conflicting congressional action or (a serious *caveat*) a direct and serious discrimination against interstate commerce as opposed to trade within the state. In this development John Harlan generally agreed with the Court's majorities. For this reason there is little point in reviewing large numbers of cases. It cannot be said that, either as the Court's spokesman or in dissent, he developed any novel principles. But it was the discretionary aspect of the application of principles that gave them the appearance of a shambles: each judge applied his own discretion, which produced frequent split decisions. Even a single individual (particularly one who, like Harlan, served for a long time) was likely to produce conclusions that were or seemed inconsistent with his own earlier ones.

This inconsistency was exacerbated by two of the period's most characteristic legal developments: the idea of substantive limits to state regulatory power and the extremely narrow interpretation of interstate commerce. An example can be provided by Harlan's opinion for a divided Court in the *Lake Shore* case in 1899. Here the Kentuckian found that an Ohio law requiring at least three trains a day (if that many ran) to stop at all towns having populations of more than three thousand was constitutional, at least in the absence of conflicting federal legislation. Train travel undeniably constituted interstate commerce, but Harlan found that even so it was within the state's police power. In dissent, Justice Shiras held that congressional inaction meant that Congress wanted commerce to be free of such restraints; he and his three dissenting brethren also thought that the law was a direct burden on interstate commerce.[50]

Harlan agreed with the Court, however, in two opposing (but unanimous) decisions reached almost concurrently, apparently because the police power was being stretched too far. Illinois had attempted to require all trains to stop at all county seat towns (even if they had to leave the main line to do so). While one may easily agree that such diversion goes too far, it is difficult to draw a clear distinction between county seats and towns of three thousand. Preventing freight trains from running at all on Sundays would seem to most observers to be a heavier burden on interstate commerce.[51]

Cases involving river transport were as troublesome as those relating to railroads. The Court, led by Harlan, had early enunciated the doctrine that state wharfage fees and bridge tolls were constitutional if reasonable and if not prohibited by Congress.[52] The question was what is reasonable, an eminently discretionary issue. Harlan's discretion led him to dissent when he felt that the charges were exorbitant, however. In one dissent he wrote, "To burden the exercise of a constitutional right with conditions which materially impair its value, or which, practically, compel the abandonment of the right rather to submit to the conditions, is, in law, an infringement of the right."[53] Further to the same effect, Harlan wrote concerning wharfage fees—this time a Baltimore levy that was lower for in-state products than for those from other states—stating what could be regarded as settled doctrine despite Chief Justice Waite's specious dissent: "No State can, consistently with the Federal Constitution, impose upon the products of other States . . . more onerous burdens or taxes than it imposes upon the like products of its own territory. . . . [Such action] must be regarded as taxation upon interstate commerce."[54]

Cases involving matters other than transportation also found the Court attempting to draw lines, based upon reason, between the Constitution's commerce clause and its own self-invented police power. The major cases fall into several categories: state liquor laws, quarantine or inspection laws, licensing acts, taxes, and, strangely, laws attempting to prohibit the sale of oleomargarine. Harlan actively participated in all of these.

Prohibition began as a state concern, and it was partly due to Supreme Court decisions that it eventually became the subject of a constitutional amendment. Liquor was indeed putatively harmful, but it was also an important item of interstate commerce, so state regulation was always suspect. John Harlan led off for the Court in the famous case of *Mugler* v. *Kansas* upholding the police power: Kansas had totally prohibited the manufacture of beer. The Court did not, however, deal with this as a matter concerning interstate commerce, so in the present connection it is important mainly for its deference to the state's legislative power to regulate its internal affairs, with great accompanying ambivalence about the extent of that power.[55] Many states went farther, however, trying to prevent liquor from entering the state. This introduced the commerce element, and the Court majority was not strongly enough opposed to the liquor trade to uphold such laws. Harlan, despite the fact that he enjoyed a glass of good Kentucky whiskey and often sent gifts of it to friends, felt that the state's power could be extended to these cases. In the *Bowman* case the Court majority held that states cannot regulate the importion of liquor without contravening the general congressional policy of free trade between states. Harlan, supported by Waite and Gray, dissented, pointing to the strange result that, following *Mugler*, a state can prohibit sale and manufacture within its borders but may find its policy frustrated by the sale of imported products. "It is inconceivable," he wrote, "that the well-being of any State is at the mercy of the liquor manufacturers of other States."[56]

Brewer, Gray, and Harlan dissented in the famous case of *Leisy* v. *Hardin*; here, Horace Gray wrote the dissent. These decisions, however, went too far for Congress, which responded with the passage of the Wilson Act, which seemingly permitted such state regulation.[57] The Court, not to be outmaneuvered, upheld the act but continued to find various state acts unconstitutional, with Harlan unvaryingly dissenting. In one case involving his home state, Harlan wrote: "I do not think that these are areas of legitimate interstate commerce. They show only devices or tricks by the express company to evade or defeat the laws of Kentucky relating to the sale of . . . liquors."[58]

The Kentuckian was not invariably to uphold the states, however. In a series of cases involving cattle or meat inspection or quarantine laws, he often championed a narrow reading of the police power. Harlan led the Court in striking down a Minnesota law requiring inspection, within twenty-four hours of importation, of cattle "on the hoof." The law's "necessary operation," he said, was to ban from the state wholesome and properly inspected meat from other states. He went on to point out (what he had ignored in the liquor cases) that "the enactment of a similar statute by each one of the states would result in the destruction of commerce."[59]

Oleomargarine, not an obviously harmful product, ran afoul of the power wielded by the dairy industry, and various states tried to regulate or prohibit it. Harlan, without adverting to interstate commerce, found that the Pennsylvania legislature had ample power to prohibit the sale of oleo, on the grounds that it could find some oleo that was indeed harmful. He followed this up with an acceptance, on the same argument, of a Massachusetts law forbidding the sale of colored oleo. But he found himself in a minority when the Court struck down a law prohibiting the importation of oleo and also when New Hampshire, in a weird exercise, prohibited the sale of all oleo not colored pink.[60] In a fairly broad reading of legislative power, he argued unsuccessfully that "if the legislature is satisfied that oleo margarine is unwholesome, or that, in the tubs, pots or packages in which it is commonly offered for sale, it looks so much like butter, that the way to protect the people against injury to health . . . or against fraud and deception . . . is to absolutely prohibit its sale, it is within the constitutional power of the legislature to do so."[61] The failure of the Court (or Harlan) to deal with oleo explicitly as an item of commerce was conspicuous in these cases, which are usually considered under the rubric of substantive due process.

In the area of taxation the major task of the Court was to prevent undue discrimination against, or prohibition of, out-of-state business. Much of the time this was routine, but in some instances it called for sophisticated judgment. Often, again, railroads were involved, especially when taxes on rolling stock were levied. For instance, when Pennsylvania imposed a tax on the Pullman Company's capital stock, apportioned by the number of miles the cars were run in the state as compared with their total mileage, the Court majority saw no constitutional defect. Justice Bradley, however, joined by Harlan and Field, found this to be a tax on interstate commerce, especially since the state could not tax the capital stock directly, as Pullman was not a Pennsylvania corporation.[62] As Harlan objected in a later case, "Under the mode of assessment pursued, property was taxed in Indiana that had no *situs* there, which was used in interstate commerce outside of Indiana, and could not properly be included in the company's railroad track and rolling stock in the State."[63] For the rest of Harlan's life the Court's doctrines kept state taxation in a state of flux.

The cases involving state power over interstate commerce do not show Harlan at his best or most characteristic. The Kentuckian at his most typical had an underlying ideology—such as a belief in national power—that guided his votes and his reasoning. This ideology was lacking here, and thus Harlan seems less sure of his ground and even at times inconsistent. One cannot say, however, that his colleagues performed any better.

14

Substantive Due Process

Over the years, probably more constitutional scholarship has concentrated on the Fourteenth Amendment's due process clause than on any other single constitutional provision.[1] Progressive historians cited it as the major instance of the Court's surrender to "the corporations" and its acceptance of laissez-faire economic theories.[2] A revisionist school of more conservative writers argues that this surrender was never more than partial but usually agrees that substantive due process was an illegitimate construction of the clause.[3] Contemporary liberals embrace it, not for its protection of economic liberties, but because it can be equally well used to protect other private rights (such as the rights to use contraceptives or to have abortions) that are on the liberal social agenda.[4] Since Justice Harlan took a full, albeit confusing, part in the development of substantive due process, any biography must deal with his attitudes on the subject.

The original Constitution imposed only two types of restraints on state legislative action: direct restraints, such as the prohibition of state taxes on imports, and indirect ones implied by the granting of power to the national government, such as the power to coin money. Altogether, these were a fairly substantial body of limitations, but they did not touch upon many of the most fundamental powers of government, which were therefore retained by the states. This essentially illimitable body of powers was dubbed the "police power," apparently first by Chief Justice Marshall.[5] It did not, however, for many years imply that there were any but the above limitations on state power.[6]

Over the years after the Civil War, however, police power gradually became a limiting concept, fully accepted by all the justices in the 1890s. Justice Field's definition in *Munn* v. *Illinois,* stating that the police power includes "whatever affects the peace, good order, morals and health of the community," was quoted in varying forms by judges and commentators after that date.[7] It clearly implied that there were limits to what legislatures could do, although the judges did not find any such limits, except in cases involving the commerce clause, until the 1890s. Conceding that limits exist, what are they and where in the Constitution are they to be found? Former

Supreme Court Justice John A. Campbell is usually given credit for originating the idea that they are contained somewhere in the words of the
Fourteenth Amendment, most probably in the privileges or immunities
clause. This idea received such rough handling by the majority in the
Slaughterhouse Cases, however, that lawyers in general dropped it, only to
return to court with the argument that the limits resided in the due process
clause instead.[8] In *Munn* v. *Illinois* in 1877 Chief Justice Waite only partially
rejected this argument: he said, in effect, that states could regulate private
business, if that business was "affected with a public interest," thereby
implying that there was a category of purely private business in which
some state regulation might be out of bounds.[9] Lawyers took to this idea
with great enthusiasm, even though Justice Miller made an ineffectual
attempt to stem the tide of cases by referring the next year to it as a "strange
misconception of the scope" of the due process clause.[10] Miller came close
to saying what seems obvious from the words of the clause: that it means
only the right to fair criminal procedures.

The concept of substantive due process is, then, illogical: the word
process cannot easily be brought to accommodate substance. Nor, it must be
added, does the clause as a whole prohibit states from depriving persons of
life, liberty, or property, so long as they do so *with* due process of law. Miller
was right, but he fought a losing battle. The spirit of the times, added to a
natural rights theory, seemed to demand limits to state action. For the
question of what these limits would be, the Court invented a sort of rule of
reason: the purpose must be reasonable, and the law must be reasonably
related to its purpose. Although this principle could easily be adapted to
the protection of private business from state regulation, it cannot be said
that the Court, or Harlan himself, consistently did so. We have already seen
that Harlan developed an opposition to big business, and he was thus
unwilling to use substantive due process as extremely as, was, say, Rufus
Peckham.

The only obvious factor about substantive due process is the wide
discretion it left judges in deciding what was reasonable. Five judges thus
could determine the fate of state legislation. In the 1880s the Court approached the concept warily, finding no state act unconstitutional. Typically, it would argue as Justice Bradley did in the *Beer* case: liquor has
"well-known noxious qualities," and therefore a state prohibition law is
well within the powers of the legislature.[11] Harlan used essentially the
same argument in a case involving inspection and condemnation of il-
luminating oil: the state condemns the oil on the grounds that it is unsafe,
which brings it within the ambit of the police power and thus makes the
law reasonable.[12]

In one little-known case, *Parkersburg* v. *Brown,* the Court unanimously
but seemingly unknowingly used substantive due process to invalidate a
state law early in the 1880s. West Virginia had enacted a law allowing cities

to issue bonds to aid private manufacturers. The Court with Justice Blatchford as spokesman held that this was an unconstitutional use of public funds for private purposes.[13] Why such use should make the law invalid was not made clear, nor was the precedent followed up.

Although *Munn* had decided that businesses affected with a public interest—obviously railroads, for instance—can be regulated and that the regulations may include price or rate fixing, it was early made clear by Harlan, among others, that the rates set or allowed by the state must be reasonable. Harlan made this perfectly explicit in a concurring opinion in *Ruggles* v. *Illinois,* averring that courts may inquire into the reasonableness of rates set by the states.[14] *Parkersburg* and *Ruggles* present the two major aspects of substantive due process: regulations for public interest businesses were to be allowed unless unreasonable (many of these turned out to involve rate fixing), but the same regulations might not be allowable for purely private businesses (for instance, rate fixing).

John Harlan's own contributions to the development of substantive due process came first in *Mugler* v. *Kansas* and *Powell* v. *Pennsylvania.* While holding that states could prohibit the sale of liquor and oleo, respectively, these cases also made it clear that if the products regulated had been completely harmless the verdict might have been different. Even oleo could be viewed by the legislature as harmful (Justice Field dissented on this point), but Harlan explicitly left a loophole. "The courts," he said, "are not bound by mere forms, nor are they to be misled by mere pretences. . . . If, therefore, a statute purporting to have been enacted to protect the public health, the public morals, or the public safety, has no real or substantial relation to those objects, . . . it is the duty of the courts to so adjudge, and thereby to give effect to the Constitution."[15]

It is obvious that Harlan had by now accepted the basic premise of substantive due process: that the courts can substitute their own judgments of the merits of legislation for the judgments of the states in "appropriate" instances. That he and his brethren—with the exception of Brother Field—were willing to allow wide latitude to the legislatures is demonstrated in *Powell,* for as one commentator says, "if there was ever a case for substantive due process, this was it. In essence the Pennsylvania margarine ban seemed simply a transfer of wealth to the dairy industry."[16]

Another way to view these cases emphasizes the Court's willingness to defer to the legislatures in cases involving the public health or morals. Harlan remarked in *Mugler* that the "deleterious social effects of the excessive use of" alcohol are sufficiently "notorious" to constitute a reasonable basis for the statute (his family experience perhaps led to this conclusion). True enough, he had to reach farther in *Powell,* for here the product was not obviously harmful; but some oleo could conceivably be, and it could easily be disguised as butter. So the law was, again, a reasonable protection of the public. The Court, however, might not be as deferential where other kinds of state regulations, or other industries, were concerned.

Harlan went along with the 6-3 majority in another case in which the Court came very close to actually using substantive due process to find a state railroad rate scheme unconstitutional. Here Minnesota had delegated the power to set rates to a commission and prohibited judicial review of the resultant rates. Justice Blatchford ruled that the state had power to delegate the power to a commission and that the actual rates set were reasonable; but he went on to declare invalid the clause prohibiting courts from reviewing the rates.[17] All that was left was for the Court to find that a specific schedule of rates violated due process. Harlan was given the ungrateful task of justifying the decision. It is true that the Court did find such an "unreasonable and unjust" schedule in 1894.[18] Not until Harlan's opinion in *Smyth* v. *Ames*, however, did the judges elucidate the standards they would use in such cases.

Smyth was unanimously decided. The chief justice did not vote in the case, and Justice McKenna had not yet been appointed when it was argued. Therefore it is listed in the records as a 7-0 decision. Harlan's opinion, not one of his best, is turgid and excessively lengthy. Perhaps these characteristics result from the fact that he was faced with a difficult job of explanation: it took him almost a year to complete his opinion.[19]

The railroads claimed that Nebraska's freight rate schedule was unconstitutional because it deprived them of "property" (profits) without due process of law. Harlan took the position that a rate need not be confiscatory (i.e., it need not deprive the railroads of all their profits or force them to operate at a loss) in order to violate constitutional rights. Railroads were instead constitutionally entitled to the opportunity to earn "a fair return on a fair valuation of the investment." In other words, they were entitled to a "reasonable" profit.

Harlan, although well educated by the standards of his day, was no economist, and few people (especially judges) were versed in transportation economics. So it is not surprising that he wandered into a morass. He had to decide several very difficult questions, all based in economics. What is a fair return? How do you figure it out? How do you determine whether the state's proposed rate schedule will permit it? The question of defining a fair return invokes not only economic questions but also questions of political prudence and even of ethics. Only in the last instance is it at all a legal question. How much ought an investor be entitled to earn on his investment? Populistic theory would argue for a low figure; courts, including Harlan, generally settled in the area of 6 percent. Capitalists might think this too low to attract future investment. It is in any case an arbitrary conclusion, but it is none the worse for that: it had at least the political virtue of not causing extreme dissatisfaction to anyone.

How to figure a fair return on a fair valuation of the property turned out to be very difficult. The Kentuckian's opinion is notable for its unwillingness to settle on any one method: "The original cost of construction, the amount expended in permanent improvements, the amount and market value of its bonds and stocks, the present as compared with the original cost of construction, the probable earning capacity of the property under particular rates prescribed by the statute, and the sum required to meet operating expenses, are all matters for consideration, and are to be given such weight as may be just and right in each case." [20] Just in case he had overlooked something of importance, Harlan added, "We do not say that there may not be other matters to be regarded in estimating the value of the property." Lawyers and utility commissions spent many years trying to figure out which of these the courts would favor and trying to persuade judges to adopt the one most to their own advantage; Justice Brandeis, many years later, opted for the so-called prudent investment theory, which, however, hardly simplified matters. [21] The Supreme Court itself largely gave up the attempt in 1944, at least to the extent of putting the shotgun—the judicial review of rates—more or less permanently behind the door. [22]

Perhaps the most difficult aspect of Justice Harlan's opinion was his guessing game revolving around the question of how this particular rate schedule would affect the income of a company. Harlan settled for taking the amount of business done by the railroad in recent years and then projecting this into the future at the new rates. This, however, involved him in making at least two untenable assumptions: that the new rates would not affect the amount of business and that the general level of business activity would remain the same. It also left out of account the possibility of increased efficiency. His prediction of what might happen was therefore likely to be at wide variance from what would actually happen.

Assuming that the state commissions contained even a modicum of good will and expertise, they were likely to do a better job than Harlan at making these complicated economic calculations. For the courts to substitute their own judgment was, then, an act of supreme supererogation. The Court's later reluctance (at least up to Harlan's death) to decide rate cases seems to indicate that the judges had at least a dim realization that they were out of their depth in the *Smyth* case. [23]

The rate-fixing cases before 1911 always involved businesses "affected with a public interest" under the *Munn* doctrine. Other substantive due process cases might or might not do so. The Supreme Court had numerous opportunities to find various state laws unconstitutional, but, except for the doubtful *Parkersburg* case, did not do so until 1896. Usually the Court merely found that the law was "reasonable" or that it was within the states' police powers. [24] Occasionally, though, the Court felt it necessary to reiterate the theory that, while it would exercise due deference to state legislative action, that deference was, as Harlan had pointed out in *Mugler*, limited by the Court's duty to strike down "unreasonable" laws.

An early occasion to do so came in *Allgeyer* v. *Louisiana* in 1897. [25] Harlan merely acquiesced in a decision that established the famous doctrine of liberty of contract. The Louisiana state law provided a fine for the sale of marine insurance in contravention of state laws. Since the sale (contract) in this case had been made in another state and premiums had been paid there, the Court felt that Louisiana was breaching the contract. The idea of liberty of contract is an old one, but it had never been imported into the due process clause before, nor has it ever been considered an absolute right. It was, though, according to *Allgeyer*, the judges' duty to decide when liberty of contract could be breached.[26]

Having thus in *Allgeyer* and *Smyth* encouraged lawyers to bring ever greater numbers of cases to court, the Supreme Court lapsed back into comparative inactivity. Harlan, indeed, had occasion in one case to remark that the Court would not find a rate invalid merely because the judges would have set a different rate than the city did.[27] He also wrote for a unanimous Court in holding that grain elevators and warehouses situated along railroad lines may be required to pay license fees, even though similar businesses elsewhere were exempt.[28]

The Court did find a few other state acts unconstitutional even before the famous, or infamous, *Lochner* decision. A statute regulating the Kansas City stockyards was held invalid because it did not include other stockyards in the state, with the Court splitting on whether this was a denial of due process or of equal protection.[29] In an early zoning case the Court held unanimously that a city cannot change its zoning to stop construction already begun under the old zoning rules.[30] With two dissents, however, Harlan wrote for the majority that a state may enact a compulsory vaccination law against the objections of Christian Scientists.[31]

Bakeries are not businesses "affected with a public interest." No one, then, would be willing to argue that they came under the *Munn* doctrine justifying state regulation. Therefore, when Lochner violated the New York law prohibiting bakeries from requiring employees to work more than ten hours a day or sixty hours a week, the argument was put on straight police power grounds: Did the state have the power to dictate hours of labor in purely private businesses? As it happened, the Court's decision seemed to be governed by precedent, for in *Holden* v. *Hardy* the Court had already upheld a Utah law fixing maximum hours for work in mines.[32] Indeed, in conference, the judges apparently voted to uphold the New York law, and John Harlan was assigned to write the opinion for the majority. Justice Peckham, in the minority, chose to use the *Allgeyer* liberty of contract doctrine (invented by himself) to argue for the law's invalidity. He was apparently able to write a more persuasive opinion than Harlan's; possibly he had, as a New Yorker, inside knowledge of the real motivations of the New York legislature. In any case, Chief Justice Fuller and justices Brown and McKenna switched their votes from *Holden*—probably also from their votes in the judicial conference—and Peckham became the writer of the Court's opinion. Since commentators and later judges alike have criticized the *Lochner* decision almost unanimously, it would seem that the inconstant judges made a serious error; indeed, only three years later they switched back again, taking both Brewer and Peckham with them.[33]

To put the matter briefly, Peckham argued that liberty of contract (here, the contract between employer and employee) was the rule, and its denial the exception. Unless New York had reasonable police power grounds for enacting the bakers' law, the rule must stand. Although the state argued that the law was intended to protect the health of bakery employees or of the general public, Peckham concluded that this was not true. The only other ground for the law woud be to regard it as a general labor regulation, and the state, Peckham argued, had no power to enact such laws under the liberty of contract doctrine. He called such laws "mere meddlesome interferences with the rights of the individual," scorning Justice Brown's argument in the *Holden* case that the state was merely protecting the equality of bargaining power between employer and employee.[34]

Peckham's opinion was so extreme that the Court practically reversed it within a dozen years. It also drew stinging dissents not only from Harlan (whose opinion, joined by White and Day, had been the original majority statement) but also from Holmes. The Yankee judge wrote a separate dissent in which, refusing with vast Olympian detachment to discuss in any detail the health conditions in bakeries or the equality of bargaining relationships, he instead attacked the whole concept of liberty of contract. Some of the most memorable Holmesianisms come from this opinion. Holmes held that legislative majorities should have their way unless the resulting statute could not be accepted by a rational and fair man. This argument blinked at the whole issue, since the majority obviously felt that this was the very test they were applying. Holmes went further, accusing the majority of using its economic predilections rather than the Constitution, since "the Fourteenth Amendment does not enact Mr. Herbert Spencer's *Social Statics.*" But of course there was also a legal theory involved—that the police power was limited to the protection of health, safety, or morality—and on this point the majority rested its case. Holmes, in other words, failed to meet the majority on its own ground.[36]

Harlan's dissent, on the other hand, had to do so, since it was originally intended to uphold the statute. Harlan went with some thoroughness into the health conditions of bakeries, concluding that sufficient evidence of health hazards existed to justify the legislature in passing the law: "I find it impossible," he wrote, "in view of common experience, to say that there is here no real or substantial relation between the means employed by the State and the end sought by its legislation." We cannot assume that the legislature has acted "in bad faith" or "without due deliberation." In such a case the Court must defer to the legislative judgment.[37] Harlan's use of the health facts (probably provided by counsel) anticipated by only three years the successful use of the "Brandeis brief." It is true that Harlan did not challenge in any fundamental way the doctrine of liberty of contract, and he certainly had no misgivings about substantive due process itself. But in the application of a rule of reason, he was willing to go farther than the majority in attributing good faith and reason to the state legislature. This is the line he drew between *Smyth* and *Lochner*, for in *Smyth* he obviously felt that the state had not applied the facts at its command reasonably.

Lochner arguably represents the most extreme use of substantive due process until the 1960s, and perhaps also the most criticized.[38] On the whole, however, the Court during Harlan's tenure used substantive due process with restraint. In only two later cases were state laws struck down. One of these found Oliver Wendell Holmes, Jr., leading the Court, which shows at least that he had no fundamental objection to using the due process clause substantively. In this case the Court struck down both a constitutional and a statutory provision of the state of Kentucky regarding the delivery and acceptance of railroad cars from one railroad to another. McKenna, joined by Harlan and Moody, dissented, feeling that the portion of the law that applied only to intrastate switching should be upheld.[39] Holmes also wrote the Court's opinion in the final case in this area, decided during Harlan's tenure, holding that the police power does not allow a state to compel railroads to install siding switches without charge on the mere request of an elevator owner. Again, Harlan and McKenna dissented, this time without opinion.[40]

If the Court had to create such a doctrine as substantive due process to protect corporate property (and most historians would oppose this), one would at least have hoped that it would be used with moderation and restraint. This is, on the whole, what Harlan and "his" Court did. Not very many of the hundreds of cases brought to the Supreme Court resulted in judgments of unconstitutionality, and in most of these the legislature could indeed be regarded as acting unreasonably. The only real exceptions (some would argue even these) occurred in *Smyth* and *Lochner*. As one writer says, "Admittedly the Court . . . had developed the due process clause as a potential check upon the arbitrariness of state and local action, but it increasingly presumed the reasonableness of governmental action and consistently refused to place any business beyond the pale of regulation."[41] Later courts, especially in the 1920s, were not to observe such restraint; but the most that one can blame Harlan and his brethren for is that they gave the Taft Court the tools.

15

Criminal Procedures in the States

If the Fourteenth Amendment's due process clause meant anything obvious, it was that all "persons" must be accorded fair treatment in state criminal proceedings. Fair treatment could most properly be interpreted as following the forms of justice that were traditionally regarded as necessary, beginning with those spelled out in the Fourth through the Eighth amendments, even though these had never been applied to the states. Even if the term *persons* was narrowed to include only freed slaves, however, the Court in practice did very little to assure this kind of due process. While it came by the 1890s to look closely at the substance of legislation—as we have seen, a farfetched reading of due process—it continued its pre-Fourteenth Amendment course of allowing the states to do pretty much as they wished in handling criminal procedures.

Concurrently, the Circuit Court of Appeals Act of 1891 gave the Court increased jurisdiction over criminal procedures in the lower federal courts. These usually involved specific congressional statutes or such typical constitutional provisions as whether or not a confession obtained involuntarily was admissible at trial. These questions are to a great degree different from those raised by cases coming to the Court under the Fourteenth Amendment's due process clause and are thus treated separately in Chapter 19.

To his lasting credit, John Harlan stood up against the refusal of his colleagues to accord even a minimal protection to persons caught in the toils of state criminal processes. He argued—to simplify a little—that if due process could be used (properly, he felt) to protect property substantively, then it could surely also be used to protect life and liberty procedurally. In a series of cases stretching over twenty-five years, he dissented from decisions holding that due process did not apply to state criminal procedures.

The attempts of various states to prevent blacks from serving on juries provided the first opportunities for the Supreme Court to apply the due process clause. Since these issues involved both procedure and the freed slaves, and jury trial was considered central to any concept of fair trial, the judges could have begun to apply the clause in the 1870s. Although they did provide some protection against racial discrimination in jury selection, they used the equal protection clause rather than due process, and the subject belongs properly in a later chapter.

Thus the Court did not really rule on the scope of due process rights until a case came before it that did not involve blacks. *Hurtado* v. *California* provided an ideal test of whether, and how far, the Court would be willing to limit states in the area of criminal procedure. In *Hurtado* the defendant in a murder case had been convicted in a trial held without a grand jury indictment. States at that time were beginning to experiment with less clumsy ways of bringing cases to court, and California had used the now-standard method of a criminal information brought by the prosecuting attorney. Hurtado claimed that this was an unfair procedure, since both custom and the Bill of Rights demanded indictment by the traditional grand jury.[1]

In order to understand the arguments in the case, one must first remember that the Bill of Rights had always been held to apply only to federal cases before the adoption of the Fourteenth Amendment.[2] Also, there is an identical due process clause buried in the Fifth Amendment in the middle of a long list of specific procedural protections including the right to a grand jury indictment. Thus Hurtado's lawyers had to argue that due process in the Fourteenth meant something more than it apparently meant in the Fifth. The state, on the other hand, claimed that since there was a separate grand jury clause, this right was not part of due process, since due process meant only what it had always meant in the Fifth Amendment.

Regarding the argument that the Fourteenth Amendment "incorporated" all of the Bill of Rights, Justice Stanley Matthews, writing for the seven-man Supreme Court majority, merely followed precedent, saying in essence that if the framers of the amendment had meant such a thing they could have said so in much plainer fashion.[3] To the more difficult question of whether grand juries were fundamental and traditional to American ideas of justice and were part of the common law, Matthews went back all the way to the Magna Carta to prove that they were not, in a scholarly and exhaustive treatise that concluded with the wisely pragmatic statement that to bind the states to the traditions of the common law would "deny every quality of the law but its age, and . . . render it incapable of progress or improvement." Due process, he said, does not include every particular of procedure that may have become traditional, but only those involving "the very substance of individual rights to life, liberty, and property," "those fundamental principles of liberty and justice which lie at the base of all our civil and political institutions." Grand jury indictment, he decided, was not that fundamental, being "merely a preliminary proceeding" that does not affect the result of the trial.[4]

Justice Harlan took issue with Matthews at every turn. First, he pointed to the obvious similarity between the words of the Fourteenth and the Fifth amendments, concluding that "that similarity was not accidental, but evinces a purpose to impose upon the States the same restrictions . . . which had been imposed upon the general government."[5] Perhaps feeling that this was a weak argument, Harlan went on to try to prove that *due process* means more than merely what a majority of the justices might feel is fundamental: it refers to "those settled usages and modes of proceeding existing in the common and statute law of England."[6] In a learned review of English law, he quoted Erskine, Blackstone, Hawkins, and other English writers to the effect that the use of information (rather than grand jury indictment) "was not consistent with . . . 'due process of law.'" This, he said, "was the understanding of the patriotic men who established free institutions upon this continent."[7] Harlan charged the majority with roaming at will among the provisions of the Bill of Rights, picking out those that they felt were fundamental. Why, he asked, is the grand jury right any less fundamental than the rule against double jeopardy or self-incrimination? According to the logic of the majority, states would not even have to maintain trial juries. In his analysis, the due process clause in the Fifth Amendment was meant to include all the other trial rights settled in English law, but some of these were enumerated in the Bill of Rights merely to make it perfectly clear that Congress could not abrogate them. So the clause in the Fourteenth Amendment has the same meaning as the one in the Fifth.[8]

Finally, Harlan turned to Matthews's argument that the states ought to be allowed a wide latitude for progressive reform in the area of criminal procedure. He implied that this might be all very well if abolition of grand juries for felonies were really progress. But all the states in 1787, and the framers of the Constitution, knew that it was not wise at all, for "in the secrecy of the investigations by grand juries, the weak and helpless . . . have found, and will continue to find, security against official oppression, the cruelty of mobs, the machinations of falsehood, and the malevolence of private persons who would use the machinery of the law to bring ruin upon their personal enemies."[9]

For all the passion and moral fervor Harlan brought to his dissent, he was not successful in persuading his colleagues or their successors that *due process* is a sort of shorthand for all of the rights contained in the Bill of Rights. Although the Court has, gradually, come to include most of the criminal procedure provisions within the concept of due process, it has always clung to Matthews's basic premise that the concept only includes those that are really fundamental: even today, grand juries do not seem to be all that fundamental, and most states have come to limit their use strictly, while the Court has never mandated their use. Due process, meanwhile, still means "what the judges say it means" in the exercise of what it must be hoped is a wise discretion.

Some judges have felt that once a precedent is set by the Court, they must follow it in future cases even if they disagree and have dissented in the first case. John Harlan, needless to say, was not of that kind, and to do him justice we must admit that such a practice carried to extremes would make it impossible for the Supreme Court ever to reverse its own decisions. The Kentuckian continued to dissent in cases from the states involving the procedural rights enumerated in the Bill of Rights until the end of his life.

In *O'Neil v. Vermont* the Court in 1892 decided (in the main strand of the majority's opinion) that O'Neil could be punished by Vermont courts for violations of the state's liquor laws even though his business was transacted in New York. Both Harlan and Justice Field objected to this (joined by Justice Brewer), and Field, indeed, got into a long and acrimonious dispute with the Chief Justice over whether or not the Vermont Supreme Court could have considered the case as one involving the federal commerce power.[10] The case, however, also presented the court with an opportunity to apply the rule against cruel and unusual punishment, a chance the majority refused. Since O'Neil had been convicted of 307 offences, the cumulative fine was $6,638.32, or, alternatively, 19,914 days in prison—more than the state's maximum sentence for manslaughter. The dissenters felt that the conviction ought to be regarded as one offense and that therefore the punishment was drastically excessive. Harlan returned to his argument that the meaning of due process was to be primarily found in the Bill of Rights, in this instance the Eighth Amendment. Field used the broader argument that cruel and unusual punishment directly violated due process even without the Eighth Amendment.[11]

Harlan wrote another major dissent in a 1900 case, *Maxwell v. Dow.* Here again the absence of grand jury indictment was an issue on which both sides (Peckham for the majority) repeated their earlier arguments. An additional issue was presented by the question of whether a state could constitutionally use an eight-man jury in a capital case. The majority held that the traditional twelve-man jury was not a fundamental right and therefore was protected neither by the privileges or immunities clause nor the due process clause of the Fourteenth Amendment. Since the argument concerning privileges or immunities was relatively new, Peckham shored up his opinion by relying upon Justice Miller's statement in an earlier case that the privileges or immunities clause in the Fourteenth Amendment can only mean what it already meant in article 4 of the original Constitution. His interpretation largely deprived the amendment's clause of any content whatever.[12]

Harlan took the occasion to review the entire question of the application of the Fourteenth Amendment to the states, especially in the light of the then-established use by the Court of the due process clause in liberty of contract and rate cases. He first went back to the privileges or immunities clause and tried to convince his colleagues that it was meant to apply the

Bill of Rights to the states. Since this argument was doomed to failure, he passed on to the due process clause. He strongly castigated the Court for being more interested in property rights than in the rights of the individual: "If, then, the 'due process of law' required by the Fourteenth Amendment does not allow a state to take property without just compensation, . . . but does allow the life or liberty of the citizen to be taken in a mode that is repugnant to the settled usages and the modes of proceeding authorized at the time the Constitution was adopted and which was expressly forbidden in the national Bill of Rights, it would seem that the protection of private property is of more consequence than the protection of life and liberty of the citizen." Then, as he often did, Harlan invoked the argument *ad horrendum*, citing the possibilities of what a state might do without falling afoul of the Supreme Court. In an interesting anticipation of a type of case that has since come to the Court, he asked what would happen should the state of Utah establish Mormonism supported by taxation. "Could its right to do so, as far as the Constitution . . . is concerned, be gainsaid under the principles of the opinion just delivered?"[13]

Harlan concluded by combating the "selective inclusion" principle established in *Hurtado* by Justice Matthews and still used in the 1990s.[14] All the rights contained in the Bill of Rights, he maintained,

> are equally protected by the Constitution. No judicial tribunal has authority to say that some of them may be abridged by the states while others may not be abridged. . . . There is no middle position, unless it be assumed to be one of the functions of the judiciary by an interpretation of the Constitution to mitigate what its members may deem the erroneous or unwise action of the people in adopting the Fourteenth Amendment. If some of the guaranties of life, liberty, and property, which at the time of the adoption of the national Constitution were regarded as fundamental and as absolutely essential to the enjoyment of freedom, have in the judgement of some ceased to be of practical value, it is for the people of the United States so to declare by an amendment to that instrument.[15]

Of course, underlying this general argument is the more specific feeling that the trial jury spoken of in the Bill of Rights is the traditional twelve-man jury provided in the common law. Since the number of jury members is not mentioned in the Constitution, however, Harlan's literalist reading was weaker than it would otherwise have been.

Most of the time Harlan tended strongly to read the Bill of Rights literally. For instance, he held for the unanimous Court that when a trial proceeds to its conclusion but there is no verdict, a new trial does not create double jeopardy and that a state need not under due process separate judicial from executive functions.[16] He joined the Court in ruling that one jailed for contempt for refusing to testify is deprived of no constitutional right.[17] Where an original conviction, Harlan said, is held on appeal to be legally defective, it is therefore a nullity, and a new trial does not constitute double jeopardy even though the defendant has spent the intervening time in prison.[18]

The old Kentuckian's last attack on the majority's approach to due process came in 1908. Albert Twining and David C. Cornell had been convicted for deception of a state bank examiner. Their appeal was based on the claim that the judge's charge to the jury, following New Jersey law, referred to the fact that the defendants had neither testified nor produced witnesses in their defense and thus deprived them of their right not to incriminate themselves, which violated due process as well as the privileges or immunities clause. Justice William H. Moody, writing for the Court, took the question of privileges or immunities seriously, reviewing the previous cases extensively and then coming down on the side of precedent: he concluded that it was "not profitable to examine the weighty arguments" in favor of applying the clause, for "the question is no longer open in this court."[19] Of course if the Court were always to treat precedent as sacred, then its mistakes could never be corrected, nor could decisions be accommodated to new conditions: it is, in other words, a thoroughly pernicious doctrine. Nevertheless, the Court even in the 1990s still observes this particular precedent: the privileges or immunities clause still resides in the Fourteenth Amendment, but it is empty of significant content. Probably what Moody actually meant to do was to confine his "doctrine" to the subject involved in the case, and he obviously thought there was some merit in Harlan's argument. Perhaps he was merely deferring to the opinions of the rest of the Court.

Turning to the due process claim, Moody went back to the old *Hurtado* argument, conceding only that due process was limited to the "settled usages and modes of proceeding existing in the common and statute law of England," modified by the judges in the light of changes rendered desirable by new circumstances. Thus Moody claimed in one sentence a vast, discretionary, natural law-like power for the judiciary. Due process was limited, too, to "those fundamental principles," discovered, of course, by the judges, that "protect the citizen in his private right, and guard him against the arbitrary action of government." Judging by early American state constitutions and court decisions, the right against self-incrimination was not fundamental. Moody was also concerned that broadening the scope of due process meant limiting the powers of the states, and "in our peculiar dual form of government, nothing is more fundamental than the full power of the state to order its own affairs and govern its own people."[20] What is fundamental, then, is to be decided (at least partly) by counting noses: What do most Americans consider to be fundamental? By this criterion, due process only requires a valid law, proper jurisdiction, adequate notice, and an adequate hearing.

Harlan, in dissent, first pointed out that the Court had departed from its usual salutary policy of avoiding constitutional issues where possible. Here, the majority had never decided—indeed, had specifically refused to decide—whether the judge's charge actually constituted forced incrimination. If it did not, there was no constitutional question for the Court to decide, and the majority was merely expressing "its opinion on an abstract question." Then, meeting the majority on its own ground, the Kentuckian reviewed the history of the privilege against self-incrimination. It had existed, he said, ever since Star Chamber days in England, and the framers of the Bill of Rights would have been "aghast" at the idea that the principle "was not among the essential, fundamental principles of English law." He cited the early state constitutions and the background of the Bill of Rights in support of his contention, concluding that the immunity was "universal in American law" by 1866. "The Fourteenth Amendment would have been disapproved," he argued, "by every State in the Union if it had saved or recognized the right of a State to compel one accused of crime . . . to be a witness against himself." Such compulsion "shocks or ought to shock the sense of right and justice of every one who loves liberty. . . . As I read the opinion of the court, it would follow from the general principles underlying it . . . that the Fourteenth Amendment would be no obstacle whatever in the way of a state law [allowing the] rack or thumbscrew, censorship, unreasonable search, or double jeopardy."[21]

Even using the *Hurtado* principle of selective inclusion (which Harlan never accepted), certainly the Kentuckian had the better of this argument, as the Court itself would come to recognize at a later time when it was concerned less with states' rights and more with applying the fundamental principles of a fair trial. The *Twining* ruling was reversed in 1965, thus justifying Harlan, even though one of the justices persisted in calling him "an eccentric exception" in his views on due process.[22]

Twining also demonstrates John Harlan's capacity to maintain harmonious relationships within the Court despite profound differences in judicial approaches. After Moody had entered his terminal illness and was thinking of resigning, he wrote the Kentuckian: "Not the least of my distress is the regret I feel in severing our judicial associations which have always been so pleasant and in the main so harmonious though I suppose you are not yet prepared to put Twining v. New Jersey into your leading Constitutional Cases but will content yourself with condemning it."[23]

16

Civil Rights

The Thirteenth Amendment, ratified in 1865, prohibited slavery or "involuntary servitude" from existing in the United States, thus setting a constitutional seal on the results of the Civil War. *Slavery,* at least in its American context, is a clear enough term that it has caused no difficulties for the courts. The words *involuntary servitude,* on the other hand, can pose problems, since they represent something less than slavery (how much?) that is still unconstitutional. Justice Harlan approached the words literally, as was his habit, and was again out of step with his brethren on the Supreme Court. Ironically, the first case calling for the interpretation of the phrase had nothing to do with the amendment's original purpose of preventing blacks from being returned to some form of semislavery. It is this fact, actually, that caused the difficulty.

In *Robertson* v. *Baldwin,* an 1887 case, a sailor had jumped ship before the end of a voyage in violation of the agreement customary when seamen sign on. Congress had provided that local officials can use compulsion to return such "deserters" to their ships; seaman Robertson claimed that this created an involuntary situation of servitude. While conceding that an element of involuntariness was involved, the majority spokesman, Justice Henry Billings Brown, sidestepped the initial issues by pointing out that the sailor's contract had been entered into voluntarily. Voluntary servitude through labor contracts is undoubtedly constitutional, and Brown argued that a voluntary labor contract does not become involuntary during its term even if the laborer desires to end it. This would seem to have been enough to settle the case, but Justice Brown went on to attempt to establish another point. He argued that laws requiring seamen to stay with their ships went back to antiquity and certainly had existed in the United States and the rest of the world at the time of the adoption of the Thirteenth Amendment. Of course, much the same argument could have been made concerning slavery itself, but Brown's point was that there existed certain well-defined forms of service that had "always been treated as exceptional" and that for this reason should not be considered as coming within the terms of the amendment.[1] He compared seamen's private contracts with military enlistments, but he did little to establish the necessity or desirability of such irrevocable forms of servitude.

Harlan, dissenting alone, argued that any "condition of enforced service, even for a limited period," constitutes involuntary servitude and that this condition for the individual exists "from the moment he is compelled against his will to continue in such service." The sailor may be sued for breach of contract, but he may not be forced to return to his ship nor charged criminally. Harlan concluded, rather exaggeratedly, perhaps, that "under this view of the Constitution, we may now look for advertisements, not for runaway [slaves]. . . but for runaway seamen."[2]

In evaluating the arguments in *Robertson,* one is struck by the fact that neither side approached the question realistically. Aside from his historical excursion, Justice Brown made no attempt to look at the reasons for the seamen's laws or the validity of these reasons in 1865 or 1897. On his side, Harlan merely applied the words of the amendment literally, at the same time leaving no doubt that his sense of injustice was aroused. He made no attempt to figure out what would happen in the real world if seamen did not have to fulfill their contracts, aside from remarking that they could be sued. Constitutional litigation tends to encourage such an air of unreality, however, and either side could argue that the important thing was the words of the Constitution (or the intentions of its framers) and that it is not the job of courts to look at the desirability of the situation created by those words.

Peonage is not mentioned in the Thirteenth Amendment, but the Court did not doubt that federal laws prohibiting it were constitutional. In *Clyatt* v. *United States,* Justice David J. Brewer defined peonage as "a status of compulsory service based on indebtedness" and a clear constitutional violation.[3] Even so, when Clyatt was accused of violating the law by sending black laborers back from Florida to their Georgia employers to work off their debts, the Court felt it could provide no relief. Even though the law was valid and there was no doubt that Clyatt had violated it, the Court found the indictment defective: it charged that the blacks were "returned" to a state of peonage, and, said Brewer, since there was no evidence that they had ever been peons, there could be no proof that they were "returned" to that status. Harlan would have none of such technicalities. He thought that being forced to work off a debt was peonage even if there had not been a preexisting status, and the fact that the lower court had sent the case to the jury for a verdict was thus perfectly proper.[4]

Since peonage had existed widely not only among black but also among Mexican laborers, it was important that the Court upheld Congress's right to prohibit it. Nevertheless, the disposition to seize upon a technicality—one that could easily have been interpreted otherwise—did not place the Court in a very good light. Harlan had no such need to dissent, and the Court partially redeemed itself when it struck down an

Alabama law that punished as stealing the failure to perform a labor contract or refund the money involved, with an irrebuttable presumption of guilt. Such a law, said Justice Charles Evans Hughes, created a condition of involuntary servitude. John Harlan silently agreed, but that hero of civil libertarians, Holmes, dissented.[5] Since the law was an obvious attempt to bind black workers to their employers, the grounds for his dissent had to be technical. On the whole, Holmes cultists tend to ignore his poor record in race cases while emphasizing his First Amendment opinions.

We are accustomed, these days, to consider the equal protection clause of the Fourteenth Amendment as one of the key provisions of the Constitution. In Harlan's day, to the contrary, the Court handled few cases involving the clause, and its treatment of those was hardly calculated to encourage other litigants to claim its protection. While constitutional arguments exist for the course the Supreme Court took, they are hardly the only arguments. As is well known, Justice Harlan in his dissents showed the Court another possible interpretation. What was lacking at the turn of the century was a disposition to protect blacks from discrimination, and Harlan eloquently demonstrated that if one has a different disposition one can easily find other interpretations of "equal protection of the laws."

The jury cases, indeed, may constitute at least a partial exception to the foregoing remarks, both because the Court as a whole made some attempt to provide for Negro rights and because John Harlan was more likely a leader than a dissenter. Nevertheless, there is no need to go over the cases in detail; Judge Loren Miller, among others, has already done so.[6] The general position taken by the Court—with the outstanding exception of Justice Stephen J. Field—was that state laws and state officials could not as a matter of policy keep blacks off grand or petit jury panels, but that no defendant, either black or white, had a right to have blacks serving on his particular jury.[7] Although the Court implied that defendants could show through evidence that blacks were prevented from serving, the kind of evidence the judges seem to have had in mind was openly stated laws or rules.[8] Only much later would a history of unvarying practice come to be regarded as sufficient evidence. The Court also strictly drew lines making it difficult for individual defendants to reach the highest level, tending to demand timely appeal from a trial verdict rather than the easier process of removal to a U.S. district court.[9]

The way these cases worked out, then, was that although a white defendant could count on having an all-white jury, a black defendant could claim no right to even a single member of his own race, as long as blacks were allowed on the panels from which the juries were selected. Then too, there was no affirmative right of blacks to serve on juries, since the Court was paying attention only to the rights of defendants as such. The right to jury service, in other words, was not regarded as a right (much less an obligation) of blacks as citizens at all. The emphasis was entirely on a concept of fair trial for black defendants. It was almost as though the Court were saying that black voting was not a right of citizenship unless a black candidate was running for office. This was, needless to say, a distinctly negative conception of the rights of citizenship. It is obvious, then, that the Court looked at jury service as an element of due process even though it might be citing equal protection as the basis for its decisions. Due process focuses on fair trial; equal protection focuses (or should focus) on the rights of citizenship.

Harlan either did not see this distinction or else agreed with his brethren on the Court, for his votes and his opinions do not show any disagreement. He and the rest of the judges can be criticized for not going far enough. Probably, as lawyers and judges, they were more familiar with the fair trial concepts and thus tended to approach jury cases from that end of the spectrum. Harlan, it is true, might have been expected to look at these questions more broadly; that he did not is partly a reflection of the way the jury cases came to the Supreme Court, for they always involved defendants already convicted at trial. No one ever claimed the right to sit on a jury or the right to be selected on jury panels. What the Court's, or Harlan's, response to such a case would have been must remain unknown.

While there are other areas of importance in the interpretation of the equal protection clause, such as state taxation and regulation of out-of-state corporations, the original intention of the clause was doubtless to secure equal treatment of the former slaves freed by the Thirteenth Amendment. In this area Justice Harlan made his enduring reputation in dissent, although even here it would be a delusion to think of him as a twentieth-century liberal. To him, equality was a constitutional principle more than it was a personal belief. His letters and those of his wife show that they had distinctly paternalistic attitudes toward their black household servants and other blacks with whom they came into close contact. Theodore Roosevelt got into political trouble when he invited blacks to the White House; there is no record of the Harlans ever having had that kind of social relations with blacks, and we have already seen the criticism John encountered by merely being seated next to Frederick Douglass at a public dinner.

This is, however, not a matter for great criticism. Harlan had by the 1880s come light years away from the Kentucky slave owner of the 1850s. That he did not go beyond his liberal contemporaries is hardly surprising. The surprise is, in fact, that he went as far as he did, and students of his life have always had difficulty in explaining his ideological shift, even to the extent of charging that it was due to mere political exigencies. There is no doubt that expediency played a role in his initial change, but we have already seen that his father, his wife, his religion, and his own experiences also influenced him. Like most of us, Harlan avoided hypocrisy by adopting his new faith thoroughly and, as always with him, single-mindedly. The sincerity of his newly adopted beliefs cannot really be challenged. Harlan was a "true believer" even when his beliefs differed vastly from those he had held previously. Although he had originally opposed the adoption of the Reconstruction Amendments, the former slaveholder came to support them more deeply than any of his Northern judicial brethren. It is this support that accounts primarily for his twentieth-century reputation as a great judge.

The Supreme Court by 1911 succeeded in practically writing off the equal protection clause as a practical device for securing black equality. It did this, first, by a strict interpretation of the enforcement clause of the Fourteenth Amendment, in other words, by blocking the efforts of the radical-led Congress to protect black rights through federal legislation. Second, the Court defined *discrimination* so narrowly that it did not reach even the most extreme state laws intended to "keep the blacks in their place." Harlan fought both of these developments, but with no support on the Court. Third, the Court generally refused to use the commerce clause to bar state legislation requiring segregation.

Indeed, the first segregation case decided by the Court found it striking down a Louisiana law—carpetbagger legislation dating from occupation days in 1869—barring segregation among passengers. In a case argued only a few weeks before Harlan took his seat, the Court held that the law could interfere with interstate commerce and was therefore within the power of Congress alone. For 1878 this was a strikingly narrow reading of state power, as we have seen earlier; it is doubtless to be accounted for by the justices' unwillingness to approve of integrated travel imposed by law. Chief Justice Waite, in fact, commented, "If the public good requires such legislation, it must come from Congress."[10] Indeed, such legislation had already been enacted by Congress in its Civil Rights Act of 1875, and when it was tested in court, the Supreme Court promptly struck it down too, partly on the pretext that the case did not involve interstate commerce. When Mississippi state law mandated segregation rather than integration, the Court reverted to its then-normal doctrine, drawing a strict line between inter- and intrastate transportation. By this time Harlan was on the Court, and he dissented (with Justice Bradley), remarking curtly that "I am unable to perceive how [the Louisiana law] is a regulation of interstate commerce and [this Mississippi law] is not."[11]

In between these two cases the Supreme Court took up the question of the power of Congress to legislate under the enforcement clause of the Fourteenth Amendment.[12] Five cases were consolidated for the argument and decision, only one from a former Confederate state. Black patrons were denied accommodation (or, at least, equal accommodation) at a San Francisco theater, the New York Opera House, a restaurant in a Kansas hotel, a room in a hotel in Missouri, and a seat in the "ladies car" of a railroad train in Tennessee. In none of the cases did a state law require such refusal; also, however, none of the states had a law requiring equal or integrated accommodation. Congress had in 1875, however, passed an equal accommodations law that prohibited denial of "full and equal enjoyment of the accommodations, advantages, facilities and privileges of inns, public conveyances . . . theaters and other places of public amusement."[13]

Were these purely private acts of discrimination? If so, could Congress regulate them under the Fourteenth Amendment's enforcement clause or, possibly, some other constitutional provision? The Court majority, led by Justice Bradley, had no doubt about either question. The equal protection clause, Bradley pointed out, reaches only state action, not private, and the state's failure to mandate equal accommodations—its action—did not constitute "action by omission." He went on to say that Congress was given no affirmative power, only corrective power, to enforce the clause. Bradley did not explicitly deny that a decision by a state court might constitute state action, but all five of these cases had been prosecuted by the United States in federal courts. He also refused to give any standing to Harlan's argument that, stemming from the public interest doctrine of *Munn* v. *Illinois*, these businesses might be considered public interest businesses and therefore became in a sense public agencies themselves. He specifically said that the Court was not considering any of these cases as commerce clause cases, which might (at least for the railroad case, using *Hall* v. *De Cuir* as a precedent) have given color to a claim of federal power. Further, Justice Bradley decided that Congress gained no affirmative power under the citizenship clause of the amendment either. Finally, refuting Harlan's argument, Bradley held that race discrimination was not a badge of slavery and therefore did not violate the Thirteenth Amendment, which has no state action requirement. Thus having comprehensively denied any power in Congress to prohibit discrimination by private agencies, Bradley left the protection of blacks to the tender mercies of the states, at least for the time being.

Alan Westin has detailed the circumstances surrounding Harlan's dissent, and it is sufficient here to point out that the Kentuckian apparently felt deeply that he had to dissent despite the fact that no one else on the Court agreed with him.[14] He took the unusual step of meeting with Senator George F. Edmunds of Vermont. Although Edmunds had originally opposed Harlan's appointment, the two had later become friends, and Edmunds had been influential in the passage of the 1875 act that was in question. The senator assured Harlan that the debates over the act had thoroughly canvassed the question of its constitutionality.[15] Edmunds wrote a memo to the justice, which gave the Kentuckian the assurance he needed to stand alone against his colleagues in the first of his great dissenting opinions. It only remained to write the opinion.

But the writing was not easy. Bradley's opinion was, at least in strictly legal terms, a strong one.[16] According to his wife, Harlan worked late at night, at first without success, to frame his opinion. Mallie wrote that, hoping it would help, she placed Chief Justice Roger B. Taney's inkstand— a memento that her husband highly prized—on his desk where he could not avoid seeing it. When Harlan next took up the task of framing his dissent—on a Sunday after church—he found Taney's inkstand there, and "the memory of the historic part that Taney's inkstand had played in the Dred Scott decision, in temporarily tightening the shackles of slavery upon the negro race in the ante-bellum days, seemed, that morning, to act like magic in clarifying my husband's thoughts in regard to the law that had been intended by Sumner to protect the recently emancipated slaves in the enjoyment of equal 'civil rights.' His pen fairly flew on that day and, with the running start he then got, he soon finished his dissent."[17] Inkstands aside, Harlan's difficulties are understandable if one remembers that the case was decided in 1883. Many of the "liberal" constitutional concepts to which we are now accustomed had not yet been developed, nor would they be for many years. In fact, Harlan was a pioneer.

Harlan began his dissent with the general charge that the majority's arguments proceeded upon "grounds entirely too narrow and artificial," sacrificing the "substance and spirit" of the Reconstruction Amendments "by a subtle and ingenious verbal criticism." Instead, he felt that the amendments should be considered in the light of their general purpose, which was to protect Negro rights: the Court's decision made such protection impossible. Proceeding to particulars, he argued that Congress had ample power to legislate under the Thirteenth Amendment, which had no "state action" limitation. His problem was to link racial segregation with the concept of slavery. He felt, obviously, that such discrimination created an inequality that could be equated with involuntary servitude. In this instance, the majority can be accused of looking at words, while Harlan is the realist. The Court finally accepted his argument many years later, but some critics still believe that his was a farfetched interpretation.[18]

Turning to the Fourteenth Amendment, the Kentuckian argued that the citizenship clause "necessarily imports at least equality of civil rights among citizens of every race in the same State" and that Congress was given the power to protect these rights, even against private interference. Although some Court precedents, particularly the Dred Scott and the *Slaughterhouse* cases, would seem to deny any such proposition, Harlan had not participated in these decisions and did not feel bound by them. There seems to be nothing intrinsically unsound about his argument given the purpose of the amendment, but the Court would have had to go against precedent to adopt it, and the majority had no disposition to do so. Even had it done so, Bradley's basic argument that Congress could not reach private action would still have stood in the way of upholding the Civil Rights Act. Harlan used the age-old idea that certain business are "common carriers," required by the state to serve the public, as an argument that (as the chief justice had said in *Munn*) they "cease to be *juris privati* only" and partake of some aspects of the state itself. Therefore their actions can be considered, to some extent, as actions of the state, particularly when the state, by not prohibiting, seems to approve their actions. "Such being the relations these corporations hold to the public," Harlan wrote, "it would seem that the right of a colored person to use . . . [them] is as fundamental in the state of freedom . . . as are any of the rights which my brethren concede to be so far fundamental as to be deemed the essence of civil freedom." Stretching the argument a bit further in order to be sure that it covered theaters, he continued, "In every material sense applicable to the practical enforcement of the fourteenth amendment . . . [these corporations] are agents of the state, because amenable . . . to state regulation." [19]

In 1883 this was a daring argument, one that few lawyers would have accepted. Nowadays, although there is still some disagreement, the state action concept has been stretched so far that the Court, even in the absence of state or federal regulation, will step in to enforce civil rights as against private action. [20] Whether the Court would accept federal regulation of purely private business is another question, although the doctrine devised to make segregated schools subject to federal taxation may indicate that it would even go that far. [21] Nowadays, too, the Supreme Court not only accepts, but carries farther Harlan's argument concerning the applicability of the commerce clause. Bradley had dismissed this, apparently because Congress had not cited the commerce clause in the Civil Rights Act and because in 1883 four of the cases could not have been conceived, even by Harlan, as constituting interstate commerce. Harlan's argument, applied only to the railroad case, was here based on precedent. We have seen that the Court, in *Hall* v. *De Cuir,* had invalidated a Louisiana law requiring integration in transportation because it interfered with interstate commerce. Why, asked Harlan, could not Congress therefore regulate railroads in this respect? It was his strongest argument, for, as he said, Congress had never been required by the Court to cite precise constitutional provisions, and its plenary power over interstate commerce was undoubted. [22]

Harlan concluded that the acceptance of the Court's opinion would

> lead to this anomalous result: that whereas, prior to the amendments congress, with the sanction of this court, passed the most stringent laws—operating directly and primarily upon states, and their officers and agents, as well as upon individuals—in vindication of slavery and the rights of the master, it may not now, by legislation of a like primary and direct character, guard, protect, and secure the freedom established, and the most essential right of the citizenship granted, by the constitutional amendments. I venture, with all respect for the opinion of others, to insist that the national legislature may,

without transcending the limits of the constitution, do for human liberty and the fundamental rights of American citizenship, what it did . . . for the protection of slavery.[23]

His dissent in the *Civil Rights Cases* was, if not Harlan's greatest, certainly his most innovative. It has been much criticized for straying too far from the words of the Fourteenth Amendment. But equally certainly, the majority—composed of many of the same judges who would stray even farther in developing substantive due process—can be criticized for not looking at the intent of the radicals who were responsible for the amendment or at the realities of black life in a segregated society. It was possibly Harlan's intimate knowledge of the slave owners' mentality that enabled him to be more realistic. The majority, it is true, exhibited more deference to (white) public opinion and to the political reality that the radicals no longer controlled Congress. If Harlan was result-oriented—that is, if he looked for and found arguments to support his conclusions—so was the majority.

As a lone dissent in a case much in the public eye, Harlan's opinion drew much comment. Newspaper reaction was mixed, as might be expected, depending much on the ideological slant of the individual editor.[24] Letters to the justice himself were, of course, almost unanimously laudatory. Retired justice William Strong called it "a *very* able opinion," continuing to aver that "the opinion of the court . . . is too narrow—sticks to the letter while you aim to bring out the spirit of the Constitution." Former Justice Noah Swayne agreed: "In my judgment," he wrote, "it is one of the great—indeed one of the greatest—opinions of the Court." Former president Rutherford B. Hayes wrote that while he might agree legally with the majority, "it was important that the *sentiment* you have so admirably expressed should be vindicated." Roscoe Conkling, his bitter opposition to the Kentuckian's appointment forgotten, wrote, "It is naked truth to say that [your dissent] . . . was read not only with admiration, but with surprise at its strength of positions. . . . That the discision [*sic*] from which it dissents, will stir potent and enduring forces, I expect; and that what you have so clearly said will be widely accepted and adopted as the truth, seen not only, but seen with the foresight of wisdom, I do not doubt."[25] Harlan was himself pleased by such sentiments, naturally, and they had the effect of hardening his own stand in future cases involving similar issues. Indeed, he probably was encouraged to believe that even when he was alone on the Court regardless of the issues involved, he lost nothing by dissenting.

Nevertheless he felt a residual guilt, or at least a lingering uncertainty, about disagreeing with all eight of his colleagues, for he wrote in a note to the chief justice: "I am glad to say that the attack of 'dis-sent-ery' of which Bro. Matthews spoke is substantially over. That the attack was, for a time, serious, is due to the *nauseous* character of the medicine which produced it.

At the out-set the discharges were all very highly *colored*, but that feature of the case has substantially disappeared, and the patient feels that he stands on firm ground." [26] He confessed to Hayes "some surprise" at being alone but said that "having determined in my own mind that the act of 1875 was constitutional, I felt bound to state fully the reasons for my dissent." [27]

Justice Bradley's reason for refusing to discuss the railroad portion of the *Civil Rights Cases* on its merits as an interference with congressional power over interstate commerce became clear some years later: he had lost his majority from *Hall* v. *De Cuir.* The Court, having no interest in protecting blacks from segregation, was willing to reverse *Hall*, at least by implication. The case in which this became clear involved a Mississippi statute decreeing racial segregation on railroad trains. The courts of the state had construed the law to apply only to passengers within its borders, and Justice David J. Brewer felt that, as interpreted, the case presented no conflict with the commerce power of Congress. The Louisiana integration law, he said, had not been limited in this fashion. Naturally, Harlan dissented again, this time with the support of Bradley. Explicitly limiting his discussion to the issue of interstate commerce, Harlan pointed out that there was really no difference between the two cases as far as their bearing on that commerce was concerned. He also adverted to the obvious result that state laws requiring integration had been held unconstitutional while those mandating segregation had been upheld, although they had identical effects on interstate commerce. [28] It should also be noted that the Court, in the Mississippi case, did not approve a criminal penalty for one who refused to occupy a segregated railroad car. Instead, it upheld the state's power to require railroads to supply separate cars for the two races. Whether anyone had to use the separate cars was a different question, one to which the Court turned its attention in the famous *Plessy* case.

Plessy v. *Ferguson* has been much criticized in recent years, but although this criticism is morally sound, much of it reveals little knowledge of the complexities of the case and the opinions. [29] Strangely, it drew comparatively little comment when it was first announced. The case arose from an organized black challenge to the Louisiana Separate Car Law of 1890, which reversed the state's earlier integration statute held invalid by the Supreme Court. The law gave train personnel enforcement power and also provided for fines applying to both the employees and to the passengers who might refuse to obey. [30] It was thus different from the earlier Mississippi law. As part of this formal challenge and after previous unsuccessful attempts to attack the law's constitutionality, Homer A. Plessy became the legal vehicle for a test case. Plessy, who was one-eighth Negro and thus defined as black by Louisiana law, was chosen by lawyers interested in the issue. He insisted on his right to a seat in the "white" car of an intrastate train and was arrested and arraigned. His lawyers challenged the trial court's jurisdiction, which was then affirmed by the state supreme court. The case was then taken by writ of error to the U.S. Supreme Court. Note that at this point Plessy had not been tried or convicted.[31]

For various tactical reasons the lawyers' briefs on both sides were excessively obscure and convoluted, characteristics shared by Justice Henry Billings Brown's opinion for a seven-man majority (Justice Brewer did not take part in the case). Although these features also infected Harlan's dissent, he was able—since he did not need to follow the lawyers' briefs— to free himself from them to some degree. In any event, Brown's turgid opinion hardly rose to the rank of a great state paper, and a century later it is the dissent that is remembered.

The Court could not deny that state action existed, and following the Mississippi case, it could deny that there was any interference with inter- state commerce. It was thus faced with the naked question of whether racial discrimination by the state violated Fourteenth Amendment rights. Of course it does, said the Court, but then it introduced a secondary issue: Does forced segregation in public accommodations constitute discrimina- tion? Justice Brown found this an iffy question. Segregation is constitu- tional if it does not evidence a purpose to relegate one race to an inferior position. "Separate but equal" thus became the key to the majority posi- tion. Brown justified this remarkable tour de force by anticipating William Graham Sumner's famous sociological dictum that "law-ways cannot change folkways." All law can do is recognize social customs. If the people of a state want to be separated from each other by race, then law may enforce this desire; such separation, without more, does not imply the inferiority of one race to the other. Only if the facilities provided for one race are inferior to those provided for the other does discrimination occur. Having no evidence to the contrary, the Court assumed that the facilities offered to Homer Plessy were equal to those offered to white passengers, and thus there was no constitutional violation.[32]

Justice Harlan's dissent, while not free of constitutional ambiguities either, did not meet the majority head-on for all its deceptive simplicity. The majority had legal precedent on its side; Harlan had sociological and semantic logic and common sense on his. Basing his argument on the proposition that the Fourteenth Amendment does not permit any public authority "to know the race of those entitled" to its protection, he went on to point out that there would be no point in segregation if it were not for feelings of superiority/inferiority. Using a "judicial notice" approach, Har- lan said that "every one knows that the statute in question had its origin in the purpose, not so much to exclude white persons from railroad cars occupied by blacks, as to exclude colored people from coaches" occupied by whites. Even if segregation was desired by the white majority, the Constitution requires "that the common government of all shall not permit the seeds of race hate to be planted under the sanction of law. . . . Our

Constitution is color-blind, and neither knows nor tolerates classes among citizens. . . . The law regards man as man, and takes no account of his surroundings or of his color when his civil rights as guaranteed by the supreme law of the land are involved."

The modern Supreme Court has revived and applied these basic principles, whether or not they are constitutionally impeccable arguments. John Harlan knew from personal experience that even in a slave society blacks and whites come into much more intimate social relationships than merely sitting in the same railway car; he also knew that jim crow laws were intended to perpetuate the inferiority symbolized by slavery. Northern judges might intone, with the agreement of Louisianan Edward D. White, that "segregation is not discrimination"; Harlan knew better. Here, if not always in his other dissents, Harlan had the stronger constitutional argument.

Many years later, Justice Felix Frankfurter, who was given to intellectual arrogance, privately referred to Harlan as "the old boy" and claimed that *Plessy* was Harlan's "one outburst of rhetoric about the color blindness of the Constitution." He also referred to this passage as Harlan's "purple patch" and as a "blow-hard sentence." [33] These remarks came in reference to Frankfurter's discovery of the Kentuckian's opinion for a unanimous Court in the *Cumming* case. [34] This case, decided in 1899, certainly does give one pause even if it does not justify Frankfurter's derogatory remarks.

Harlan's opinion in *Cumming* is, on the surface at least, disingenuous coming from the writer of the dissents surveyed above. Nevertheless, the case contains technical complexities that may partially explain Harlan's stand, and segregation was not among the issues presented to the Court. Then too, Harlan may have felt that yet another dissent—he had already decided that he would have to dissent in *Maxwell* v. *Dow* in the same session—would make him appear to be the "eccentric exception" that Frankfurter was later to call him. [35]

Like many Southern states, Georgia in the 1890s still had not established universal public school systems. Richmond County at that time partially subsidized the cost of private high school education for white children, segregated by sex. It had also maintained a public high school for black boys (not girls), charging them tuition. When the county decided to close the black high school, which had about sixty students, in order to use the facilities for a black grade school accommodating three hundred, the plaintiffs asked for equitable relief, claiming that equality demanded that the subsidization of white students also cease. The trial court granted this relief, but the Georgia Supreme Court reversed the decision. The plaintiffs went to the Supreme Court on a writ of error.

The plaintiffs made no claim that segregation in education was an issue: everyone seemingly accepted it, at least in the existing circumstances. Harlan, possibly in deference to his judicial brethren, treated the case on its facts. He asked what would be gained by denying high school education to whites as well as blacks, pointed out the advantages for black grade school children, noted that there were private black high schools that cost almost the same as the former public one, and ended by maintaining that the equitable relief sought was inappropriate since it would create other inequities. He also adverted to the unfairness of the fact that the county provided no high school education for black girls and would not do so even were the relief granted.

This is all perfectly straightforward in technical terms, but it still seems a little odd that Harlan wrote the opinion (let alone that he voted with the majority). When his emotions were involved, he seldom was satisfied with legalities. In fact, however, nothing the Supreme Court could do in the case would accomplish any useful purpose for the black plaintiffs. Real relief could only come by going entirely outside the framework of the case as presented in order to issue a mandamuslike order for the school board to maintain high schools for both races (and both sexes) even at the cost of raising its school tax rate. This was a type of action that the Supreme Court never used until the 1950s.

An admirer of Harlan would at least wish that he had refused to be the Court's spokesman in the case. There was an obvious injustice to the black students, and it was insensitive of him not to have seen this (if indeed he did not). No justice, however, remains free of inconsistency if he stays on the Court very long, not even Holmes or Frankfurter. Indeed, the *Cumming* opinion could well have been written by either of them, since they both frequently hid behind technicalities. Harlan, however, ordinarily did not, which makes his role in *Cumming* an enduring puzzle.

The Kentuckian returned to his dissenting mode in several other Thirteenth and Fourteenth Amendment cases, however. In one, certain private parties were accused of a conspiracy to prevent blacks, in effect, from securing employment in certain occupations. Since only private acts were involved, the majority held that there was no Fourteenth Amendment right concerned and decided on the basis of the Thirteenth, holding that U.S. courts had no jurisdiction over such a charge. Harlan, this time with Justice William R. Day's support, dissented; he argued that Congress could legislate and had legislated against private conspiracies of this nature.[36] What had happened was that a group of blacks, attempting to work for a lumber company, had been chased off by a white mob. The Court's decision thus left black rights to the tender mercies of white rabble-rousers and the uncertain protection of the state courts.

Harlan also dissented, this time without opinion, from a decision extending the *Plessy* doctrine explicitly to interstate trains: railroads can require segregation in the absence of legislation by Congress. In this case the railroad was being forced to obey a state law, which made the expansion of "separate but equal" especially obvious. Given the state of political affairs of the early twentieth century, Congress was unlikely to legislate.[37]

John Harlan's final opinion on the subject—again a dissent, and one of his most famous—came in the *Berea College* case. Berea College, a private institution, had for many years admitted both whites and blacks. In 1904 the Kentucky legislature enacted a law prohibiting any "school, college or institution where persons of the white and negro races are both received as pupils for instruction." Convicted and fined by a Kentucky court, the college appealed to the Supreme Court. Although the Kentucky courts had based their decisions squarely on the race question, Justice Brewer sedulously avoided it. The college, he said, was a corporation chartered by the state, and as such it could be regulated even in ways that might be inapplicable to individuals. The Kentucky law was merely an amendment to the college's charter, and as such it was constitutionally permissible. Brewer's evasive reasoning commanded only a bare majority. Holmes and Moody concurred but preferred the idea that there was no Fourteenth Amendment violation. Day dissented without opinion.[38]

To Harlan it was obvious that the Kentucky legislation was intended to apply to all biracial instruction whether or not it was carried on by a corporation. He wrote: "It is a reflection upon the common sense of legislators to suppose that they might have prohibited a private *corporation* from teaching by its agents, and yet left individuals and unincorporated associations entirely at liberty, by the same instructors, to teach the two races. . . . There is no magic in the fact of incorporation which will so transform the act of teaching the two races in the same school at the same time that such teaching can be deemed lawful when conducted by private individuals, but unlawful when conducted by the representatives of corporations." Concluding with a rhetorical flourish, Harlan asked, "Have we become so inoculated with prejudice of race that an American government . . . can make distinctions between . . . citizens in the matter of their voluntary meeting for innocent purposes, simply because of their respective races?"[39] The Court's answer was obvious.

Harlan and the Court were also concerned about discrimination on the West Coast against the Chinese. The primary political concern was the economic competition imposed on whites by members of a race that worked harder and at lower wages. The Court began on the right foot by invalidating a city ordinance that had given discretionary power to withhold consent to operate a laundry. If the law is administered so that it discriminates against Chinese laundry operators, it is unconstitutional even if the law is nondiscriminatory on its face.[40]

There was no federal protection of the Chinese residents of Nicolaus, California, however, when private intimidation forced them out of the community and prevented them even from doing business or working there. While allowing that Congress could pass protective legislation under the treaty with China, Chief Justice Waite found that it had not done so. Aside from the treaty, he found that no national law could be constitutionally applied: the case involved private, not state, action, and laws applying to "citizens" could not be used for the Chinese. Harlan, in dissent, argued that Congress had legislated properly under section 5 of the Fourteenth Amendment. Stephen J. Field also dissented, on the grounds that the treaty was self-executing and thus needed no special legislation. Both dissenters also wanted to use a broader interpretation of the word citizen.[41]

A later case found the members of the Court flip-flopping. A six-man majority led by Justice Horace Gray finally found, after long wrangles in the judicial conference, that children born in the United States of Chinese parents are "native born" (in the words of the Fourteenth Amendment) and thus are citizens. Chief Justice Fuller, even after long private arguments, was able to convince only John Harlan—of all people—to follow him in dissent, claiming that citizenship follows the parents. Fuller may have been afraid of congressional reaction in that age of Chinese exclusion policies, but in the event there was none.[42] Why Harlan followed him is a minor mystery. Of course, the amendment was written with the protection of the freed slaves in mind, not of Chinese immigrants, but even so the majority's more expansive interpretation is to its credit. Both opinions were exhaustive, relying on history and precedent, but Gray's, said Senator Edmunds, reflected the sense of Congress. The famous newspaper humorist Mr. Dooley nevertheless asked wryly, "If cats were born in an oven wud they be biscuits?"[43]

The story of the Fifteenth Amendment during the Waite and Fuller years strongly resembles the history of the Fourteenth. That is, the Supreme Court showed a tendency to narrow the effect of the amendment, with John Harlan often in dissent. It is true that even Harlan used restrictive interpretation at times. In an early case involving the exclusion of blacks from juries, one of the claims of the blacks was that Delaware law limited the suffrage to whites and then limited the right to jury service to qualified voters. Harlan's opinion made the obvious point that the state law about voters was unconstitutional after the adoption of the Fifteenth Amendment, but he refused to grant relief on those grounds since there was no evidence that the state any longer enforced the law anyway. He went on to base relief on the mere fact that no blacks had ever served on juries in the state.[44]

The Court was unanimous in believing that Congress could legislate to prevent private interference with the right of blacks to vote in federal elections.[45] But Harlan felt called upon to dissent when the majority held that nontribal Indians were not citizens and thus did not have the right to vote. His dissent, joined by William B. Woods, pointed out that the state expected such persons to perform the duties of citizens such as paying taxes and serving in the state militia. Why then should it not accord them the rights of citizenship?[46]

Mississippi law also required one to be a qualified voter in order to be a juror; but contrary to Delaware, the state did not explicitly bar blacks from voting. Instead it swept the "circle of expedients" to keep them from qualifying to vote, such as requiring a literacy test. The Court said, however, that none of the disqualifying laws discriminated on their faces against blacks: they apply equally to both races, and thus they are constitutional. Strangely, Harlan lent his silent acquiescence to this farrago.[47]

The Kentuckian returned to the fray, however, in a somewhat similar case from Alabama in 1903. Here Alabama tied the vote to literacy and the ownership of considerable property and wrote these qualifications into the state constitution. There was a deadline for registration, as well. All these expedients were confessedly to be used as bars to Negro voting. Thus the Supreme Court could hardly close its eyes to the purpose and effect of the provisions. In an opinion notable for its casuistry, Justice Holmes said that the Supreme Court could not control voting in state elections. He went on to a discussion of technical law, concluding that the case was inappropriate for equitable relief: "Equity," he said, "cannot enforce political rights." Then he left the whole question to white public opinion in Alabama. He did say that Congress could perhaps deal with the situation, but by the 1900s Congress was no longer in the mood to do any such thing—a fact with which Holmes must have been very familiar.[48] This disastrous opinion brought three dissents from an otherwise pliant Court. Henry Billings Brown dissented without opinion, David J. Brewer thought that the Court could deal with the question on nonequity grounds, and Harlan pointed out the questionable nature of an opinion that denied jurisdiction but then went on to deal with the merits of the case.

Harlan and Brown again dissented, but without opinion, in a case from Kentucky involving the question of whether Congress could punish a white man for bribing a black man to refrain from voting. The majority held that the law was unconstitutional because it applied to an individual act, contrary to the terms of the Fourteenth and Fifteenth amendments.[49]

These cases left blacks in the situation of not having anywhere to turn when either states or individuals prevented them from voting, as long as the state law was devious enough in accomplishing its purpose. Harlan, of course, disagreed with this, and he was the only justice who consistently did so.

Harlan's overall record in civil rights cases was, for his period, a radical one. If he did not always vote as a latter-day liberal would have wished (especially where state action was involved), one ought to remember that much of the time he was completely isolated on the Court and on the far left of general public opinion. He should not be judged by the standards of a later generation. At least he was not, like the majority, searching madly for narrow or technical interpretations of constitutional provisions in order to prevent blacks from successfully asserting rights that now seem clearly to have been stated in the Reconstruction Amendments.

A fitting, if perhaps unduly laudatory, assessment of Harlan's record was written in a letter to him from Senator Jonathan P. Dolliver:

When the *Supreme Court* passes upon the record of all earthly decisions one thing will be made manifest, and that is that running through all the opinions of your court there has been at least one great calm voice of protest against wasting the riches of civil liberty which a past generation earned for those who have followed. You have spoken the word to which we must return if American society is to develop on lines of sympathy with our institutions. A great body of outcast citizens, victims of prejudice and injustice, cannot permanently live in the United States without destroying the frame of government which we have inherited. The individual man, now being eliminated from all our industries and nearly all our commerce, must come back to his own, or the foundations of our system of government are all taken away. Your voice in the civil rights cases and the trust and tax cases, is the chief guide and monitor of these confused times, directing the social progress of the nation in channels consistent with the permanence of our affairs. I hope that voice may long be potent, and that your life may be spared to see the victory of this market place over every effort to subject the community, under whatever pretense, to the evil of monopoly and organized greed.[50]

17

The Income Tax

Although Justice Harlan is best known today for his powerful dissents in the racial discrimination and criminal procedure areas, he was most famous, or infamous, to his contemporaries for his emotionally delivered dissenting opinion in the income tax cases.[1] The swirl of controversy surrounding these cases has never died completely, even though the adoption of the Sixteenth Amendment reversed the decisions themselves. Dispute has centered around the constitutional arguments, the political attitudes of the judges, the sectional nature of the votes, leaks to the newspapers, and the heated dissension among the members of the Court—dissension that spilled over into open court.[2]

The income tax law was enacted in August 1894. In view of the fact that taxpayers' suits, at least in advance of payment, were illegal, one might wonder how a case got to the Supreme Court so quickly that it was argued in March 1895. The fact is that the entire Court, excepting only Harlan, was almost indecently eager to decide the issue. No other justice objected to the presentation of a "friendly" suit, in which Pollock as a stockholder could sue his own company, asking for an injunction against payment of the tax.

In 1881 the Court had unanimously upheld a Civil War income tax.[3] Such taxes, however, had never been a regular part of the federal revenue structure, and a peacetime tax was regarded by those who would have to pay it as dangerously progressive, even socialistic. While this may account for the political furor, it does not justify a constitutional argument, especially in the face of the preceding decision.

The tax covered all sources of income, but in addition to claiming that the entire law was unconstitutional, its opponents also segmented their arguments, asserting that even if a tax on personal income from one source might be held valid, that on income from other sources might be invalid. Finally, they asserted that the law was inseparable, and thus if one levy were unconstitutional, they all were. While the constitutional arguments varied somewhat depending upon the particular application of the tax being discussed, the basic issue was whether an income tax, as such, constituted a direct tax within the meaning of either of the two direct tax clauses in the Constitution.[4]

Much of the folklore surrounding the case results from the troubling fact that Justice Howell E. Jackson was terminally ill at his home in Tennessee and thus did not participate in the hearing or decision of the first case. This left the Court susceptible to a tie vote that would have the effect of upholding the tax, since the lower courts had denied the injunctions requested. Diehard opponents of the tax would then, as they did, ask for a rehearing, hoping for a full Court that could in effect reverse the first decision, or at least provide a clear majority.

The so-called Harlan leak provides another part of the legend. The first case was argued in early March 1895, and the decision was announced with opinions on April 8, a Monday. On Saturday the sixth the Chicago *Tribune* came out with a front-page spread that accurately forecast not only the decision but also the voting lineup of the judges and intimate details of what had occurred in the judicial conference. In view of the usual secrecy surrounding the Court's predecision discussions and votes, there was obviously a leak somewhere. It had to be one of the judges, the Court clerk, or someone close to a judge. Of the judges, Harlan and Chief Justice Fuller had the closest ties in Chicago: the Kentuckian because he had been assigned to the Chicago circuit court for so many years and because he had two sons who were prominent practicing attorneys in the Windy City; and Fuller because the city was his home and he had practiced there for years. Historians have for some reason assumed that Harlan was the source of the leak, without adducing any affirmative evidence, perhaps because he obviously felt so strongly about the case. Any such leak would, of course, have been a serious breach of Court custom, if not ethics.[5] "The *Tribune* story gave an entirely disproportionate amount of space," writes Fuller's biographer, Willard King, to Harlan's "individual view on a feature of the law which was barely mentioned in the opinions."[6] Aside from this negative evidence, no one has ever succeeded in pinning the guilt on anyone. The only fact that stands beyond dispute is that a *Tribune* reporter did profit from an inside source.

Peculiarly, the newspaper may have been wrong about one aspect of the April decision: the actual vote. It announced the four protax justices as being Harlan, Henry Billings Brown, George Shiras, Jr., and Edward D. White. But the Court, contrary to its usual custom, did not announce who took which side, doubtless because, with a tie vote, no one could dissent. Since the chief justice, Stephen J. Field, Harlan, and White each wrote opinions, their votes are obvious. But we have only the *Tribune* story about which of the four remaining justices stood on which side.

Understanding what happened in the first case necessitates the examination of a few details. The points decided by the Court were both against the validity of the tax. First, the Court held unanimously (8-0) that the tax as applied to income from state and municipal bonds was unconstitutional because it limited the power of the states to borrow money, which all eight judges felt was protected by the federal system as embodied in the Constitution. Second, the majority—Harlan and White dissented—held that the tax on rents and other income from real estate was a "direct tax." Since it was obviously not apportioned according to the populations of the states, it was thus unconstitutional. Having thus held major portions of the tax invalid, however, the Court was unable to proceed further because it was evenly divided on the other questions presented. The decision of the circuit court was thus reversed only on the two points.

Did these actions necessitate holding the entire tax law unconstitutional because of inseparability? Only four judges felt that it did, so the Court had to proceed to a discussion of the application of the law to income from personal property. Again the judges divided evenly. This left the law in force, but only in a truncated and unsatisfactory form. Neither the public nor the Court was happy with such a result, which accounts for the eagerness and speed with which the Court granted a rehearing and then heard the second case. The Court, in fact, decided to rehear the entire case.

Howell E. Jackson thus accidentally caused the entire imbroglio that necessitated a second hearing, for his fifth vote on either side would have disposed of the case. There was thus great pressure put upon him either to resign (in which case President Cleveland would undoubtedly have replaced him with someone favorable to the tax) or to proceed to Washington for the rehearing, ill as he was. Some impression of the Court's eagerness to settle the case quickly is reflected in Jackson's letter to the chief justice only a week after the first decision: "[If] it is the wish of the court to have the matter disposed of at the present term I will make the effort to come to Washington & participate in the rehearing which could be set for some day early in May. . . . It seems highly important that the whole matter should be finally and speedily settled. Its settlement now will prevent much embarrassment and prevent a multitude of suits."[7]

In addition, both sides undoubtedly put extreme pressure on Jackson to decide the case their way. Indeed, under the circumstances, all of the other justices were under similar pressure to change their votes. In any event, after the ailing Tennesseean struggled to Washington, the final result showed his presence to have been unnecessary, since one of the other judges changed his vote so that the antitax side had a clear majority no matter how Jackson voted.

It is one of history's little practical jokes that, although Jackson voted in favor of the tax, it was nevertheless struck down. Who was the fifth man? If the *Tribune*'s leaked story is accurate, he would have to have been George Shiras, Jr. This has never been validated, however, and despite much speculation, no one knows who changed. Indeed, with the shifting battle lines shown by the first decision, it is even possible that no one did.[8] We know for certain only that the writers of opinions in the first case—the chief justice, Field, White, and Harlan—did not change their positions.

The rehearing was argued early in May, and the decision came down

May 20. This time Chief Justice Fuller, who again wrote for the antitax faction, had a majority for each question, with the result that the entire tax was declared unconstitutional. Jackson, somewhat to everyone's surprise, dissented with an opinion, as did Brown, White, and Harlan. The case was over, and the income tax was dead; it only remained for the Democrats to come into power again with enough votes in Congress to reverse the Court by adopting the Sixteenth Amendment.

Aside from the newspaper leak, what was John Harlan's role in all this? He undoubtedly felt even in 1894 that the Congress had the power to enact an income tax. Although written much later, a letter to Gus Willson summarizes his attitude about the wisdom and policy, if not the constitutionality, of such a tax:

> It is a curious fact in my experience that I never knew a *very* rich man who was not astute in attempting to evade the payment of his proper share of taxes. Those whose *business* in life is to clip coupons from bonds as a general rule are indignant at the thought of being required to pay taxes. The fury of socialism is equalled by the fury with which *mere* millionaires, taking them as a class, and corporations, resent any attempt to make them pay their share. . . . Many millionaires as they walk the streets, complain in their own minds that Tom, Dick and Harry whom they meet as they pass along, contribute nothing in the way of taxes to the Government. But those fellows forget that the men who are not able to pay taxes are those who, in time of trouble, give their lives to maintain their government and thereby protect the property of the well-to-do people of the country.[9]

This does not indicate that Harlan thought that the income tax law of 1894 was without fault. Indeed, he probably agreed with his son James, who wrote:

> The law as it stood before it reached the court at all was a bad law, and I think you ought to say so. And then you ought to point out clearly that it is bad as a legislative measure. And then proceed to show how impossible it is for the courts to review the legislature's action, simply because of its bad judgment. You see what I have in mind. Thousands of people are glad of the result, because they thought the exemptions of the law were bad. They do not stop to think that the court has denied to the general government a power of vast importance. You ought to bring this all out clearly. As a matter of fact, in my judgment, an income tax is the most righteous and just tax that can be laid.[10]

While Harlan did not follow all of his son's suggestions, he clearly agreed with the sentiments expressed.

This all suggests that the Kentuckian, when the cases came to the Court, followed his political sentiments rather than the Constitution's command. But there is no reason why the two are necessarily inconsistent. Nor, of course, was Harlan unique among his fellow judges. Stephen J.

Field, particularly, made this quite obvious when he wrote, in his opinion in the first case: "The present assault upon capital is but the beginning. It will be the stepping stone to others, larger and more sweeping till our political contests will become a war of the poor against the rich; a war constantly growing in intensity and bitterness."[11] Nor is there evidence that other judges felt less strongly about the political aspects of the case. Willard King argues strongly that those from the wealthy states opposed the tax while those from the poorer states favored it. While his argument is not entirely persuasive, it does indicate that the judges approached the case, in the first instance, as a political rather than a constitutional issue.[12]

The chief justice, in arguing that the tax was a direct tax and thus unconstitutional unless apportioned, had a major job of getting around the earlier decisions of the Court, principally *Hylton* v. *United States* and *Springer* v. *United States*.[13] The result was persuasive mainly to the already persuaded. Fuller placed great reliance on his interpretation of what the framers of the Constitution meant, pointed out that *Hylton* did not involve an income tax, and claimed that *Springer* was limited to emergency situations such as the Civil War.[14] White, in an exhaustive dissent in the first case, disagreed about the framers' intent but placed major emphasis on the precedents and the Court's duty to follow them.[15] Both opinions were largely legalistic, although Fuller did approach his own predilections when he wrote: "If by calling a tax indirect when it is essentially direct, the rule of protection could be frittered away, one of the great landmarks defining the boundary between the nation and the states of which it is composed would have disappeared and with it one of the bulwarks of private rights and private property."[16]

Harlan's dissent in the first case was conditioned by the fact that he agreed with White. Therefore he wrote only briefly, to emphasize his feeling that, first, the Court should have dismissed the case for lack of jurisdiction, since it did not allow taxpayer suits. Second, he merely stated, depending on White for argument, that the tax on the income from real estate was not a direct tax. Third, he agreed with the rest of the Court that the tax on municipal bond income was unconstitutional.[17]

The great pressures on the Court came between the two hearings. Newspaper editorials on both sides, statements by political leaders, and letters to the judges were numerous. Harlan, for instance, received a long letter from his Paris friend Senator John T. Morgan arguing that the direct tax clauses applied to slaves only and that after the adoption of the Thirteenth Amendment these clauses no longer had any effect.[18] This was an argument Harlan did not accept, but the kind of pressure it illustrates was unusual enough that Morgan was semiapologetic about writing the letter.

Harlan entered the fray more openly in the second case, and some of his actions incurred the wrath of antitax newspapers and the wonderment of spectators in the courtroom.[19] Fuller and White were largely left to repeat the arguments they had used in April. Urged on by his sons and by Judge William Howard Taft—a close friend from the sixth circuit court, which had upheld the tax—Harlan felt that more ought to be said than White was likely to say. There were affirmative arguments for the constitutionality of the income tax, he thought, that did not rely solely on precedent. The more he thought about it and the more the implications of Field's rash charges of socialism sank in, the more disturbed the Kentuckian became. By decision day he was quite worked up; he had not yet finished drafting his dissent, so his oral remarks in court were partly extemporaneous. Fuller's biographer, obviously partisan, wrote: "Justice Harlan delivered an extemporaneous dissent in which he banged his fist on his desk and glared at the Chief Justice. The *Nation* said: 'Remembering . . . that it was to the Southern members mainly that we owed the insertion of the income tax in the tariff-reform bill, it is not surprising that of the four judges who stood by the tax three should be Southerners. Nor is it surprising, remembering Justice Harlan's antecedents, that he should have made himself their mouthpiece in the most violent political tirade ever heard in a court of last resort.'"[20] Future attorney general Philander C. Knox remarked, "I should hate to use any such language about the Court as it said about itself yesterday."[21]

These are grave—or at least sensational—charges to make about a dignified Supreme Court justice. In mitigation, one should keep in mind that, as King admits, all of the dissents were heated. Why pick on Harlan especially? Apparently this was for two reasons: he was the most newsworthy and charismatic of the dissenters, and he did allow his anger to get the best of his judgment, even if the above charges are partly hyperbolic. Of course, Harlan's own version of what happened that day is quite different. He wrote to his sons James and John:

Do not be at all alarmed by the reports sent out by lying newspaper correspondents as to what occurred in court last Monday, or as to the views expressed by the minority about the decision. The statement that I gestured in the face of the Chief Justice has not the slightest foundation in truth. The Chief is always courteous and would never give anyone occasion to be rude towards him, and he knows that I was not rude to him on Monday. The fact is that Justice Field, who has acted often like a mad man during the whole of this contest about the income tax, bothered the Chief Justice on his left and Gray on his right, with sharp running comments on my opinion as it was being read. Offended by his unseemly conduct and discourtesy, I turned sharply towards him and read part of my opinion directly at him. This was observed by many in the bar, and it was perhaps the occasion of the statement by the newspaper correspondents to the effect that I glared at some of my associates who were in the majority. Oftentimes heretofore when delivering opinions in important cases, I was told by the marshal and some others that I did not raise my voice high enough, and was not distinctly heard. As this case was of vast importance, I determined that I should be heard. So I read my opinion in a clear, distinct, audible tone of voice, which, I am told, rang through the courtroom so that everyone present heard each word of the opinion and took it for what it was worth. My voice and manner undoubtedly indicated a good deal of earnestness, and I am quite willing that it should have been so interpreted. I felt deeply about the case, and naturally the extent of my feeling was shown by my voice and manner. I read my dissent deliberately, and it took an hour. Not a human being in the large crowd present but what kept his eye upon me from beginning to close. Occasionally I made a gesture, but not raising my hand at all high nor using it in any particularly conspicuous way.[22]

Harlan, in fact, probably protests too vigorously to be entirely believed, and truth probably lies, as so often, somewhere between the extremes. A paper by Henry H. Ingersoll, at least, does stress Harlan's vigor and earnestness without charging him with discourtesy.[2]

Considering the furor raised over Harlan's courtroom actions, his written opinion seems almost pallid and anticlimactic. Observing that the meaning of the term *direct tax* to the framers of the Constitution was so doubtful that one ought not to conclude anything from it, Harlan claimed that this fact made it the more desirable to observe the Court's unbroken line of precedents, stretching all the way back to *Hylton*, practically contemporaneous with the Constitution's framing. After reviewing these precedents, the Kentuckian pointed out that they led to one conclusion: an income tax cannot be a direct tax. Harlan then turned to the practical facts behind the case: "In its practical operation this decision withdraws from national taxation not only all incomes derived from real estate, but tangible personal property, '*invested* personal property, bonds, stocks, investments of all kinds' and the income that may be derived from such property." Of course, he admitted, these things could be taxed if the tax were apportioned by the populations of the states, but it was obvious that "no such apportionment can possibly be made without doing gross injustice to the many for the benefit of the favored few in particular states." This state of affairs would be disastrous, preventing the national government from such taxation "however sorely the administration in power may be pressed to meet the moneyed obligations of the nation."[24]

Adverting to the charges of socialism raised by lawyer Rufus Choate and Justice Field, he averred that they were merely irrelevant, since "with the policy of legislation of this character, this court has nothing to do. . . . We deal here only with questions of law." Then, deserting questions of law, Harlan claimed that income taxes per se are "just and equitable" as a means of spreading the tax burden among the people. Regarding the chief justice's claim that income taxes could only be imposed as an emergency power, Harlan rejected the idea that the Supreme Court should or could judge whether an emergency exists: this can only be done by Congress.

Taking his cue from Field, Harlan made his peroration frankly political. With the eloquence to which he could occasionally rise, the justice concluded: "The practical effect of the decision today is to give certain kinds of property a position of favoritism and advantage inconsistent with the fundamental principles of our social organization, and to invest them with power and influence that may be perilous to that portion of the American people upon whom rests the larger part of the burdens of government, and who ought not to be subjected to the dominion of aggregated wealth any more than the property of the country should be at the mercy of the lawless." [25]

The other justices in dissent were just as impassioned. White feared that "the red spectre of revolution would shake our institutions to their foundations." Jackson referred to the decision as "the most disastrous blow ever struck at the constitutional power of Congress." [26] Brown, no raving liberal, nevertheless painted the most lurid picture of all:

> The decision involves nothing less than a surrender of the taxing power to the moneyed class. . . . Even the spectre of socialism is conjured up to frighten Congress from laying taxes upon the people in proportion to their ability to pay them. . . .
>
> While I have no doubt that Congress will find some means of surmounting the present crisis, my fear is that in some moment of national crisis this decision will rise up to frustrate it and paralyze its arm. I hope it may not prove the first step towards the submergence of the liberties of the people in a sordid despotism of wealth. [27]

Congress, although it had to wait until the next Democratic administration, averted (at least for a time) the calamities feared by the dissenters by, at their invitation, initiating the Sixteenth Amendment.

As for Harlan, he was thoroughly excoriated by conservatives and just as enthusiastically praised by protax elements. He was probably most proud of the personal commendations received from friends and family. Howell Jackson, back in Nashville enduring his final illness, referred to his colleague's "vivid dissenting opinion which is a great improvement on the opinion as read from the Bench. I congratulate you on this dissent, which will fully vindicate the position of the minority—and will, I am sure, be regarded by the Bench and bar of the country as the soundest view of the question. It seems to me unanswerable." Judge William Howard Taft based his agreement mostly on the wisdom of following precedent, but he was considerably more restrained in praising Harlan's opinion: "You certainly present your premises and conclusions most forcibly. . . . I hope it is not presuming in me to suggest that some of your expressions separated from the context are capable of being twisted into meanings which you would be the last to intend and are likely to be thus seized upon by unscrupulous persons to foment the very bitterness of controversy which I know both from your present opinion, and your lifelong views you strongly deprecate." Harlan's son James contented himself with saying that "I am utterly in sympathy with your view of the case."[28]

Embodying one of the great constitutional issues of the nineteenth century, the income tax cases (not untypically) were decided in accordance with the personal predilections of the judges. Whether any Court could have divorced itself from its individual and collective prejudices is doubtful. John Harlan at least had the wisdom to stand in the flow of history, as he so often seemed to do.

18

The Insular Cases

The American empire—the words have an almost antiquated ring. It is difficult to remember that we still have an empire of sorts and even more difficult to recall that there was once a great debate over whether democracy was consistent with the holding of colonies. Even though Americans decided after the Spanish-American War to acquire and keep noncontiguous areas populated largely by people of other ethnic, political, and cultural backgrounds, the American conscience has always been troubled over the question of whether we should keep people permanently in a status of second-class citizenship. This troubled conscience accounts for the fact that we did not keep Cuba and that we later granted the Philippines independence and Hawaii and Alaska statehood. The retention of Puerto Rico still troubles us.

It is no surprise to find that the Supreme Court had its role to play in all this. True, the Court never ruled on the constitutionality of holding foreign territories as colonies, but the consequent questions of the extent to which the Constitution applied to the new territories mightily exercised the justices over a period of years. The extremes of opinion on this subject were well expressed by Senator Francis G. Newlands of Nevada: "The difference between the imperialists and the anti-imperialists on this question is that the imperialists wish to expand our territory and contract our Constitution. The anti-imperialists are opposed to any expansion of territory which, as a matter of necessity arising from the ignorance and inferiority of the people occupying it, makes free constitutional government impracticable or undesirable."[1]

In 1901 Justice Harlan's good friend William Howard Taft had been commissioner and was then governor general of the Philippines, and Harlan's son James was shortly to be appointed attorney general of Puerto Rico. In these positions, in close touch with local conditions, both might have been expected to have opinions on questions touching the islands. Whatever ideas James had are not recorded, but Taft's letters are available, and he expressed what might be expected of an island administrator. The strong-minded Kentuckian, however, did not agree. Harlan wrote Taft in

July 1900: "Our next term is likely to be a most important one; chiefly because we may be called on to declare the extent of the powers of Congress, over our new possessions. I hear there is a case on the docket which will compel us to face the issue. It is a great question, and worthy of serious, deliberate consideration. I have impressions, but no fixed opinions."[2] The governor general accepted the implied invitation to comment. His first response was noncommittal: "You can be sure that we shall look with great interest to the consideration of constitutional features of the extension of American rule to these Islands. . . . The question of a right of trial by jury and by indictment, and the question of extending the United States tariff laws to these Islands are of course the two points which will most affect us in our work."[3]

Harlan, somewhat incautiously, strongly intimated that he felt that residents of possessions ought to have all the rights of citizens, commenting that some of the Republican campaigners in the 1900 presidential election had put the party "in the position of being allies to the great trusts, and as holding some views about the powers of Congress and of the President over our new possessions that may well create (and I think have created) some alarm among the people who do not wish any radical departure from the principles underlying our system of Govt."[4] Obviously, Harlan placed himself among those who were "alarmed." This, in turn, alarmed the portly Taft, and he tried cautiously to nudge his friend into a more "realistic" position. He described at some length the difficulties of administering justice in a culture where people were habituated to bribery and were largely uneducated peasants. Knowing Harlan, however, Taft no doubt felt that he could not persuade the justice to change his mind, for he concluded: "However, if you conclude that we must have juries here we shall do the best we can by raising their qualifications to prevent the administration of justice from being an entire laughing stock, as it is now under Filipino judges."[5]

This exchange occurred largely before any of the insular cases had reached the Supreme Court, and months before the first one was actually decided. Taft's opinions, as a realistic colonial administrator, were doubtless known (at least in general) to the rest of the judges; if they did not persuade Harlan, who could be very stubborn and self-righteous, they may have influenced others.

The insular cases covered most of the decade following 1900 and involved numerous decisions. The more significant cases were decided by a sharply divided Supreme Court, with Justice Edward D. White leading one faction, composed of himself, George Shiras, Jr., Joseph McKenna, and Horace Gray (and later, Oliver Wendell Holmes, Jr.). The "antiimperialist" side comprised Chief Justice Fuller, Harlan, David J. Brewer, and Rufus Peckham (and later, William R. Day). This left Henry Billings Brown as the "swing man." Brown did not change his opinions, but since they were based on a third theory about the status of the colonies, he was sometimes to be found on either side when it came to voting and often provided the fifth vote that decided several of the cases.

The first case stemming from the Spanish-American War gave no hint of the judicial imbroglio that would later ensue. Since Congress had already decided to occupy Cuba only until a new native government could be formed, the Court could unanimously—with Harlan as spokesman—decide that, even though it was under occupation, it remained foreign territory and thus that American citizens must submit to Cuban trial practices even if they did not include all the rights of persons tried in the United States.[6] The length of the military occupation makes no difference, said the Court.

More significant, partly because they were so thoroughly divisive, were the tariff cases decided during the same session of the Court. These involved the newly acquired territory of Puerto Rico and its status under the tariff uniformity clause of the Constitution.[7] Put simply, these cases posed this question: When, if ever, did Puerto Rico (or the Philippines, Hawaii, or Alaska) become part of the United States for purposes of this clause? At the extremes, answers were simple. One side could say that territories that were not on their way to becoming states could have separate tariff systems, that is, they were not part of the United States. The other side argued that any territory held by the United States was part of the United States and that therefore the tariff uniformity clause applied. One might guess, of course, that the Supreme Court would not find the question that simple to answer.

The three cases decided on May 27, 1901, provide apt illustrations of the Court's fragmentation on the tariff question. Brown was the only justice who could be found on the majority side in all three cases. In the first of these, Brown held that during the period after the peace treaty with Spain but before Congress had enacted any tariff legislation, Puerto Rico was not a foreign country and therefore could not collect tariffs on goods coming in from the rest of the United States. Harlan, the chief justice, Brewer, and Peckham agreed. Gray dissented alone, while McKenna's dissent was joined by White and Shiras, holding that at the relevant time Puerto Rico was not yet part of the United States and thus could impose tariffs.[8]

In the *Dooley* case the same lineup of judges, but with White now writing for the four dissenters, held that although the President as commander in chief could impose tariffs on U.S. goods during military occupation before the peace treaty, once the treaty went into effect this power lapsed.[9] Finally, also on May 27, the Court held—with no majority opinion—that Congress could allow Puerto Rico to have a tariff.[10] Brown's ability to shift sides resulted from his feeling that, once the treaty recognized the island as a U.S. possession, it placed it in a constitutional vacuum. While not foreign territory, neither was it part of the United States. It was thus not subject to the tariff clause.

None of the other justices shared Brown's approach. Justice White led one side in the development of a theory of "incorporation." According to this idea, Congress could do pretty much as it pleased with a territory as long as that entity had not been incorporated. Although White was not clear about how incorporation took place, he had no doubt that it was not the result of a treaty, by itself, but flowed from some affirmative action of Congress indicating that the colony "had reached that state where it is proper that it should enter into and form a part of the American family." This, he said, Congress had not done. Fuller, seconded by Harlan, held that all U.S. territory was subject to all of the Constitution's commands. Harlan, particularly, had stinging remarks to make about the idea of incorporation, which, he charged, "has some occult meaning which my mind does not apprehend. It is enveloped in some mystery which I am unable to unravel."[11] Basically, the dissenters argued that the Constitution was a compact of the people, not of the states, and that the people encompassed all American territory. Thus the power of Congress is constitutionally limited for noncontiguous territories just as it is for the continental part of the nation organized into states.

Being the man he was, Harlan preferred to put his dissent into his own words, even though he said little that was very different from Fuller's opinion. Perhaps he felt that Fuller was not emotional enough. In any case, as he wrote to Taft,

> It was not my original purpose to write a dissenting opinion. . . . I had intended to stand upon the opinion prepared by the Chief Justice for himself, Brewer, Peckham and myself in the Downes case. But Friday night before . . . Downes was decided, I concluded to say something on my own responsibility which was suggested by certain parts of Brown's and White's opinions. My friend Brown particularly had said some things which I was unwilling to pass without explicitly referring to them. Hence my dissent which you have perhaps seen and read. It expresses views about which I feel strongly. I am sorry to say, and you will be shocked to learn, that the greater part of my dissent was written on the Sabbath. I stayed away from Church to do the work. Horrible! But my ox was in the ditch, and had to be gotten out in some way.[12]

Taft, as governor general, saw little to praise in the dissenters' position. But since the Kentuckian was a good friend, he had to say something. Leaving no doubt where he stood, he blunted his criticism with a joke.

> I have read your opinion in the Insular cases, and as you say, there seems to be no doubt where you stand. I have read the other opinions too. I do not know who it is that said so, but it amused me very much when I heard it, that the position of the Court was in this wise: that four of the judges said the constitution did follow the flag, that four of them said it did not follow the flag, and one said, "It sometimes follows the flag and sometimes does not, and I will tell you when it does and when it does not." However, I sincerely hope, without

expressing any decision on the law of the subject, that the five judges who carried the Court in these other cases on the main question will reach the conclusion that we have the power to impose duties on imports coming from the United States, merely as a practical question in government.[13]

In private, Harlan found it difficult to let the matter drop. During the summer vacation he conducted regular correspondence with the chief justice, adverting frequently to both the cases already decided and those still awaiting decision. In one letter he wrote caustically: "You have, I take it, become established in your summer home, and have banished all thought about insular cases. Indeed, it must be assumed that you are indifferent as to what becomes of the foundations or the dome, or the superstructure, during the vacation. That is my condition. . . . I am even unconcerned as to what effect the tariff will have upon the rice-eating Mindanoans. If it should be applied without an act *incorporating* that country into the United States, my prediction is that there is [?] ahead if not mischief, when we reassemble in October."[14] Joking aside, Harlan was worried about the results of two more cases that had already been argued but that the Court had held over to the next session for decision. Concerned about what Brown would do, he conducted a lengthy summer correspondence with Fuller about tactics for these cases. First, he suggested,

> I think it would be well for you to prepare something on the Fourteen Diamond case to be used as a concurring or dissenting opinion as the situation may require. I do not feel sure that we will hold the judgment in that case. In the De Lima case something was said about the treaty not taking effect . . . until there was delivery of possession by the ceding power. It will be said that we had not obtained such possession in the Philippines. . . . I have some apprehension that Brown may accept this view. If so whatever you write will become or can be turned into a dissenting opinion.[15]

The chief justice accepted this suggestion and wrote opinions for both the *Fourteen Diamond Rings* case and the second *Dooley* case. The first was destined to become the majority opinion, the second a dissent, in both cases because of Brown's iconoclastic views. In the same letter Harlan expatiated on his real concerns about these decisions: "The more I think of these questions, the more alarmed I am at the effect upon our institutions of the doctrine that this country may acquire territory inhabited by human beings anywhere upon the earth, and govern it at the will of Congress, and without regard to the restrictions imposed by the Constitution upon governmental authority. There is a danger that we give away the safeguards of real freedom, and give us parliamentary in the place of constitutional government."[16]

Although he fought the good fight, Justice Harlan was destined to lose, at least in the short run, by the margin of Brown's vote. After receiving

Fuller's draft opinion, Harlan explained more fully his concerns about Brown.

> I have received and read (& herewith return) your concurring opinion in the Diamond Rings case. It covers the ground fully. . . . If Brown indicates to you when court meets that he intends to adhere to his vote it will not be necessary, I take it, for us to have a concurring opinion. In that event you could let him have your opinion as embodying your views & thus make it certain that he will say all that ought to be said. My fear that Brown might change his vote in the Diamond case arose from what he said, and his manner of saying it when he asked that the Diamond case go over to the next term.[17]

Although Fuller acquiesced in this, he sent his opinion also to Brown, who then decided to let Fuller's become the Court's opinion while he wrote a brief concurrence.

The two cases lying behind these elaborate tactical discussions were finally decided in December 1901. In *Dooley*, Brown wrote for the imperialist side that the Constitution's prohibition on export taxes did not apply to Puerto Rico, since the island was no longer foreign territory. Fuller, in dissent, pointed out that Congress could not impose export taxes on trade from one state to another and that this principle must surely apply to federally held territories as well. Obviously Harlan agreed.[18]

In the *Fourteen Diamond Rings* case Chief Justice Fuller merely applied the *De Lima* rule (as Brown had developed it) to the Philippines, assuming that its status was the same as that of Puerto Rico. This, too, was a 5-4 decision.[19] By the time the next insular case came to the Court, Holmes had replaced Gray. Although in general John Harlan welcomed Holmes to the bench, he did have reservations regarding America's island possessions. He commented on this in another of his summer letters to Chief Justice Fuller: "Holmes will, undoubtedly, be a valuable accession to our Court, though this opinion is based upon his reputation rather than [any] . . . personal knowledge I have of his ability. It is satisfying to observe that the appointment is favorably regarded by the country. The indications in the papers are that he is sufficiently 'expansive' in his views to suit those who think that it is the destiny of the United States to acquire and hold outlying possessions 'outside of the Constitution.' But we will see."[20] Harlan proved to be correct in this regard, for Holmes lined up solidly behind Edward D. White's imperialist faction on the Court.

Hawaii v. *Mankichi* demonstrated the solidity of the two factions in an almost classic manner. The resolution of Congress annexing the Hawaiian Islands provided that no existing Hawaiian law contrary to the Constitution could be applied. Mankichi had been tried without a grand jury indictment and convicted by a nonunanimous jury. Justice Brown rejoined the White faction, writing an opinion that relied on the theory that only fundamental constitutional provisions were intended to be applied by Congress and that therefore Mankichi had been properly convicted.[21]

Justice White, doubtless feeling the weakness of this argument, wrote a concurring opinion in which he claimed that Hawaii had not yet been incorporated when the case was decided and that therefore the Constitution did not apply regardless of the annexation resolution. Of course the four antiimperialists dissented. Fuller held that the language of the resolution was unambiguous and that it made no exceptions for nonfundamental trial practices. Although Harlan agreed with this, he went farther in a separate opinion, disagreeing with White. He argued that Hawaii was, indeed, incorporated (*organized* was the word he preferred) and that its citizens were therefore entitled to all constitutional protections; in fact, annexation by itself had achieved that result. "It is impossible for me," he wrote, "to grasp the thought that that which is admittedly contrary to the supreme law can be sustained as valid."[22]

Justice Harlan had an opportunity to lead the Court, with only White dissenting, in a case holding that the federal district court in Puerto Rico was bound by the same rules regarding the makeup of grand juries as those in the continental United States. Grand jury practice was, he said, "a matter of substance, which cannot be disregarded without prejudice to an accused."[23] A similarly sized majority held that Congress was free to provide tax systems in territories—in this case Alaska—different from those in the United States. What Harlan thought of this is unknown, since he did not vote in the case.[24]

The Court, on the same day, went back to its fractionated mode, with Harlan in the majority, in another case from the Philippines. Here the islands' supreme court had accepted an appeal by the government after the defendant had been acquitted. Day wrote the opinion, holding that this violated the double jeopardy rule, thus at least temporarily joining the antiimperialist faction. But Holmes and Brown wrote dissents, joined by White and McKenna.[25]

The embattled Kentuckian had to dissent, this time alone, in a fourth case decided on the same day, the Court's last sitting in the spring of 1904. Justice Day held that a libel conviction obtained in Manila without a jury trial was valid, since at the time the case was tried Congress had neither incorporated the islands nor imposed the Constitution on them; Congress need not impose the requirement of jury trial under such conditions. Harlan, as one might expect, felt that jury trial was a fundamental right of all U.S. nationals no matter where they were located.[26]

Regardless of the ponderousness of his official opinions on the subject, Harlan retained his sense of humor about the insular cases. He wrote to Taft (who was back in the United States as secretary of war), inviting him to visit the Harlans' vacation home on the St. Lawrence River:

Consider yourself now summoned. Whether in the event of disobedience, there shall be a jury, will rest in the *discretion* of the Court; for remember, this place is outside of the Constitution. . . . Until it is *incorporated* . . . the law will be such as the Sovereign, the President of the Murray Bay Golf Club, wills [it to] be at the time of his action. And remember also, that the jeopardy clause has no application in these *possessions*. Here, all are subjects. . . . This is the finest air in the world, and it will help you to get out of your system the loose ideas of *fundamental* law, and plant you on the solid soil of the Constitution.[27]

By about 1904 all the major territories had been "incorporated" even by Justice White's strict standards, and the only remaining questions had to do with how widely different their laws could be from American domestic law. Although the justices often disagreed in specific cases, the sharp cleavages evinced in the insular cases disappeared. In effect, White's theory dominated: before incorporation, Congress, not the Constitution, governed the rights that might be extended to the peoples of the island territories and Alaska.

Behind these profound disagreements were widely differing views of the judicial function. White's theory was what can best be called realistic. To him, the peoples of the territories were in no real sense Americans: they had differing cultures, languages, religions, and traditional legal institutions. Moreover, the populations were largely uneducated and illiterate. In such circumstances it seemed wise to allow Congress to decide what measure of rights should be extended, rights that might vary according to the particular territory involved and that could then be broadened as the territory became more Americanized.

The Harlan/Fuller approach was, as was common with the Kentuckian, based on a strict construction of the Constitution, to which was added a deep belief in the rightness of the Bill of Rights. The island possessions were, to Harlan, America extended; there was no constitutional logic to a differentiation between the rights of citizens of Utah territory and those of the Philippines.

Both approaches have validity, and there appears no reason to argue which is "right." To the student of Harlan's judicial career, his opinions in the insular cases are fully consistent with his strict constructionist approach and with his opinions in the civil rights cases. Any other view would have been impossible. Harlan lived up to his judicial faith in the strict command of the Constitution.

19

Other Issues

John Marshall Harlan's reputation as a jurist was made principally in the areas surveyed in preceding chapters. Obviously he participated in the Court's activities fully, however. He wrote numerous opinions, both for the majority and in dissent, on other issues, not all of which involved constitutional questions. It is worth looking briefly at the more important of these other areas, if only to illustrate the breadth of the subjects upon which Supreme Court justices had to formulate opinions in Harlan's time. As in the earlier chapters, we will concentrate on those areas in which the Kentuckian wrote opinions that either led the Court or disagreed with it. Harlan's influence on the development of constitutional law is most obvious in such cases. The more subtle kinds of influence that every justice exercises to some degree through informal associations with his colleagues, through discussion in the judicial conference, and through comment on successive drafts of opinions are difficult to demonstrate, although they are in some ways more significant. For nineteenth-century judges, particularly, influence can usually be demonstrated only by results achieved.

First Amendment cases illustrate these considerations. The Supreme Court did not deal with very many of these, especially from the states. Of sixteen cases dealing at least tangentially with free expression, however, Harlan wrote opinions in only two. Whether he was influential beyond contributing his vote in the rest one cannot say.

The Supreme Court cannot be said to have contributed very much to First Amendment jurisprudence during the Harlan years, and the contributions it did make have been mostly reversed or rendered irrelevant in later years. No single justice—not even the redoubtable Holmes—can be cited as a champion of civil liberties in this era. Of Harlan's two opinions, only one could be called libertarian.

The Kentuckian led the Court in deciding that the indictment in obscenity cases need not include the material claimed to be obscene. The defendant's only right is to be reasonably informed of the nature of the charge against him. Harlan went on to say that it could be assumed that everyone using the mail knows what is obscene. This is good Victorian stuff, even if patently untrue. No one could today make such an assumption, despite Justice Potter Stewart's observation that even if he could not define obscenity, "I know it when I see it." Even in 1896 justices White and Shiras dissented on the grounds that the indictment was not specific enough.[1]

As usual, Harlan was more prescient when dissenting. In 1907 Oliver Wendell Holmes, Jr., wrote a majority opinion upholding a Colorado contempt citation for a newspaper criticism of its courts, written while the case criticized was still pending. Holmes left aside the question of whether the Fourteenth Amendment's due process clause applies freedom of the press to the states. He emphasized instead that free speech is only freedom from prior restraint, not freedom from punishment subsequent to publication. He also pointed out the difficulties posed for the proper administration of justice if newspapers could influence judges and jurors while a case was in progress.[2] Dissenting, Harlan wrote that free speech is an attribute of national citizenship, expressing the iconoclastic view that the First Amendment should therefore be applied to the states through the privileges or immunities clause of the Fourteenth Amendment. Justices Hugo Black and William O. Douglas have in later years expressed the same view about the use of contempt citations for news articles, but based upon the due process clause. Felix Frankfurter, however, has followed the Holmes doctrine.[3]

Despite the obvious fact that the rights of criminal procedures established in the Fourth through the Eighth amendments applied to the actions of federal courts and law enforcement officials, the Supreme Court ruled in very few criminal appeals until the 1890s. Even then, appeals in federal cases directly involved the relevant constitutional provision or congressional act, whereas appeals from state courts had to involve the meaning of *due process.*

Until the 1890s Congress did not provide for criminal appeals to the Supreme Court in federal cases. Thus, aside from an occasional appeal from a federal territory, the Court had no opportunity to establish itself as a supervisor of the federal court system's procedures in criminal cases. Justice Harlan, in fact, wrote only one opinion in a criminal case before 1890. It came from the courts of the District of Columbia and raised the question of whether the Constitution's jury trial provision applied to the District in misdemeanor cases. Harlan, for a unanimous court, held that Constitution applied the common law jury practices as of the date of its adoption, and thus it did extend to at least some misdemeanors. The jury trial provision, he added, did undoubtedly apply to all federal courts.[4]

The lack of appeal rights in federal criminal cases became a concern of Congress because many district courts handling trials thus had the power of final decision. One court in particular, that of the western district of Arkansas, presented problems because it had jurisdiction over all crimes committed in the lawless neighboring "Indian Territory" of what is now Oklahoma. This court, located in Fort Smith, had only one judge, who was not only overburdened but also predisposed to impose death sentences without much regard for legal niceties. This "hanging judge," Isaac C. Parker, whose severity "is attested by the fact that he sentenced 160 men to die and hanged 79 of them," was active over a period of more than twenty years. The only recourse of defense lawyers (some of whom, in their turn, were not overnice in their methods) was to ask the President for commutation or pardon.[5]

Judge Parker's methods were naturally called to the attention of Congress, which responded in 1889 by empowering the Supreme Court to reexamine, reverse, or affirm his death sentences on writ of error.[6] Thus the judges in Washington were given the burden of handling all appeals in capital cases from Parker's court without regard to whether the error cited by the convicted defendant was a constitutional or legal one, or merely a mistake of fact. That Parker was too extreme is shown by the rough handling his verdicts received in the Supreme Court, which was not in general predisposed in favor of convicted criminals: the Court reversed thirty-one of the forty-four death sentences appealed to it from Parker's court.

Considering his record in *Maxwell v. Dow* and other cases from the states, one would expect Justice Harlan to be a leader in voting for such reversals, not because he favored criminals but because he believed in strict adherence to established legal procedures. In fact, the Court usually voted unanimously in the Fort Smith cases, so whatever influence the Kentuckian had is impossible to ascertain.

Congress followed the 1889 law with another that increased the Court's jurisdiction in federal criminal cases generally. After 1891 the Court's role in reviewing and supervising the lower federal courts' criminal work became a substantial part of its caseload.[7] Over time, the Court became the arbiter not only of constitutional cases involving the Fourth through the Eighth amendments but of all criminal laws—including procedural matters— enacted by Congress, and a growing number of judge-made rules involving procedure and jurisdiction.

Justice Harlan played a surprisingly modest role in this development, which indicates that the general trend of decisions was one that he agreed with or (less likely) that he could bring the rest of the judges to accept. Most decisions were unanimous, and even when they were not the dissenters often did not write opinions. Thus there are only a few cases in which Harlan had an identifiable position differing from some or most of the rest of the Court.

In 1896 Harlan led a six-man majority in a forgery case from Judge

Parker's Fort Smith district. He held that if there was a lack of evidence that the defendant had been properly arraigned and had been given a chance to plead, the trial was invalid and had to be returned for a new trial. While the principle involved here seems orthodox, Justice Peckham pointed out for the dissenters that the whole course of the trial was such that the Court ought to infer that the defendant was arraigned and did plead, even in the face of the lack of positive evidence.[8] In 1914 the Court reversed its earlier decision.[9]

The Court was even more seriously split a year earlier in a murder case from California that raised various issues, mainly about the effects of a confession by one of two defendants. The five-man majority, with Harlan writing for the Court, held that the confession could be used at trial against both defendants, but the Kentuckian went on to reverse the decision because, he said, of questions of the admissibility of the confession, especially as against the second defendant. The confession, he also ruled, was voluntary even though made in custody, and the jury could properly convict for a lesser offense than murder even though the charge was murder. Brewer (with Brown) dissented on the question of the admissibility of the confessions, while Gray (with Shiras) felt that the trial judge allowed improper submissions to the jury. That the judges took their differences seriously is indicated by the fact that Harlan felt it necessary to write an exhaustive opinion running to almost fifty pages, while Gray's learned dissent was even longer (seventy-three pages). The disagreements on the Court possibly account for the fact that the case did not become a major precedent.[10] Harlan felt that his efforts had been rewarded when he received a complimentary letter from one of America's most prestigious jurists, Judge John F. Dillon of Iowa: "On my return from the West I found a copy of your great judgment in the case of Sparf against the United States on my table. It is enough to say that your opinion meets the highest demands of this great and important question of historical, constitutional and legal interest therein discussed, and I am sincerely obliged to you for a copy of it."[11]

Another case producing a divided court, with Harlan leading the majority, concerned the question of whether a person who received stolen stamps with the intent to use or sell them had committed a criminal offense. The law provided that the conviction of the thieves could be used as conclusive evidence, indeed, as the only evidence, against the receiver. Harlan argued that such a presumption of guilt violated the constitutional provision that an accused person must be able to confront the witnesses against him. Brown and McKenna dissented but did not write opinions, and Brewer was absent.[12]

When a federal grand jury investigated possible violations of the antitrust laws by the American Tobacco Company, the Court had to decide on the effects of immunity bath legislation. Congress, in an attempt to secure testimony, had passed a law providing general immunity for corporate executives who were asked to testify and to provide company records. Although Justice Brown considered several questions along the way, the general effect of his opinion for a five-man majority was that persons could be forced to testify under this law. Harlan and McKenna wrote separate concurrences disagreeing with portions of Brown's opinion. The Kentuckian was especially concerned about the majority's holding that although corporations could not claim protection under the Fifth Amendment's self-incrimination clause, they were protected by the Fourth Amendment's search and seizure provision—a seeming contradiction. He felt that corporations ought not to be protected by either amendment, since they were not "persons" entitled to such protection. Brewer and Fuller also dissented, taking the opposite tack: that corporations were protected by both amendments.[13]

Surveying Justice Harlan's opinions in federal criminal appeals cases, one is struck primarily by the fact that the sometimes acrimonious differences that marked his relations with his colleagues are largely absent here. This is probably because the Court's decisions in this area were largely unexceptionable. True, controversy over immunity bath legislation has never ceased, but most of the time the Court was operating in areas that were noncontroversial—at least at the turn of the century—and involved subjects with which the justices, as lawyers, were conversant.

The American federal system as envisaged in the Constitution contains several built-in conflicts between state and federal powers. One of these results from the fact that the states were left with a complete power of taxation, limited only (as the Supreme Court has made clear) by direct constitutional command, by interference with federal instrumentalities or powers, and later by the due process and equal protection clauses of the Fourteenth Amendment. Federal control over such aspects of interstate commerce as navigable streams, bridges, and railroads provides obvious possibilities for such interference by states, even when Congress has not exercised its powers. State taxes may, even without intent, discriminate against interstate business in favor of local enterprise or may place intolerable burdens on the conduct of interstate enterprises. For this reason the Supreme Court as early as *Gibbons* v. *Ogden* and *Brown* v. *Maryland* had to decide when, if ever, state taxes were unconstitutional because they trenched upon federal interstate and foreign commerce powers.[14] The details of such state tax laws provide a complex body of constitutional law marked by frequent shifts of judicial doctrine, especially as the definition of *commerce* broadened.

During Harlan's tenure, because of congressional inaction plus the Court's generally narrow interpretation of *interstate*, the high tribunal tended to allow states to tax rather freely, a tendency with which the

Kentuckian frequently disagreed. In fact he dissented—often alone (but often with Justice White) and frequently without opinion—in twenty-nine cases, all of which found the majority allowing a state tax. On the other hand, Harlan wrote majority opinions in only three such cases. In most of the dissents, he objected that the state tax interfered with interstate commerce to an unacceptable degree, although he was capable of finding other reasons for dissent in some cases.

A typical example of these cases, in which White wrote the dissent joined by Harlan, Field, and Brown, came when the majority held that Ohio could tax the pro rata share of all of a company's property. White, in dissent, wrote that "the recognition of a right to take an aliquot proportion of the value of property in one state and add it to the intrinsic value of property in another state and there assess it, is in substance an absolute denial and overthrow of all the great principles announced from the beginning . . . on the subject of interstate comerce."[15]

The views of John Harlan in such cases were thoroughly consistent with his lifelong nationalism. If he could read a case as an interference with the powers of Congress, even unused, he was likely to do so. He did not, however, make them the objects of a public crusade. This fact indicates that his emotions were not deeply involved, since, as we have seen, he was not one to keep silent when they were.

In the litany of American constitutional law, the separation of powers has always played a prominent, if misleading, part. One aspect of this has been the general question of how much, and what kinds, of power may be given to the executive by the legislature. The general doctrine underlying this is that delegated power may not be redelegated. That is, power given to Congress by the people in the Constitution may not be given away by Congress to any other agency. There are, nevertheless, many circumstances in which Congress may, for reasons of lack of time or expertise, wish to give some executive agency some powers that it could constitutionally exercise itself. If such grants of power were truly grants of "legislative" power, they would run afoul of constitutional doctrine.

Through the years the Supreme Court has thus been asked to define *legislative power*. Justice Harlan, as it happens, had the opportunity to establish one of the basic doctrines governing such a definition. In the McKinley Tariff Act of 1890, in general a high tariff act, a few items, mainly sugar, were removed from the duty list. As a sop to protectionist sentiment in the dominant Republican party, however, the president was empowered to restore the tariff on sugar, molasses, tea, coffee, or hides if he found that a country exporting these products to the United States was imposing duties on American goods that he considered to be "reciprocally unequal and unreasonable." This power was challenged on the grounds that it was an unconstitutional delegation of legislative power.

Although the plaintiff raised several questions, that of delegation was the most significant. In upholding the tariff act, Justice Harlan spoke for a seven-man majority, finding that there was no improper delegation. All Congress had done, he said, was to provide that "suspension should take place upon a named contingency." The role of the president was not legislative at all: he acted as a "mere agent of the lawmaking department to ascertain and declare the event upon which its expressed will was to take effect." Lucius Q.C. Lamar, joined by Chief Justice Fuller, lamented the new powers given to the executive.[16] This is, in other words, one of the relatively few instances in which Harlan, speaking for the Court, set a lasting precedent.[17] The fact that there was a dissent indicates that there was a constitutional alternative, which makes Harlan's stand the more significant, especially coming as it did during a period of weak presidents and a dominant Congress.

Personal injury cases do not always, or even typically, present constitutional issues; nor are they usually federal cases. One may wonder, then, why the Supreme Court rather frequently had to handle appeals in such cases. They mostly came before 1891 as a result of the Court's diversity jurisdiction. Most of these cases involved employee, passenger, or third-party suits against railroads for damages resulting from accidents. Injuries on railroads were exceedingly common in the nineteenth century and also the early twentieth, until federal safety regulations combined with the increasing cost to the railroad companies gradually reduced the injury rate. The Supreme Court played a role in this by, eventually, sanctioning the states' abrogations of the common law fellow-servant rule and the rule of no liability without fault. These changes in state law made it easier for injured persons to collect damages from the only entity having the ability to pay: the company.[18]

This, however, happened after Justice Harlan's death. In the meantime all the Court could do was to broaden the definition of *fellow-servant* and that of contributory negligence. The Court was not always willing to do these things, so there is a good deal of ambivalence in its decisions. The Kentuckian, with his large heart and his distrust of corporate enterprise, could be expected to favor definitions and interpretations that made it easier for corporations to be sued successfully. Most of the time this is what he did.

This was illustrated early in his career in his opinion for a unanimous Court in *Pennsylvania Co.* v. *Roy* in 1880. Here a passenger injured by the accidental fall of a sleeping car berth sued the railroad company. The company claimed that since sleeping cars were operated under rental agreements with the Pullman Company, which also provided the employees, it was not liable for the injury. Harlan's handwritten notes on the case reveal his approach, which was accepted by his brethren. Mistakes in syntax can be attributed to the fact that he was writing hasty notes, rather than a finished essay. "The Railroad Company," he wrote, "is bound to use the utmost care in providing for the safety of its passengers—To this end it must provide *sufficient* apparatus, careful servants. Instead of completing the transportation by using its own cars it chooses to use the car belonging to another corporation for an additional charge. It is as much bound for the safety of those cars as they would be if they owned to them. . . . They could not contract for exemption of liability on account of defects in any of the agencies it employs to complete the transportation."[19]

Harlan's tendency to favor the injured party was shown both in majority and in dissenting opinions. In one case he held, for the majority, that it was proper for a judge to insert the words *or other employees* in the railroad's requested instruction to the jury that they must find for the company in the absence of negligence by it. Since the jury had found that the conductor of a streetcar was negligent in a case in which a passenger was injured when leaving the car, these words had the effect of making the company liable.[20]

Harlan, however, was frequently found in dissent. When a person was killed in an accident, Justice Shiras wrote a majority opinion holding that the railroad could not be sued in Arkansas since it was a Missouri corporation. Harlan, alone, dissented, arguing that the railroad was recognized by Arkansas as a corporation there, so in effect it had a "home" there, as well as in Missouri.[21]

Harlan felt more strongly in another case, since it reversed a doctrine announced by the Court in an earlier case with him in the majority. George Shiras, Jr., was again responsible for the majority opinion, which held that a railroad conductor is not a vice principal of the company, and therefore the company is not liable for his negligence. This left the conductor himself liable, and he was unlikely to be able to pay damages. Harlan, again alone, dissented not merely because the precedents were not being followed but also on policy grounds: "As the conductor commands the movements of the train and has general control over the employees connected with its operation, the company represented by him ought to be held responsible for his negligence. . . . If in such case the conductor be not a vice-principal, it is difficult to say who among the officers or agents of a corporation . . . ought to be regarded as belonging to that class."[22] As the lone survivor of the Court making the first decision, Harlan perhaps felt more strongly than he might otherwise have done, but the dissent represents his consistent opinion. Again, in dissent he often rode the wave of the future: corporations are now commonly held liable for all sorts of accidents from which the traditional common law absolved them.[23]

20

Man, Politician, Judge

What manner of man was John Marshall Harlan? At this date, and with the documentary gaps existing, one cannot say with certainty, perhaps, and yet some things have become obvious. Harlan was, first of all, the quintessential family man. A tender and loving husband, a concerned and caring father, and a responsible son and sibling—these characteristics shine through everything that is known about Harlan. His relations with Mallie can be adduced from various sources: their letters to each other, Mallie's recorded reminiscences, and the testimony of family members as well as outsiders. John quite certainly was not a dominating husband. He made decisions in consultation with his wife, who seems to have been a strong and very intelligent person in her own right. Nor was Harlan the type to be a philanderer; there is not even a rumor to indicate that he was ever unfaithful or even flirtatious (as Holmes, for instance, was). Perfect marriages probably exist only in fiction, but we know of no specific defects in Harlan's.

Nor was he a Victorian dictatorial father. On the contrary, he seems to have been very modern in the openness with which he dealt with his children. He was supportive when and to the extent that they wanted or needed his help: for instance, he pulled all the strings he could to gain a judicial career for his son James, and probably James's appointments as attorney general of Puerto Rico and later as a member of the Interstate Commerce Commission were secured partly as a result of Harlan's influence. He was proud of the success attained by his other two sons, who did not rely on his support. Two of his daughters never married and remained at home with their parents. The Harlans seemed eager (not merely willing) to take the responsibility of caring for their infant granddaughter, despite the facts that money was tight and John and Mallie were already beyond middle age. The fact that the Harlans' sons were responsible for financing and arranging the building of their home in Washington remains as outward testimony to the gratitude and affection that existed between them and their parents.

The same general pattern of caring and responsibility characterized

Harlan's relations with his extended family. Upon his father's death he became the head of the family, by default, since neither of his living older brothers appeared capable of doing so. He settled his father's estate and provided support for his mother, despite his own meager income. As his brother James's wife, Amelia, died early and James himself slowly descended into alcoholism and drug addiction, John assumed some of the responsibility for their affairs. He also aided their son, who was also an alcoholic. He used his influence to help his brother-in-law, Dr. Hatchitt, secure federal jobs; he was willing to take another brother-in-law, Francis Cleveland, as a law partner (although Cleveland proved not to have the ambition to move to Louisville). Harlan appears to have shouldered these responsibilities willingly, even though they must at times have been both irksome and distasteful, as well as financially burdensome.

Throughout his life Harlan showed a pronounced talent for making and keeping friends (with the outstanding exception of Benjamin Bristow). Old friends, even Democrats like Tom Crittenden, rallied round during the fight in the Senate for his appointment to the Court. His relationships within the Court and on circuit were uniformly harmonious. He enjoyed society, and if he was not intimate with all of his Court colleagues, he was at least on amicable terms with practically all of them. He had the ability to shrug off judicial or political disagreements and remain friendly with his opponents. The bitter battles with Justice White over the antitrust and insular cases did not prevent the two from living on friendly, if not close, terms. Even with the crusty Holmes, with whom Harlan had little in common, there was nothing resembling feuding or open dislike, at least outside the judicial conference.

Harlan always retained the saving grace of being able to laugh at himself, and as we have seen, he was also able to take jokes made by others about him without outward irritation. Nor was he one to stand much on his personal dignity. His portraits invariably show a stern and dignified man, but he was in fact neither stern nor particularly dignified. He liked to ride on the platform of Washington streetcars so that he could talk to the conductors, or, sitting inside, he would cut an apple in half and offer one piece to his neighbor. He always had a twinkle in his eye and was ready for the light banter in which friends often indulge. He always, also, enjoyed the relationships with young people that came through his teaching in the Sunday School and in his law school professorship. If he hit a home run at the annual bar association picnic, one of the younger men was always ready to run around the bases for the portly judge.

Along with these attractive traits, Harlan had, of course, others that were either neutral or unattractive. When the occasion demanded seriousness, jokes and badinage were of course forgotten: his judicial opinions are monuments of a rather heavy-handed seriousness. He could easily be stirred to anger, as the income tax episode demonstrates, and this anger was not always displayed in the proper forum. He often seemed arrogant and self-righteous, especially in dissenting opinions. He also seemed politically intolerant, but he lived in a time when this was the rule. He was ambitious as well. Of course, no one succeeds without a measure of ambition, but Harlan was often accused of changing his opinions or acting in ways that were perhaps designed solely to further his career. This characteristic, if indeed the charges are valid, showed itself mostly in his pre-Court political life and in his estrangement from Bristow.

Harlan's political ambitions, fed by his father, stemmed from an initial deep attachment to Henry Clay and to Clay's version of Whig beliefs. These consisted largely of a fundamental nationalism. With a name like John Marshall, Harlan could hardly give credence to Jeffersonian ideas of states' rights. While Clay and the national Whig party lived, the Harlans could count on political advancement in Kentucky. Once the grand old man was gone and slavery became the great fundamental issue of national politics, the Kentucky Whigs were placed in a dilemma from which there was in the end no escape. Replacement parties tended strongly to be based on free soil and eventually antislavery doctrines; while for a brief time in their Know-Nothing period Kentucky Whigs could emphasize nativism and downplay slavery, this was both discreditable to them and in the longer run doomed to failure. John Harlan was later apologetic about this period of his political life, which was in any case mercifully brief. Once secession loomed on the horizon, the Whigs fell back on Constitutional Unionism, again ignoring slavery as an issue.

The fight for the Union led inevitably to an antislavery position, but this too was a losing issue in Kentucky even while the fighting continued. Harlan temporarily adopted—for the only time in his life—a states' rights position, arguing not for slavery but for the sovereign right of each state to decide this issue for itself. This accounts for his support of McClellan and for the Conservative Unionists' brief flirtation with the Kentucky Democrats immediately after the cessation of hostilities. By 1868 Harlan decided that he had no stomach for that solution, even though he could probably have risen far in state politics as a Democrat. By opting to join the Republican party, he was able to keep faith with his basic ideas, at the cost of having to support the Reconstruction Amendments and reconciling himself to the probability that he could never win a statewide electoral contest. Keeping the party alive in Kentucky gave him at least some hope that Republican administrations in Washington would satisfy his ambition by appointing him to high federal office.

It was this ambition that eventually led to trouble with Harlan's law partner Ben Bristow. Harlan would have been happy to be the éminence grise behind Bristow's presidential success. Once it became clear that Bristow could not be nominated and that Hayes would not give Ben any political preferment, however, Harlan felt free to pursue his personal ambitions. That this course of action appeared to Bristow as a betrayal was perhaps natural, but neither man seems to have been greatly at fault. Bristow's political star rapidly flickered out, although he became a successful and moderately wealthy New York lawyer; Harlan was so happy and proud to be a Supreme Court justice that he at once gave up any more strictly political ambitions.

John Harlan's success as a politician was due equally to his ambition, to luck, to hard work, and to ability. He was neither more nor less ethical than the better politicians of his day: certainly he stood higher than Blaine, Conkling, or Morton. All Republicans of his day had come through the chaotic partisan wars of the 1850s caused by the rise of antislavery as an issue and the death of the Whig party. Kentuckians, especially, because no successful party could stand against slavery, were unlikely to find their way directly into the Republican party until after the slavery issue had been settled. Harlan was always a strong, almost fanatic, partisan for his beliefs. That these beliefs changed in some ways due to political exigencies should not surprise anyone.

As a Supreme Court justice, however, Harlan for the first time in his life did not need to pay attention to partisan political necessities. He was able to revert to his basic Whig nationalism, which he saw as being written into the Constitution, reinforced by a strongly nationalistic interpretation of the Reconstruction Amendments. If this set of constitutional beliefs brought him into conflict with the rest of the Court—as it often did—there was nothing except peer pressure to prevent him from dissenting. Harlan, a proud and stubborn, not to say self-righteous, man, was willing to disregard this pressure.

Holmes once called Harlan "the last of the tobacco-spittin' judges." Holmes may have meant this literally. It also has a possible philosophical meaning, for, as I hope this book demonstrates, Harlan was very much a nineteenth-century man and judge. If he reached conclusions agreeable to 1930s New Dealers and 1950s liberals, he did so through the use of thoroughly nineteenth-century theories and ideals.

Harlan was heavily influenced in the 1870s and 1880s by the rise of what Karl Llewellyn calls the "Formal Style" of judging, which relies heavily upon reasoning logically from a set of precedents with little attention to the fact-situation or the wisdom of the result. Harlan's opinions, like those of most of his brethren, are usually dry, excessively verbose, and studded with case references, so much so that the reader's sense of what the judge is saying can easily be lost. It is customary to assume that such opinions represent a closing of the law to creativity, expansiveness, and progress, but such is obviously not the case. Creativity did not disappear, but judges tended to drive it underground by claiming and believing that their conclusions were the only ones possible based on text and precedent. Justice Harlan, however, was aware that judges can use even the formal style to achieve desirable results. As Llewellyn points out, however, judges often with "almost random irregularity jumped legal traces" and reached good conclusions "by way of bad logic, or by distortion of authority or fact, or by main strength." Thus, Harlan's "great" opinions, usually dissents, have often been criticized for their weakness in strictly constitutional terms. Harlan was often at least subconsciously aware that the majority was using good logic to make bad law; his own tendency, when his deepest convictions were involved, was the reverse. He consequently has not become known as a great judicial craftsman.

The same can be said for the literary qualities of his opinions. Most of the time his opinions were as verbose and dull as were those of his contemporaries, with the notable exception of Justice Holmes. But when his emotions were deeply stirred, his prose took on a grand quality that had little to do with the law of the case. To some extent Harlan realized this; he often remarked to his law students that if the justices did not "like an act of Congress, we don't have much trouble to find grounds to declare it unconstitutional." At the same time he was, however, much attached to the doctrine of judicial self-restraint and continually inveighed against what he saw as the majority's tendency to act as a superlegislature. This produced some inconsistencies, as the difference between his approach in *Smyth* v. *Ames* and that in *Lochner* v. *New York* demonstrates. He doubtless would have felt that some contradictions were a small price to pay for the achievement of good law.

It is one of the ironies of constitutional history that this nineteenth-century man, with his deeply flawed judicial philosophy, so often reached conclusions in dissent that later Court majorities have also reached. What looks at first glance like prescience was actually almost a historical accident. During his years on the Court Harlan proved to be a greater man than judge. Yet if one disregards the niceties of craftsmanship and realizes that all Supreme Court judges, regardless of the methods they use, tend strongly to reach conclusions already at least inchoately formulated in their heads, one can only give credit to Harlan's greatness of heart, while deploring the narrow social views that led to the constitutional doctrines propounded by his colleagues. It is for these reasons that John Harlan was a great judge. He could not lead the Court; indeed, much of the time his dissents did not persuade even one of his brethren. The greatness of his contemporaries lay in their influence on the rest of the Court's members, and this is where Field, Miller, and Bradley shone. Harlan's influence was on the future, as was that of Holmes.

This influence was greatest in three areas. First (because most commonly acknowledged today) stands the broad use of the Fourteenth Amendment to attempt to achieve equality. That this has gone far beyond anything conceived possible (or even desirable) by Harlan himself is no detraction from his great accomplishment in his own day. He stands out as the only justice who took such a position before the 1930s. Second, Harlan greatly influenced the use of a broader interpretation of the Fourteenth Amendment to secure greater due process protection in the area of criminal law. While later judges both broadened and in other ways narrowed Harlan's incorporation theory, they have nevertheless achieved the protections he sought and in some respects gone beyond them. Third, the broad reach of the power of the national government was perhaps first and most strongly advocated by Harlan in his arguments for an expanded meaning of the word *commerce* and in his attempt to maintain a less restrictive interpretation of the Interstate Commerce Act. Here again the New Deal Court went far beyond anything Harlan could have predicted, although it is likely that he would have agreed.

Harlan signally failed, however, to influence the future use of the Sherman Antitrust Act. Here his attempt to read a strict interpretation into the law was probably unrealistic and thus doomed to failure. This area, in fact, reveals most clearly the nineteenth-century character of Harlan's jurisprudence.

Where Harlan was ambivalent—as in the use of substantive due process to limit state regulation of corporate property—later history is complex. For while the Court in the 1940s entirely gave up the attempt to limit such state actions, its acquiescence in the great growth of congressional regulation under the commerce clause has limited the states' powers perhaps more severely. It has become obvious that "liberal" Courts, too, are willing to use substantive due process to prevent states from doing other things that the judges disapprove, such as the limitation of the right of abortion or the right to order the sterilization of habitual criminals.

Harlan's quickest vindication undoubtedly came when the Sixteenth Amendment operationalized his belief that there could be a federal income tax. The fact that he had support from three of his colleagues is perhaps significant. It led to greater questioning of the majority's decision, and Harlan could not be stigmatized by comments such as that of Felix Frankfurter, who called him an "eccentric exception" in his views of the criminal process envisaged by the due process clause.

Nevertheless, in his result-orientation Harlan never cut completely loose from the words of the Constitution unless it was in the one area in which the whole Court agreed: substantive due process. In all his other opinions his interpretation of the relevant text was at least plausible; it was the intent of the framers and, more basically, wise public policy that led to his differences with his brethren.

Of the other great judges who served with Harlan, he probably resembled Stephen J. Field most closely; even though the two often disagreed about the desired result, both were more or less openly doctrinaire and result-oriented. The most objective, because he did not seem to care about the policy result very deeply, was Oliver Wendell Holmes, Jr.; the best legal craftsmen were Samuel Miller and Joseph Bradley. Oddly, it is the craftsmen who are most nearly forgotten today, while of the five, Harlan is now—perhaps temporarily—the most admired.

This book has attempted a "warts and all" portrait of this admirable and admired judge. It is probable that he is nowadays admired for somewhat the wrong reasons. Nevertheless, he stands out among his colleagues because he was so like them, yet more so: strong-minded, enthusiastically partisan, warm-hearted, and humanitarian. If Chief Justice Marshall is the great judge of our formative period, then Harlan is perhaps the great judge of the whole period following Marshall's death until at least the accession of Justice Holmes. This places him in no mean company and could well stand as his epitaph.

Chronology

1833	June 1	Born at Old Stone House, Mercer (now Boyle) County, Kentucky.
1835		Moved to Harrodsburg (Mercer County).
1840		Moved to Frankfort.
1848-50		Attended Centre College, Danville.
1850-52		Attended law school at Transylvania University, Lexington.
1851		Appointed adjutant general of Kentucky.
1853		Admitted to the Kentucky Bar, Frankfort.
1854		Elected city attorney of Frankfort. Joined American ("Know-Nothing") party.
1856	Dec. 23	Married Malvina French Shanklin of Evansville, Indiana.
1858		Elected county judge of Franklin County (Frankfort).
1859		Ran unsuccessfully for Congress as member of Opposition party.
1861		Moved to Louisville.
	Oct.	Formed Tenth Kentucky Infantry and became colonel in Union army.
1862	Jan. 19-20	Battle of Mill Springs (Logan's Crossroads).
	April 6-7	Battle of Shiloh (Pittsburg Landing).
	Oct. 8	Battle of Perryville.
	Oct.	Acted as brigade commander.
	Dec.	Skirmish at Hartsville, Tennessee.
	Dec. 29-30	Skirmish at Rolling Fork, Kentucky.

1863	Feb.	Nominated to be brigadier general. Resigned from army. Moved to Frankfort.
	Aug.	Elected attorney general of Kentucky as member of Union party.
1864		Supported Democrat General George McClellan for president as member of Conservative Union party.
1865		Opposed adoption of Thirteenth Amendment.
1867	Jan.	Nominated, to be U.S. senator as member of Conservative Union party, but defeated.
	Aug.	Ran for reelection as attorney general as member of Conservative Union party, but was defeated. Moved to Louisville.
1868		Became member of Republican party; campaigned for Grant for president.
1870		Added Benjamin Bristow as law partner.
1871		Argued before U.S. Supreme Court in *Watson* v. *Jones*, 13 Wall. 679 (1872). Ran for Governor as Republican, and lost. Supported Reconstruction Amendments.
1872		Defeated as candidate for U.S. Senate.
1873		Appointed special prosecutor for the United States in Kentucky civil rights cases.
1874		Bristow became secretary of the Treasury.
1875		Defeated again in race for governor.
1876	June	Led Kentucky delegation to Republican National Convention pledged to Bristow; swung votes to Hayes on sixth ballot.
1877	April	Member of Hayes's Louisiana Commission.
	Oct. 16	Nominated to Supreme Court by Hayes.
	Dec. 3	Confirmed by Senate.
	Dec. 10	Sworn in as associate justice.
1883	Oct. 15	Dissent in *Civil Rights Cases*, 109 U.S. 3.
1884	March 3	Dissent in *Hurtado* v. *California*, 110 U.S. 516.
1887	Dec. 5	Opinion for Court in *Mugler* v. *Kansas*, 123 U.S. 623.

1889		Began teaching constitutional law at Columbian (later George Washington University) Law School.
1892	Aug.	To Paris as member of arbitration commission in Bering Sea fur seal dispute with Great Britain.
1893	Oct.	Return to United States.
1895	Jan. 14	Dissent in sugar trust case, 156 U.S. 1.
	April 8 and May 20	Dissents in income tax cases, 157 U.S. 429, 158 U.S. 601.
1896	May 18	Dissent in *Plessy* v. *Ferguson,* 163 U.S. 537.
1898	March 7	Opinion for Court in *Smyth* v. *Ames,* 169 U.S. 466.
1900	March 5	Dissent in *Maxwell* v. *Dow,* 176 U.S. 581.
1901	Jan. 14-Dec. 2	Dissents and opinions for Court in insular cases, 182 U.S. 1, 182 U.S. 222, 182 U.S. 244, 183 U.S. 176.
1904	March 14	Opinion for Court in *Northern Securities* case, 193 U.S. 197.
1905	April 17	Dissent in *Lochner* v. *New York,* 198 U.S. 45.
1908	Jan. 6	Dissent in *Employers' Liability* case, 207 U.S. 463.
	Nov. 9	Dissent in *Berea College* case, 211 U.S. 45.
	Nov. 16	Dissent in *Twining* v. *New Jersey,* 211 U.S. 78.
1911	May 15	Concurring in *Standard Oil Co.* case, 221 U.S. 1.
	May 29	Concurring in *American Tobacco Co.* case, 221 U.S. 106.
	Oct. 14	Death, of pneumonia, Washington, D.C.

A Note on Sources

One of the problems in dealing with nineteenth-century men and women is the usual absence of personal records and correspondence. Until late in the century there were no typewriters or carbon paper. Unless one had a feeling that one's papers would be important later, one kept no copies. John and Malvina Harlan, for instance, evidently wrote hundreds of letters and notes to each other, of which a scant dozen or so remain. John often kept files of his incoming correspondence, but he was not so faithful in recording outgoing materials. The files that he did keep are quite often unreadable. A good deal does remain, though, and more can be gleaned by sorting through the papers of his correspondents. This, however, still leaves gaps that the biographer can only fill in by intelligent inference.

Harlan's own papers consist of masses of financial and legal materials from his days as a practicing attorney; of many letters that he received dating from about 1855 to his death; of letters (not many) that he wrote; and of scrapbooks of political and personal memorabilia and newspaper clippings. This, plus printed copies of some of his speeches, constitutes Harlan's personal "paper trail." Among these papers are also some autobiographical notes in which he recalls various parts of his life; the "one-day diary" giving his side of the Bristow controversy; and his wife's invaluable set of recollections written about 1915. These are of widely varying interest and value, but they constitute an important set of bio-historical materials without which no biography of Harlan could be written. These papers, partially duplicatory, are held by the University of Louisville (UL) and by the Library of Congress (LC).

Other valuable sources of letters to, from, or about Harlan are the papers of his personal or political friends. These are somewhat fugitive in nature, and I am not sure that I have found all of them. The more important are located at the Filson Club Library in Louisville (mostly correspondence with John Bruner and Augustus Willson); the Library of Congress (mainly papers of Benjamin Bristow, William Howard Taft, Theodore Roosevelt, and various Supreme Court justices); and the Hayes Memorial Library (latterly, the Hayes Presidential Center), which holds the papers of Chief

Justice Waite and President Rutherford B. Hayes. A valuable source for the later Court period is the papers of Chief Justice Fuller held by the Chicago Historical Society (CHS). I have also obtained materials from the Kentucky Historical Society, Yale University Library, the Ohio Historical Society, and the Massachusetts Historical Society.

I have not hesitated to resort to secondary sources for general historical and background materials. In addition, the biographies of Harlan's colleagues on the Court and of other prominent people of the period have been of great value, principally those of chief justices Waite and Fuller; associate justices Field, Miller, White, and Holmes; and, among politicians, Bristow, Hayes, Garfield, Roosevelt, Taft, and Hughes.

All scholars know that librarians are among the most cheerfully helpful people in the world. I cannot possibly thank them individually, but I could not have done this work without them.

Notes

1: Kentucky Childhood, 1833-1854

1. Harlan's son, Richard Davenport Harlan, became interested in the family's genealogy, and the results of his researches are contained in the Harlan Papers held by the Library of Congress, hereafter cited as LC.   **2.** The Old Stone House was built in 1800 near the headwaters of the Salt River—a tiny stream at this point, and now apparently no longer fed by the "never-failing spring" that probably accounted for the Harlans' settlement of the place. The house was on a rise overlooking the little rivulet. The family property descended through Harlan's uncle and then his cousin Wellington. Upon Wellington Harlan's death it was inherited by his wife, "Jinkie," and it was passed on by her to a niece, Irene Moore. It was acquired by a Mr. Stockton in 1954 as part of his farm, and as late as 1983 the old man, then eighty-seven, still owned it. The remains of the Old Stone House could still be seen: much damaged by time and storms, the four walls of the original house still stood, but the remains of the later additions were nothing but piles of rubble covered by the encroaching grass. The house was placed on the National Register in 1978, but nothing has been done to preserve or restore it. The house is a mile or so off the highway from Danville to Perryville, only a few miles west of Danville.   **3.** James Harlan to Charles Lanman, Sept. 3, 1858, Lanman Papers, Filson Club.   **4.** While in Harrodsburg—the family apparently moved there when John was only a year old—the Harlans lived in a house on the hilltop now occupied by the famous Beaumont Inn. Their occupancy from 1834 to 1841 preceded a string of schools for girls that predated the inn.   **5.** Information on James Harlan is derived from the entry under his name in the *Dictionary of American Biography* (hereafter *DAB*) 8: 267; from a typewritten copy of a thirty-two-page autobiographical letter written by John Harlan to his son Richard, dated July 4, 1911, and contained in the Harlan Papers held by the law school, University of Louisville (hereafter UL); and from a few scattered recollections of unknown date that Harlan wrote as answers to questions from an unknown source, contained in LC. These latter two will be referred to below as Autobiographical Letter and Recollections.

6. Clark McMeekin, *Old Kentucky Country* (New York: Duell, Sloan and Pearce, 1957), p. 94. According to McMeekin, over five hundred people died within three weeks in Lexington alone. Apparently the disease was Asiatic cholera, and there was no known treatment; see Allen J. Share, *Cities in the Commonwealth: Two Centuries of Urban Life in Kentucky* (Lexington: Univ. Press of Kentucky, 1982), pp. 61-63.   **7.** Eleanor Talbot Kinkead, *Young Greer of Kentucky* (Chicago: Rand McNally, 1895), p. 5.   **8.** Quoted by Lawrence S. Thompson, *Kentucky Tradition* (Hamden, Conn.: Shoe String Press, 1956), p. 18.   **9.** James Harlan to Charles Lanman, Sept. 3, 1858, Lanman Papers, Filson Club.   **10.** Actually, Moore won. The election, however, was contested in Congress on grounds of fraud. A new election was ordered, which Letcher won. See articles on Letcher and Moore in *DAB* 11: 193; 13: 139-40. The characterization of Letcher is from P.V. Major, "The Frankfort Bar," in H. Levin, ed., *The Lawyers and Lawmakers of Kentucky* (Chicago: Lewis Pub. Co., 1897), p. 108.

11. Recollections, pp. 3-4.   **12.** For most of the period during which Harlan lived in Frankfort, the main family residence was located at the corner of Wapping and Wilkinson streets. In this neighborhood some of the most prestigious families of the state also lived: the Crittendens, Letcher, Morehead, Vest, and U.S. Supreme Court justice Richard Todd. The house—no longer existent—is described as having been "a large three story frame house." See Alice E. Trabue, *A Corner in Celebrities* (Louisville: George G. Fetter Co., 1923), p. 56.
13. Autobiographical Letter, p. 2.   **14.** Harlan, "The Know-Nothing Organization, etc.," undated memo, Harlan Papers, LC, p. 1.   **15.** Champ Clark, *My Quarter Century of American Politics*, 2 vols. (New York: Harper and Brothers, 1920), 1: 18-20. Although life in the state capital would have been somewhat more sophisticated, Frankfort was a small town, boys were boys, and conditions were probably not all that different.
16. James Lane Allen, *The Blue Grass Region of Kentucky* (New York: Harper and Brothers, 1899), pp. 87-116.   **17.** *Kentucky State Journal* (Frankfort), Nov. 24, 1908.   **18.** Both Harrodsburg (Mercer County) and Frankfort (Franklin County) were then, as they are now, county seats.   **19.** The Harlans are recorded on the membership rolls of the First Presbyterian Church of Frankfort. The church edifice, which still stands on Main Street only a block from the Harlan residence, was built in 1848. Church records list John as Sunday School superintendent in the late 1850s and his wife as organist during the same period. W.H. Averill, *A History of the First Presbyterian Church, Frankfort, Ky.* (Cincinnati: Monfort and Co., 1902), pp. 159, 225. My attention to these matters was suggested by the kindness of the Reverend Mr. Averill's granddaughter, Miss Margaret Averill.   **20.** Quoted from a typed manuscript by Malvina Shanklin Harlan, "Some Memories of a Long Life, 1854-1911" (unpublished, 1915), Harlan Papers, UL, pp. 27ff.
21. Ibid., p. 29.   **22.** William J. Simmons, *Men of Mark: Eminent, Progressive and Rising* (1887; New York: Arno Press, 1968), pp. 613-16. I am indebted to Professor Charles Wynes of the University of Georgia for calling this relationship to my attention.   **23.** Rayford W. Logan and Michael R. Winston, eds., *Dictionary of American Negro Biography* (New York: W.W. Norton, 1982), pp. 287-88.   **24.** Cincinnati *Enquirer,* Sept. 22 and 25, 1897. The Cleveland *Gazette* published a note on the death of his mother, April 25, 1885.   **25.** A.S. Paxton (or Poston?) to Harlan, July 9, 1868, Harlan Papers, LC.
26. James Harlan to Harlan, July 27, 1888; also references in letters dated Sept. 23, 1887, and June 19, 1988. Harlan Papers, UL.   **27.** Robert Harlan to Harlan, Feb. 9, 1878, Harlan Papers, LC.   **28.** *Franklin Roundabout,* April 4, 1885, UL; Autobiographical Letter, p. 5.
29. Undated biographical note probably written by Harlan himself although in the third person, LC, p. 2. Referred to hereafter as Biographical Note.   **30.** James Harlan to Charles Lanman, Sept. 3, 1858, Lanman Papers, Filson Club.
31. Malvina Harlan, "Some Memories," pp. 29-30.   **32.** Walter A. Groves, "Centre College—the Second Phase, 1830-1857," *Filson Club History Quarterly* 24 (Oct. 1950): 328. This is the best source on Centre College life during the Harlan period.   **33.** Ibid., p. 317; see, for Young, *DAB* 20: 629.   **34.** Groves, "Centre College,", p. 313.   **35.** Ibid., p. 320.
36. Ibid., pp. 326-27.   **37.** Ibid., p. 327.   **38.** Written July 30, 1849, Harlan Papers, LC.   **39.** Quoted from the college catalog in Groves, "Centre College," p. 327.   **40.** Ibid., p. 329.
41. Ibid., p. 331.   **42.** John H. Gaines to Harlan, undated letter, Harlan Papers, UL.
43. Groves, "Centre College," p. 315.   **44.** John D. Wright, Jr., *Transylvania: Tutor to the West* (Lexington: Univ. Press of Kentucky, 1975), p. 165.   **45.** Both William Strong and Ward Hunt attended law schools briefly, however.
46. George Robertson, *Scrapbook on Law and Politics, Men and Times* (1855); cf. *DAB* 16: 22. For Marshall, see *DAB* 12: 329.   **47.** Robertson, *DAB* 16: 22.   **48.** *DAB* 19: 260.   **49.** Robertson, *Scrapbook,* p. 330.   **50.** Public remarks at Transylvania University, as reported in Louisville *Courier-Journal,* Nov. 24, 1908.
51. Share, *Cities,* p. 330.   **52.** On life in Lexington circa 1850, see Share, *Cities,* pp. 27-30.   **53.** Harlan, "My Appointment as Adjutant General of Kentucky and My First

Meeting with James G. Blaine," undated, Harlan Papers, UL.   **54.** Malvina Harlan, "Some Memories," pp. 30-31.   **55.** Lewis Franklin Johnson, *The History of Franklin County, Ky.* (Franklin, Ky.: Roberts Printing Co., 1912).
56. Harlan's Law Ledgers, 1854, Harlan Papers, UL.   **57.** Recollections.

2: Kentucky Lawyer-Politician, 1855-1860

1. Thomas T. Crittenden to John R. Dunlap, Nov. 27, 1907, Harlan Papers, LC. See *DAB* 4: 549.   **2.** Malvina Harlan, "Some Memories," p. 1. Harlan's size—he was six foot three and had a large frame—apparently ran in the family. Besides other relations such as his great-uncle Silas, John's own father was, at least by the standards of those days, a very large person. One source describes James Harlan in his maturity as "the huge, brawny, fair-haired, near-sighted generous attorney general, James Harlan, gigantic in body and mind, a living, slow- speaking, incarnate digest of the decisions of the Kentucky court of appeals, as well as those of the supreme court of the United States." Major, "Frankfort Bar," p. 108.   **3.** Harlan Papers, LC.   **4.** Malvina Harlan, "Some Memories," pp. 4-7.   **5.** Unsigned letter from a Shanklin female cousin residing in Evansville to Richard D. Harlan, dated only Jan. 30 but probably written around 1930, Harlan Papers, LC.
6. Malvina Harlan, "Some Memories," pp. 4-7   **7.** Ibid., p. 10.   **8.** Ibid.
9. Ibid.   **10.** Ibid., p. 20.
11. Ibid., p. 21.   **12.** Ibid., pp. 30A-30B.   **13.** Ibid., p. 44. The Harlans were to have six children: the other three were John Maynard, born Dec. 21, 1863; Laura Cleveland, born Jan. 7, 1871; and Ruth, born Sept. 7, 1875.   **14.** Malvina Harlan, "Some Memories," pp. 7A, 12.
15. President Young's gradual emancipation proposal for the state constitution was never adopted. The most famous of Kentucky abolitionists, Cassius M. Clay, was tolerated but had no influence: his press was politely carried to Ohio with the understanding that he would not bring it back into Kentucky. See E. Merton Coulter, *The Civil War and Readjustment in Kentucky* (Chapel Hill: Univ. of North Carolina Press, 1926), p. 6. James Harlan, Sr., vehemently opposed abolitionism in a letter to D. Howard Smith dated Aug. 5, 1851, in which he just as vehemently defended his action in serving as counsel for two free blacks who had been shanghaied back into slavery, Harlan Papers, UL.
16. See principally the following: Louis Hartz, "John M. Harlan in Kentucky, 1855-1877," *Filson Club History Quarterly* 14, no. 1 (Jan. 1940): 17-40; David G. Farrelly, "Harlan's Formative Period: The Years before the War," *Kentucky Law Journal* 46 (1958): 367; Alan F. Westin, "John Marshall Harlan and the Constitutional Rights of Negroes: The Transformation of a Southerner," *Yale Law Journal* 66 (1957): 637; Thomas L. Owen, "The Pre-Court Career of John Marshall Harlan," M.A. thesis, Univ. of Louisville, 1970.   **17.** James Harlan to John B. Bruner, Nov. 10, 1858, Bruner Papers, Filson Club.   **18.** Malvina Harlan, "Some Memories," pp. 24-25, 26- 27.   **19.** Ibid., pp. 26-27.   **20.** Ibid., p. 28.
21. Ibid.   **22.** See Owen, "Pre-Court Career," pp. 12-15, for indications of Harlan's resort to expediency on the slavery issue for political reasons; and pp. 66ff. for his initial opposition to the Thirteenth and Fourteenth amendments, also politically expedient.
23. The political history of the period from 1845 to the Civil War, more specifically as it affected the Whig party and its successors, is dealt with excellently and succinctly in David M. Potter, *The Impending Crisis* (New York: Harper and Row, 1976). See also Michael F. Holt, *The Political Crisis of the 1850's* (New York: John Wiley, 1978); Don E. Fehrenbacher, *Slavery, Law, and Politics: The Dred Scott Case in Historical Perspective* (New York: Oxford University Press, 1981).
24. For the situation in Kentucky, see, for instance, Albert D. Kirwan, *John J. Crittenden: The Struggle for the Union* (Lexington: Univ. of Kentucky Press, 1962).   **25.** See esp. Owen, "Pre-Court Career."
26. Harlan, "Know-Nothing," p. 1.   **27.** The career of the Know-Nothing movement in Kentucky is ably surveyed in Agnes G. McGann, *Nativism in Kentucky to 1860* (Washington,

D.C.: Catholic University of America, 1944). For its impact on the national political scene, see references in note 23.   **28.** Frankfort *Commonwealth,* May 7 and 9, 1856.   **29.** Harlan, "Know-Nothing," pp. 1-2. The American party was organized as a semisecret society, complete with initiations, oaths, and rituals.   **30.** As noted earlier, Thomas T. Crittenden was the nephew of the leading Kentucky Whig after Clay's death, John J. Crittenden, who served the state both as U.S. senator and as governor. For Morehead, see *DAB* 13: 157-58; for Thomas Crittenden, see *DAB* 4: 550-51. The characterization of Morehead is from Major, "Frankfort Bar," p. 108.

31. Harlan, "Know-Nothing," pp. 5-6.   **32.** Malvina Harlan, "Some Memories," pp. 30-30A.   **33.** Louisville *Daily Journal,* July 29, 1856.   **34.** Frankfort *Commonwealth,* July 23, 1855.   **35.** Lexington *Observer and Reporter,* July 25, 1855.

36. Paris *Western Citizen,* July 6, 1855; Lexington *Observer and Reporter,* Aug. 1, 1855; Louisville *Daily Journal,* July 25, 1855.   **37.** See Leonard Koester, "Bloody Monday," Louisville *Courier-Journal Magazine,* Aug. 31, 1955. For the general national background of the Know-Nothing movement, see Potter, *Impending Crisis,* pp. 241ff.   **38.** Frankfort *Commonwealth,* May 21, 1856. For Breckinridge, see *DAB* 3: 7-10.   **39.** Undated handwritten fragment, Harlan Papers, UL.   **40.** Lewis Collins, *History of Kentucky,* rev. ed. by Richard H. Collins (Louisville: John P. Morgan and Co., 1924), 1: 80.

41. Benjamin Hardin, as quoted in Washington *Star,* April 16, 1905.   **42.** Autobiographical Letter.   **43.** Louisville *Daily Journal,* Feb. 23 and 24, June 1, 1859.   **44.** Old Whigs accused Simms of leaving the party because he had failed to receive its nomination either for the state senate or for Congress, which he felt he deserved; see Paris *Western Citizen,* June 10, 1859. But it is more likely that he left the party for the same reason the Harlans did; it was no longer a vehicle for winning. Like many other Southern Whigs, however, he moved to the Democratic party, as it was more congenial in its attitude toward slavery. Simms later served in the Senate of the Confederacy for Kentucky's "rump" delegation. See *DAB* 17: 170-71.   **45.** Harlan, "Know-Nothing," p. 6.

46. Savoyard, "John Marshall Harlan," Washington *Post,* Oct. 26, 1902. Savoyard apparently got some of his information directly from Harlan, and perhaps from other politicians as well.   **47.** Paris *Western Citizen,* June 10, 1859.   **48.** Savoyard, "Harlan." Davis was a very prominent, and fiery, Whig and Unionist.   **49.** Paris *Western Citizen,* June 10, 1859; Frankfort *Commonwealth,* July 29, 1859; Louisville *Weekly Journal,* Feb. 23, 1859.   **50.** Cynthiana *News* as quoted in Frankfort *Tri-Weekly Commonwealth,* May 30, 1859.

51. Paris *Western Citizen,* July 8, 1859; Frankfort *Tri-Weekly Commonwealth,* May 30, Aug. 15, 1859.   **52.** Lexington *Statesman,* as quoted in Frankfort *Tri-Weekly Commonwealth,* May 28, 1859.   **53.** Kirwan, *Crittenden,* p. 341.   **54.** Harlan, "Know-Nothing," p. 7.   **55.** Ibid.

56. Potter, *Impending Crisis,* p. 417.   **57.** The "Address" is found in the John B. Bruner Papers, Filson Club.   **58.** On Beriah Magoffin, see *DAB* 12: 199-200. The best source on political events in Kentucky during the Civil War period remains Coulter, *Civil War.*

3: Kentucky Unionist, 1861

1. Share, *Cities,* pp. 39, 46-64.   **2.** Ibid.   **3.** Eighth U.S. census, 1860, Population, pp. 183-85. While some immigrants were found all over the state, most settled in Louisville and in the Kentucky suburbs of Cincinnati.   **4.** On the Brandeis and Dembitz families, see Alpheus T. Mason, *Brandeis: A Free Man's Life* (New York: Viking, 1946). Brandeis's brother-in-law, Lewis Dembitz, was a prominent Louisville attorney by 1860 and a staunch Unionist.
5. On Bullock (1807-89), see Levin, ed., *Lawyers and Lawmakers,* p. 163. The partnership was apparently broken up when Harlan joined the army, and probably because Bullock eventually became a Democrat, it was never reestablished.

6. Joseph Holt (1807-94) was commissioner of patents from 1857 to 1859, postmaster general in 1859, and secretary of war in 1860 and 1861. He became a strong Lincoln supporter and was judge advocate general from 1862 to 1875. See *DAB* 9: 181-83.   **7.** Harlan to Joseph Holt, March 11, 1861, Kentucky State Historical Library.   **8.** Ibid.   **9.** The situation in the winter and spring of 1861 and the events of the succeeding summer and fall are exceedingly confused. See Coulter, *Civil War,* pp. 18-124; Steven A. Channing, *Kentucky: A Bicentennial History* (New York: W.W. Norton, 1977), pp. 70-128; W.H. Perrin, J.H. Battle, and G.C. Kniffin, *Kentucky: A History of the State* (Louisville: F.A. Battey, 1887), pp. 350ff.; Lowell H. Harrison, *The Civil War in Kentucky* (Lexington: Univ. Press of Kentucky, 1975); Robert Emmett McDowell, *City of Conflict: Louisville in the Civil War* (Louisville: Louisville Civil War Roundtable, 1962); James A. Rawley, *Turning Points of the Civil War* (Lincoln: Univ. of Nebraska Press, 1966), esp. pp. 11-45; Thomas Speed, *The Union Cause in Kentucky* (New York: G.P. Putnam's Sons, 1907).   **10.** Louisville *Daily Journal,* Jan. 10, 1861. Senator John J. Crittenden proposed a series of constitutional amendments that would have protected slavery south of the traditional "thirty-six thirty" line. The plan was obviously not acceptable in the North, but Southerners took its failure to mean a complete unwillingness on the part of Lincoln and the Republicans to negotiate.

11. For James Speed (1812-87), see Levin, ed., *Lawyers and Lawmakers,* pp. 282-84; *DAB* 17: 440-41.   **12.** Quoted in Speed, *Union Cause,* p. 27. John C. Breckinridge was Buchanan's vice president; he later became a Confederate general. *DAB* 3: 7-10.   **13.** Speed, *Union Cause,* pp. 30-31.   **14.** Frankfort *Commonwealth,* March 1, 1861.   **15.** Speed, *Union Cause,* p. 117, quoting Harlan; Malvina Harlan, "Some Memories," pp. 40, 50.

16. McDowell, *City of Conflict,* pp. 47-48.   **17.** Autobiographical Letter, p. 11.
18. Speed, *Union Cause,* pp. 119-21, quoting Harlan.   **19.** Coulter, *Civil War,* pp. 51-52, 95. Harlan campaigned actively around Frankfort and Lexington for John J. Crittenden, who defeated Simms, the incumbent Democrat.   **20.** Ibid., pp. 96-98.

21. Malvina Harlan, "Some Memories," p. 45.   **22.** Quoted in Perrin, Battle, and Kniffin, *Kentucky,* pp. 495-96.   **23.** Harlan, "Civil War of 1861," undated (probably 1903) autobiographical note, thirteen typed pages, Harlan Papers, LC, pp. 6-11.   **24.** *Brady and Davis* v. *Louisville & Nashville Railroad,* Case 50705, Jefferson Circuit Court Records, 1861; cf. Louisville *Daily Journal,* July 3 and 12, 1861.   **25.** Harlan, "Civil War," pp. 5-6.

26. Malvina Harlan, "Some Memories," pp. 50-51.   **27.** Ibid., pp. 52-53. According to Harlan, the announcement was actually written by Prentice: see Harlan, "Civil War," p. 11.
28. Malvina Harlan, "Some Memories," pp. 52-53. Mrs. Harlan had some interesting comments on her "exciting" boat trip to Evansville.

4: Union Soldier, 1861-1863

1. McDowell, *City of Conflict,* pp. 46-48; William T. Sherman, *Memoirs* (New York: D. Appleton and Co., 1875), 1: 197-99.   **2.** Alfred Pirtle, "My Early Soldiering, etc.," typed manuscript, 1919, Filson Club. Pirtle was a long-time friend of the Harlans who served in the Zouaves.   **3.** Harlan, "Some Experiences as a Captain of Home Guards," undated typed manuscript, 5pp., Harlan Papers, LC.   **4.** Ibid.   **5.** Ibid.

6. Basil W. Duke, *Reminiscences of General Basil W. Duke* (Garden City, Doubleday, Page and Co., 1911), pp. 72-77. Duke went on to be second in command of Morgan's Raiders; *DAB* 5: 495-96.   **7.** Harlan, "The Union Cause in Kentucky in 1861 and the Raising of a Regiment by Me," undated typed manuscript, 20 pp., Harlan Papers, LC, p. 8. Willich became a brigadier general. Stewart Sifakis, *Who Was Who in the Civil War* (New York: Facts on File, 1988), p. 720.   **8.** Shelby Foote, *The Civil War: A Narrative* (New York: Random House, 1958), vol. 1: 176-79.   **9.** Speed, *Union Cause,* contribution by Harlan, pp. 196-99. Colonel James B. Steedman became a major general and a hero at Chickamauga. Speed S. Fry, another Kentuckian, became a brigadier general but was not a successful soldier. Sifakis, *Who Was Who,* pp. 619, 231-32.   **10.** Autobiographical Letter, p. 21.

11. Thomas Speed, *Union Regiments of Kentucky* (Louisville, 1897), pp. 368-69; Foote, *Civil*

War, p. 569.   **12.** Harlan, Autobiographical Letter, p. 21.   **13.** Ibid., pp. 22-23.   **14.** The main facts about this campaign are taken from Foote, *Civil War*, pp. 650-61.   **15.** Autobiographical Letter, pp. 23-24. Brigadier General Joshua W. Sill was killed at Murfreesboro.
   16. Foote, *Civil War*, p. 715.   **17.** Malvina Harlan, "Some Memories," p. 53; Autobiographical Letter, p. 24. Unfortunately, almost all of this correspondence has disappeared.
18. Frederick H. Dyer, *A Compendium of the War of the Rebellion*, (Des Moines: Dyer Pub. Co., 1908).   **19.** Autobiographical Letter, p. 25.   **20.** Foote, *Civil War*, pp. 726-43.
   21. Autobiographical Letter, pp. 27-28.   **22.** Autobiographical Letter, pp. 28-29.
23. Dyer, *Compendium*.   **24.** Basil W. Duke, *A History of Morgan's Cavalry*, ed. with introduction and notes by Cecil Fletcher Holland (Bloomington: Indiana Univ. Press, 1960), p. 309.
25. Dyer, *Compendium*.
   26. Duke, *History*, pp. 309-16.   **27.** Autobiographical Letter, pp. 29-30.   **28.** Duke's recollections of the raid cover pp. 325-43 of his *History*.   **29.** The most reliable strength report is probably Harlan's own report in *The War of the Rebellion: A Compilation of the Official Records of the Union and Confederate Armies*, ser. 1, vol. 20, pt. 1, p. 137.   **30.** Ibid.
   31. Speed, *Union Regiments*, p. 370.   **32.** Autobiographical Letter, p. 31.   **33.** Ibid., p. 30. Harlan's brother William was by 1863 unfit for legal work, for unknown reasons, but James was a working lawyer, although subject to bouts of alcoholism. Harlan's memory, in other words, played him false here.   **34.** Resolution, Harlan Papers, UL.

5: Into the Political Wilderness, 1863-1867

   1. There is scattered correspondence regarding Wellington's claims as late as 1868. See, for instance, letter from James G. Hatchitt to Harlan, Nov. 2, 1868, Harlan Papers, LC.
2. Harlan to James B. Beck, Oct. 31, 1877, Harlan Papers, LC. Boyle (1818-71) was a Danville, Kentucky, lawyer who served as Union commander of the District of Kentucky, 1862-64. See Ezra J. Warner, *Generals in Blue* (Baton Rouge: Louisiana State Univ. Press, 1964), p. 40. Warner says that Boyle's "civilian policy alienated all but the most zealous Union sympathizers"; see Coulter, *Civil War*, pp. 151ff. Beck (1822-90) was the Democratic senator for Kentucky (1876-90); he had been John C. Breckinridge's law partner. *National Cyclopaedia of American Biography* (hereafter *NCAB*) 3: 418.   **3.** At least that was Mallie's recollection. Malvina Harlan, "Some Memories," p. 57.   **4.** Ibid.   **5.** Undated printed notice in Harlan Papers, LC.
   6. Louisville *Daily Journal*, March 20, 1863.   **7.** Louisville *Daily Commercial*, July 8, 1863.   **8.** The story of this campaign is most fully and clearly told in Coulter, *Civil War*, pp. 170-78. Coulter is, however, somewhat biased, and his remarks should not always be taken at face value. See Owen, "Pre-Court Career," pp. 45-60, for details of Harlan's activities that I have chosen not to repeat.   **9.** Frankfort *Commonwealth*, May 13, June 24, June 17, Aug. 21, 1863.   **10.** Coulter implies differently: *Civil War*, p. 178. Bramlette defeated Wickliffe about sixty-eight thousand to eighteen thousand, and Harlan won by a similar—perhaps greater— margin. See Thomas D. Clark, *A History of Kentucky* (Lexington: John Bradford, 1954), p. 341.
   11. Clark, *History of Kentucky*, p. 63. Champ Clark (1850-1921) served as a Democratic senator from Missouri, Speaker 1911-19; *DAB* 4: 121-22.   **12.** The politics of McClellan's nomination are discussed in James A. Rawley, *The Politics of Union: Northern Politics during the Civil War* (Hinsdale, Ill.: Dryden Press, 1974).   **13.** "Report of the Meeting of the Conservative Union National Committee at Cincinnati, Thursday, December 3, 1863," John B. Bruner Papers, Filson Club.   **14.** Frankfort *Commonwealth*, April 20, 1864. The committee was also to support Bramlette for vice president. The Republican breakaway was led by Robert J. Breckinridge (the former vice president's uncle) and Benjamin H. Bristow. See Coulter, *Civil War*, pp. 180-81. The majority was led by former governor Robinson, Governor Bramlette, Guthrie, Prentice, and Bruner.   **15.** Lexington *Observer and Reporter*, May 23, 1864.
   16. Coulter, *Civil War*, p. 183.   **17.** Louisville *Daily Journal*, Sept. 24, 1864.   **18.** New Albany *Ledger*, Oct. 4, 1864. See also Harlan Papers, LC; and a reprint of the speech in Matilda

Gresham, *Life of Walter Quintin Gresham* (Chicago: Rand McNally, 1919), 2: 823-25. Oliver P. Morton (1823-77) served as Republican governor of Indiana and, briefly, as senator; *DAB* 13: 262-64.   **19.** Harlan to James B. Beck, Oct. 31, 1877, Harlan Papers, LC.   **20.** Malvina Harlan, "Some Memories," p. 61.

21. Ibid.   **22.** Ibid.   **23.** Ibid., p. 59.   **24.** Ibid., p. 62.   **25.** B.D. Lacy to Harlan, Nov. 28, 1864, Harlan Papers, LC.

26. William Johnson to Harlan, Sept. 20 and 26, 1863, Harlan Papers, LC.   **27.** James Langden to Harlan, Aug. 18, 1864, Harlan Papers, LC.   **28.** D.G. Mitchell to Harlan, Dec. 22, 1864, Harlan Papers, LC.   **29.** *Jones* v. *Commonwealth*, 64 Ky. (1 Bush) 34 (1866).
30. *Commonwealth* v. *Palmer*, 65 Ky. (2 Bush) 570 (1866).

31. *Bowlin* v. *Commonwealth*, 65 Ky. (2 Bush) 5 (1867).   **32.** The Thirteenth Amendment bars slavery and "involuntary servitude." It was sponsored by Lincoln and went into effect at the end of 1865. Peculiarly enough, Maryland, Missouri, West Virginia, and even Tennessee had abolished slavery before that. Of the slave states that remained loyal to the Union, only Delaware and Kentucky waited to be forced by the amendment. In March 1865 the Freedman's Bureau was given general powers of relief and guardianship over the (primarily black) refugees left by the abolition of slavery.   **33.** Ross A. Webb, *Benjamin Helm Bristow, Border State Politician* (Lexington: Univ. Press of Kentucky, 1969), pp. 45-49; Coulter, *Civil War*, pp. 258ff.   **34.** Quoted in Cincinnati *Gazette*, Aug. 2, 1865.   **35.** Perrin, Battle, and Kniffin, *Kentucky*, p. 474.

36. Letter from Harlan to John W. Combs, June 1, 1865, quoted in Lexington *Observer and Reporter*, June 10, 1865.   **37.** Frankfort *Commonwealth*, July 28, 1865.   **38.** Cincinnati *Commonwealth*, July 20, 1866.   **39.** Speech of Harlan at Glasgow, Ky., reported in Cincinnati *Commercial*, July 20, 1866.   **40.** Lexington *Observer and Reporter*, Feb. 24, 1866.

41. These complicated shifts and maneuvers are described in Coulter, *Civil War*, pp. 287-311. See also Owen, "Pre-Court Career," pp. 61-95.   **42.** Cincinnati *Weekly Gazette*, July 13, 1866.   **43.** Coulter, *Civil War*, pp. 304-7. Actually it was difficult to know which side was joining which, since both were obviously weak. Edward H. Hobson was a Union soldier principally known for chasing Morgan's Raiders; *DAB* 9: 96.   **44.** Cincinnati *Gazette*, July 2, 1866.   **45.** Cincinnati *Commercial*, July 20, 1866.

46. Reported later in Louisville *Courier-Journal*, June 3, 1871.   **47.** Louisville *Courier*, July 17, 1866.   **48.** Louisville *Courier*, July 18, 1866.   **49.** Frankfort *Tri-Weekly Yeoman*, July 21, 1866.   **50.** Cincinnati *Gazette*, Dec. 1, 1866. The vote is reported in Coulter, *Civil War*, p. 309.

51. These events are summarized in Coulter, *Civil War*, p. 317. The final vote was Davis 78, Bristow 41. Cf. Owen, "Pre-Court Career," pp. 85-86.   **52.** Coulter, *Civil War*, pp. 317-20.
53. Louisville *Democrat*, March 7, 1867; Frankfort *Semi-Weekly Commonwealth*, March 11, 1867, Bruner Papers, Filson Club.   **54.** Lexington *Observer and Reporter*, March 9, 1867.
55. Harlan to John Bruner, March 11, 1867, Bruner Papers, Filson Club.

56. Ibid.; Frankfort *Semi-Weekly Commonwealth*, March 22, 1867. The platform, among other things, charged that the Democratic "resolutions are mere platitudes intended to mean nothing." See "Address of the Union Democracy to the People of Kentucky", as reported in Louisville *Democrat*, March 9, 1867.   **57.** Perrin, Battle, and Kniffin, *Kentucky*, pp. 478-79.
58. Louisville *Democrat*, April 12, 1867.   **59.** Frankfort *Semi-Weekly Commonwealth*, March 8, 1867; Louisville *Democrat*, April 14, 1867.   **60.** Coulter, *Civil War*, p. 325; for details, see pp. 323ff.

61. Ibid., pp. 27-28, 358-359.   **62.** Louisville *Democrat*, July 24, 1867.   **63.** Perrin, Battle, and Kniffin, *Kentucky*, pp. 478-79; Owen, "Pre-Court Career," pp. 93-94.

6: Kentucky Republican, 1868-1875

1. Even though James remained in Frankfort for the time being, William's remaining affairs were turned over to John's brother-in-law, Dr. James G. Hatchitt, who had become postmaster at Frankfort. See letters from Hatchitt to Harlan, April 17, May 4, and July 28, 1968, Harlan Papers, LC.	**2.** Little other information is available about Newman (1819-73); he edited a treatise, *Pleading and Practice under the Civil Code of Kentucky* (1871). See Levin, ed., *Lawyers and Lawmakers*, pp. 770-71.	**3.** Crab Orchard was popular as a spa in the nineteenth century because of its mineral springs. See Thomas D. Clark, *Kentucky: Land of Contrast* (New York: Harper and Row, 1968), p. 240.	**4.** Harlan to J.G. Hatchitt, July 15, 1873, Harlan Papers, UL.	**5.** When sober, James was apparently an excellent lawyer, and some thought him superior to John. He was selected to be vice chancellor of the Louisville Court of Chancery in the early 1870s.

6. F.L. Cleveland to Harlan, April 16, July 17, 1868, Harlan Papers, LC.	**7.** James Harlan Cleveland (1865-1906) was at Princeton with the Harlan boys, graduating in 1885, and went to the University of Berlin with young John Maynard Harlan in 1885-86. He became a prominent Ohio Democrat. One of his children was named John Marshall Cleveland. See *Appletons' Cyclopedia of American Biography* 9: 99-101.	**8.** After Judge Newman's death in 1873, his widow frequently made application to the firm for financial help.	**9.** Harlan wrote on May 17, 1870, to one client: "We will be greatly obliged if you would have that claim paid. We need the money—otherwise, we should not press it." To S.C. Hawthorne, Harlan Papers, UL. Similarly, he wrote to P.H. Jordan on Aug. 15, 1870: "Send us the fee in the Forsch case—It is pay-day with us. You rich fellows must pay your poor lawyers promptly." Harlan Papers, UL.	**10.** John W. Finnell (1824-?) was a state legislator, briefly editor of the Frankfort *Commonwealth*, Kentucky secretary of state from 1848 to 1852, and state adjutant general from 1861 to 1863. He practiced law in Covington. Finnell remained in Louisville only two years, returning to Covington to resume his law practice in 1872. He was, of course, a prominent Republican. See Levin, ed., *Lawyers and Lawmakers*, pp. 726-27).

11. For details on Bristow (1832-96), see Webb, *Bristow*.	**12.** Willson (1846-1931) became, in his turn, a leading Republican in the state and served as its second Republican governor, from 1907 to 1911; *DAB* 20: 312.	**13.** The site of the office is now occupied by a bank. The house has also disappeared, and its location is part of highway I-65.	**14.** On the general situation within the Presbyterian faith in Kentucky after the war, see Coulter, *Civil War*, pp. 395-98; the case itself is thoroughly though confusingly described in Charles Fairman, *Reconstruction and Reunion, 1864-88*, part 1 (New York: Macmillan, 1971), pp. 901-17.	**15.** *Watson* v. *Avery*, 65 Ky. (2 Bush) 332 (1867).

16. *Jones* v. *Watson*, unreported, U.S. Circuit Court for the District of Kentucky, May 11, 1869.	**17.** Henry Pirtle (1798-1880), was a native of Kentucky who had practiced law in Louisville since 1825; he had been in partnership with James Speed and later with Bland Ballard. He was chancellor of the Louisville chancery court from 1850 to 1856 and taught law at the University of Louisville. He was a strong Republican, and his son James was a close friend of Harlan's. Bland Ballard (1819-79), a strong Unionist, was U.S. district court judge for Kentucky from 1861 until his death. Thomas W. Bullitt (1838-?) was a Centre College graduate and, like Harlan, an active Presbyterian. See Levin, ed., *Lawyers and Lawmakers*, pp. 239-42, 158-59, 236-38.	**18.** Fairman, *Reconstruction*, pp. 909-10.	**19.** Ibid., pp. 910-12.	**20.** *Watson* v. *Jones*, 13 Wall. 679 (1872).

21. In *Presbyterian Church* v. *Hull Church*, 393 U.S. 440 (1969).	**22.** The published correspondence is in the Harlan Papers, LC. Letter to J.B. Huston, Jan. 1, 1868, Harlan Papers, UL. The reference is to the Kentucky court's recent treatment of the Louisville church case.
23. See "Speech of John M. Harlan, before the Committee on Judiciary," Frankfort *Commonwealth*, Feb. 22, 1867.	**24.** Coulter, *Civil War*, p. 398. A letter from W.J. McKnight, dated Sept. 27, 1869, indicated that the litigants were thinking of trying to get this case, too, into federal court by the diversity route; the letter also expresses some doubt about the attitudes of Judge Ballard. Harlan Papers, LC. In a letter to A. Beatty on June 4, 1873, Harlan called the final decision "a great victory for the College, and in connection with the decree rendered here in the Federal Court renders the title to the property perfectly secure." Harlan Papers, UL.
25. See letters from John F. Caldwell of Campbellsville, Nov. 22, 1870; and R.M. Bradley of Lancaster, March 22, 1871. Harlan Papers, LC.

26. A.H. Adams to Bristow, March 21, 1873, Bristow Papers, LC.   27. Letter from A.H. Clark of Hopkinsville, Aug. 6, 1870, Harlan Papers, LC.   28. Harlan was also a lawyer in another Negro voting case, in an action to oust the municipal officials of Lexington because of the exclusion of blacks from the polls: see brief of John M. Harlan, *Watson* v. *Bradshaw,* in Kentucky Court of Appeals, 1874. This brief is located in the library of the U.S. Supreme Court.   29. Harlan to Bristow, Sept. 16, 1871, Bristow Papers, LC.   30. Wharton to Bristow, Sept. 24, 1871, Bristow Papers, LC. Bristow was solicitor general at the time, or he would probably have been asked instead of Harlan.

31. Harlan to Bristow, Sept. 27, 1871, Bristow Papers, LC.   32. Harlan to Bristow, Sept. 29, 1871, Bristow Papers, LC.   33. Telegram, Attorney General George H. Williams to Harlan, Feb. 11, 1873, Harlan Papers, LC.   34. Box 36, clipping file, Harlan Papers, LC. 35. Harlan to Bristow, Nov. 16, 1870, Bristow Papers, LC.

36. Frankfort *Weekly Commonwealth,* March 20, 1868. Reports of his 1868 campaign activities are in the same paper, July 24, Oct. 2 and 23, 1868.   37. Louisville *Courier Journal,* July 6, 1875.   38. He admits this in his letter to James B. Beck, Oct. 31, 1877, Harlan Papers, LC.   39. Harlan conducted extensive correspondence on behalf of the *Commercial,* only some of which still exists in the Harlan Papers, LC and UL.   40. For instance, he was invited by his old wartime subordinate, William H. Hays, to speak at Columbia, Kentucky, in late Oct., 1868, in support of Hays's candidacy (probably for Congress). Hays to Harlan, Oct. 17, 1868, Harlan Papers, LC.

41. Harlan to Bristow, Nov. 16, 1870, Bristow Papers, LC.   42. Recollections, pp. 15-16, 17-19.   43. Harlan to John G. Cozine, May 25, 1875, Harlan Papers, UL. Theodore C. Tracie to Harlan, June 3, 1878; U.S. Commissioner of Pensions J.H. Baker to Harlan, Jan. 30, 1872; Harlan to Hiram S. Powell, Nov. 28, 1871; N.R. Black to Harlan, Dec. 5, 1871; Harlan to Thomas H. Fox, March 6, 1873 (refusing to intercede in a contest between two Republicans); W.H. Polk to Harlan, Aug. 17, 1871; E.P. Vimont to Harlan, Oct. 16, 1871; Harlan to Stanley Matthews, May 28, 1877; E. Case and H.C. Callett to Harlan, Jan. 8, 1872; Alf Allen to Harlan, Dec. 29, 1871; Harlan Papers, LC.   44. Harlan, for instance, wrote a long letter urging the appointment of U.S. district court judge Ballard to a vacancy in the circuit judgeship: Harlan to W.W. Belknap (secretary of war), Dec. 15, 1869, Filson Club. See also telegram from Harlan and others to President Grant on another appointment, Dec. 13, 1874, Harlan Papers, UL.   45. Tracie to Harlan, June 3, 1878, Harlan Papers, LC.

46. Harlan to Finnell, July 19, 1873, Harlan Papers, UL.   47. Harlan to Matthews, May 28, 1877, Hayes Papers, Hayes Presidential Center.   48. Harlan to W.R. Holloway, Oct. 4, 1876, Harlan Papers, UL.   49. Richard Smith to Rutherford B. Hayes, June 6, 1877, Hayes Papers, Hayes Presidential Center.   50. David C. Farrelly, "A Sketch of John Marshall Harlan's Pre-Court Career," *Vanderbilt Law Review* 10 (1956-57): 222.

51. John Marshall Harlan II to Morris L. Ernst, Dec. 14, 1955, Harlan Papers, LC. 52. The quotations are taken from a summary of Harlan's campaign statements, including both his 1871 and 1875 campaigns, prepared by the Louisville *Commercial,* Nov. 1, 1877, to aid in the battle for his confirmation as Supreme Court justice. A copy appears in the Harlan Papers, LC.   53. Coulter, *Civil War,* pp. 434-37.   54. Louisville *Commercial,* May 18 and 24, 1871.   55. Louisville *Courier-Journal,* May 28 and 31, 1871.

56. J.R. Duncan to Editor, Louisville *Commercial,* June 7, 1871. The letter was turned over to Harlan and never published. It is now in the Harlan Papers, LC. On Leslie, see *Biographical Encyclopedia of Kentucky* (Cincinnati: J.M. Armstrong & Co., 1878), pp. 660-61.   57. Louisville *Commercial,* July 29, 1871; Cincinnati *Daily Gazette,* May 24, 1871.   58. Louisville *Commercial,* July 29, 1871; Louisville *Courier-Journal,* May 31, 1871.   59. Louisville *Commercial,* June 3, 1871.   60. Rumsey Wing to Harlan, Oct. 6, 1871, Harlan Papers, LC.

61. D.R. Carr to Harlan, Sept. 9, 1871, Harlan Papers, LC.   62. Alan F. Westin, "Ride-in!" *American Heritage* 13 (August 1962): 57.   63. Coulter, *Civil War,* p. 437.   64. Harlan to J.B. Bruner, Aug. 26, 1871, Bruner Papers, Filson Club.   65. D.O. Farrand, chairman of Wayne County Republican Committee, to Harlan, Oct. 12, 1872; Charles Kirtley to Harlan, Sept. 30 and Oct. 9, 1872; E. Case to Harlan, Sept. 29, 1872. Harlan Papers, LC.

66. Collins, *History of Kentucky*, 1: 221. But Harlan's close friend Walter Evans, who was in the legislature at the time, wrote, "We are about to vote for the Hon. R. Tarvin Baker for Senator tomorrow"; Evans to Harlan, Jan. 20, 1872, Harlan Papers, LC.   67. See letters from Harlan to H.V. Boynton, July 23, 1873; W.A. Merriweather, July 11, 1873; S.L. Woodford, July 3, 1873; E.H. Hobson, June 30, 1873; Harlan Papers, UL. John T. Croxton to Harlan, Oct. 29, 1871, Harlan Papers, LC.   68. Harlan to "Ewing" (the paper's business manager), July 11, 1873, regarding "this reform movement," Harlan Papers, UL; Harlan to J.B. Bruner, Aug. 26, 1871, Bruner Papers, Filson Club.   69. Evans to Harlan, June 19, July 7, 1873, Harlan Papers, LC.   70. Letter to his old friend Thomas T. Crittenden, who had just been elected to Congress from Missouri as a Democrat, July 3, 1873, Harlan Papers, UL.

71. David Davis to Harlan, undated, Harlan Papers, UL.   72. Louisville *Courier-Journal*, May 13, 1875; Harlan to A.S. Poston, May 17, 1875, Harlan Papers, UL.   73. D.C. Wintersmith to Harlan, May 22, 1871, Harlan Papers, LC; Harlan to Wintersmith, May 25, 1871, Harlan Papers, UL.   74. On McCreary, see *Biographical Encyclopedia of Kentucky*, pp. 45-46.   75. Washington *Post*, Feb. 15, 1916. In the same article McCreary says that he spoke to President Hayes in support of Harlan's Supreme Court nomination.

76. Louisville *Courier-Journal*, April 26, 1903.   77. Cincinnati *Enquirer*, Nov. 14, 1908, typed copy with marginal notes apparently in Harlan's handwriting, Harlan Papers, UL. 78. Ibid.   79. See *American Annual Cyclopedia and Register of Important Events* (New York: D. Appleton and Son, 1876), 15 (1875): 417.   80. John D. White to Harlan, June 2, 1875, Harlan Papers, UL.

81. Harlan to A.G. Wickoff, chairman of the Ohio Republican State Committee, Aug. 18, 1875, Harlan Papers, UL.

7: Kingmaker, 1876

1. Their only contacts after 1877 seem to have been the formal occasions when Bristow argued cases before the Supreme Court.   2. Harlan to Bristow, Oct. 11, 1871, Bristow Papers, LC.   3. Bristow to Grant, Dec. 22, 1873, as cited in Webb, *Bristow*, pp. 129-31. 4. These events are recounted from Bristow's point of view in Webb, *Bristow*, pp. 113-32. 5. Davis to Bristow, June 15, 1874, Bristow Papers, LC.

6. For the Whiskey Ring events, see Webb, *Bristow*, pp. 133-212; William B. Hesseltine, *Ulysses S. Grant, Politician* (New York: Dodd, Mead, 1935), pp. 375-88.   7. Jewell to Harlan, Dec. 26, 1875(?), Harlan Papers, LC.   8. Harlan to Bristow, Feb. 17, 1875, Hayes Papers, Hayes Presidential Center.   9. Harlan to Bristow, May 11, 1875, Bristow Papers, LC. 10. Harlan to Bristow, May 19, 1875, Harlan Papers, UL.

11. Harlan to J.H. Reno, Dec. 17, 1875, Harlan Papers, UL.   12. Bristow to Harlan, Jan. 22, 1876, Bristow Papers, LC.   13. Bristow to E.A. Starling, Jan. 27, 1876, Bristow Papers, LC.   14. Harlan to Bristow, Jan. 24, 1876, Bristow Papers, LC.   15. Harlan's papers in the Library of Congress contain replies sent from many states and from all over Kentucky.

16. Gresham, *Life* 2: 456-57; cf. Harlan to Gresham, May 25, 1876, Gresham Papers, LC.   17. Boynton to Harlan, Jan. 30, 1876, Harlan Papers, LC.   18. Boynton to Harlan, March 15, 1876, Harlan Papers, LC. Medill was editor of the Chicago *Tribune*, Smith of the Cincinnati *Daily Gazette*, and Halstead of the Cincinnati *Commercial*. Reed was an editorial writer for the Cincinnati *Gazette*.   19. Reported in Lodge journal, Feb. 25 and 29, 1876, Lodge Papers, Massachusetts Historical Society.   20. Bluford Wilson to Harlan, May 23, June 6, 1876, Harlan Papers, LC.

21. Bristow to Harlan, April 17, 1876, Bristow Papers, LC.   22. On Hayes as a "passive runner," see Harry Barnard, *Rutherford B. Hayes and His America* (Indianapolis: Bobbs-Merrill, 1952), pp. 277-83.   23. A vivid account of the convention is given in a long letter from a Cincinnati observer, William C. Cochran, to his mother, dated June 18, 1876, Hayes Papers, Hayes Presidential Center.   24. This story, which appears to be reliable, is told in Barnard,

Hayes, pp. 284-86. William Henry Smith also played a role in Harlan's Supreme Court appointment. He was an active Republican leader and an early Hayes supporter—in Hayes's first campaign for governor of Ohio—who later became the general agent for Associated Press in Chicago. None of his newspaper responsibilities prevented him from being active in politics—a fact that was true of many journalists in those days, including Boynton. **25.** Cochran letter, Hayes Papers, Hayes Presidential Center.

26. Barnard, *Hayes*, p. 290.   **27.** Cochran letter, Hayes Papers, Hayes Presidential Center.   **28.** Ibid.   **29.** Telegram, Bristow to Harlan, June 16, 1876, Harlan Papers, LC. **30.** New York *Times*, June 17, 1876.

31. Bristow to Harlan, June 20, 1876, Bristow Papers, LC.   **32.** Harlan to Bristow, June 19, 1876, Bristow Papers, LC.   **33.** Barnard, *Hayes*, pp. 288-94.   **34.** This is Webb's analysis; see Webb, *Bristow*, pp. 242-50.   **35.** Gresham, *Life* 2: 459. Boynton to Bristow, June 16, 1876; Gresham to Bristow, June 16, 1876; Bristow Papers, LC.

36. See, for instance, *Harper's Weekly*, July 8, 1876.   **37.** Webb, *Bristow*, pp. 253-60.

8: The Fruits of Success, 1877

1. After Greeley's nomination in 1872 by the Liberal Republicans, the Democrats also nominated him. Despite the defection, Grant's popularity remained strong enough, combined with the still lively memories of the war, to carry the Republicans to an easy victory. See Earle D. Ross, *The Liberal Republican Movement* (Seattle: Univ. of Washington Press, 1970); and also Wilbur J. Granberg, *Spread the Truth: The Life of Horace Greeley* (New York: Dutton, 1959). **2.** See John Bigelow, *The Life of Samuel J. Tilden*, 2 vols. (New York: Harper and Brothers, 1895).   **3.** Letter dated July 8, 1876, reprinted in Charles Richard Williams, *The Life of Rutherford Birchard Hayes* (Columbus: Ohio State Archaeological and Historical Society, 1928), 1: 460-62.   **4.** To Governor Edward F. Noyes of Ohio, July 14, 1876, Harlan Papers, UL. **5.** Since Harlan did not know Hayes, he apparently sent the letter through a mutual friend, W.D. Bickham. Harlan to Hayes, June 21, 1876, Hayes Papers, Hayes Presidential Center.

6. Hayes to W.D. Bickham, June 25, 1876, Hayes Papers, Hayes Presidential Center. **7.** Ibid.   **8.** Harlan to Marshall Jewell, July 21, 1876, Harlan Papers, UL. Jewell had just been fired from his position as postmaster general. He was a former governor of Connecticut (1869-73) and ambassador to Russia. He was a strong Bristow supporter. *DAB* 10: 65. **9.** Harlan to Jewell, July 17, 1876, Harlan Papers, UL. Also see a letter in similar terms to Carl Schurz, July 30, 1876, Harlan Papers, UL.   **10.** Harlan to W.M. Randolph of Memphis, Tenn., Sept. 22, 1876, Harlan Papers, UL.

UF92 11. "Speech of Gen. Harlan," Sept. 18, 1876, Salem, Ind., handwritten manuscript, Harlan Papers, UL. Apparently Harlan gave pretty much the same speech throughout the campaign: a shorter version, but verbatim in parts, also in his own handwriting, is marked "Indiana, October, 1876," Harlan Papers, UL.   **12.** James D. Williams (1808-80). See *Biographical Directory of the Governors of the United States* (Westport, Conn.: Meckler Books, 1978), 1: 407.   **13.** J.H. Reno to Harlan, Sept. 28, 1876. Harlan Papers, LC.   **14.** Telegram, Harlan to Grant, Dec. 12, 1876, Harlan Papers, UL.   **15.** Harlan to Boynton, July 29, 1876, Harlan Papers, UL. Wharton (1839-87) had fought in the Tenth Kentucky under Harlan and served as an assistant to Bristow when he was U.S. attorney in Louisville; *NCAB* 5: 288.

16. Harlan to George W. Gallup, Aug. 1, 1876, Harlan Papers, UL.   **17.** Harlan to W.T. Sherman, Aug. 3, 1876, Harlan Papers, UL. See also a similar but much more detailed letter to Representative John D. White (Kentucky's only Republican congressman), July 28, 1876, Harlan Papers, UL.   **18.** The best treatments are C. Vann Woodward, *Reunion and Reaction* (Boston: Little, Brown, 1966); and Kenneth M. Stampp, *The Era of Reconstruction* (New York: Knopf, 1965).   **19.** Boynton to Bristow, Oct. 15, 1876, Boynton Papers, Hayes Presidential Center.   **20.** Boynton to Bristow, Nov. 14, 1876, Boynton Papers, Hayes Presidential Center. **21.** Webb, *Bristow*, p. 264.   **22.** Biographical Note, p. 10. External evidence indicates

that things had not gone quite that far. In a letter of March 5, 1877, W.C. Goodloe wrote Harlan from Washington that the president had changed his mind. So if John went to Washington at all, he must have been forewarned. Goodloe to Harlan, March 5, 1877, Harlan Papers, LC. Still another factor may have been a vague feeling, as reported by one correspondent, that "some good men think him [Harlan] 'shallow,' and criticise him severely for 'want of fidelity to principle' and for grave 'inconsistency.' " W.D. Bickham to Hayes, Feb. 14, 1877, Hayes Papers, Hayes Presidential Center.   **23.** Webb, *Bristow,* p. 265; Barnard, *Hayes,* p. 416.
24. Gresham, *Life* 2: 456-57.   **25.** Oliver P. Morton to Hayes, March 1877, Hayes Papers, Hayes Presidential Center.

26. Barnard, *Hayes,* pp. 416-17. Hayes eventually demanded Thompson's resignation when he accepted the chairmanship of the American Committee for the Panama Canal Company at twenty-five thousand dollars a year; *NCAB* 3: 202. Barnard was unfair to Devens, who had been a good general and who "was recognized as one of the strongest members of a strong cabinet"; *DAB* 5: 260-62.   **27.** Webb, *Bristow,* p. 266. On Carl Schurz, see *DAB* 16: 466-70.   **28.** S.D. Brown to Harlan, March 17, 1877, Harlan Papers, LC.   **29.** This episode is described in some detail in Charles Richard Williams, *Diary and Letters of Rutherford B. Hayes* (Columbus: Ohio State Archeological and Historical Society, 1924), 2: 33ff. For Nicholls, see *DAB* 13: 487-88.   **30.** Charles B. Lawrence (1820-83) was justice of the Illinois Supreme Court from 1865 to 1870, chief justice 1867-70; *NCAB* 5: 437. Joseph R. Hawley (1826-1905) was an "original" Republican, an editor, and a Union soldier. He served as governor of Connecticut, 1866-67; congressman, 1872-74, 1879-81; and senator, 1881-1905; *DAB* 8: 421-22. John C. Brown (1827-89), a Tennessee Confederate soldier, served in the state legislature, 1869-70, and as Democratic governor, 1870-74; *DAB* 3: 135-36. Wayne MacVeagh (1833-1917) was a Pennsylvania lawyer and Union soldier. He was the son-in-law of Simon Cameron, Republican boss of Pennsylvania, although he opposed Cameron politically. MacVeagh served as attorney general under Garfield. He was a lifelong reformer; *DAB* 12: 170-71.

31. Bristow to Dennison, telegram and letter, March 15, 1877, Bristow Papers, LC. For Dennison, a former Ohio governor, see *DAB* 5: 241-42.   **32.** Boynton to Bristow, March 31, 1877, Boynton Papers, Hayes Presidential Center.   **33.** Boynton to Bristow, April 8, 1877, Boynton Papers, Hayes Presidential Center.   **34.** Boynton to Bristow, April 3, 1877, Boynton Papers, Hayes Presidential Center.   **35.** Ibid.

36. Boynton to Bristow, April 8, 1877, Boynton Papers, Hayes Presidential Center.
37. Harlan to Bristow, April 13, 1877, Bristow Papers, LC. Also April 9, 1877, Bristow Papers, Hayes Presidential Center.   **38.** Boynton to Bristow, April 15, 1877, Boynton Papers, Hayes Presidential Center. Eli H. Murray had been U.S. marshal for Kentucky until Grant dismissed him; he was a close friend of Harlan's. Bluford Wilson was a prominent Illinois Republican who had been Bristow's solicitor of the Treasury; see *NCAB* 33: 363-64.   **39.** Citations of the diary refer to it as it is reprinted in David G. Farrelly, "John M. Harlan's One-Day Diary," *Filson Club History Quarterly* 24 (1950): 158.   **40.** Ibid. Grammatical errors in the text are given verbatim; undoubtedly Harlan, an excellent grammarian, wrote in the heat of passion and did not go back to correct his mistakes.

41. See letter, Boynton to Bristow, June 16, 1877, in which Boynton accuses Harlan of being behind public attacks on Bristow. Boynton to Bristow, Aug. 15, 1877, reports that Boynton is "quite prepared to hear that [Harlan] is hard at work for the Judgeship." Also see letters dated Sept. 9 and 29, October 3, 10, 21, and 28, Nov. 4, 1877. All in Boynton Papers, Hayes Presidential Center.   **42.** Webb, *Bristow,* pp. 270ff.   **43.** Miller to William Pitt Ballinger, May 6, 1877, quoted in Charles Fairman, *Mr. Justice Miller and the Supreme Court* (Cambridge, Mass.: Harvard University Press, 1939), p. 358.   **44.** MacVeagh to Harlan, May 12, 1877, Harlan Papers, UL.   **45.** Augustus E. Willson to Richard D. Harlan, April 11, 1920, Harlan Papers, LC.

46. Farrelly, "One-Day Diary," p. 358.   **47.** Harlan to Bristow, April 9, 1877, Hayes Papers, Hayes Presidential Center.   **48.** Harlan to Bristow, April 13, 1877, Hayes Papers, Hayes Presidential Center.   **49.** Miller to Ballinger, May 6, 1877, cited in Fairman, *Mr. Justice Miller,* p. 358.   **50.** Williams, *Diary,* 3: 419.

51. Farrelly, "One-Day Diary." Edward F. Noyes, a former governor of Ohio, was close to Hayes, who appointed him minister to France; *DAB* 13: 587.   **52.** Webb, *Bristow*, p. 271. Simon Cameron (1799-1889) was a sometime senator and secretary of war, long-time Republican boss of Pennsylvania, and a defender and practitioner of the spoils system; *DAB* 3: 437-39.   **53.** MacVeagh to Hayes, Aug. 21, 1877, Hayes Papers, Hayes Presidential Center.

9: Political Reward, 1877

1. Army pay was suspended for the first quarter of the new fiscal year in order to avoid an earlier (hot summer) session. See Williams, *Diary* 2: 81. On March 18 Justice Miller wrote to a friend that the vacancy would not be filled "until the Senate is in session again." Miller to William Pitt Ballinger, cited in Fairman, *Mr. Justice Miller*, p. 352. But Miller at that time had no idea that it would be October before the Senate reconvened.   **2.** Miller to Ballinger, cited in Fairman, *Mr. Justice Miller*, p. 352. Miller consistently misspelled the name "Woods."
3. William B. Woods (1824-87) had been an Ohio legislator. He settled in Alabama after the war and, as a Republican, was appointed U.S. circuit court judge in 1869; see *DAB* 20: 505-6. Henry Clay Caldwell (1832-1915), born in Maine, served in the Iowa legislature but was in 1864 appointed by Lincoln as U.S. district court judge for Arkansas, serving in that capacity until 1890, when he was made a circuit court judge. He retired in 1903; see *DAB* 3: 408.   **4.** Quoted in John P. Frank, "The Appointment of Supreme Court Justices: Prestige, Principles and Politics," *Wisconsin Law Review* 188 (1941): 205.   **5.** Miller to Ballinger, May 6, 1877, in Fairman, *Mr. Justice Miller*, p. 358.
6. Thomas Drummond (1809-90) was a U.S. district court judge in Illinois from 1850 to 1869; Grant promoted him to the circuit court in 1869, a post he occupied until 1884. *NCAB* 20: 111-12.   **7.** Miller to Ballinger, May 6, 1877, in Fairman, *Mr. Justice Miller*, p. 358.   **8.** The politics of the appointment—especially as regards Harlan—are surveyed ably in Ellwood W. Lewis, "Document: The Appointment of Mr. Justice Harlan," *Indiana Law Journal* 29 (1953): 46.   **9.** MacVeagh to Hayes, Aug. 21, 1877, Hayes Papers, Hayes Presidential Center.
10. Charles W. Fairbanks to an unknown recipient merely called "My dear Uncle," Sept. 25, 1877, Hayes Papers, Hayes Presidential Center.
11. Hayes to Smith, Sept. 29, 1877, Hayes Papers, Hayes Presidential Center.
12. Smith to Hayes, Oct. 3, 1877, Hayes Papers, Hayes Presidential Center.   **13.** Smith to Hayes, Oct. 10, 1877, Hayes Papers, Hayes Presidential Center.   **14.** C.B. Lawrence to Hayes, Aug. 31, 1877, Hayes Papers, Hayes Presidential Center.   **15.** Miller to Ballinger, Nov. 21, 1877, quoted in Fairman, *Mr. Justice Miller*, p. 369.
16. Hayes called him "an eager candidate." Williams, *Diary*, p. 471. Timothy O. Howe (1816-83) was a justice of the Wisconsin Supreme Court; Republican senator, 1861-78; and postmaster general in Arthur's cabinet, 1881-83. *DAB* 9: 297-98.   **17.** Fuller to Hannibal Hamlin, Oct. 29, 1877, Fuller Papers, Chicago Historical Society (hereafter CHS). Hamlin was a senator from Maine and had been vice president during Lincoln's first term.   **18.** George F. Edmunds (1828-1919) served in the Senate from 1866 to 1891. He was regarded as "the ablest constitutional lawyer in Congress" but was also noted for his "lack of amiability and contentious nature." *DAB* 6: 24-27. Zachariah Chandler (1813-79) was Republican boss of Michigan; senator, 1857-75; and secretary of the Interior under Grant, 1875-77. *DAB* 3: 618.
19. Speed to Edmunds, Nov. 10, 1877, quoted in Frank, "Appointment," pp. 208-9.
20. Roscoe Conkling (1829-88), a competitor for the presidential nomination in 1876, was senator from New York from 1867 to 1881 and one of the most powerful figures in that body. See David M. Jordan, *Roscoe Conkling of New York* (Ithaca, N.Y.: Cornell Univ. Press, 1971).
21. Miller to Ballinger, Oct. 28, 1977, quoted in Fairman, *Mr. Justice Miller*, p. 366.
22. Willson to Richard D. Harlan, April 11, 1930, Harlan Papers, LC.   **23.** Harlan to Hayes, Oct. 31, 1877, Hayes Papers, Hayes Presidential Center.   **24.** Harlan to Beck, Oct. 31, 1877, Filson Club.   **25.** Crittenden to Harlan, Nov. 21 and 27, 1877; Crittenden to his brother (otherwise unidentified), Nov. 10, 1877; Harlan Papers, UL. Senator Daniel W. Voorhees

(1827-97) was an influential Democratic senator from Indiana from 1877 to 1897; *DAB* 19: 291. John G. Carlisle (1835-1910) served in the House from Kentucky from 1877 to 1890 and was Speaker for three terms. He was regarded as a "great" Speaker. He was senator, 1890-93, and secretary of the Treasury under Cleveland, 1893-97; *DAB* 3: 494-96. Stanley Matthews (1824-89), a Republican senator from Ohio, 1877-79, was nominated for the Supreme Court by Hayes in 1880 but failed of confirmation. Nominated again by Garfield, he served until his death in 1889; *DAB* 12: 418-20. Samuel B. Maxey (1825-95) was a Confederate general and senator from Texas, 1875-87; *DAB* 12: 435-36.

26. Harlan to Beck, Oct. 31, 1877, Filson Club.   **27.** Boynton to Bristow, Dec. 10, 1877, Boynton Papers, Hayes Presidential Center. One W.H. Painter used Boynton's information for a broadside attack on Harlan's character. He wrote: "I think a man who is by his own confession a *particeps criminis* to the late debauchery & revolution at New Orleans will be a dishonor to the bench." Painter to Edmunds, Oct. 4, 1877, quoted in Lewis, "Document," n. 79.   **28.** John Ledwick to Kirkwood, Nov. 17, 1877, quoted in Lewis, "Document," p. 70. Samuel J. Kirkwood (1813-94) was governor of Iowa and Republican senator, 1877-81; he also served as secretary of the Interior under Garfield. *DAB* 4: 436-37.   **29.** William Brown to Edmunds, Nov. 19, 1877, quoted in Lewis, "Document," n. 88.   **30.** W.F. Bullock to Hayes, Sept. 10, 1877, Hayes Papers, Hayes Presidential Center.

31. Letter to Hayes signed by Chief Judge W. Lindsay, Will S. Pryor, J.M. Elliott, and M.H. Cofer, Sept. 7, 1877, Hayes Papers, Hayes Presidential Center.   **32.** Lewis N. Dembitz to Hayes, Sept. 26, 1877, Hayes Papers, Hayes Presidential Center.   **33.** E.B. Martindale of Indianapolis to Hayes, Sept. 25, 1877, Hayes Papers, Hayes Presidential Center.   **34.** Beck to Harlan, probably Nov. 19, 1877, Harlan Papers, UL.   **35.** As cited in Lewis, "Appointment"; diligent search has failed to uncover a more adequate official source. All of the dates given in the text after Nov. 19 are uncertain, since no official record exists of when the Senate did what.

36. This is the date that seems to be indicated in Beck's letter to Harlan, Nov. 30, 1877, Harlan Papers, UL.   **37.** Ibid.   **38.** Malvina Harlan, "Some Memories," p. 79.

10: Associate Justice, 1877-1887

1. Malvina Harlan, "Some Memories," p. 80. Mallie says, in fact, that Mrs. Hayes collected her in her carriage and sat beside her at the ceremony.   **2.** Harlan to Hayes, Oct. 19, 1877, Hayes Papers, Hayes Presidential Center.   **3.** Finnell to Harlan, Dec. 4, 1877, Harlan Papers, UL.   **4.** Malvina Harlan, "Some Memories," p. 83.   **5.** Ibid.

6. 17 Statutes at Large of the USA, 485 (1873); 32 U.S. Statutes at Large, 825 (1903).   **7.** Finnell to Harlan, Dec. 30, 1877, Harlan Papers, UL.   **8.** Finnell to Harlan, Dec. 14, 1877, Harlan Papers, LC.   **9.** Harry James Brown and Frederick D. Williams, eds., *The Diary of James A. Garfield* (East Lansing: Michigan State Univ. Press, 1973), 3: 552, Dec. 12, 1877.   **10.** Harlan to Waite, July 31, 1888, Waite Papers, LC.

11. Two good biographies of Waite exist: C. Peter Magrath's excellent work, *Morrison R. Waite: The Triumph of Character* (New York: Macmillan, 1963); and Bruce R. Trimble, *Chief Justice Waite: Defender of the Public Interest* (Princeton: Princeton Univ. Press, 1938).   **12.** Miller to Ballinger, Dec. 5, 1875, quoted in Fairman, *Mr. Justice Miller*, p. 373.   **13.** Magrath, *Waite*, p. 321.   **14.** The best summary of Clifford's life and career was written by William Gillette, in Leon Friedman and Fred L. Israel, eds., *The Justices of the United States Supreme Court, 1789-1969* (New York: Chelsea House, 1969), pp. 963-75.   **15.** There is no biography of Swayne. The sketch above is drawn from the William Gillette essay in Friedman and Israel, eds., *Justices*, pp. 989-99.

16. See Fairman, *Mr. Justice Miller*.   **17.** For Field, see principally Carl Brent Swisher, *Stephen J. Field, Craftsman of the Law* (Washington, D.C.: Brookings Institution, 1930); and Robert McCloskey's article in Friedman and Israel, eds., *Justices*, pp. 1069-89.   **18.** There is no biography of Strong. See Stanley I. Kutler's article in Friedman and Israel, eds., *Justices*, pp.

1153-61.　**19.** Bradley deserves a full biography; unfortunately none exists. The best brief treatment is Friedman's article in Friedman and Israel, eds., *Justices*, pp. 1181-200.　**20.** See Stanley I. Kutler in Friedman and Israel, eds., *Justices*, pp. 1221-29.

21. These figures are approximate and were gleaned from the *United States Reports*, vols. 118-22.　**22.** The jurisdictional problems and consequent overload of the dockets of the federal courts are surveyed (in lawyer's language) in Felix Frankfurter and James M. Landis, *The Business of the Supreme Court* (New York: Macmillan, 1928), pp. 56-102.　**23.** The writ of error was the predecessor to the present writ of certiorari, but whereas the Court has almost complete discretion over the issuance of certiorari, it had little choice whether or not to take cases in error.　**24.** Waite to Harlan, April 20, 1878, Waite Papers, LC.　**25.** Harlan to Waite, Dec. 15, 1877; Harlan to Waite, Dec. 22, 1877. Waite Papers, LC.

26. Waite to his wife, May 5, 1878, Waite Papers, LC.　**27.** He wrote: "Bradley has not read an opinion (even one) since you were taken ill. Judge Field hasn't done better." Miller to Waite, Jan. 25, 1885, Waite Papers, LC.　**28.** The best description of Woods's Supreme Court career is that of Louis Filler in Friedman and Israel, eds., *Justices*, pp. 1327-36.　**29.** Matthews deserves greater recognition than he has received. There is a good summary of his life by Louis Filler in Friedman and Israel, eds., *Justices*, pp. 1351-61.　**30.** Harlan to Gray, April 18, 1881; Harlan to Garfield, March 15, 1881; Harlan Papers, LC. Like Matthews and Bradley, Gray still lacks any adequate biographical treatment; see Louis Filler in Friedman and Israel, eds., *Justices*, pp. 1379-89.

31. See Arnold M. Paul's treatment in Friedman and Israel, eds., *Justices*, pp. 1401-14; also the more sympathetic anonymous article, "Samuel Blatchford; 'Workhorse' of the Court," *Supreme Court Historical Society Quarterly* 4 (Summer 1982): 4-5, 8.　**32.** All figures are calculated from the *United States Reports* for the indicated sessions.　**33.** Harlan to Waite, June 17, 1885, Waite Papers, LC.　**34.** Harlan to Waite, Sept. 8, 1884, Waite Papers, LC. **35.** James Harlan to Harlan, May 20, 1884, Harlan Papers, UL.

36. Harlan to Bullitt, Oct. 17, 1880, Harlan Papers, UL.　**37.** Harlan to Bullitt, Oct. 27, 1880, Harlan Papers, UL.　**38.** Malvina Harlan, "Some Memories," pp. 96, 105.　**39.** Ibid., p. 105.　**40.** Richard D. Harlan to President William Howard Taft, Jan. 23, 1909, Taft Papers, LC.

41. Shackleford Miller to Augustus Willson, March 30, 1888; Willson to Harlan, same date. Harlan Papers, LC.　**42.** James S. Harlan to Harlan, Jan. 7, no year given, Harlan Papers, LC.　**43.** Harlan to Waite, March 31, April 3, 5, 14, May 8, 10, 24, 1882, Waite Papers, LC.　**44.** Harlan to Malvina Harlan, June 8, 1882, Harlan Papers, LC.　**45.** Letters and receipts, F.L. Ballard to Harlan, Aug. 1, 1878; March 27, April 18, 1879. Harlan Papers, UL.

46. John M. Butler to Harlan, June 2, 1880, Harlan Papers, UL. Butler was Mallie's cousin and a prominent Indianapolis attorney who was close to the Harlans for many years. **47.** James S. Harlan to Harlan, Dec. 14, 1879, Harlan Papers, UL.　**48.** James Harlan to Harlan, undated, Harlan Papers, UL.　**49.** Harlan to James S. Harlan, July 20, 1881, Harlan Papers, UL.　**50.** Barrett McGurn, "Law Clerks—A Professional Elite," *Yearbook* (Supreme Court Historical Society, 1980), pp. 98, 99-100. Provision for "stenographic clerks," to be paid not more than $1,600, was made by Congress soon after Attorney General Augustus H. Garland made the proposal in 1885.

51. Edith Harlan to former President R.B. Hayes, July 9, 1881, Hayes Papers, Hayes Presidential Center.　**52.** Strong to Harlan, Sept. 6, 1880, Harlan Papers, UL.　**53.** Harlan to Waite, Nov. 9 and 10, 1882, Waite Papers, LC.　**54.** Malvina Harlan, "Some Memories," p. 102.　**55.** Ibid., p. 104.

56. James began scratching out the "Willson" from the firm's letterhead in May 1882. James Harlan to Harlan, May 22, 1882, Harlan Papers, UL.　**57.** Willson to Harlan, Sept. 12, 1880, Harlan Papers, UL. Willson says that "the Judge" got drunk on the train on his way back to Louisville from Block Island. James also hospitalized himself in St. Louis in 1883, but the "cure" proved to be only temporary; James Harlan to Harlan, Oct. 30, 1883, Harlan Papers, UL.　**58.** Harlan to Henry Harlan, July 10, 1889, Harlan Papers, UL.　**59.** Lillie Cleveland to Harlan, Jan. 26, 1880. See also the letter from Francis Cleveland to Harlan, March 12, 1880, accusing his sister-in-law of deliberately prejudicing Lillie against him. This estrangement had long-term effects: after Francis's death, James Harlan accused young Harlan Cleveland of callousness and completely ignoring his sister; James Harlan to Harlan, Sept. 23, 1887. All letters in Harlan Papers, UL.   60. See esp. J.G. Hatchitt to Malvina Harlan, March 7, 1891, Harlan Papers, LC.

61. James Harlan to Harlan, Aug. 26, 1887, Harlan Papers, UL.   62. Malvina Harlan, "Some Memories," p. 108.   63. Harlan to W.A. Maury, June 18, 1893, Harlan Papers, UL.
64. Harlan to James S. Harlan, Sept. 15, 1880, Harlan Papers, UL.   65. For instance, he became embroiled in a fight to save the position of his friend Eli Murray as governor of Utah Territory and actively promoted the career of Willson.

66. There is a useful discussion of some of the seventh circuit court's work in Gresham, Life, vol. 2.   67. Harlan to Walter Q. Gresham, March 20, 1887, Gresham Papers, LC.
68. In re Coy, 31 Fed. Rep. 794 and 127 U.S. 731 (1888).   69. The episode is discussed briefly in Allan Nevins, Grover Cleveland, a Study in Courage (New York: Dodd, Mead, 1944), p. 438. A much fuller discussion, although apparently biased, can be found in Gresham, Life, 2: chap. 38.   70. Harlan to Woods, Dec. 24, 1888, Harlan Papers, LC.

71. Woods to Harlan, Dec. 25, 1888, Harlan Papers, LC.   72. Harlan to Woods, Dec. 30, 1888, Harlan Papers, LC.   73. Woods to Harlan, Jan. 2, 1889, Harlan Papers, LC.
74. Woods to Harlan, Jan. 3, 1889, Harlan Papers, LC.   75. Harlan to Woods, Jan. 11, 1889, Harlan Papers, LC.

76. Harlan to Claypool, Jan. 21, 1889, Harlan Papers, LC.   77. Harlan's activities on the Bering Sea commission are described in Chapter 11.   78. Harlan dissented from a bank-ruptcy decision that went against Willson: see Louisville Trust Co. v. Comingor, 184 U.S. 18 (1902). Harlan voted for his nephew in Cincinnati, Hamilton & Dayton Railroad Co. v. Thiebaud, 177 U.S. 615 (1899); but he voted against him in Gregg v. Metropolitan Trust Co., 197 U.S. 183 (1904), and again in Great Western Mining & Mfg. Co. v. Harris, 198 U.S. 561 (1904). James S. Harlan won a case unanimously: Succession of Serralles v. Esbri, 200 U.S. 103 (1905); and James and John, acting together, won (with two dissents) in Perez v. Fernandez, 202 U.S. 80 (1905).   79. Mifflin v. R.H. White Co., 190 U.S. 260 (1902). Holmes joined the Court on Dec. 8, 1902; the case was argued on April 30, 1903, and decided unanimously on June 1.   80. In at least the following three cases Peckham was absent: New Orleans v. Warner, 175 U.S. 120 (1899); New Orleans v. Warner, 180 U.S. 199 (1900); and Knowlton v. Moore, 178 U.S. 41 (1899).

81. Harlan to Theodore Roosevelt, July 5, 1906, Taft Papers, LC.   82. Harlan to Eli Murray, Feb. 9, 1881, Harlan Papers, UL.

11: Associate Justice, 1887-1897

1. Harlan to Waite, July 1, 1887, Harlan Papers, LC. Although Lamar was undistinguished as a judge, he was important enough politically to stimulate some interest among biographers. See W.A. Cate, Lucius Q.C. Lamar, Secession and Reunion (Chapel Hill: Univ. of North Carolina Press, 1935); James B. Murphy, L.Q.C. Lamar, Pragmatic Patriot (Baton Rouge: Louisiana State Univ. Press, 1973). See the article by Arnold M. Paul in Friedman and Israel, eds., Justices, pp. 1431-51.   2. Quoted from Irving Schiffman's article on Fuller in Friedman and Israel, eds., Justices, p. 1479.   3. Harlan to Fuller, April 3, 1888, Fuller Papers, CHS.   4. Harlan to Fuller, May 30, 1888, Fuller Papers, CHS. Cleveland was to marry the youngest daughter of Justice Matthews: see Matthews to Rutherford B. Hayes, May 17, 1888, Hayes Papers, Hayes Presidential Center.   5. Harlan to Fuller, May 30, 1888, Fuller Papers, CHS.

6. Harlan to Fuller, May 3, 1888, Fuller Papers, CHS.   7. Harlan to Fuller, Dec. 13, 1892, Fuller Papers, CHS.   8. Harlan to Fuller, Nov. 29, 1888, Fuller Papers, CHS. The reference to Gray is partly illegible and thus uncertain.   9. Harlan to Fuller, May 21, 1894, Fuller Papers, CHS.   10. Harlan to Fuller, Dec. 18, 1898, quoted in Willard L. King, Melville Weston Fuller

(Chicago: Univ. of Chicago Press, 1950), p. 245. King's book is the most complete treatment of Fuller's life.

11. See Brewer's remarks as reprinted in *Dinner Given by the Bar of the Supreme Court of the United States to Mr. Justice John Marshall Harlan in Recognition of the Completion of Twenty-five Years of Distinguished Service on the Bench, December 9th, 1902*, pp. 33-37 (privately printed, n.d.).

12. Harlan to Brewer, April 21, 1893, Brewer Papers, Yale University Library. There is no biography of Brewer; some rather one-sided views may be gleaned from Arnold M. Paul's article in Friedman and Israel, eds., *Justices*, pp. 1515-34.   **13.** Quoted in *Central Law Journal*, Oct. 24, 1890, p. 333.   **14.** Friedman and Israel, eds., *Justices*, pp. 1577-92.   **15.** Fuller to his wife, Jan. 1, 1892, Fuller Papers, CHS.

16. See George Shiras III, *Justice George Shiras, Jr., of Pittsburgh* (Pittsburgh: Univ. of Pittsburgh, 1953).   **17.** Harlan to Bradley, Feb. 23, 1889, Harlan Papers, LC. The "Utah case" is *Calton* v. *Utah*, 130 U.S. 83 (1889).   **18.** Jackson to Harlan, Dec. 5, 1894, Harlan Papers, LC. There is a brief treatment of Jackson's life and career by Irving Schiffman in Friedman and Israel, eds., *Justices*, pp. 1603-15. The Plumley case is *Plumley* v. *Massachusetts*, 155 U.S. 461 (1894).   **19.** For White, see the excellent biography by Robert B. Highsaw, *Edward Douglass White, Defender of the Conservative Faith* (Baton Rouge: Louisiana State Univ. Press, 1981).

20. Surprisingly little has been written about Peckham. The major source is Richard Skolnik's brief article in Friedman and Israel, eds., *Justices*, pp. 1685-703.

21. The "dirty day's work" story appeared in Charles Evans Hughes, *The Supreme Court of the United States* (New York: Columbia Univ. Press, 1928) pp. 75-76. Hughes was apparently told the story by Harlan. But Charles Alan Wright argues that Harlan must have forgotten what really happened; see "Authenticity of 'A Dirtier Day's Work' Quote in Question," *Supreme Court Historical Society Quarterly* 13 (Winter 1990): 6-7. Harlan to Fuller, Oct. 4, 1897. Fuller Papers, CHS.   **22.** King, *Fuller*, p. 230. See Matthew McDevitt, *Joseph McKenna, Associate Justice of the United States* (Washington, D.C.: Catholic University Press, 1946) for a rather uncritical biography.   **23.** Harlan registered a complaint about this work load to Waite: "I returned yesterday from my Circuit having been continuously at work there (except for one week) since May 30. It has been the severest Circuit work that I have had since coming into the Court. And what is worse; the cases which I was compelled to bring home with me will occupy the remainder of my vacation." Harlan to Waite, July 1, 1887, Harlan Papers, LC.   **24.** Seven constitutional cases were decided in the 1878 session, but by 1895 the number had risen to twenty-eight. Figures derived from *United States Reports*.   **25.** King, *Fuller*, pp. 230-33.

26. Harlan to Fuller, Sept. 11, 1891, Fuller Papers, CHS. The case is *Briggs* v. *Spaulding*, 141 U.S. 132 (1891). See King, *Fuller*, pp. 173-76.   **27.** This statement is generally true even though Justice Robert H. Jackson accepted appointment (to the dismay of at least one colleague, Hugo L. Black) as the American judge for the Nuremberg trials of Nazi war criminals after World War II.   **28.** His oldest son was in Europe at the time because of Richard's wife's health, and of the two daughters living at home, Richard had taken the older (Laura) with them. So the justice and his wife took Ruth (the younger) and their granddaughter Edith. A long description of the trip—primarily from the viewpoint of the women—appears in Malvina Harlan, "Some Memories," pp. 114-38.   **29.** Malvina Harlan, "Some Memories," pp. 115-16.   **30.** The fullest treatment of the fur seal controversy is James Thomas Gray, "American Fur Seal Diplomacy," Ph.D. diss., Univ. of Georgia, 1971; a brief but lively treatment appears in Thomas A. Bailey, *A Diplomatic History of the American People*, 9th ed. (Englewood Cliffs, N.J.: Prentice-Hall, 1974), pp. 410-14.

31. Lord James Hannen (1821-94) was a British judge for thirty years; one commentator said of him, "If there has been a greater Englsh judge during . . . my life . . . it has not been my good fortune to see him or to know him." *DNB* 22: 811-12. On his illness during the arbitration sessions, see Harlan to Fuller, April 24, 1893, Fuller Papers, CHS.   **32.** Bailey, *Diplomatic History*, p. 413.   **33.** Harlan to Eli Murray, Feb. 15, 1893, Harlan Papers, UL. See also Harlan to Richard Harlan, July 17, 1893, Harlan Papers, LC, for text of a motion made by Harlan to define the arbitration commission's jurisdiction.   **34.** Harlan to Brewer, March 30, 1893, Brewer Papers, Yale University Library. (Translated by a colleague of mine who wishes to remain anonymous.)   **35.** Harlan to Harrison, Dec. 23 and 27, 1893, Harrison Papers, LC.   **36.** Frankfurter and Landis, *Business*, p. 100.   **37.** Harlan to Willson, Dec. 24, 1891, Harlan Papers, UL.   **38.** Richard D. Harlan, "Justice Harlan and the Game of Golf," *Scribner's Monthly* 62 (November 1917): 626-35.   **39.** Augustus Willson to Richard Harlan, April 11 (year unknown), Harlan Papers, LC.   **40.** I have not been able to discover the exact date of James's death, and the story of how he died is perhaps apocryphal.

    41. Willson to Richard Harlan, April 11 (year unknown), Harlan Papers, LC.   **42.** W.L. Wilson to Harlan, May 16, 1900; Harlan Cleveland to Harlan, Feb. 24, 1899; numerous letters in 1899 and 1900 from J. Harlan Hiter to Harlan. Harlan Papers, UL.   **43.** E. Alfred Grant to Harlan, June 16, 1911, Harlan Papers, UL.   **44.** King, *Fuller*, p. 86.   **45.** John Scholfield to President Harrison, Nov. 12, 1892 (Scholfield was a judge on the Illinois Supreme Court); Robert Rae to President McKinley, Feb. 6, 1899; Harlan Papers, UL. Also, Harlan to Fuller, March 25, April 16, 1893, Fuller Papers, CHS.

    46. John Maynard Harlan to Harlan, April 19, 1898; to Malvina Harlan, March 31, 1898. Harlan Papers, UL.   **47.** John Maynard had three daughters in addition to the one son. **48.** These activities are recorded in the justice's scrapbooks, in Mallie's memoir, and in references by his sons. These can be found in the Harlan Papers, LC and UL.   **49.** Memorandum, author unknown, undated, Harlan Papers, UL.

12: Associate Justice, 1897-1911

    1. Harlan to Augustus Willson, March 13, 1893, Harlan Papers, UL.   **2.** Harlan to Willson, Sept. 25, 1906, Harlan Papers, LC.   **3.** Harlan to William Howard Taft, Nov. 13, 1892, Taft Papers, LC.   **4.** Taft to Moody, Aug. 3, 1906, Harlan Papers, LC.   **5.** Taft to Moody, Aug. 30, 1906, Taft Papers, LC.

    6. Harlan to Willson, June 16, 1907, Willson Papers, Filson Club.   **7.** See their separate dissenting opinions in *Lochner* v. *New York*, 198 U.S. 45 (1905), and the discussion below in Chapter 14.   **8.** David P. Currie, "The Supreme Court and the Bill of Rights: Full Faith and Credit," *University of Chicago Law Review* 52 (1985): 900.   **9.** David J. Danelski and Joseph S. Tulchin, eds., *The Autobiographical Notes of Charles Evans Hughes* (Cambridge, Mass.: Harvard Univ. Press, 1973), p. 168.   **10.** Quoted in Francis Biddle, *Mr. Justice Holmes* (New York: Charles Scribner's Sons, 1942), p. 111.

    11. The literature, biographical and otherwise, on Holmes is too voluminous to be cited fully. Probably the best is Silas Bent, *Justice Oliver Wendell Holmes* (New York: Vanguard, 1932).   **12.** Undated memorandum, author unknown. Probably written by one of Harlan's law students, Harlan Papers, LC.   **13.** An inadequate biography of Day is Joseph E. McLean, *William Rufus Day: Supreme Court Justice from Ohio* (Baltimore, Md.: Johns Hopkins Univ. Press, 1946). A good summation of his career can be found in Friedman and Israel, eds., *Justices*, pp. 1773-89, by James F. Watts, Jr.   **14.** James F. Watts, Jr., in Friedman and Israel, eds., *Justices*, pp. 1809-10.   **15.** *Swift & Co.* v. *United States*, 196 U.S. 375 (1905).

    16. For Moody, the best source is the Watts article in Friedman and Israel, eds., *Justices*, pp. 1801-21.   **17.** Malvina Harlan, "Some Memories," pp. 146-48.   **18.** "When I came to the Court, Justice Harlan was particularly earnest in expressing his pleasure at my appointment, and during the year that I sat with him, he was like a father to me." Danelski and Tulchin, eds., *Autobiographical Notes*, p. 164.   **19.** Henry F. Pringle, *The Life and Times of William Howard Taft* (New York: Farrar and Rinehart, 1939), 1: 264, 265.   **20.** King, *Fuller*, p. 303.

    21. Ibid.   **22.** Taft to Mrs. Taft, July 10, 1905, quoted in Pringle, *Taft*, p. 311.   **23.** Taft to Lurton, May 22, 1909, quoted in Pringle, *Taft*, p. 530.   **24.** In the 1909 session neither Peckham nor Moody wrote any opinions for the Court. Brewer wrote only twelve, Fuller and

Harlan eighteen each. This left McKenna with twenty-four, White with twenty-five, Day with twenty-seven, and Holmes with thirty-four. Lurton, who replaced Peckham midway through the term, nevertheless wrote nineteen opinions.   **25.** Merlo J. Pusey, *Charles Evans Hughes*, 2 vols. (New York: Macmillan Co., 1951); Pringle, *Taft*; John E. Semonche, *Charting the Future: The Supreme Court Responds to a Changing Society, 1890-1920* (Westport, Conn.: Greenwood Press, 1978).

26. Taft to Chauncey M. Depew, Oct. 15, 1910, quoted in Pringle, *Taft*, p. 534.   **27.** Taft to Hughes, April 22, 1910, quoted in Pringle, *Taft*, p. 532.   **28.** Semonche, *Charting the Future*, p. 248.   **29.** Cited in Pringle, *Taft*, p. 533.   **30.** J.J. Leary, Jr., *Talks with T.R.*, quoted in Pringle, *Taft*, p. 533.

31. Pringle, *Taft*, pp. 534-35.   **32.** Semonche, *Charting the Future*, p. 248.   **33.** Holmes to Sir Frederick Pollock, Sept. 24, 1910, in Mark DeWolfe Howe, ed., *Holmes-Pollock Letters*, 2 vols. (Cambridge, Mass.: Harvard Univ. Press, 1941), 1: 170.   **34.** Pusey, *Hughes* 1: 278. **35.** Pringle, *Taft*, p. 534.

36. Alpheus Thomas Mason, *William Howard Taft, Chief Justice* (New York: Simon and Schuster, 1964), p. 35; Semonche, *Charting the Future*, p. 248.   **37.** Pringle, *Taft*, p. 534. **38.** Pusey, *Hughes* 1: 278.   **39.** Chicago *Inter-Ocean*, Dec. 29, 1910.   **40.** Undated, Harlan Papers, UL.

41. Lurton to Harlan, Sept. 8, 1910; Harlan to Lurton, Sept. 12, 1910. Harlan Papers, LC.   **42.** Harlan to H.B.F. Macfarland, Aug. 5, 1910, Harlan Papers, LC.   **43.** Harlan to Day, July 22, 1910, Harlan Papers, LC.   **44.** Ibid., from copy sent to Day.   **45.** Day to Harlan, July 25, 1910, Harlan Papers, LC.

46. Highsaw, *White*, pp. 57-59.   **47.** Taft to Harlan, July 13, 1910, Taft Papers, LC. **48.** Danelski and Tulchin, eds., *Autobiographical Notes*, p. 169.   **49.** Joseph B. Foraker, *Notes of a Busy Life* (Cincinnati: Stewart and Kidd, 1916), 2: 405-6.   **50.** 218 U.S. 245 (1910).

51. These figures have been calculated from the *United States Reports*, vol. 218, p. 245, to vol. 219, p. 526.   **52.** 219 U.S. 346 (1910); 219 U.S. 219 (1910).   **53.** Almon C. Kellogg to Richard D. Harlan, May 27, 1930, Harlan Papers, UL.   **54.** Dean E.G. Lorenzen to Harlan, June 27, 1910, Harlan Papers, LC.   **55.** Margaret Snow to Harlan, May 26, 1910, Harlan Papers, UL.

56. Harlan to A.B. Brown, July 29, 1910, Harlan Papers, LC.   **57.** Harlan to Walter C. Clephane, Aug. 4, 1910, Harlan Papers, LC.   **58.** Harlan Papers, LC.   **59.** John M. Harlan, "Memorial on Building a National Presbyterian Church in Washington," May 16, 1905, Harlan Papers, UL.   **60.** Harlan to George M. Wrong, Aug. 22, 1904, Harlan Papers, LC. Harlan apparently held this post from 1900 until his death.

61. Harlan was presented with a loving cup, in appreciation of his services, by the Young Men's Bible Class at Christmas 1903. Harlan Papers, UL.   **62.** Harlan to Roosevelt, June 25, 1908, Harlan Papers, UL.   **63.** Henry W. Jessup to Richard D. Harlan, June 9, 1930, Harlan Papers, UL.   **64.** Harlan to Taft, Nov. 18, 1905, Taft Papers, LC.   **65.** Richard D. Harlan to Taft, Jan. 23, 1909, Taft Papers, LC. Taft replied that "you can count on my moving heaven and earth at any time in bringing about a proper compensation for Judges." Taft to Richard Harlan, Jan. 31, 1909, Taft Papers, LC.

66. There is a letter from Laura to Taft, dated Sept. 5, 1923, in which she thanks Taft for his letter of condolence to Mrs. Harding upon the death of her husband. Taft Papers, LC. **67.** For Richard's early career, see *NCAB* 33: 46-47.   **68.** There is a brief summary of James's career in *Who Was Who in America* (Chicago: A.N. Marquis, 1942), I: 520.   **69.** For John Maynard, see *NCAB* 45: 534-35.   **70.** John Maynard Harlan to Augustus Willson, Oct. 13, 1911, Willson Papers, Filson Club.

71. Malvina Harlan, "Some Memories," p. 187.   **72.** Ibid., pp. 186-87.   **73.** J.E. Hoover to Richard D. Harlan, Oct. 11, 1911, Harlan Papers, UL. (This is not J. Edgar Hoover of FBI fame.) Charles Henry Butler, the Court reporter, was a close friend of the Harlan family. Butler was a relative of John Maynard Harlan's wife and had been in Richard's class at Princeton. Cf. Charles Henry Butler, *A Century at the Bar of the Supreme Court of the United States* (New York: G.P. Putnam's Sons, 1942), p. 142.

13: Justice Harlan and Interstate Commerce

1. An able treatment, focusing on the Court's treatment of the issue, can be found in Semonche, *Charting the Future.*   2. Harlan to Willson, Dec. 1, 1905, Willson Papers, Filson Club. The sentence in brackets was crossed out by Harlan but left readable.   3. Ibid. 4. *United States* v. *E.C. Knight Co.*, 156 U.S. 1 (1895), dissenting opinion, p. 44.   5. *Standard Oil Co. of New Jersey* v. *United States*, 221 U.S. 1 (1911), concurring opinion, p. 83.

6. See especially Holmes's effective dissenting opinion in *Northern Securities Co.* v. *United States*, 193 U.S. 197 (1904), a case in which Harlan wrote the major opinion for the majority. 7. *United States* v. *E.C. Knight Co.*, opinion of the Court, p. 12.   8. The decision was 7-1. Howell Jackson was absent due to his final illness.   9. Epilogue to Felix Frankfurter, *The Commerce Clause under Marshall, Taney and Waite* (Chicago: Univ. of Chicago Press, 1964), p. 116.   10. See *Kidd* v. *Pearson*, 128 U.S. 1 (1888), concerning the constitutionality of a state prohibition law.

11. *United States* v. *E.C. Knight Co.*, dissenting opinion, pp. 33, 35-36, 42, 44. 12. William F. Swindler, *Court and Constitution in the 20th Century: The Old Legality* (Indianapolis: Bobbs-Merrill, 1969), p. 31.   13. *Mandeville Island & Farms* v. *American Crystal Sugar Co.*, 334 U.S. 219 (1948).   14. *Swift & Co.* v. *United States*, 196 U.S. 375 (1906).   15. See, for instance, Swindler, *Court and Constitution*, pp. 24-29; John A. Garraty, *The New Commonwealth, 1877-1890* (New York: Harper and Row, 1968), pp. 121ff.; Jonathon Lurie, *Law and the Nation, 1865-1912* (New York: Knopf, 1983), p. 37. On the other hand, one writer claims that "the ambiguity of the act seems to have been the subsequent contribution of the Supreme Court." Harold U. Faulkner, *Politics, Reform and Expansion, 1890-1900* (New York: Harper and Row, 1959), p. 101.

16. *United States* v. *Trans-Missouri Freight Association*, 166 U.S. 290 (1897), p. 312. 17. Ibid., dissenting opinion, p. 344.   18. Ibid., p. 318.   19. *United States* v. *Joint Traffic Association*, 171 U.S. 505 (1898), p. 572.   20. *Hopkins* v. *United States*, 171 U.S. 578 (1898), p. 588. See also *Anderson* v. *United States*, 171 U.S. 604 (1898).

21. *Addyston Pipe & Steel Co.* v. *United States*, 175 U.S. 211 (1899).   22. For a discussion of the background of this case, see William Letwin, *Law and Economic Policy in America: The Evolution of the Serman Antitrust Act* (New York: Random House, 1965), pp. 187-217. 23. *Northern Securities Co.* v. *United States*, 193 U.S. 197 (1904), pp. 345-46, 351-52.   24. Ibid., dissenting opinion of White, p. 368.   25. Ibid., dissenting opinion of Holmes, pp. 410, 411.

26. Semonche, *Charting the Future*, p. 173.   27. *Continental Wall Paper Co.* v. *Louis Voight & Sons Co.*, 208 U.S. 227 (1909).   28. *Standard Oil Co. of New Jersey* v. *United States*, 221 U.S. 1 (1911); *United States* v. *American Tobacco Co.*, 221 U.S. 106 (1911).   29. Danelski and Tulchin, eds., *Autobiographical Notes*, p. 170.   30. *Standard Oil*, Harlan concurring opinion, pp. 83, 90.

31. *American Tobacco*, Harlan concurring opinion, p. 191.   32. *Standard Oil*, Harlan concurring opinion, pp. 102, 105.   33. *Loewe* v. *Lawlor*, 208 U.S. 247 (1908).   34. *Gompers* v. *Bucks Stove and Range Co.*, 221 U.S. 418 (1911).   35. Harlan to Taft, June 7, 1905, Taft Papers, LC.

36. *Interstate Commerce Commission* v. *Alabama Midland Railway*, 168 U.S. 144 (1897), dissenting opinion, pp. 176, 177. The specific question was whether Congress had given the ICC the power to prescribe railroad rates.   37. *United States* v. *Delaware & Hudson Co.*, 213 U.S. 366 (1909), Harlan dissent, pp. 418-19.   38. *In re Debs*, 158 U.S. 564 (1895). Justice Brewer wrote the Court's opinion.   39 *(First) Employers' Liability Cases*, 207 U.S. 463 (1908). 40. 35 U.S. Stats. at Large, 65, c. 149, and 36 Stat. U.S. Stats. at Large, 291, c. 143.

41. *Adair* v. *United States*, 208 U.S. 161 (1907).   42. *Champion* v. *Ames*, 188 U.S. 321 (1903). The dissent was written by Chief Justice Fuller, who was joined by justices Brewer, Shiras, and Peckham. Harlan's opinion is more fully explicated in Semonche, *Charting the Future*, pp. 155-57.   43. C.H. Pritchett, *The American Constitution* (New York: McGraw-Hill, 1959), p. 235.   44. *Hipolite Egg Co.* v. *United States*, 220 U.S. 45 (1911). Justice Hughes, with Harlan and

Day, dissented, wanting a more expansive construction of the law than Holmes gave it.
45. *Hammer v. Dagenhart*, 247 U.S. 251 (1918).

46. See J. Willard Hurst's minor classic, *Law and the Conditions of Freedom in the Nineteenth Century* (Madison: Univ. of Wisconsin Press, 1956), for a fascinating treatment of the opening of the West to private enterprise, especially railroads, through state action.   **47.** Winston Churchill, *Coniston* (New York: Macmillan, 1906), and *Mr. Crewe's Career* (New York: Macmillan, 1908); Frank Norris, *The Octopus* (New York: Doubleday Doran, 1901).   **48.** Lawrence M. Friedman, *A History of American Law*, 2d ed. (New York: Simon and Schuster, 1985), pp. 445-46.   **49.** David P. Currie, *The Constitution in the Supreme Court: The First Hundred Years, 1789-1888* (Chicago: Univ. of Chicago Press, 1985), pp. 403-4.   **50.** *Lake Shore & Michigan Southern Railway Co. v. Ohio*, 173 U.S. 285 (1899). The Court, with Harlan in the majority, also upheld a Georgia law prohibiting freight trains from running on Sundays; see *Hennington v. Georgia*, 163 U.S. 299 (1896).

51. *Illinois Central Railroad Co. v. Illinois*, 163 U.S. 142 (1896); *Cleveland, Cincinnati, Chicago & St. Louis Railway Co. v. Illinois*, 177 U.S. 514 (1900).   **52.** For instance, wharfage fees were upheld by Harlan in *Packet Co. v. St. Louis*, 100 U.S. 423 (1879), following *Packet Co. v. Keokuk*, 95 U.S. 80 (1877).   **53.** *Transportation Co. v. Parkersburg*, 107 U.S. 691 (1882) at 711.   **54.** *Guy v. Baltimore*, 100 U.S. 434 at 439, 443 (1880).   **55.** *Mugler v. Kansas*, 123 U.S. 623 (1887). This question will be discussed more fully in Chapter 14.

56. *Bowman v. Chicago & North Western Railway* Co., 125 U.S. 465 (1888) at 517. See also *Kidd v. Pearson*, n. 10.   **57.** *Leisy v. Hardin*, 135 U.S. 100 (1890); Wilson Act, chap. 728, 26 U.S. Statutes at Large 313 (1890).   **58.** *Adams Express Co. v. Kentucky*, 206 U.S. 129 (1907) at 141. See also *Rhodes v. Iowa*, 170 U.S. 412 (1898); *American Express Co. v. Kentucky*, 214 U.S. 218 (1908).

59. *Minnesota v. Barber*, 136 U.S. 313 (1890), 321. See also *Brimmer v. Rebman*, 138 U.S. 78 (1891); *Voight v. Wright*, 141 U.S. 62 (1891); *Lindsay & Phelps Co. v. Mullen*, 176 U.S. 126 (1900). But the Court upheld inspection or quarantine laws—in some cases with Harlan's approval—in such cases as *Compagnie Française de Navigation à Vapeur v. Louisiana State Board of Health*, 186 U.S. 380 (1902); *Reid v. Colorado*, 187 U.S. 137 (1902); *Patapsco Guano Co. v. North Carolina Board of Agriculture*, 171 U.S. 345 (1898); *General Oil Co. v. Crain*, 209 U.S. 211 (1908).   **60.** *Powell v. Pennsylvania*, 127 U.S. 678 (1888); *Plumley v. Massachusetts*, 155 U.S. 461 (1894); *Schollenberger v. Pennsylvania*, 171 U.S. 1 (1898); *Collins v. New Hampshire*, 171 U.S. 30 (1898).

61. *Schollenberger*, p. 30.   **62.** *Pullman's Palace Car Co. v. Pennsylvania*, 141 U.S. 18 (1890).   **63.** *Cleveland, Cincinnati, Chicago & St. Louis Rwy. Co. v. Backus*, 154 U.S. 439 (1894).

14: Substantive Due Process

1. It would be impossible to cite even the more significant books and articles that deal with this subject. Some of them are referred to in the text and notes that follow.   **2.** An example is Swindler, *Court and Constitution*, chaps. 7, 12, 17.   **3.** A good example is Semonche, *Charting the Future*. Also see my own *American Constitutional Development, 1877-1917* (New York: Harper and Row, 1972), chap. 6.   **4.** These writers often do not comment on the cases of the earlier era, but their approval of more recent decisions involves necessarily an acceptance of the theory developed by the Waite and Fuller courts, if not the practice. See, for example, Philip Bobbitt, *Constitutional Fate* (New York: Oxford, 1982).   **5.** In *Willson v. Black Bird Creek Marsh Co.*, 27 U.S. 245 (1829).

6. See, for instance, the arguments of justices McLean and Grier in the *License Cases*, 46 U.S. 504 (1847); and various arguments in the *Passenger Cases*, 48 U.S. 283 (1849).   **7.** Dissenting in *Munn v. Illinois*, 94 U.S. 113 (1877) at 145. John Harlan was not appointed to the Court until after this decision was reached.   **8.** *Slaughterhouse Cases*, 83 U.S. 36 (1873).   **9.** *Munn*, p. 125.   **10.** *Davidson v. New Orleans*, 96 U.S. 97 (1878) at 104. Harlan must be assumed to have agreed with this statement at the time: in fact, only Bradley (in a concurring opinion) expressed any misgivings about it.

11. Justice Bradley for the Court in *Beer Co.* v. *Massachusetts*, 97 U.S. 25 (1878) at 33.
12. Harlan for the Court in *Patterson* v. *Kentucky*, 97 U.S. 501 (1878).   **13.** *Parkersburg* v. *Brown*, 106 U.S. 487 (1882).   **14.** *Ruggles* v. *Illinois*, 108 U.S. 526 (1883).   **15.** *Mugler* v. *Kansas*, 123 U.S. 623 (1887) at 661; see *Powell* v. *Pennsylvania*, 127 U.S. 678 (1888).
     16. Currie, *Constitution*, p. 378.   **17.** *Chicago, Milwaukee & St. Paul Railway Co.* v. *Minnesota*, 134 U.S. 418 (1890). Justices Bradley, Gray, and Lamar dissented, with Bradley arguing that the judiciary had no proper role to play in rate-making and accusing the Court of, in effect, reversing its decision in *Munn* v. *Illinois*. *Munn* was, however, narrowly upheld in *Budd* v. *New York*, 143 U.S. 517 (1892), and again in *Brass* v. *North Dakota ex rel Stoeser*, 153 U.S. 391 (1894), with Harlan in the majority in both cases.   **18.** *Reagan* v. *Farmer's Loan & Trust Co.*, 154 U.S. 362 (1894).   **19.** *Smyth* v. *Ames*, 169 U.S. 466 (1898). The case was argued—with William Jennings Bryan as counsel for the state of Nebraska—April 5-7, 1897; Harlan's opinion was not read until March 7, 1898—an unusually long gestation period for those days.   **20.** *Smyth* v. *Ames*, p. 547.
     21. See his opinion in *Southwestern Bell Telephone Co.* v. *Public Service Commission*, 262 U.S. 276 (1923).   **22.** *Federal Power Commission* v. *Hope Natural Gas Co.*, 320 U.S. 591 (1944). This story is surveyed briefly in Pritchett, *American Constitution*, pp. 587ff.   **23.** Up to 1911 the Court decided only the following rate cases and did not find any of the rates invalid: *Atlantic Coast Line Railroad Co.* v. *Florida ex rel Ellis*, 203 U.S. 256 (1906); *Seaboard Air Line Railway* v. *Florida ex rel Ellis*, 203 U.S. 261 (1906); *Alabama & Vicksburg Railway Co.* v. *Mississippi Railroad Commission*, 203 U.S. 496 (1906); *Prentis* v. *Atlantic Coast Line Co.*, 211 U.S. 210 (1908); *Knoxville* v. *Knoxville Water Co.*, 212 U.S. 1 (1908); *Wilcox* v. *Consolidated Gas Co.*, 212 U.S. 19 (1909).   **24.** For instance, see Harlan's opinion for the Court in *Chicago Life Insurance Co.* v. *Needles*, 113 U.S. 574 (1884), in which he held that adjudication by a competent state tribunal, after full opportunity for defense, could deny the right to operate in the state to a corporation against which adequate grounds had been established upon reasonable statutory provisions. In *Missouri Pacific Rwy. Co.* v. *Humes*, 115 U.S. 512 (1885), Justice Field held that a state law requiring railroads to build and maintain fences and cattle guards on penalty of double damages did not violate due process.   **25.** Two cases antedating *Allgeyer* by a few months—but not involving the doctrine of liberty of contract—have been largely ignored by commentators. See *Missouri Pacific Rwy. Co.* v. *Nebraska*, 164 U.S. 403 (1896), which invalidated a state law requiring a railroad to allow, on the same terms, the building of an additional grain elevator; and *Gulf, Colorado & Santa Fe Rwy. Co.* v. *Ellis*, 165 U.S. 150 (1897), invalidating a state law requiring railroads to pay attorney fees and costs for plaintiffs who won suits against the railroad.
     26. *Allgeyer* v. *Louisiana*, 165 U.S. 578 (1897), unanimous decision with opinion written by Justice Peckham.   **27.** *San Diego Land & Town Co.* v. *National City*, 174 U.S. 739 (1899).
28. *W.W. Cargill Co.* v. *Minnesota*, 180 U.S. 452 (1901).   **29.** *Cotting* v. *Kansas City Stock Yards Co. and Kansas*, 183 U.S. 79 (1901). See also Harlan's opinion in *Connolly* v. *Union Sewer Pipe Co.*, 184 U.S. 540 (1902), for another decision on equal protection grounds.   **30.** *Dobbins* v. *Los Angeles*, 195 U.S. 223 (1904).
     31. *Jacobsen* v. *Massachusetts*, 197 U.S. 11 (1905).   **32.** *Holden* v. *Hardy*, 169 U.S. 366 (1898). This case resulted in a 5-2 decision, with Brewer and Peckham dissenting.   **33.** *Muller* v. *Oregon*, 208 U.S. 412 (1908). This unanimous decision upheld an Oregon law restricting women's hours of labor to ten a day. Brewer, in fact, wrote the opinion.   **34.** *Lochner* v. *New York*, 198 U.S. 45 (1905).   **35.** *Bunting* v. *Oregon*, 243 U.S. 425 (1917), upheld an Oregon statute imposing a ten-hour day for all industrial workers: this was just the kind of general labor regulation *Lochner* had invalidated.
     36. *Lochner*, pp. 75ff.   **37.** Ibid., pp. 69ff.   **38.** Probably its only competitor is a federal case—*Adkins* v. *Children's Hospital*, 261 U.S. 525 (1923)—in which a much more conservative Supreme Court invalidated a minimum wage law for women in the District of Columbia.   **39.** *Louisville & Nashville Railroad Co.* v. *Central Stock Yards Co.*, 212 U.S. 132 (1909).
40. *Missouri Pacific Railway Co.* v. *Nebraska*, 217 U.S. 196 (1910).
     41. Semonche, *Charting the Future*, p. 424.

15: Criminal Procedures in the States

1. *Hurtado* v. *California*, 110 U.S. 516 (1884). Justice Field did not participate.   **2.** See *Barron* v. *Baltimore*, 32 U.S. 243 (1833).   **3.** See *Walker* v. *Sauvinet*, 92 U.S. 90 (1876), denying that the states had to provide juries in civil suits.   **4.** *Hurtado*, pp. 528ff.   **5.** Ibid., dissenting opinion, p. 541.

6. Here he quoted from *Murray* v. *Hoboken*, 59 U.S. 272 (1856), pp. 276-77.   **7.** *Hurtado*, dissenting opinion, p. 545.   **8.** Ibid., pp. 546-50.   **9.** Ibid., pp. 554-55. Harlan dissented again on the same issue, but without opinion, in *Bolln* v. *Nebraska*, 176 U.S. 83 (1900).   **10.** For details of this side of the controversy, see King, *Fuller*, pp. 169ff.

11. *O'Neil* v. *Vermont*, 144 U.S. 516 (1892).   **12.** *Slaughterhouse Cases*, 83 U.S. 36 (1873); *Maxwell* v. *Dow*, 176 U.S. 581 (1900).   **13.** *Maxwell*, dissenting opinion, pp. 614, 615-16.   **14.** See Justice Benjamin Cardozo's opinion for the Court in *Palko* v. *Connecticut*, 302 U.S. 319 (1937).   **15.** *Maxwell*, dissenting opinion, p. 616.

16. *Dreyer* v. *Illinois*, 187 U.S. 71 (1902).   **17.** *Jack* v. *Kansas*, 199 U.S. 372 (1905).   **18.** *Schoener* v. *Pennsylvania*, 207 U.S. 188 (1907).   **19.** *Twining* v. *New Jersey*, 211 U.S. 78 (1908) at 98.   **20.** Ibid., pp. 99ff.

21. Ibid., dissenting opinion, pp. 116, 118, 123, 125.   **22.** Justice Felix Frankfurter, concurring in *Adamson* v. *California*, 332 U.S. 46 (1947). *Twining* was reversed explicitly in *Griffin* v. *California*, 380 U.S. 609 (1965).   **23.** Moody to Harlan, July 3, 1910, Harlan Papers, LC.

16: Civil Rights

1. *Robertson* v. *Baldwin*, 165 U.S. 275 (1897) at 282.   **2.** Ibid., dissenting opinion, pp. 292, 301, 303.   **3.** *Clyatt* v. *United States*, 197 U.S. 207 (1905).   **4.** Ibid., dissenting opinion, p. 223.   **5.** *Bailey* v. *Alabama*, 219 U.S. 219 (1911).

6. Loren Miller, *The Petitioners* (Cleveland: World Publishing Co., 1966), chap. 8.

7. The Court made this point in numerous cases; Harlan did so, for instance, in his opinion for the Court in *Bush* v. *Kentucky*, 107 U.S. 110 (1882).   **8.** For statutes, *Strauder* v. *West Virginia*, 100 U.S. 300 (1879), is the leading case; for judges and other state officials, the first case is *Ex parte Virginia*, 100 U.S. 339 (1879).   **9.** Harlan, for instance, insisted that a motion to dismiss should be taken at trial, and that habeas corpus should not be used to bypass the state appellate process. See his opinions for the Court in *In re Wood*, 140 U.S. 278 (1891); *Andrews* v. *Swartz*, 156 U.S. 272 (1885); and *Gibson* v. *Mississippi*, 163 U.S. 565 (1886).   **10.** *Hall* v. *De Cuir*, 95 U.S. 485 (1878).

11. *Louisville, New Orleans and Texas Railway* v. *Mississippi*, 133 U.S. 587 (1890).   **12.** Section 5 of the amendment provides that "Congress shall have power to enforce, by appropriate legislation, the provisions of this article."   **13.** *Civil Rights Cases*, 109 U.S. 3 (1883).   **14.** Alan F. Westin, "John Marshall Harlan and the Constitutional Rights of Negroes: The Transformation of a Southerner," *Yale Law Journal* 66 (1957): 674-85.   **15.** Ibid., p. 674; Edmunds to Harlan, Dec. 1, 1882, Harlan Papers, UL.

16. At least, it was strong in the opinion of some commentators; by implication, at least, this is what Currie seems to say in *Constitution*, pp. 398-402.   **17.** Malvina Harlan, "Some Memories," pp. 97-102.   **18.** For instance, see Currie, *Constitution*, pp. 400-401. The Court validated Harlan in *Jones* v. *Alfred H. Mayer Co.*, 392 U.S. 409 (1968).   **19.** *Civil Rights Cases*, dissenting opinion, pp. 39, 58-59.   **20.** See, for instance, *Shelley* v. *Kraemer*, 323 U.S. 1 (1947), outlawing private restrictive covenants on the grounds that state court enforcement is state action; and *Runyon* v. *McCrary*, 427 U.S. 160 (1976), requiring private schools to admit blacks, using a freedom to contract argument.

21. See *Bob Jones University* v. *United States*, 461 U.S. 725 (1983); and *Goldsboro Christian Schools* v. *United States*, 461 U.S. 574 (1983).   **22.** *Civil Rights Cases*, dissenting opinion, p. 60. In the Civil Rights Act of 1964 Congress claimed the right under the commerce clause to

regulate public accommodations, including hotels and restaurants (if not theaters), and the Supreme Court upheld the statute. See *Katzenbach* v. *McClung*, 379 U.S. 294 (1964); and *Heart of Atlanta Motel* v. *United States*, 379 U.S. 241 (1964).　**23.** *Civil Rights Cases*, dissenting opinion, p. 53.　**24.** See Westin, "Harlan," pp. 682-85, for a survey of newspaper comment.
25. Strong quoted by Harlan in an undated note to Mallie; Swayne to Harlan, Nov. 20, 1883. Harlan Papers, UL. Hayes to Harlan, Nov. 28, 1883, Hayes Papers, Hayes Presidential Center; Conkling to Harlan, Dec. 27, 1883, Harlan Papers, UL.
　26. Harlan to Waite, undated, Harlan Papers, LC.　**27.** Harlan to Hayes, Nov. 30, 1883, Hayes Papers, Hayes Presidential Center. Harlan felt similarly bound to dissent when the Court held that a treaty with China gave the federal government no power to deal with private action discriminating against Chinese; see *Baldwin* v. *Franks*, 120 U.S. 679 (1887).
28. *Louisville, New Orleans & Texas Railway* v. *Mississippi*, 133 U.S. 587 (1890). See also *Chesapeake & Ohio Railway Co.* v. *Kentucky*, 179 U.S. 388 (1900), upholding a similar Kentucky law; Harlan dissented without opinion.　**29.** *Plessy* v. *Ferguson*, 163 U.S. 537 (1896). Readers wishing more detailed treatment are referred to Charles A. Lofgren's excellent case study, *The Plessy Case: A Legal-Historical Interpretation* (New York: Oxford Univ. Press, 1987).　**30.** *Laws of Louisiana*, 1890, pp. 152ff (no. 111).
　31. For details, see Lofgren, *Plessy*, chap. 2.　**32.** For reasons of brevity and a desire to emphasize fundamentals, I have not followed Lofgren's excellent analyses of either Brown's or Harlan's opinions: see Lofgren, *Plessy*, chap. 8. Brown's opinion appears in 163 U.S. 537 (1896) at 537-52. Harlan's dissenting opinion covers pp. 553-64.　**33.** Frankfurter to Alan Westin, May 30, July 9, 1958, Harlan Papers, LC. Professor Westin was at the time engaged in writing a biography of Harlan.　**34.** *Cumming* v. *Richmond County Board of Education*, 175 U.S. 528 (1899).　**35.** Frankfurter's concurring opinion in *Adamson* v. *California*, 332 U.S. 46 (1947).
　36. *Hodges* v. *United States*, 203 U.S. 1 (1906).　**37.** *Chiles* v. *Chesapeake & Ohio Railway Co.*, 218 U.S. 71 (1909).　**38.** *Berea College* v. *Kentucky*, 211 U.S. 45 (1908).　**39.** Ibid., dissenting opinion, pp. 62, 69. Harlan asked the court clerk to change the words *prejudice of race* to *the virus of race prejudice*, but for some reason the change was never incorporated into the official report. Cf. undated letter, Harlan to Charles H. Butler, Harlan Papers, LC.　**40.** *Yick Wo* v. *Hopkins*, 118 U.S. 356 (1886). The opinion was written by Justice Matthews for a unanimous Court.
　41. *Baldwin* v. *Franks*, 120 U.S. 679 (1887).　**42.** *United States* v. *Wong Kim Ark*, 169 U.S. 649 (1898).　**43.** Cited in King, *Fuller*, pp. 237-38.　**44.** *Neal* v. *Delaware*, 103 U.S. 370 (1881).　**45.** *Ex parte Yarbrough*, 110 U.S. 651 (1884).
　46. *Elk* v. *Wilkins*, 112 U.S. 94 (1884).　**47.** *Williams* v. *Mississippi*, 170 U.S. 213 (1890). The opinion was written by Justice Joseph McKenna.　**48.** *Giles* v. *Harris*, 189 U.S. 475 (1903).
49. *James* v. *Bowman*, 190 U.S. 127 (1903).　**50.** Dolliver to Harlan, Dec. 19, 1909, Harlan Papers, LC. Dolliver was a prominent progressive Republican senator from Iowa.

17: The Income Tax

　1. *Pollock* v. *Farmers' Loan and Trust Co.*, 157 U.S. 429 (1895); and 158 U.S. 601 (1895).
2. For general background and discussion, see the following (mostly critical of the decision): Matthew Josephson, *The Politicos* (New York: Harcourt, Brace, 1938), pp. 106-10; Edward S. Corwin, *Court over Constitution* (Princeton, N.J.: Princeton Univ. Press, 1938), pp. 182ff.; Semonche, *Charting the Future*, pp. 62ff. Biographies that have dealt extensively with the case include Edward S. Martin, *The Life of Joseph Hodges Choate*, 2 vols. (London: Constable, 1920), 2: chap. 1; King, *Fuller*, chaps. 15-16; Highsaw, *White*, chap. 8; and Swisher, *Field*, chap. 15. Any standard constitutional history also deals extensively with the cases. Readers should be warned that almost all writers on the subject have presented one side or the other as if it were correct. This comment does not exclude myself.　**3.** *Springer* v. *United States*, 102 U.S. 586 (1881). Justices Field and Harlan were the only holdovers from this decision.　**4.** The two

clauses are as follows: "Representatives and direct taxes shall be apportioned among the several states . . . according to their respective numbers" (art. 1, sec. 2); and "No capitation or other direct tax shall be laid, unless in proportion to the census" (art. 1, sec. 9).   **5.** For further details about the leak, see King, *Fuller,* pp. 205-6. See Chicago *Tribune,* April 6, 1895, p. 1.

6. King, *Fuller,* p. 206.   **7.** Jackson to Fuller, April 15, 1895, Fuller Papers, CHS. **8.** For an analysis of this question reviewing the various possibilities, see King, *Fuller,* pp. 218-21.   **9.** Harlan to Willson, undated, Harlan Papers, UL.   **10.** James S. Harlan to Harlan, May 2, 1895, Harlan Papers, UL.

11. *Pollock,* p. 607.   **12.** King, *Fuller,* pp. 214-15.   **13.** *Hylton* v. *United States,* 3 Dall. 171 (1796), involved the question of whether a federal tax on carriages used for hire was a direct tax. The Court held that it was not, with various judges attempting to define *direct tax.* **14.** Probably the best defense of Fuller's two opinions appears in King, *Fuller.*   **15.** For analysis of White's two dissents, see Highsaw, *White,* and Semonche, *Charting the Future.*

16. *Pollock,* p. 583.   **17.** Ibid., pp. 653-54.   **18.** Morgan to Harlan, March 15, 1895, Harlan Papers, UL.   **19.** A dramatic and apparently largely accurate contemporary portrayal of courtroom events—which does not bear out some of the charges against Harlan— appeared in a paper by Henry H. Ingersoll, "The Revolution of 20th May, 1895," read to the Tennessee Bar Association in July 1895 and later privately printed. A copy is contained in the Harlan Papers, UL.   **20.** King, *Fuller,* pp. 215-16.

21. Cited in David Farrelly, "Justice Harlan's Dissent in the Pollock Case," *Southern California Law Review* 24 (1951): 175, n. 4.   **22.** Harlan to James S. and John M. Harlan, May 27, 1895, Harlan Papers, UL.   **23.** Ingersoll, "Revolution."   **24.** *Pollock,* pp. 640-665, 671, 672.   **25.** Ibid., pp. 674, 676, 679, 685-88.

26. Ibid.,pp. 714, 706.   **27.** Ibid., p. 695.   **28.** Jackson to Harlan, June 25, 1895. Harlan Papers, LC. Taft to Harlan, May 27, 1895; Harlan Papers, UL. James S. Harlan to Harlan, May 2, 1895; Harlan Papers, UL. James was accurately guessing what his father would write.

18: The Insular Cases

1. Quoted in Carl Brent Swisher, *American Constitutional Development,* 2d ed. (Boston, 1954), p. 475.   **2.** Harlan to Taft, July 16, 1900, Taft Papers, LC.   **3.** Taft to Harlan, Sept. 22, 1900, Taft Papers, LC.   **4.** Harlan to Taft, Nov. 5, 1900, Taft Papers, LC.   **5.** Taft to Harlan, Jan. 7, 1901, Taft Papers, LC.

6. *Neely* v. *Henkel,* 180 U.S. 109 (1901), and 180 U.S. 126 (1901).   **7.** Art. 1, sec. 8: "The Congress shall have Power [t]o lay and collect Taxes, Duties, Imposts and Excises . . . ; but all Duties, Imposts and Excises shall be uniform throughout the United States."   **8.** *De Lima* v. *Bidwell,* 182 U.S. 1 (1901). See also *Goetze* v. *United States,* and *Crossman* v. *United States,* 182 U.S. 221 (1901), the latter of which applied the same conclusions to Hawaii.   **9.** *Dooley* v. *United States,* 182 U.S. 222 (1901). See also *Armstrong* v. *United States,* 182 U.S. 243 (1901).   **10.** *Downes* v. *Bidwell,* 182 U.S. 244 (1901).

11. Ibid., dissenting opinion, p. 375.   **12.** Harlan to Taft, July 22, 1901, Taft Papers, LC.   **13.** Taft to Harlan, Oct. 21, 1901, Harlan Papers, UL.   **14.** Harlan to Fuller, June 14, 1901, Fuller Papers, CHS.   **15.** Harlan to Fuller, July 8, 1901, Fuller Papers, CHS.

16. Ibid.   **17.** Harlan to Fuller, Aug. 16, 1901; cf. Sept. 2, 1901. Fuller Papers, CHS. **18.** *Dooley* v. *United States,* 183 U.S. 151 (1901).   **19.** *Fourteen Diamond Rings* v. *United States,* 183 U.S. 176 (1901).   **20.** Harlan to Fuller, Aug. 18, 1902, Fuller Papers, CHS.

21. *Hawaii* v. *Mankichi,* 190 U.S. 197 (1902).   **22.** Ibid., p. 241.   **23.** *Crowley* v. *United States,* 194 U.S. 461 (1904).   **24.** *Binns* v. *United States,* 194 U.S. 486 (1904).   **25.** *Kepner* v. *United States,* 195 U.S. 100 (1904).

26. *Dorr* v. *United States,* 195 U.S. 138 (1904); see also *Secundino Mendezona* v. *United States,* 195 U.S. 158 (1904).   **27.** Harlan to Taft, June 8, 1904, Taft Papers, LC.

19: Other Issues

1. *Rosen* v. *U.S.,* 161 U.S. 29 (1896).   **2.** *Patterson* v. *Colorado,* 205 U.S. 454 (1907). **3.** See their respective opinions in *Bridges* v. *California,* 314 U.S. 252 (1941).   **4.** *Callan* v. *Wilson,* 127 U.S. 540 (1888).   **5.** Isaac C. Parker (1838-96) was perhaps the most notorious of the so-called hanging judges of the Old West. Two books recount his career: one, wholly favorable to him, is Glenn Shirley, *Law West of Fort Smith* (New York: Henry Holt, 1957); the other, more objective, is Fred H. Harrington, *Hanging Judge* (Caldwell, Idaho: Caxton Printers, 1951). A good brief description of this affair can be found in Semonche, *Charting the Future,* pp. 51-56.

6. Act of Feb. 6, 1889, chap. 113, 25 U.S. Stats. at Large, 655-56.   **7.** Circuit Court of Appeals Act, chap. 517, 26 U.S. Stats. at Large, 826 (1891).   **8.** *Crain* v. *U.S.,* 162 U.S. 625 (1896). Brewer and White were the other dissenters.   **9.** In *Garland* v. *Washington,* 232 U.S. 642 (1914).   **10.** *Sparf and Hansen* v. *United States,* 156 U.S. 51 (1895). The case covers 133 pages in the *United States Reports.*

11. Dillon to Harlan, April 5, 1895, Harlan Papers, UL.   **12.** *Kirby* v. *United States,* 174 U.S. 47 (1899).   **13.** *Hale* v. *Henkel,* 201 U.S. 43 (1906).   **14.** *Gibbons* v. *Ogden,* 9 Wheat. 1 (1824); and *Brown* v. *Maryland,* 12 Wheat. 419 (1827).   **15.** *Adams Express Co.* v. *Ohio State Auditor,* 165 U.S. 194 (1897), dissenting opinion, p. 242.

16. *Field* v. *Clark,* 143 U.S. 649 (1892).   **17.** In *Panama Refining Co.* v. *Ryan,* 293 U.S. 388 (1935), and *Schecter Poultry Corp.* v. *United States,* 295 U.S. 495 (1935), a conservative majority struck down New Deal legislation for excessive delegation.   **18.** See, for instance, *New York Central Railroad Co.* v. *White,* 243 U.S. 188 (1917).   **19.** *Pennsylvania (Railroad) Co.* v. *Roy,* 102 U.S. 451 (1880). Harlan's notes are in the Harlan Papers, UL.   **20.** *City & Suburban Railway* v. *Svedborg,* 194 U.S. 201 (1904).

21. *St. Louis & San Francisco Railway Co.* v. *James,* 161 U.S. 545 (1896).   **22.** *New England Railroad Co.* v. *Conroy,* 175 U.S. 323 (1900), reversing *Chicago, Milwaukee & St. Paul Railway Co.* v. *Ross,* 112 U.S. 377 (1884).   **23.** In the interests of brevity, only a few representative cases have been mentioned.

Index of Cases Cited

General Index

FLORIDA STATE UNIVERSITY

3 1254 01137 0372

LUIS

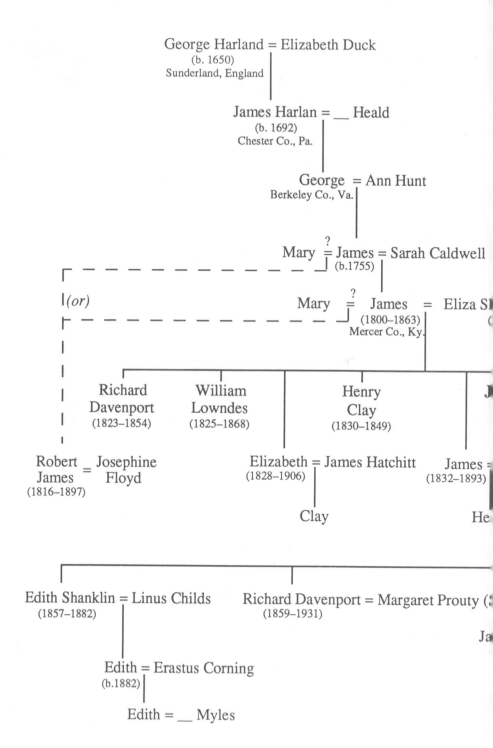

George Harland = Elizabeth Duck
(b. 1650)
Sunderland, England

James Harlan = __ Heald
(b. 1692)
Chester Co., Pa.

George = Ann Hunt
Berkeley Co., Va.

Mary $\overset{?}{=}$ James = Sarah Caldwell
(b.1755)

(or)

Mary $\overset{?}{=}$ James = Eliza S|
(1800–1863)
Mercer Co., Ky.

Richard
Davenport
(1823–1854)

William
Lowndes
(1825–1868)

Henry
Clay
(1830–1849)

Robert = Josephine
James   Floyd
(1816–1897)

Elizabeth = James Hatchitt
(1828–1906)

James =
(1832–1893)

Clay

He

Edith Shanklin = Linus Childs
(1857–1882)

Richard Davenport = Margaret Prouty (|
(1859–1931)

Ja

Edith = Erastus Corning
(b.1882)

Edith = __ Myles